ARMING AND DISARMING

A History of Gun Control in Canada

From the École Polytechnique shootings of 1989 to the political controversy surrounding the elimination of the federal long-gun registry, the issue of gun control has been a subject of fierce debate in Canada. But in fact, firearm regulation has been a sharply contested issue in the country since Confederation. *Arming and Disarming* offers the first comprehensive history of gun control in Canada from the colonial period to the present.

In this sweeping, immersive book, R. Blake Brown outlines efforts to regulate the use of guns by young people, punish the misuse of arms, impose licensing regimes, and create firearm registries. Brown also counters popular assumptions about Canadian history, suggesting that gun ownership was far from universal during much of the colonial period, and that many nineteenth-century lawyers – including John A. Macdonald – believed in a limited right to bear arms.

Arming and Disarming provides a careful exploration of how social, economic, cultural, legal, and constitutional concerns shaped gun legislation and its implementation, as well as how these factors defined Canada's historical and contemporary "gun culture."

(Osgoode Society for Canadian Legal History)

R. BLAKE BROWN is an associate professor in the Department of History at Saint Mary's University.

ARMING AND DISARMING

A History of Gun Control in Canada

R. BLAKE BROWN

Published for The Osgoode Society for Canadian Legal History by
University of Toronto Press
Toronto Buffalo London

Reprinted in paperback 2013

ISBN 978-1-4426-4639-1 (cloth)
ISBN 978-1-4426-2637-9 (paper)

∞

Printed on acid-free paper

Library and Archives Canada Cataloguing in Publication

Brown, R. Blake
Arming and disarming : a history of gun control in Canada /
R. Blake Brown.

(Osgoode Society for Canadian Legal History)
Includes bibliographical references and index.
ISBN 978-1-4426-4639-1 (bound). – ISBN 978-1-4426-2637-9 (pbk.)

1. Gun control – Canada – History.   2. Firearms – Law and legislation –
Canada.   I. Title.   II. Series: Osgoode Society for Canadian Legal
History series

HV7439.C3B76 2012   363.330971   C2012-905645-6

University of Toronto Press acknowledges the financial assistance to its
publishing program of the Canada Council for the Arts and the
Ontario Arts Council.

Canada Council   Conseil des Arts
for the Arts   du Canada

University of Toronto Press acknowledges the financial support of the
Government of Canada through the Canada Book Fund for its
publishing activities.

Contents

Foreword

THE OSGOODE SOCIETY
FOR CANADIAN LEGAL HISTORY

The topic of gun control is never far from the public eye in this country, taking centre stage whenever a dramatic shooting occurs and invariably featuring in debates about Canadian-American distinctions. *Arming and Disarming: A History of Gun Control in Canada* is the first comprehensive history of the subject, and we are delighted to be the publishers of what will be the standard work. Professor R. Blake Brown's account of both gun use and its regulation from the early periods of European settlement to the controversy over the gun registry tells us a complex and at times contradictory story. Gun control is far from merely a contemporary concern. At many times in our history Canadian governments have evinced concern about gun ownership and use. Yet that concern has often been about who should have access to what sorts of firearms, and the urge to regulate has been tempered by campaigns to encourage gun use as a manly pursuit useful for training citizens to be well versed in the practice of using firearms. Canadians' own views of the subject have not been uniform, with marked differences between urban and rural dwellers and across regions. This book is thus a rich piece of social, cultural, political, and legal history.

The purpose of the Osgoode Society for Canadian Legal History is to encourage research and writing in the history of Canadian law. The Society, which was incorporated in 1979 and is registered as a charity, was founded at the initiative of the Honourable R. Roy McMurtry, formerly attorney general for Ontario and chief justice of the province, and officials of the Law Society of Upper Canada. The Society seeks to stimulate the study of legal history in Canada by supporting researchers, collecting oral histories, and publishing volumes that contribute to legal-historical scholarship in Canada. It has published eighty-eight books on the courts, the judiciary, and the legal profession, as well as on the history of crime and punishment, women and law, law and economy, the legal treatment of ethnic minorities, and famous cases and significant trials in all areas of the law.

Current directors of the Osgoode Society for Canadian Legal History are Robert Armstrong, Kenneth Binks, Susan Binnie, David Chernos, Thomas G. Conway, J. Douglas Ewart, Violet French, Martin Friedland, John Gerretsen, Philip Girard, William Kaplan, Horace Krever, C. Ian Kyer, Virginia MacLean, Patricia McMahon, R. Roy McMurtry, Dana Peebles, Paul Perell, Jim Phillips, Paul Reinhardt, Joel Richler, William Ross, Paul Schabas, Robert Sharpe, Mary Stokes, and Michael Tulloch.

The annual report and information about membership may be obtained by writing to the Osgoode Society for Canadian Legal History, Osgoode Hall, 130 Queen Street West, Toronto, Ontario, M5H 2N6. Telephone: 416-947-3321. E-mail: mmacfarl@lsuc.on.ca. Website: www .osgoodesociety.ca.

R. Roy McMurtry
President

Jim Phillips
Editor-in-Chief

Acknowledgments

This book, like all others, has resulted from the skill, hard work, and insight of many people.

The editor-in-chief of the Osgoode Society for Canadian Legal History, Jim Phillips, backed this project from its inception and offered extremely valuable advice on its themes, structure, and content. Marilyn MacFarlane handled all of the administrative issues that arose. The talented staff of the University of Toronto Press greatly improved the manuscript. Special thanks to Len Husband and Wayne Herrington at the Press, and copy editor Ian MacKenzie. Sandra Barry assisted in the preparation of the index.

Several people commented on the manuscript, or parts thereof. The blind reviewers enlisted by the Osgoode Society asked many penetrating questions. Donald Fyson read a version of chapter 1, and Bill MacFarlane offered a gun-owner's take. In addition, undergraduate students in my 2011 seminar class at Saint Mary's University, "Guns, Violence, and the Law," offered comments on several chapters.

Funding support from several organizations allowed for the timely completion of this book. The Social Sciences and Humanities Research Council provided a substantial grant. The Foundation for Educational Exchange between Canada and the United States of America (Fulbright Canada) awarded me a Visiting Research Chair at Vanderbilt University in 2008. Fulbright granted extra travel funds to locate a place for my family to stay in Nashville. Joel Harrington, Vanderbilt's assistant provost for international affairs, quickly solved every dilemma I faced in Nashville, from locating housing to solving emergency child care issues. Esther Enns, dean of the Faculty of Arts, and Kevin Vessey, dean of the Faculty of Graduate Studies and Research at Saint Mary's University, proved strong supporters of this work. Saint Mary's University awarded an Internal Research Grant for New Faculty and an Internal Research Grant for Established Faculty to complete parts of the necessary research. I also owe thanks to my colleagues in the Department of History who supported my request to take an unpaid leave of absence to take up the Fulbright chair.

The research funding from the Social Sciences and Humanities Research Council and Saint Mary's allowed me to employ several research assistants without whose assistance this project would remain far from completed. Thanks to Saint Mary's undergraduate students David Reynolds, Joana Galante, Angela Kinsman, Julie Reynolds, Lisa McNiven, Michael Hughes; Saint Mary's graduate students Daryl Leeworthy, Tammy Morgan, and Harris Ford; and law students from the Schulich School of Law at Dalhousie University: Jan Jensen, Kate Saldanha, and Susanna Ashley.

Many organizations and businesses kindly granted permission for me to reproduce images, including the Nova Scotia Museum, Library and Archives Canada, the Glenbow Museum, the City of Toronto Archives, Savage Arms, the Royal British Columbia Museum, Sears Canada, Uluschak Creative Concepts, the Canadian Wildlife Federation, the *Orangeville Citizen*, the *Winnipeg Free Press*, Sun Media, the *Globe and Mail*, and the Canadian Press.

Thanks also to the *Journal of the Canadian Historical Association* and the *Canadian Historical Review* for permitting me to republish material that first appeared on their pages.

I owe both thanks to my wife, Jennifer Llewellyn, for talking through ideas presented in this book, and apologies for my tendency to write late into the night, edit manuscripts on camping trips, talk to research assistants when on vacation, and be grumpy when work proceeds too slowly. Finally, my two young sons, Owen and Elliott, consistently remind me that there are more important things in life than the number of publications on one's resume.

Figures

Abbreviations

AO	Archives of Ontario
B.C.A.C.	British Columbia Appeal Cases
B.C.J.	British Columbia Judgments
C.C.C.	Canadian Criminal Cases
CIHM	Canadian Institute for Historical Microreproductions
C.S.C.	Consolidated Statutes of Canada
C.S.L.C.	Consolidated Statutes of Lower Canada
DCB	*Dictionary of Canadian Biography*
D.L.R.	Dominion Law Reports
LAC	Library and Archives Canada
MG	Manuscript Group
M.R.	Manitoba Reports
N.B.R.	New Brunswick Reports
O.J.	Ontario Judgments
O.L.R.	Ontario Law Reports
O.R	Ontario Reports
RG	Record Group
R.S.C.	Revised Statutes of Canada
R.S.N.B.	Revised Statutes of New Brunswick
R.S.N.S.	Revised Statutes of Nova Scotia
R.S.O.	Revised Statutes of Ontario
S.A.	Statutes of Alberta
S.B.C.	Statutes of British Columbia

S.C.	Statutes of Canada
S.C.R.	Supreme Court Reports
S.L.C.	Statutes of Lower Canada
S.M.	Statutes of Manitoba
S.N.	Statutes of Newfoundland
S.N.B.	Statutes of New Brunswick
S.N.S.	Statutes of Nova Scotia
S.O.	Statutes of Ontario
S.P.E.I.	Statutes of Prince Edward Island
S.S.	Statutes of Saskatchewan
S.U.C.	Statutes of Upper Canada
U.C.C.P.	Upper Canada Common Pleas
W.W.R.	Western Weekly Reports

ARMING AND DISARMING

A History of Gun Control in Canada

Introduction

Many progressive Canadians take pride in policy differences between Canada and the United States. They suggest that the existence of publicly funded, universal health care proves that Canada is a caring and compassionate society, and that the abolition of the death penalty indicates that the nation abhors violence. Gun control is also a key distinction. Jean Chrétien, for example, suggests in his memoirs that gun control is "a core value" that helps "define the difference between Canadians and Americans."[1] While the United States is allegedly filled with "gun nuts" defended by the all-powerful National Rifle Association, Canada is a place of "peace, order, and good government" – a nation whose citizens tolerate firearm regulation to ensure public safety.

Michael Moore's 2002 Oscar-winning documentary, *Bowling for Columbine*, drew upon the popular perception of the two nations' differing gun cultures and firearm laws. Moore explored the causes of the 1999 Columbine High School massacre in which twelve students, one teacher, and the two teenage shooters died, and, more broadly, what contributed to the high level of interpersonal violence in the United States. Moore argued that violence in America stemmed from, among other factors, a climate of fear caused by breathless media reports and an antagonistic history of race relations. He contrasted American and Canadian attitudes towards firearms, suggesting that Canadians expressed less concern with crime and security, and thus felt less necessity to possess arms for self-defence.[2] While Moore lauded Canadians for their sensible approach to guns, he failed to report that Canadians were in fact embroiled in a heated debate over their nation's firearm laws. In 1995, the Liberal government had passed the *Firearms Act*, which tightened gun laws in a number of ways, most controversially by creating a national registry of all firearms. The *Firearms Act* met with substantial opposition, and gun control became an issue in every subsequent federal election.

The heated public debates over gun control demonstrated a remarkable lack of awareness of how and why Canada regulated firearms in the past. Many Canadian historians publicly lament that politicians and public servants make little use of scholars' work that sheds light on complex historical phenomena. In discussing gun control, however, politicians and bureaucrats should be excused, because academics have paid little attention to the history of Canadian firearm regulation. Some fine studies exist on particular pieces of legislation, such as Susan Binnie's examination of several state security statutes in the last half of the nineteenth century and Gérald Pelletier's article on late-nineteenth- and early-twentieth-century firearm laws, as well as the pioneering work of legal historian Martin Friedland.[3] But for most periods of Canadian history, we know little and must depend on the work of criminologists, political scientists, interested amateurs, or historians who allude to gun laws in their work on other subjects.[4]

In comparison to the limited Canadian literature on firearm regulation, there is a growing body of work on the history of gun laws in Britain. Scholars of British gun control offer very polarized conclusions regarding the propriety and effectiveness of gun control. Joyce Lee Malcolm has published two books that, respectively, argue for the existence of a historic constitutional right in England for individuals to bear arms, and that English gun laws led to more crime, not less. On the other hand, Lois Schwoerer criticizes Malcolm's work, suggesting, for instance, that the English right to bear arms included important limitations that Malcolm underemphasizes.[5]

This scholarly division of opinion in Britain is but a skirmish compared with the larger academic battle over the right to bear arms in the United States. The second amendment of the 1789 *Bill of Rights* states that a "well regulated Militia, being necessary to the security of a free State, the right of the people to keep and bear Arms, shall not be infringed." The modern American gun control debate deeply affects the academic exchange over the meaning of this provision. Some scholars argue that the amendment provides no, or almost no, protection against government regulation of firearm ownership, because it guaranteed that states could arm and maintain militias. The other extreme view is that the amendment dictated an unmitigated right of individuals to possess weapons.[6] Some scholars, seeking a middle ground, argue that the provision guaranteed individuals the right to keep and bear arms, but that it had to be exercised collectively. It thus linked gun ownership to the civic obligation of military service.[7]

Despite such efforts to find a compromise, the historical literature on gun control is better known for the extent to which scholars have allowed personal opinions to shape the outcomes of their research. The most infamous illustration of this is the scandal that engulfed Michael Bellesiles's 2000 book *Arming America: The Origins of a National Gun Culture*. Bellesiles argues that firearm ownership was exceptional in the United States in the seventeenth, eighteenth, and early nineteenth centuries, even on the frontier, and that guns became common only with industrialization in the mid-nineteenth century. The firearms industry relied on state investment and did not fear government regulation. The entwinement of firearms with American history, Bellesiles argues, was an "invented tradition" born of dime novels, advertising campaigns by arms manufacturers, and the Civil War experience that collectively transformed guns into symbols of freedom and masculinity. *Arming America* received awards upon its publication, then ridicule for, at best, inaccurate citations, or, at worst, academic fraud. Bellesiles's factual errors and interpretative bias eventually forced him to resign from his tenured position at Emory University.[8]

The present book has a different focus than *Arming America* and makes distinct claims. At its core, *Arming and Disarming* provides a legislative history of gun control in Canada. *Gun control* is a frequently used but rather imprecise term. It refers to a wide range of regulatory provisions that shaped the possession, use, sale, transfer, and registration of weapons, as well as criminal laws designed to punish those who intentionally or unintentionally misused firearms. In exploring the history of such laws in Canada, this book asks some basic, yet unanswered, questions: When were arms regulated, and by whom? Where and how were they regulated? These questions are relatively easy to answer through an examination of legislative materials and criminal statistics. The more difficult challenge is to explain the existence of guns controls and why the law changed. Answering such "why" questions takes more than a narrow political analysis; it requires a careful exploration of how social, economic, cultural, legal, and constitutional concerns shaped gun legislation and its implementation. Together, these factors defined Canada's "gun culture" – that is, the values and attitudes expressed towards firearms that the public or some part of the public held. As will be shown, changes in Canadian gun culture led to legislative action ... or inaction. A broader perspective also means that the history of gun control can shed light on changing attitudes towards minorities, definitions of masculinity, liberal thought, state formation, constitutional rights, and a host of other topics, for, as Martin Friedland recognized in the mid-1970s, a "history of Canada, social, political and economic, could be written based on the history of our gun control legislation."[9]

Writing a history of Canadian firearm controls and gun culture requires the consideration of a wide array of primary and secondary sources. Primary sources examined that deal with firearm laws include colonial, provincial, and federal statutes, parliamentary debates, regulations, Orders in Council, local by-laws, and archival records of key politicians. Additional primary sources, including police reports, crime statistics, judicial decisions, policy papers, and government reports, shed light on the implementation of gun legislation. Still other sources offer insight into attitudes towards firearms: travel accounts, department store catalogues, militia reports, hunting and police periodicals, petitions, polling data, personal correspondence, and a broad array of newspapers and popular journals. These primary sources are situated in the existing historical literature. While work on the history of Canadian firearm regulation is scarce, scholars have explored many topics that relate to gun control and use, such as hunting, the militia, cadets, state formation, environmentalism, militarism, consumer culture, crime, imperialism, gender, legal change, social reform, and youth culture.

***

Arming and Disarming offers several core arguments. The most basic is that there exists a surprisingly long history of gun regulation in Canada. Firearm laws predate Confederation; in fact, they date from the beginnings of a European presence in what became British North America. The earliest laws attempted to limit Aboriginal Peoples' access to guns. Attempts to prevent the arming of Native Peoples points to another core argument: legislators frequently passed gun laws meant to disarm particular ethnic, racial, or political groups deemed suspicious. At various times, legislators have, to choose a few examples, created laws to disarm Irish labourers, Aboriginal Peoples, immigrants, and alleged Bolsheviks. Fear has thus motivated much of Canada's firearm legislation – politicians often invoked racist, ethnocentric, and xenophobic rationales for stronger gun control.

The importance of such motivations is undoubtedly unsurprising to Canadian academic historians who, for several decades, have cast light on how such nefarious factors frequently shaped public policy. However, there is more to the story of gun control than how Canadians targeted minorities and sought to impose draconian legislation. Legislators also responded to real problems of violence caused by the availability of increasingly dangerous arms. Politicians grappled with the introduction of revolvers, modern rifles, and automatic weapons. In addition, the infamous cases of murder, attempted murder, suicide, and mass shootings that pepper Canadian history often motivated legislative responses. *Perceptions* of high crime thus proved important, but so too did *actual* spikes in crime and the introduction of dangerous arms. For example, rising levels of violent crime in the late 1960s and early 1970s led to efforts to pass ambitious new gun controls.

American companies manufactured many of the modern firearms that concerned Canadian legislators in the late nineteenth and twentieth centuries. This fact illustrates that a study of Canadian gun culture and firearm control cannot be offered in isolation. Canadian politicians drew legislative inspiration from Britain and the United States. In addition, cultural attitudes towards Britain and America frequently played a role in efforts to tighten (or loosen) domestic gun laws. Canadians, for example, first voiced an awareness of an emerging distinction between American and Canadian attitudes to firearms in the 1860s. Since then, fear of replicating American levels of interpersonal violence helped Canada adopt a legislative framework that regulates firearms more fully than the laws of most jurisdictions in the United States. Legal rules imposed by Ottawa (and to some extent, by the provinces) gradually shaped gun ownership patterns such that many of the most dangerous types of firearms became relatively uncommon. While Canadians owned large numbers of shotguns and rifles, the number of handguns and fully automatic weapons in circulation remained comparatively modest.

While several factors encouraged the state to impose gun regulations, others mitigated the desire to pass new laws. One such factor is that the state lacked the ability to adequately enforce gun laws for large swathes of Canadian history.[10] For decades, politicians invoked the perceived inability of the state to ensure compliance as a reason to avoid regulating arms. Not until the 1970s did many political leaders believe the state apparatus sufficiently strong to overcome popular resistance to the regulation of hunting rifles and shotguns. The burgeoning bureaucracy, as well as technological innovations (i.e., computers), eventually increased the state's confidence that it could enforce ambitious gun laws, even a national registry of all firearms.

Ideas concerning the constitution and rights also mitigated the state's willingness to impose strict gun controls. While Canada lacked a written constitution protecting individual rights until the *Charter of Rights and Freedoms*, old constitutional principles imported from Britain grounded a belief in an individual's right to possess arms. This helped stymie calls for gun control in the nineteenth century. In the twentieth century, Canadians largely forgot this English right, but the increasing hegemony of liberal ideology meant that opponents of gun control could disparage proposals meant to encourage collective public safety if they seemed to threaten an individual's right to property or to protect one's person.[11]

The widespread use of firearms for practical purposes also discouraged gun control efforts. Rural citizens employed firearms to kill pests, hunt for food, and protect property. One must take care, however, to avoid assuming that all rural Canadians had arms at all times for, as will be shown, rural gun ownership was far from universal. Country residents who owned guns for practical purposes did not motivate much legislative action, nor did those who used firearms for entertainment, such as target shooting.

When the government did act, farmers, target shooters, and recreational hunters generally opposed efforts to regulate firearms. Their intense opposition often stemmed from the belief that guns were more than practical instruments. By the late nineteenth century, business emphasized the beauty, safety, and power of weapons in an effort to encourage gun ownership amongst recreational shooters and hunters, many of whom resided in Canada's growing urban centres. Firearm manufacturers and retailers also tied gun ownership to masculinity, emphasizing that owning and using a gun made one a man. Firearms thus became consumer items used to define owners' self-identity and self-worth. Handling a gun transformed boys into men, and white-collar clerks into rugged "sportsmen." American novels, radio and television programs, and films buttressed this view by offering portrayals of freedom-loving western cowboys and brave soldiers.

A final important factor limited the scope of gun laws: governments of British North America and Canada often *promoted* the use of firearms by citizens deemed trustworthy. For most of Canadian history, the state encouraged loyal subjects to join the militia, volunteer units, or the regular armed forces to help defend the country. Governments financially supported shooting associations and encouraged boys and youth to practise with rifles. Rather than seek to disarm citizens, the state developed their acumen in the arts of war. Governments thus made few attempts to limit citizens' access to long guns, with the result that Canada became a heavily armed nation compared to many other developed democracies.[12]

**

This study is organized chronologically into six chapters. Each chapter devotes attention to changing firearm technology, gun use, cultural attitudes towards firearms, motivations for gun control, arguments offered to oppose new legal measures, and the details of new firearm laws.

Chapter 1 examines gun culture and firearm regulation in what became Canada, before 1867. It explores the use of guns by early French and British communities in northern North America, as well as how Aboriginal Peoples adopted firearms. During periods of settlement, Europeans possessed a substantial number of guns to hunt for food and defend themselves. However, by the mid-nineteenth century, firearms became less important in the more established areas of British North America. The creation of successful farms, subsiding concern with foreign invasion, and declining fear of Aboriginal Peoples made weapons less necessary. A spike in interest in firearms occurred by the 1860s, however. People concerned about a possible invasion by the United States celebrated the invention of the breech-loading rifle, believing that this new weapon would allow British North America to repel an American attack. As a result, governments encouraged men to join militia and volunteer units, and to form rifle shooting associations. Rather than regulate firearms, colonial leaders hoped to arm and train as many civilians as possible. Although British North America was not awash in firearms for most of the pre-Confederation period, governments at times regulated the ownership and use of guns. Authorities sought to prevent the discharge of guns in urban spaces, limit the possession of weapons at public meetings and polling places, and control gun possession or use when fears rose of foreign invasion or of domestic ethnic, class, or political upheaval.

Chapter 2 demonstrates how the new Canadian state continued to encourage the ownership and use of rifles in the quarter century after

Confederation. The federal government supported the Dominion of Canada Rifle Association and reorganized the nation's militia to encourage loyal citizens to become expert marksmen. Ottawa, however, deemed some groups less than trustworthy and sought to limit their access to arms. The Fenian threat led to some legislation, as did the Northwest Rebellion of 1885. Chapter 2 also demonstrates that the federal government increasingly opposed having citizens own and use another technologically innovative weapon: the modern revolver. British- and American-made revolvers flooded into Canada after Confederation.[13] Increasingly inexpensive because of the miracles of industrial production, revolvers found their way into the hands of many urban residents by the 1870s. This resulted in a perceived spike in the number of accidents, shootings, and suicides. A special worry was that young, working-class men carried pistols to demonstrate their manliness. Legislators responded, but with trepidation. They largely banned the carrying of revolvers, required retailers to keep records, and prevented the sale of pistols to people under sixteen years of age. Parliament did not put in place stricter gun laws for several reasons. Many politicians doubted the ability of law enforcement officials to effectively implement firearm regulations, and assumed that gun laws would only disarm the law abiding. In addition, a number of leading politicians, most importantly John A. Macdonald, believed that British subjects possessed a right to guns grounded in the English *Bill of Rights*, albeit a right limited to men of property.

Chapter 3 explores firearm control and gun culture from roughly the 1890s to the beginning of the Great War, a time when the ownership of firearms became increasingly entwined with dominant definitions of masculinity. Worries over the negative effects of modernity on men's health and character resulted in the growth of recreational hunting by urban, middle-class men. Travelling to rural areas and using a rifle to shoot game became an important means for men to secure their manliness. The state once again encouraged gun use, this time because many imperialists believed that Canada could help Britain in a future war only if citizens trained as marksmen. The state thus renewed its support for rifle associations and shooting, going so far as to train boys and youth in use of weapons and establishing a domestic arms industry. Once again, however, the state did not want *all* Canadians to use guns. Governments encouraged firearm ownership and use by traditional British stock. Numerous politicians, newspaper editors, and other public figures, however, called for legislation to prevent new immigrants from acquiring and using arms. Ottawa and the provinces thus passed new laws regulating handguns.

The desire to limit firearm use by "untrustworthy" residents also shaped gun control from the Great War to the Second World War – the period covered in chapter 4. The onset of war in 1914 led many Canadians to worry about the ownership of arms by enemy aliens. This resulted in the decision to temporarily disarm recent immigrants from Germany and Austria-Hungary. At the end of the war, concerns continued about the ownership of firearms by potential enemies of the state. Parliament passed legislation to regulate gun ownership by aliens, and even, for a brief period, required all Canadians to acquire a firearm permit for most weapons. Fears of subversive activity eventually subsided, such that Ottawa repealed most of these gun controls. During the 1920s, however, many Canadians continued to express frustration with the widespread availability of pistols, a vexing problem that Canadians never fully resolved. Criminal use of handguns sparked public fears, as did the prominence of guns in youth culture, and the misuse of firearms by police. Despite calls for action, governments did little during the 1920s. The onset of the Great Depression sparked new worries about public disorder that resulted in stronger firearm legislation. The creation of a handgun registry represented a key demarcation point in the comparative histories of gun control in Canada and the United States. The handgun registry also reflected the state's growing confidence that it could successfully regulate at least one category of guns. This belief grew in intensity in the Second World War, when Ottawa established a national registry for all weapons. Although temporary, the registry foreshadowed future attempts to closely track gun ownership.

The state imposed stricter regulations after the Second World War. Chapter 5 examines both the calls for stronger gun control from the end of the war until 1980 and the ferocious resistance voiced by hunters, gun collectors, and target shooters. By the 1960s, a new argument emerged: that *all* firearms, including hunting rifles and shotguns, were potentially dangerous guns needing regulation. As the state shifted its attention to the ownership and use of "ordinary" weapons, firearm owners organized themselves to prevent state intervention. Motivated by strong liberal beliefs in an individual right to property and to freedom from government regulation, as well as gendered ideas of the value of firearm ownership, many firearm owners passively or actively resisted new gun controls. This opposition prevented the Liberal government of Prime Minister Pierre Trudeau from passing ambitious new regulations in 1976. The government instead adopted a law in 1977 that generally left alone average gun owners and instead focused on the criminal use of arms.

Gun owners' success in stymying increased state regulation would be short-lived, however, as shown in chapter 6, which examines the gun control issue from 1980 to the election of Stephen Harper as prime minister in 2006. A lull in the debate over firearm regulation in the 1980s ended abruptly with the December 1989 massacre of fourteen women at the École Polytechnique in Montreal. For the first time, women played a prominent and sustained role in the issue, with women's groups arguing that a woman's right to freedom from gun violence trumped a man's right to own a firearm for recreation. The Montreal Massacre resulted in the passage of modest legislation by the Progressive Conservative government of Prime Minister Brian Mulroney, much to the consternation of gun owners who had supported the Conservatives. Ottawa subsequently demonstrated a growing belief that the state could aggressively regulate arms. In 1995, Liberal Prime Minister Jean Chrétien's government passed the *Firearms Act*, which, among other measures, created a national firearm registry for all guns. The rocky implementation of this legislation, however, laid bare the limits of the modern state's power. Gun owners resisted so strongly that the *Firearms Act* taxed the financial, administrative, and police powers of Ottawa. As a result, the long-gun registry's future remained in continuous doubt, and the topic of gun control did not disappear.

1

"Every man has a right to the possession of his musket": Regulating Firearms before Confederation

Canadians have become accustomed to heated debates over gun control. However, unbeknownst to most, the question of whether the state should allow citizens to freely possess and use arms has a long history. This chapter explores how and why firearms were regulated before 1867 in what became British North America. Economic trends, cultural attitudes, labour strife, civil unrest, firearm technology, constitutional thought, and foreign threats all shaped the extent to which firearms were used and regulated.

Levels of gun ownership changed over time and differed between locales before Confederation. During periods of settlement, Europeans possessed a substantial number of guns to hunt for food, shoot pests, and defend themselves. By the mid-nineteenth century, however, interest in firearms declined in the more established colonies. The decline of subsistence hunting, subsiding concern with foreign invasion, and declining fear of Aboriginal Peoples made guns less necessary. Beginning around 1860, however, British North Americans renewed their interest in firearm ownership and use. Shooting spiked in popularity because of technological improvements to rifles and the belief that modern arms would help defend the colonies against the American behemoth.

Modest levels of firearm ownership resulted in few calls for stronger gun control. Even when circumstances called for gun control, the state doubted its ability to successfully implement regulations. Some legislators also believed that the British constitution bestowed a right to bear arms to men of property. That some leading political and legal figures held such a belief is absent from the existing literature examining constitutional and political thought in British North America.[1] Despite their reticence, authorities at times regulated the ownership or use of arms. Gun laws fell into three categories. First, authorities sought to prevent the discharge of guns in urban spaces. Second, governments placed limits on the possession of weapons at public meetings and polling places. Third, colonial legislators periodically passed laws limiting gun possession or use when fears rose of foreign incursion, or ethnic or class upheaval.

Firearms Technology and Gun Ownership before the Mid-Nineteenth Century

Explaining the history of firearm regulation requires some sense of the extent to which inhabitants possessed guns. It unfortunately is very difficult to determine with precision the level of gun ownership at almost any time in Canadian history. This is unsurprising, since quantifying firearm ownership has also bedevilled historians in Britain and the United States. A historian of gun regulation in England admits that "we have no way of knowing how many Englishmen actually owned firearms."[2] However, the available evidence does suggest that firearm ownership was not universal before Confederation, especially in the mid-nineteenth century in the more established areas of British North America.

Europeans brought firearms to North America, but the number of weapons at any particular time or place depended on their perceived usefulness. Gun technology often made firearms imperfect implements for the colonial context. When John Cabot arrived off the coast of northeastern America in 1497, the most advanced European firearm used a matchlock firing system. This gun, sometimes referred to as "arquebus," had a smooth barrel. Loading entailed pouring powder and ball down the barrel, then ramming the shot and powder into place with a ramrod. After placing a small amount of powder into the "flashpan," the shooter pulled the trigger, causing an arm holding a glowing match tip to swing down, thus igniting the powder in the pan, sparking the powder in the barrel and causing the gun to fire. A weakness particular to matchlocks was the need for a lit match. Men could be caught without lit matches, in which case their matchlocks were useless, while rain could dampen powder or extinguish the match. The match also made loading the matchlock dangerous – the owner had to carefully keep the ember and gunpowder at a safe distance to avoid a potentially disastrous accident.[3]

The desire to overcome the matchlock's weaknesses led gun-makers to develop new firing mechanisms. The wheelock offered one solution. It used sparks created by a spinning metal wheel contacting a piece of iron pyrite to ignite the powder in the pan, thus causing the gun to discharge. The wheelock bettered the matchlock by eliminating the need to keep a lit match. Wheelocks had other weaknesses, however. They were expensive and complicated weapons that only the most skilled gunsmiths could build and repair. This prevented the wheelock from fully replacing the matchlock, although the gun developed a following among the wealthy. The complexity of wheelocks made them especially unsuited to the North American frontier. The flintlock musket offered a simpler solution to the matchlock's weaknesses. It used a piece of flint hitting a striking plate, or frizzen, to create sparks that ignited the primer. Flintlocks possessed several advantages. The flintlock operated without a match, and, unlike the wheelock, was relatively cheap and easy to repair. As a result, it became the most common firearm in what became British North America until well into the nineteenth century.[4]

Regardless of their firing mechanism, smooth-bore muskets possessed several weaknesses. Early arquebuses were heavy and cumbersome, although later muskets became smaller and lighter. Loading a musket took at least thirty seconds and usually required the owner to stand, thus exposing him to enemy fire. Compared to modern weapons, muskets also often misfired and required frequent cleaning to prevent barrels building up a powder residue. Finally, muskets lacked accuracy, with short effective ranges of approximately one hundred metres. This led to the practice of discouraging shooting accuracy amongst soldiers. Instead, massed musketeers devastated enemies at short range. Despite the limitations of such firearms, early French colonists often armed themselves in case of conflict with Aboriginal Peoples or other Europeans. The Iroquois discovered this in 1609, when Samuel de Champlain famously used a firearm to kill two Iroquois chiefs.[5]

The Aboriginal Peoples who experienced muskets found them startling, and many attempted to procure firearms. Aboriginal Peoples, however, tended to use guns to supplement their traditional weapons, rather than replace them, at least until the development of the repeating rifle in the nineteenth century. Aboriginal Peoples recognized the

Figure 1: Aboriginal Peoples integrated firearms early into their traditional lifestyles, as this Mi'kmaq petroglyph of men hunting a porpoise with a musket demonstrates.
Source: Ethnology Collection, Nova Scotia Museum, Halifax, NS, 10.23.82

limitations of such weapons, but desired them because they frightened Aboriginal enemies who lacked guns, became a sign of prestige, and allowed Native groups to unsettle fearful Europeans.[6]

England and France initially banned trading weapons with North American Native Peoples. However, when authorities in New France refused to provide firearms, Aboriginal Peoples procured guns from Dutch traders. After Charles de Montmagny succeeded Champlain as governor of Quebec in 1636, the French could sell guns to Native Peoples who had converted to Christianity. The French provided these weapons to their allies as part of the fur trade, and placed gunsmiths at western outposts so that Natives could repair their firearms.[7]

The English also traded guns to Aboriginal Peoples, mostly through the Hudson's Bay Company, established in 1670. Figures for the number of guns sold or traded exist for nineteen of the company's first thirty years. It distributed at least 10,100 muskets and 100 pairs of pistols and

Figure 2: This image of a Mi'kmaq encampment circa 1791 demonstrates the use of muskets in everyday life of Aboriginal Peoples in pre-Confederation Nova Scotia.
Source: Ethnology Collection, Nova Scotia Museum, Halifax, NS, N-9410

may have provided as many as 16,000 arms. During its first hundred years of operations, the company purchased over 480 trade guns per year on average and in some years ordered over 1000. Like the French, the Hudson's Bay Company also employed gunsmiths to repair the arms of employees and Native Peoples.[8]

Many French colonials became adept at using firearms to hunt and to protect themselves from attacks by foreign powers or hostile Aboriginal Peoples. Firearm ownership, however, though widespread, was never universal in New France. When an English privateer captured Quebec in 1629, his inventory of captured French possessions included just nineteen firearms. The quantity of weapons in New France increased when the French Crown sent military forces to protect the fledgling colony. In addition, in 1669 France ordered the creation of colonial militia companies composed of all able-bodied men between the ages of fifteen and sixty. Many militiamen, however, could not afford a musket.

Large families often possessed a gun for the head of the household only and perhaps for the eldest son, thus leaving younger sons unarmed. Militiamen thus often expected authorities to provide arms; otherwise, they brought only the "oldest and most useless firearms to a muster."[9] When war broke out between France and England in 1744, Canada had 11,285 militiamen but only 7,260 muskets, many unworkable.[10]

Like the residents of New France, not all British colonials possessed arms. Britain was slower than France to establish permanent settlements in what became Canada. After Britain took possession of Acadia in 1713 and then New France in 1763, the British populations in these conquered territories initially remained small, limited mainly to soldiers and government officials. Traders operated in the west, and a few settlers struggled to live year round in Newfoundland during the first half of the eighteenth century. Substantial levels of British immigration occurred with the founding of Halifax in 1749, the Planter migration, and the Loyalists. Many of these early British settlers armed themselves to hunt, fend off animals, or defend themselves from feared attacks by Aboriginal Peoples. Loyalist immigrants, for example, thus noted the important place of hunting in early Upper Canadian life. Elizabeth Simcoe, wife of the first lieutenant governor, reported that their family's diet at York included several types of wild game, including duck, pigeon, deer, and raccoon. Thomas William McGrath reported as late as 1832 that many settlers in Upper Canada carried small arms when walking along roads so they could shoot any game that suddenly appeared.[11]

When agriculture became established, however, farmers had less need to participate in subsistence hunting. Crops and livestock supplanted hunting as the primary means of providing food, although farmers undoubtedly retained some firearms to kill pests and protect property. In addition, prevailing conceptions of ideal land use discouraged hunting by farmers. Hunting was "associated with idleness," Jeffrey McNairn notes, for it drew settlers' attention away from establishing successful farms and was thus "incompatible with economic development."[12] While Catharine Parr Traill noted in 1855 that inhabitants of Upper Canada's backwoods sold hunted meat in more settled areas, nineteenth-century gun sales at country stores suggest a gradual reduction in the use of firearms in rural areas.[13] Douglas McCalla concludes that "there was a heritage of firearms in rural society from pioneer days, but it was not universal and it was markedly diminishing at mid-century." He estimates that Upper Canada imported almost

125,000 pounds of gunpowder in 1861. Even if all of this went to civilian use, each household used only five ounces. The relatively small amount of gunpowder imported "scarcely suggests widespread and extensive shooting by most families."[14]

The transition from subsistence hunting to agriculture occurred of course in different places at different times. Acadians prior to the Deportation established prosperous farms that produced large quantities of food. By the end of the seventeenth century, Acadians still hunted, but it provided just part of their diet.[15] In comparison, the challenges of farming in other parts of the Maritime colonies resulted in more hunting by a "sizable minority" of "rural households whose farms failed to produce subsistence."[16] The Canadian west experienced a later transition from subsistence hunting to agriculture. The ratio of Canadians who declared themselves "hunters" in the 1881 census indicates the importance of using guns to hunt food in the early European settlement of the west (and the reduced importance of hunting in the more established colonies). In Manitoba, the ratio of hunters to the general public was 1:55. The ratio was 1:57 in British Columbia, and 1:43 in the North-West Territories. The eastern provinces, in comparison, had lower ratios of full-time hunters: Quebec (1:1200), New Brunswick (1:3400), Nova Scotia (1:3900), and Ontario (1:2100). The importance of wild animals in the food supply eventually declined in the west as well. By the beginning of the twentieth century, with farms established and game herds depleted, sports hunters lobbied governments to shorten hunting seasons, require hunting licences, and prevent hunters from selling meat to consumers. Only in the Yukon and the north did the gun continue to provide wild meat well into the twentieth century.[17]

Other factors contributed to a decline in firearm ownership. By the mid-nineteenth century, many British North Americans no longer desired weapons out of fear of Aboriginal Peoples. During the early to mid-nineteenth century, many Native groups in the eastern colonies experienced a substantial decline in their strength vis-à-vis the growing European population. Both the English and French had developed strong ties with Aboriginal groups during their colonial competition for control of North America. Settlers often feared attacks by Aboriginals that either sided with an opposing European power or generally expressed hostility to foreign incursions into their territory. But, by the mid-nineteenth century, the fear of potential attacks by Native Peoples subsided in what became eastern Canada. Once Acadia and New France fell permanently into British hands, the influence of Aboriginal nations began to decline in Quebec and the Maritimes, while in New-foundland the death of the last Beothuk in 1829 removed one group tra-ditionally antagonistic to the European presence. As well, disease and alcohol stressed Aboriginal societies. As Native societies weakened, so did colonials' perceived need to own a firearm for protection.[18]

The creation of more effective law-enforcement institutions also de-creased British North Americans' interest in gun ownership, especially in urban areas. Various municipalities, often drawing inspiration from police reforms in Britain and the United States, began to professional-ize policing.[19] The establishment of new police forces led citizens to rely less on themselves for the preservation of the public peace, and, as views changed about who should respond to crime, citizens likely felt less urgency to own firearms for protection.

The end of duelling also contributed to modest levels of gun own-ership by the mid-nineteenth century. Duels usually occurred over a perceived slight that cast doubt on the honour of one of the partici-pants. The practice allowed upper-class men to demonstrate their vir-tue and courage under the threat of death. Most countries officially banned duelling. For example, England outlawed duels in the seven-teenth century. But courts and juries proved unwilling to convict men who murdered others in properly conducted duels, and, as a result, duelling continued, and the practice migrated across the Atlantic to the North American colonies.[20] Early duellists in what became Canada fought with swords, but after the British conquest of New France, pis-tols replaced swords. Firing a pistol took considerably less skill than fencing, which broadened the appeal of duelling by making it easier to participate.[21] Duelling was in vogue in British North America in the early nineteenth century among elite men, such as lawyers, and, to a lesser extent, military officers. These men sought to create a society that encouraged hierarchy and paternalism, and duelling became integral to how they defined their class and masculinity. Duelling therefore, ac-cording to Cecelia Morgan, was "a public display of masculine courage for the eyes of all society to see and record, particularly those of the du-ellists' own class."[22] Opponents of duelling called it a barbaric practice and suggested that men should avoid demonstrations of male honour through physical violence. The critique of duelling also stemmed from the colonial reform movement that opposed the hierarchy that duelling represented. Such criticisms resulted in a decline in duelling, and few duels took place after the 1840s.[23] With the decline, men had no need for a well-crafted set of duelling pistols.

Militia laws of British North America often required men to own and use weapons, but governments often failed to enforce these regulations. The colonial militia laws differed in important ways from the British model. In Britain, the distaste for standing armies made the militia an important body. Britain, however, did not arm all men. In the seventeenth century, Parliament created different divisions of militia. All able-bodied men between the ages of sixteen and sixty could be required to appear for a "general muster." Musters occurred infrequently and offered participants little military training, but they provided opportunities to select those deemed most loyal to the government because of their social status, political views, and religion to serve in the "trained band." The responsibility of arming and drilling fell upon men of property, and the members of the trained band did not retain militia firearms. A new militia act in 1757 dictated the selection of thirty thousand men by lot to serve for three years. The British government also took over responsibility for supplying arms to the militia, although it kept these weapons out of the hands of the militiamen, except when needed to train or fight.[24]

The vulnerability of the early British settlements in North America meant colonies passed laws requiring broader militia participation. In most of the thirteen colonies, all able-bodied free white men between sixteen and sixty had to possess a gun and could be called out for militia service. Nova Scotia followed their example. A 1749 proclamation provided for military training of all men between sixteen and sixty. The colony received representative government in 1758 and in the same year passed a militia act requiring militiamen to provide their own weapon. New Brunswick passed a similar law soon after it became a separate colony in 1784, calling for most men between sixteen and fifty years of age to enrol and keep at home a weapon, bayonet, nine cartridges of gunpowder, and nine bullets, as well as one pound of good gunpowder. Prince Edward Island passed its first militia act in 1780, not long after it became a separate colony in 1777. The island government required all men between sixteen and sixty to bear arms and attend muster.[25]

The militia systems of the pre-Confederation Canadas also required universal participation but demanded less in terms of gun ownership. The 1777 militia ordinance for Lower Canada required militia service of most able-bodied men and obliged militia officers to call out their companies to inspect arms and fire at marks. The law, however, did not require men to own a gun. The 1787 Lower Canada militia ordinance dictated that a militiaman's failure to bring his firearm to muster could result in a fine but again did not dictate gun ownership. By 1803, Lower Canada still did not require men to have a weapon but did stipulate that militia members provide an account of the number of firearms in their possession.[26] Upper Canada became a distinct colony in 1791 and passed a militia act in 1793 requiring most men between sixteen and fifty to enrol in the militia but did not force them to supply their own arms. This changed by 1808, by which time Upper Canada dictated that each militiaman had to provide himself a firearm with at least six rounds of ball and sufficient powder, unless his commanding officer excused him from the requirement because he could not procure a weapon.[27]

These militia laws did not result in all men either owning or using arms. Prince Edward Island legislators acknowledged that many men lacked guns. The 1780 legislation recognized that "many of the Settlers of this place cannot bear the expence [sic] of purchasing Fire Arms and Ammunition." The colony thus excused them from keeping arms in good order until the government provided weapons.[28] While the colony received some arms from Britain, in 1803 Lieutenant Governor Edmund Fanning claimed that Prince Edward Island's defence consisted of "a small and dispersed Body of Unarmed and Undisciplined Militia." In 1812, the island had 546 serviceable muskets for its 2,643 militia members.[29] In New Brunswick, the requirement in the 1787 act that militiamen provide their own arms proved impossible to enforce, because many of the Loyalist immigrants had sold their muskets out of financial necessity. Those who brought arms often arrived with their weapons in terrible condition. At the outbreak of the War of 1812, New Brunswick possessed only 437 weapons, of which 253 were deemed unserviceable, to arm the colony's militia of four thousand members. By the 1820s, New Brunswick owned 455 muskets, thirty-eight pistols, and eighteen carbines to arm a militia of ten thousand.[30] In Nova Scotia, Thomas Chandler Haliburton noted in 1829 that the colony's militia "have no uniforms, nor are they now generally armed," while in 1842 the adjutant-general of the colony said the militia was in a "deplorable state."[31] In 1851, the Speaker of the Nova Scotia Assembly asked whether the militia law should even be included in the revised statutes, since the law had "fallen into disuse, although an annual act gave the governor power to call it into operation."[32] Nova Scotia's militia also lacked sufficient arms. By 1857, the Nova Scotia militia had 4,863 firearms, most of which were broken and outdated.[33]

The militia of Upper Canada similarly lacked arms. The propagation of the "militia myth" in the late nineteenth century established an erroneous belief that the militia served as the backbone of the defence of early Upper Canada, especially during the War of 1812. In fact, regular forces largely took responsibility for defending British possessions in North America, in part because militia members often proved reluctant to serve. The militia was also ineffective because of a lack of firearms. After the British attack on the *Chesapeake* in 1807 led to fears of war with the United States, Isaac Brock chose not to call out the Upper Canada militia, because of a paucity of available firearms. While the law required militia members to bring their own arms to train, many men lacked the means to procure a weapon. The government distributed several thousand muskets in Upper Canada between 1795 and 1812, but most were soon lost, broken, or sold. In 1822, Robert Gourlay thus observed that Upper Canada militiamen were "imperfectly armed" although required by law to own weapons.[34] Such statements support McCalla's claim that firearms ownership, even in rural Upper Canada, was not universal.

The Lower Canada militia also lacked enough firearms. In 1807, the colony's 54,072 militiamen possessed only 10,044 muskets. By 1815, this number decreased to just under 7,500 for the colony's 53,929 militiamen. In 1827, the number of official militia members had increased to 79,542, but the number of muskets in their possession grew to only 10,403. The most careful historical study of the militia's arms concludes that fewer than 20 per cent of Lower Canada's militia had a weapon in the early nineteenth century.[35] This lack of arms hampered efforts to defend the eastern townships of Quebec in the War of 1812. In April 1813, militia leader Lieutenant-Colonel Henry Cull pleaded for arms because of the lack of privately owned guns. Cull noted that "with the few old Firelocks, fowling pieces, Pitchforks, etc. that we could muster, it is not very probable that our defence would redound much to our Honor or the advantage of the Country." Later, in October 1813, Cull again noted that the local militiamen required arms because "the very few rusty neglected fowling pieces that some few men (addicted to Hunting) have to snap three or four times probably at a Partridge are not worthy to be reckon'd."[36] In the late 1820s, Lower Canada militia officers took roll-calls on muster days but organized little or no drilling or shooting.[37]

The amalgamation of Upper Canada (which became known as Canada West) and Lower Canada (Canada East) into the United Province of Canada in 1841 did not result in the creation of a well-armed militia.

By the mid-nineteenth century the institution was in disrepair. According to Canada's leading military historian, the colonial militias were "unarmed, untrained, and by the 1840s, unorganized."[38] The Crimean War of 1853 to 1856 saw a brief burst of interest in the militia. For example, the Province of Canada's 1855 *Militia Act* allowed for the creation of an active militia of five thousand to be armed, equipped, and paid five shillings per day for ten days of training. Interest soon waned, however, and the province did not renew the 1855 act in 1858.[39] The weakness of the various militias in British North America meant that most inhabitants of the colonies did not become acquainted with weapons or purchase guns because of compulsory military service.

The lack of firearms in the Canadas was evident in the extent to which men involved in the uprisings of 1837 and 1838 had guns. Many of the men who assembled to support William Lyon Mackenzie's rebellion in 1837 came unarmed. Similarly, many of the participants in the Lower Canadian rebellion required guns, and the rebellion's leaders constantly pursued additional weapons. According to Allan Greer, the rural patriots were "pathetically short of arms." While there were "hunting fusils hanging in many an habitant cabin," they tended to be "old and unreliable, and in any case there were only enough for a small proportion of the insurgents."[40]

The limited use of firearms in violent crime further indicates the level of gun ownership in what became eastern Canada in the first half of the nineteenth century. While people feared crime, few murderers killed with guns. In 1857, the *Globe* reported on an elderly man who had shot his stepson but noted that it was "not often we are called upon to record man-shooting in Canada."[41] Even the most violent cities experienced relatively small numbers of homicides using guns. Halifax in the eighteenth and nineteenth centuries had a substantial military garrison. Soldiers drank, caroused, visited brothels, and occasionally killed, with the result that Halifax was one of the most violent cities in North America. Nevertheless, few murderers used guns. Similarly, in Lower Canada, a relatively violent society in the first half of the nineteenth century, civilians rarely employed firearms in murders. Even most soldiers in Lower Canada preferred to use swords or bayonets when they became involved in interpersonal violence.[42]

Regulating Firearms before the Mid-Nineteenth Century

While the number of firearms in circulation appears modest, authorities still regulated the possession or use of guns in three different situations. Some laws limited the discharge of firearms in urban areas. Legislators passed a second set of measures to prevent violence at polls and at public meetings. The third group of laws prevented the possession of firearms in places and at times that unrest, or potential unrest, threatened the state or its goals.

Several colonies and communities limited the discharge of weapons in urban areas. Such shooting posed several obvious problems. Noisy gunfire could constitute a nuisance, startling horses and causing injuries to their riders or bystanders. Guns discharged in heavily populated areas could also accidentally strike people or property. As well, a desire to prevent fires long motivated the regulation of gunpowder and guns in urban areas.[43]

Some colonial legislatures banned shooting in urban centres. In 1758, Nova Scotia outlawed the "unnecessary" firing of guns in Halifax and by 1807 extended the ban to other towns in the colony. Prince Edward Island banned the unnecessary firing of guns in Charlottetown.[44] The Newfoundland legislature noted in 1835 that "many accidents have occurred and much inconvenience arisen from the custom of unnecessarily discharging Guns and other Fire Arms" in St John's and several other communities "during the season of Christmas and on the occasion of other festivals." Newfoundland thus banned the discharge of guns without a reasonable cause in a number of communities.[45] The Canadas also had a tradition of regulating the discharge of firearms in urban areas. In the eighteenth century, Montreal, Quebec City, and Trois-Rivières outlawed shooting guns within their boundaries,[46] and other communities followed suit in the nineteenth century.[47] By 1852, Hamilton included in its nuisance by-laws a provision that "no person shall fire any gun or other fire arms ... within the City."[48] Toronto also had a measure against the discharge of guns among its nuisance and preservation of order by-laws. Quebec City created perhaps the strictest municipal gun law when, in 1865, it forbade anyone from carrying a firearm in public places. [49] These by-laws were thus relatively common. While local governments did not usually limit the ownership of arms, they sought to regulate usage in areas of high population density.

A second group of gun control measures sought to prevent the use of firearms at polling places and public meetings. The Canadas experienced frequent election-day violence in the mid-nineteenth century. In 1842, the Province of Canada passed legislation allowing an election returning officer or a deputy returning officer to demand offensive weapons, including firearms, from anyone in possession of such arms. People who refused could be punished with a fine of up to twenty-five pounds and/or imprisonment of up to three months. Seized weapons could be returned following the election. To prevent arms from flowing into a polling area, the legislature also banned anyone who had not been resident in the polling district in the previous six months from coming within two miles of a polling place with a firearm. Doing so could lead to a hefty fine of up to fifty pounds and/or six months' imprisonment.[50]

The Province of Canada created similar provisions to prevent men arming themselves while attending public meetings. Legislation enacted in 1843 allowed any justice of the peace within whose jurisdiction a public meeting had been called to demand offensive weapons. Failure to hand over a weapon could result in a smaller fine than on election days – up to forty shillings. If the owner peaceably and quietly delivered the weapon, he or she could apply to have the gun returned. As an added protection, no armed person could approach within two miles of any public meeting. The fine for an infraction of this ban was again high, although lower than carrying weapons close to a polling place – up to a twenty-five pound fine and/or imprisonment for up to three months. Those exempted from these bans included the sheriff, justices of the peace, mayors or high bailiffs of a city or town, and constables or special constables.[51]

Perceived threats to the state or its goals resulted in the third group of firearm controls. These laws generally shared two common characteristics. First, legislators typically sought to limit the possession or use of guns by groups deemed dangerous, rather than to regulate all citizens. Second, legislators erected temporary measures that did not permanently disarm inhabitants. This reflected the sense that legislators had no need or right to permanently interfere with gun ownership. Between the 1750s and the 1840s, three episodes resulted in this type of legislation: the British conquest of Canada, the 1837–8 rebellions in the Canadas, and the Irish influx and canal riots of the 1840s.

The British victories over France in northern North America in the eighteenth century resulted in efforts to regulate arms amongst the French populations. Following the capture of Acadia in 1710, Britain remained concerned about a French uprising. As a result, British authorities attempted to secure oaths of allegiance from the Acadian population. Although those efforts usually failed, the British allowed the Acadians firearms until just before the Deportation. In June 1755, British forces seized approximately four hundred firearms. Lieutenant Governor Charles Lawrence subsequently issued a proclamation that any inhabitants found with firearms would be "treated as Rebells to

His Majesty." Acadians responded by surrendering almost three thousand guns.[52] The seizure of firearms prior to the Deportation reflected the desire to limit firearm ownership by a group deemed dangerous, but the Deportation meant that, in this unusual case, disarmament was permanent.

After the fall of Canada, Britain seized, then regulated, arms. The British initially disarmed inhabitants and obliged the French to swear an oath of allegiance to the British Crown.[53] Robert Monckton issued a proclamation following Britain's victory at Quebec City in 1759 permitting the defeated French to return to their parishes, take possession of their lands, and practise their religion, provided that they "surrender their arms, take the oath of fidelity and remain peaceably in their homes."[54] In 1760, after the French surrender at Montreal, all inhabitants who had not turned in their arms were ordered to do so. This resulted in the delivery of many guns in some areas. For example, the almost six hundred residents of Trois-Rivières and its suburbs delivered 212 firearms to authorities, while the roughly 331 inhabitants of Maskinongé handed in 128 guns.[55]

The British soon allowed some French Canadians to use tightly regulated weapons. To control the countryside, the British allowed former Canadien militia leaders firearms. In 1761, the British also permitted a small number of arms for hunting in the Trois-Rivières district. Authorities distributed firearms and gun permits "for the relief of the inhabitants" and intended that "guns and permits should be lent mutually and of good will from one to another among the inhabitants of the same parish." Captains of the militia ensured that the arms remained longest in the possession of those "who are poorest" so that they could hunt. In addition to these shared guns, the governor also provided a firearm and permit to the seignior and an arm and permit to the curé.[56] The British, however, distributed only a small number of guns. For example, the residents of Maskinongé had surrendered 128 firearms to authorities. The British subsequently allowed one weapon for the curé and eight arms for the inhabitants to share. Similarly, the roughly 566 residents of Machiche had delivered 179 guns to the government, but received just five weapons to share.[57] Even when added to the small number of arms held by the officers and sergeants of the militia, it is clear that a much smaller proportion of French Canadians possessed arms immediately after the fall of New France.

Officials sometimes complained that Canadians misused weapons provided for hunting, or possessed guns illegally. The military governor of Quebec, James Murray, complained that many French Canadians hid their arms and used them illegally. He thus banned workers and artisans from carrying arms in Quebec City in 1761.[58] In 1762, the acting captain of militia at Yamaska received word that more guns than permits had been distributed, and thus he had to search for arms. Residents had to hand surplus weapons to authorities, and the British threatened severe punishment for people who possessed excess guns in the future.[59] Two years later, in March 1764, the government ordered the inhabitants of Batiscan and Rivière Batiscan to surrender their arms to authorities in Trois-Rivières, because they refused "so insolently to employ them for the welfare of the public." They thus did not "deserve to have them for their personal interest." Further, the British ordered the search for and seizure of arms acquired illegally in the parish. Owners of houses in which authorities found guns faced a twelve dollar fine.[60]

These limitations on gun ownership ended when the civil government that replaced the military regime in August 1764 did not reintroduce the measures. The Lower Canada militia ordinance of 1777 required the calling out of militiamen for the inspection of their arms. Authorities designed the ordinance to encourage militia service during the period of the American Revolution, using a ban on gun ownership as a stick. Anyone who refused to serve faced several penalties, including being "rendered incapable" of keeping or bearing firearms.[61] The militia law of 1787 lacked this particular penalty, likely because the crisis caused by the American Revolution had ended.

The 1837–8 rebellions in Upper and Lower Canada also led to the passage of legislation designed to disarm potential rebels. Upper Canada acted because men had "clandestinely and unlawfully assembled" and had "practiced Military Training and Exercising in Arms, to the great terror and alarm of Her Majesty's loyal Subjects." While many rebels in fact lacked arms, Upper Canada banned meetings for the purpose of drilling or practising in the use of arms, threatening violators with incarceration for up to two years. The government permitted magistrates to seize arms if one or more witnesses under oath provided evidence of possession for a purpose dangerous to the public peace. The legislation also enabled justices to issue warrants to conduct searches of homes or other buildings for firearms. If the occupant refused admission, the house or building could be entered by force. Further, the legislation allowed for authorities to arrest and detain any person found carrying arms "in such manner and at such times" as to afford "just grounds of suspicion that the same are for purposes dangerous to the public peace."[62] The legislation allowed for the eventual return of seized guns. Upper Canada made these measures temporary – they expired once the fear of further rebellion subsided.

Beginning in 1838, the Special Council that administered Lower Canada after the outbreak of rebellion issued ordinances that imposed gun regulation. Although similar to Upper Canada's law, the Lower Canada measure possessed slightly more draconian provisions, presumably because of the more serious nature of the Lower Canada rebellion. A justice of the peace or other authorized person could seize firearms from any person in the province, with the exception of guns in the hands of military forces or government officials. Unlike Upper Canada, Lower Canada did not require credible witnesses to provide evidence to take such action. The ordinance also permitted justices of the peace or other authorized persons to enter dwellings or other buildings to look for weapons, but, unlike in Upper Canada, did not require a warrant. All seized weapons went to one of several secure locations, including the police offices in Montreal, Quebec, or Trois-Rivières, the office of the clerk of the peace in Sherbrooke, or a military post. Resisting implementation of the act could result in three months in jail. Another difference from the Upper Canada legislation was that the Lower Canadian law did not include provisions for the return of seized weapons. A final difference was that the Lower Canada ordinance eventually became permanent: initially to expire 1 January 1840, it was continued until 1 June 1840, then made permanent.[63]

There was British precedent for these Canadian measures, although Lower Canada created a law in some ways more stringent than the British antecedents. Following the Peterloo Massacre of 1819, the British Parliament passed legislation designed to prevent a feared revolution, including an act to prevent unlawful training in the use of arms or military drill. It differed from the measures in Upper Canada in the available punishments. Courts could sentence persons who trained others in the use of arms to seven years' transportation or two years' imprisonment. Persons who attended a meeting to receive training in arms faced a penalty of up to two years' incarceration. Another response was the 1820 *Seizure of Arms Act*, which allowed justices of the peace in counties marked by disturbances to seize arms. The Upper Canada act was most similar to the British statute in that both, unlike the Lower Canadian ordinance, included some procedural safeguards, such as the requirement that authorities acquire a warrant to search homes.[64]

An 1845 act designed to disarm canal workers represented the third example of gun legislation meant to respond to threats to the state or its goals. In the early 1840s, the Province of Canada contracted out the construction of several canals. There were, however, never enough jobs for the large number of job seekers. This created social tensions around canals, as did fluctuations in the demand for labour and traditions of animosity between Catholics and Protestants and between immigrants from different parts of Ireland. Workers complained of poor wages, and local residents expressed concern over the existence of large groups of rowdy, unhappy young men.[65]

When canal workers rioted or fought amongst themselves, they used a variety of weapons, including fists, clubs, swords, pikes, and pitchforks. Workers also sometimes succeeded in procuring guns, causing great concern for colonial officials. In 1843, for example, a number of workers on the Lachine Canal had firearms. Labour battles involving canal workers near Williamsburg, Upper Canada, in 1844 resulted in frequent complaints by officials and local residents that canal workers possessed guns. The tendency of canal men to acquire weapons by breaking into the homes of local residents proved an especially worrying practice.[66] For example, in November 1844, five justices of the peace from the Cornwall area reported that labourers daily tried to steal firearms, often with success, and had even attempted to capture caches of militia weapons.[67] Justices of the peace and other inhabitants from the County of Dundas claimed that labourers had "forcibly broken open houses and taken out fire-arms," and were "furnishing themselves with arms and ammunition by various means, and from various sources."[68] By early 1845, reports indicated that Welland Canal construction workers had supplied themselves with weapons, possibly by bringing them in from Buffalo.[69]

Authorities had few means to disarm canal workers. An engineer convinced a number of armed labourers at the Beauharnois Canal to hand their weapons to officials, although they eventually returned these guns because they had no legal right to retain them.[70] In November 1844, fear of armed construction workers at the Lachine Canal led Governor General Charles Metcalfe to order the disarmament of the labourers using the 1838 Lower Canada measure for seizing weapons. The resulting sweep of canal workers' residences resulted in the seizure of fifty-one firearms. A similar sweep of residences at the Beauharnois Canal resulted in the seizure of just two arms. The small number reflected the modest size of the workforce on the Beauharnois Canal, the limited availability of guns, or, perhaps, that news of the search spread quickly amongst the workers, who responded by hiding their arms.[71] Authorities remained nervous, despite the seizures. In January 1845, a stipendiary magistrate of the Lachine Police said that his force could do little to control the canal workers because of the small size of the police force and because labourers were "in possession of large quantities of fire-arms."[72]

The fear of armed canal workers led to legislation in 1845 allowing for limitations on gun possession at public works. Unlike the 1838 disarming statute, which applied only to Canada East, the 1845 act applied to the entire Province of Canada. The attorney general for Canada East, James Smith, deemed the existing tools of the criminal justice system insufficient to police the hordes of men building public works.[73] Anti-Irish sentiments played a substantial role in the passage of the legislation. Assemblyman George Macdonell of Dundas encouraged legislative action because, he said, canal workers liked to pillage arms from local inhabitants, fight amongst themselves, and generally act like a "horde of savages." Similarly, Edward Hale, an English-educated businessman representing Sherbrooke, supported the bill because it was "well known" that the Irish were "warm-blooded, and apt to quarrel."[74]

The legislature created an act flexible enough to disarm canal workers when and where required. It allowed the governor in council to proclaim the act in force in areas in which public works, such as canals, were under construction. The state could employ two prongs of the legislation to keep order. First, the legislation permitted the formation of a mounted police force to assist magistrates. Second, the act could ban all public works construction employees from possessing a firearm. Unlike the 1838 Lower Canada measure, the 1845 law allowed for the return of weapons. When a weapon was delivered to a local magistrate, the owner would receive a receipt showing that the gun had been deposited. Once the act ceased to be in force, authorities would return the arm. Weapons kept illegally could be seized and ownership forfeited to the government, which could sell such confiscated arms. The government threatened hefty potential penalties of between ten and twenty-five pounds for concealing, or assisting in the concealment of, weapons. To encourage enforcement, informers received half of these fines. Moreover, the legislation allowed justices of the peace to authorize searches for and seizure of weapons from any person or household with sufficient evidence suggesting the presence of a weapon. Anyone found carrying a weapon could also be arrested. Like most such laws, the government made the act temporary – it remained in force for two years, although the legislature extended it several times until it finally expired in 1860.[75]

Despite the serious canal violence, aspects of the 1845 measure created controversy in the Assembly. The debates over the legislation shed light on attitudes to firearms in the Canadas and, most importantly, on the perceived constitutional right of British subjects to possess arms for their own defence. While the bill ultimately passed by a wide margin, opponents of the proposed law issued several complaints. A major concern was that disarming citizens threatened to violate the British constitution. Attorney General James Smith suggested that the government could not, in normal circumstances, disarm inhabitants, but he deemed acceptable this targeted and temporary measure. He admitted that the powers applied for were "great, but when taken into consideration with the circumstances of the case, they were very limited." To allay fears that the measure violated the rights of Englishmen, Smith suggested that many of the canal workers would eventually move to the United States upon the completion of the canal work. As a result, "nothing could arise from this bill which would be injurious to the rights of citizens of the country." Smith also noted that he would consider a "general disarming measure" to be "an atrocious one," but his bill targeted only dangerous inhabitants. When some legislators worried that the 1845 legislation might result in the disarming of citizens living near a canal, Smith assured them that this would not occur.

Other legislators also suggested that the act risked trampling established liberties. Former attorney general for Upper Canada, Robert Baldwin, felt reluctant to grant "great and arbitrary powers" to the executive, and compared the proposal to the Irish coercion acts – the various laws passed to suppress dissent and impose order in Ireland. He nevertheless supported the legislation. While "it could never be pleasant" to "restrict the liberties of the subject" in the context of public works violence, "the restriction for a time might prevent its loss for ever." Assemblyman Thomas Cushing Aylwin, a reformer, lawyer, and former solicitor general for Lower Canada, voted against the bill. In attacking the legislation, he invoked the memory of the controversial Irish coercion acts, claiming that the proposed law was "one of those disarming Bills" which had "aroused the indignation of the people of Britain and Ireland, not once but a dozen times." He called the plan an "unconstitutional exercise of power" that targeted the poor and left alone men of high standing who walked about armed. Reformer Joseph-Édouard Cauchon, a journalist who was called to the bar but did not practise, also believed the proposed act arbitrary and unjust, and thus voted against the bill.[76]

It is somewhat unclear which constitutional principle it was that critics of the act had in mind. They may have been concerned that the act would infringe on the right to property by taking firearms, albeit briefly. The Toronto *Globe* had expressed this view after the 1844 attempts to disarm canal workers. It argued that the government had to limit such action to situations dangerous to the public. "As a general rule," suggested the *Globe*, "every man has a right to the possession of his musket, or other weapons, as much as any other kind of property," and it was "only when an unlawful use of those arms is about to be made, either collectively or individually, that the government has a right to deprive the owners of them."[77]

It is more likely, however, that critics of the legislation felt unease with the potential infringement of the right to bear arms found in the English *Bill of Rights* of 1689. Article VII provides "that the Subjects which are Protestants may have Armes for their defence suitable to their Condition and as allowed by Law."[78] William Blackstone repeated, and disseminated, this right. He called Article VII an "auxiliary right": "The fifth and last auxiliary right of the subject ... is that of having arms for their defence, suitable to their condition and degree, and such as are allowed by law."[79] Like the American Second Amendment, Article VII has provoked scholarly debate about its meaning. A minority of scholars, most prominently Joyce Lee Malcolm, argue that the provision guaranteed a broad right to the mass of Englishmen to bear arms.[80] The majority position is that the guarantee contained several important limitations. Lois Schwoerer offers this view, noting that only Protestants had the right to arms, which reflected the strong hostility to Catholics in English society. As well, the provision had a class limitation, for men could only be armed "suitable to their Condition." This, says Schwoerer, "reflected the social and economic prejudices of upper-class English society."[81] After all, the upper class did not want *all* Protestants armed. The right to possess arms was associated with property ownership – men without property had little or no right to bear arms.

The 1845 debates over gun regulation demonstrated that some British North Americans held dear the right to bear arms, at least the right of men of property to bear arms as described by Schwoerer. The Glorious Revolution and the English *Bill of Rights* held a privileged place in the conception of "British justice" espoused by many nineteenth-century Canadian lawyers. As well, Blackstone was important in the education of nineteenth-century common law lawyers, many of whom had begun to espouse liberal views regarding rights and property by the 1840s.[82] It is thus unsurprising that some members of the bar expressed a belief in the right to possess arms. Lewis Drummond, a Catholic, Irish-born lawyer, provided the clearest evidence that a belief in the right to bear arms existed in the minds of some Canadian legislators. Drummond called the bill a "tyrannical and arbitrary measure," expressly invoking the "constitutional right that all men possessed to keep and carry arms for the protection of their property." Drummond generally supported the cause of Irish canal workers, but he refused to extend the right to bear arms to them, because they lacked property. In his view, labourers had "no property to protect, they were too poor to acquire any, and therefore it was better that a little should be sacrificed to prevent the loss of a single life, or the commission of an act of violence." The "possession of arms among these men, when driven by the arbitrary acts of the contractors, or want, to acts of violence, might tend to serious consequences, and therefore their being deprived of them [i.e., firearms] would contribute to the peace of the country and their own welfare."[83] Men without property, such as the canal workers, could thus not claim full rights of British citizenship, including a right to a gun. Drummond's overt comments, and the more opaque statements of Baldwin, Aylwin, Cauchon, and Smith, suggest that a limited right to bear arms – to protect property – was a relatively common view in the mid 1840s, at least amongst men with some legal training. No member of the Assembly, it should be noted, spoke against such a right.[84]

Fear of rowdy Irish immigrants also led to legislation in New Brunswick and Nova Scotia. A series of violent battles took place between Orangeman and Irish Catholic immigrants in New Brunswick in the late 1840s. In many instances, both sides, aware of rising tensions, collected firearms before taking part in pitched battles. This led the colony to pass legislation in 1849 that dictated that people who openly carried "dangerous and unusual weapons" in any public place in a manner calculated to create terror and alarm could be imprisoned for up to twelve months.[85] Nova Scotia, which also experienced Irish Catholic versus Orange violence, adopted an identical provision by 1851.[86] New Brunswick further targeted "deadly weapons" in 1861. The legislature suggested that the "practice of carrying deadly weapons about the person" was "attended with great danger, and tends to aggravate the consequences of sudden quarrels." The legislature thus banned any person from carrying various weapons, including daggers, metal knuckles, skull-crackers, slung shots, or "other offensive weapon."[87] The legislation, however, included no mention of guns, and two factors suggest against the view that "other offensive weapon" included firearms. First, legislators who identified the need for action did not indicate the existence of a gun problem.[88] Second, New Brunswick legislators likely shared the view of their Upper Canadian compatriots that men of property had a right to own and carry firearms for self-defence. A similar law passed in the Province of Canada had not placed limits on carrying firearms. In 1859, the Province of Canada prohibited the carrying of daggers, dirks, iron knuckles, skull crackers, slung shots, or "other offensive weapons of a like character."[89] Lawyer John Prince introduced the measure in the Legislative Council, arguing that weapons made for assassination and murder should be less available. Weapons like the bowie knife were "un-English" and were "used only by cowards." The law, however, did not apply to firearms. The bill introduced in the legislature had mentioned pistols, but legislators removed the reference in the final act. The views of the government leader may explain this decision. John A. Macdonald, as will be shown in chapter 2, generally opposed firearm regulation throughout his career.[90]

A Growing Interest in Firearms

The limited number of guns in the established regions of British North America meant that firearms posed slight danger in normal circumstances. A relatively unarmed citizenry was not, however, a permanent condition. Beginning around 1860, a growing number of people expressed interest in gun use and ownership. A desire to defend the colonies against possible attacks from the United States partly helps explain this interest. The United States became a major military power during the American Civil War. When the war began in April 1861, the United States Army consisted of approximately sixteen thousand soldiers. By the war's conclusion, 2.5 million men had served in the Union Army alone, and the North had produced as many as 3 million firearms.[91]

High tensions with the United States revitalized interest in the colonial militias. New Brunswick established two classes of militia in 1862. The first class, the sedentary, consisted of all men between eighteen and forty-five. The second class, the active, consisted of volunteers who promised to drill six days each year. Nova Scotia also passed a new militia act in 1862. The legislation required universal compulsory militia training. By the end of 1864, over 56,000 men had enrolled in Nova Scotia militia regiments (although there were enough rifles only for officers and non-commissioned officers). Prince Edward Island enacted a new militia law that established volunteer, general, and sedentary units. The Province of Canada also passed legislation to develop the militia.[92] The militia service required by these new measures exposed more inhabitants of British North America to firearms.

The "volunteer movement" became another outlet for men to gain experience with guns. Volunteers formed their own companies, elected officers, chose equipment, and trained themselves. By the early 1860s, volunteer rifle companies established themselves across British North America. In 1860, Nova Scotia alone had thirty-six volunteer companies, with almost 2,300 men enrolled. The popularity of volunteering was short-lived but significant. The volunteer movement required frequent meetings for drill and shooting practice. Inhabitants of rural areas found it almost impossible to meet a more rigorous schedule of meetings and had limited resources to pay for ammunition and drill instructors. Some units thus disbanded.[93] However, for a brief period, many urban men joined and, as a result, became more familiar with firearms.

Several factors motivated the volunteer movement. The Crimean War spurred interest in the formation of volunteer militia units, as did the British decision to reduce the size of its military forces in British North America. The visit of the Prince of Wales to British North America in 1860 provided further motivation volunteering. As the Prince of Wales travelled across the colonies, volunteer units formed for the opportunity to parade before Queen Victoria's son, or perhaps even to meet him.[94] British Columbians also valued volunteer companies as defenders against Aboriginal Peoples. Volunteer rifle units "would operate as a deterrent" to Aboriginal aggression and thus "might prevent what it would require many regiments of Her Majesty's troops to remedy."[95]

Volunteering also became popular because of the social aspects of the movement. Canadian volunteer units acted as bastions of middle-class propriety, nativism, and masculinity, especially in urban centres. The election of officers made volunteer units similar to the many fraternal associations popular in the mid-nineteenth century. Units often offered a wide variety of activities for members, such as rifle shooting, curling competitions, and dinners.[96] For instance, at the annual meeting of Scottish Volunteers in Halifax in 1863, a "sumptuous supper" was provided by the officers. Bagpipes played, and volunteers gave toasts "drunk with enthusiasm" to Queen Victoria, the Prince and Prin-

Figure 3: Volunteering grew in popularity in part because of the social
aspects of the movement, including dinners, such as this dinner in Montreal
in honour of the bandmaster of a Montreal rifle brigade.
Source: *Canadian Illustrated News* 6, no. 21 (23 November 1872): 324

cess of Wales, and other members of the royal family.[97] Advocates of
volunteering further claimed that participation affirmed one's manliness and social position. As the *British Columbian* suggested, there was
"something noble and manly in being able to defend oneself," and thus
"young men should be trained to defend this their adopted soil."[98]

The interest in volunteering was also motivated, in part, by technological improvements to weapons that made arms more deadly, accurate, and easier to use. By the end of the American Civil War, the
industrial production of firearms moved gun making from the artisan's
workshop to the factory. Industrial manufacturing allowed for the mass
production of weapons that incorporated several important technological improvements: rifled arms largely replaced smooth-bore weapons;
breech-loading guns supplanted muzzle-loaders; cartridges became
self-contained; and arms could hold several rounds of ammunition.[99]

The widespread use of rifling made firearms more accurate and extended their range. The ball fired by smooth-bore muskets had to be

small enough to be rammed into the barrel. When the gun went off, the ball ricocheted off the sides so that its trajectory was determined by its final bounce out of the weapon. Muskets could be made more accurate by rifling the inside of the barrel. Gun makers had long known that grooving the barrel so that the projectile would spin made arms more accurate, but smooth-bore weapons remained popular because of the challenges of rifling. Rifled weapons took longer to load. As well, rifled muskets developed a gunpowder residue and thus required frequent cleaning. Rifled guns also cost more. As a result, some European nations created special rifle units to harass enemies at long range but continued to arm most soldiers with smooth-bore muskets. Rifle technology, however, took a great step forward when Claude-Étienne Minié developed a new type of muzzle-loaded ammunition. When fired, the base of the "Minié ball" expanded, forcing it to connect to the rifling in the gun's barrel. This led the bullet to spin as it emerged from the rifle and also helped clean the barrel of residue. This innovation was then improved upon further. In the 1850s, for example, the British Snider-Enfield rifle fired a "cylindro-conoidal" projectile, that is, a lead cylinder with a cone nose. Rifled weapons such as the Snider-Enfield had an effective range three times that of smooth-bore muskets.[100]

The creation of breech-loaded weapons marked another key technological advancement. The most famous of the early breech-loading weapons was the "needle gun" developed by the Prussian Johann Nikolaus von Dreyse. His weapon used a long needle-shaped firing pin to ignite a primer in a paper cartridge. After each shot, the Dreyse rifle could be loaded again by using a sliding bolt action mechanism. The Prussian army began adopting Dreyse breech-loaders in the 1840s and used them in several campaigns. In Prussia's victorious war against Austria in 1866, for example, Prussian soldiers took advantage of the technology to lie prone and fire six shots for every one shot fired by the Austrians. Other European states soon developed breech-loading designs. For example, Britain converted Snider-Enfield rifles to load at the breech, then adopted a new model, the Martini-Henry. These weapons affected military tactics. Armies stopped bringing together massed infantry formations to fight in close quarters, and cavalry became more vulnerable to long-range fire.[101]

Developments in ammunition in the late nineteenth century made these breech-loading rifles even more efficient. Firearms using older "black powder" gunpowder spewed smoke, but new, more powerful smokeless powder increased the range of weapons and meant that impenetrable smoke no longer obscured battlefields. As well, metal cartridges eventually replaced paper ones, allowing for easier loading.[102]

The deadliness of the nineteenth-century rifle increased further with the invention of repeating rifles that held several shots in a magazine. Various American companies began producing such weapons for use in the Civil War. Christopher Spencer patented a rifle in 1860 that carried seven cartridges. Oliver Fisher Winchester had operated a factory producing men's dress shorts, but in 1857 he purchased the Volcanic Repeating Arms Company. He reorganized it into the New Haven Arms Company, and then, in 1867, into the Winchester Repeating Arms Company. Winchester's chief gun designer, Benjamin Tyler Henry, had developed the Henry repeating rifle (patented in 1860) that saw extensive use in the Civil War and became the first of a series of Winchester guns.[103]

Rifled weapons came to dominate the firearm market, although one smooth-bore weapon also eventually became popular: the shotgun. Shotguns normally fired a number of small pellets, or "shot." The shot spread out after firing, and thus shotguns lacked accuracy at long ranges. The power of each projectile was relatively low, but the dispersion pattern of the projectiles made shotguns useful for hunting birds and small game. Gun makers eventually improved the design of shotguns that sustained the popularity of such weapons. John Browning revolutionized shotgun design when, in 1887, he introduced a repeating shotgun, and later, a pump action design.[104]

British North Americans took note of, and then embraced, technologically advanced long guns. In 1866, for example, several men tested Henry's repeating rifle and boasted that they fired fifteen shots in just 13.5 seconds.[105] The *Globe* suggested arming volunteer units with modern weapons, since the "immense superiority" of breech-loading, repeating rifles "over the ordinary breech-loading rifle, can no more be questioned than the value of the needle gun as compared with the Austrian musket."[106]

Canada did not produce its own modern rifles in the 1860s, but foreign manufacturers made them widely available. After the conclusion of the American Civil War, businesses sold off vast numbers of unnecessary weapons in the open market, including in the Canadian market. In 1866, a Boston merchant attempted to sell part of a huge stockpile of rifles by advertising in Toronto. The company offered ten thousand used rifles for $1.25 each, and ten thousand new rifles for $5.25 each. These rifles had "been in use in the late war."[107] The war's end also

Figure 4: The introduction of breech-loaded magazine rifles revolutionized
long guns in the nineteenth century.
Source: Glenbow Archives, NA-1811-26

meant that American gun manufacturers looked to foreign markets, including Canada. Businesses in British North America soon offered various models of modern rifles. The Province of Canada armed a handful of the Queen's Own Rifles with Spencer repeating rifles to repulse the Fenian raiders.[108]

Access to these technologically advanced guns helped spur interest in rifle associations, which proved even more important than the volunteers in encouraging firearm use. The British National Rifle Association established in 1859 provided a model for similar organizations that appeared throughout British North America during the 1860s. The Upper Canada Rifle Association existed by 1862, and Quebec had a provincial rifle association by 1869. There was rifle shooting in St John's, Newfoundland by the mid-1860s, a provincial rifle association in New Brunswick by 1867, and a rifle association in Prince Edward Island by 1875, although the island had hosted popular rifle-shooting competitions since the early 1860s. Local rifle associations also formed. For instance, Nova Scotians formed a colonial rifle association affiliated with the British National Rifle Association in 1861, but also organized several county-level associations.[109] The sudden popularity of rifle shooting led the Toronto *Globe* to declare in 1864 that rifle matches "have come greatly into vogue of late years."[110]

Rifle associations enticed members by holding target-shooting matches, offering awards and cash prizes for winning shooters. The Upper Canada Rifle Association, for instance, held its first shooting competition on the Garrison Common in Toronto in 1862, offering a range of prizes for various competitions. In 1864, shooting associations awarded more than eight thousand dollars in prize money in shooting competitions throughout the Province of Canada, and in 1865 23,301 men participated in rifle shooting. There was a similar level of interest in Nova Scotia. The first annual rifle match run by the Nova Scotia association consisted of six separate competitions. In one, the winner received a medal donated by the British National Rifle Association, as well as five pounds contributed by the provincial association. These prizes attracted substantial numbers of participants. In 1865, for example, three hundred competitors entered the annual Nova Scotia shooting match.[111]

More than prizes drew men to rifle associations. Shooting advocates believed that acumen in firing breech-loading, repeating rifles would allow British North Americans to defend themselves against an American attack. The *Globe* suggested that "if every man in Canada, between the ages of eighteen and forty-five, could put a bullet through a target at six hundred yards, a long step would be taken towards safety."[112] Writers in other newspapers agreed. For example, in 1866 the *Grand River Sachem* suggested that arming Canadians with modern weapons would make Canada more secure, for "25,000 men armed with breech-loading repeating rifles, would be equal to 100,000 men armed with the muzzle-loading Enfield, or any other similar arm."[113] Advocates of rifle shooting drew parallels between the breech-loading rifle and the historic English longbow, suggesting that Canadians trained in rifle shooting would defeat an opponent in the same way English longbowmen annihilated French forces in the Hundred Years' War. "Time was when England had a national weapon," suggested the *Globe* in 1860, and "she is now likely to have one again." "The English bowmen decided the day at Crescy, at Poitiers, and at Agincourt," and what in one day was done "with the bow can be more easily done in hours by the rifle."[114] Training men to use modern guns thus proved especially appealing to those wanting to defend the Canadas against a feared American attack.[115]

Proponents of rifle use also believed it created opportunities for socializing in a context emphasizing men's martial prowess. Men living in urban centres in the mid- to late nineteenth century sought out chances to remove themselves temporarily from their domestic lives and to assert their manliness. Rifle shooting provided such an opportunity. Early advocates of rifle training thus constantly emphasized the "manly" character of the activity. According to historian K.B. Wamsley, rifle shooting, "with its publicized images of protection, strength and military power," was an activity that "sustained the gender order."[116] Rifle shooting could make any man feel alive, even one typically cloistered in the confines of an office or whose physical limitations prevented participation in sports played by healthier or younger men. The *Globe* made the point bluntly: "As a manly sport, practice with the rifle has no equal."[117] Participation in rifle shooting benefited the whole nation, for the nation's men became more masculine.

Gun Control from the American Civil War to Confederation

The American Civil War thus encouraged British North Americans to take up rifles. The war and its aftermath also spurred a final flurry of firearm regulations meant to protect the state. The first measure followed the 1864 St Albans Raid in which a small contingent of Confederate soldiers used Canada as a base to raid St Albans, Vermont. The

Figure 5: Provincial Rifle Match, Montreal, 1870. Rifle-shooting competitions encouraged Canadians to own and use rifles in the nineteenth century. As the dress of many in this image suggests, elite Canadians proved strong proponents of shooting.
Source: Canadian Illustrated News 2, no. 8 (20 July 1870): 120

event caused an international furore that risked drawing British North America into an armed conflict with the United States. One response of the Province of Canada meant to deflate tensions was 1865 legislation to prevent outrages on the frontier. The act allowed for the deportation of aliens and created stiff penalties for assisting an attack on a foreign state. The legislation also sought to control weapons that could be used in cross-border raids. It permitted the seizure of weapons of war held for the purpose of a military raid beyond the borders of the colony, or held for a purpose dangerous to the public peace within the Province of Canada.[118]

The Civil War also played a role in legislation meant to disarm the Fenians. Irish-American Civil War veterans launched two raids into the Canadas and a raid against New Brunswick. These attacks created substantial fears and led to restrictions on the use of firearms. The Province of Canada passed legislation that largely copied the measures passed in

Upper Canada following the rebellion of 1837. The government sought to ban the unlawful training of people to use arms. The governor in council could declare the act in force across the province, or just in specific areas. It prohibited all meetings for training or drilling, or being trained in the use of arms, without lawful authority. The legislature also permitted authorities to seize arms if the weapons were kept for a purpose dangerous to the public peace. One difference from previous legislation was that the 1866 act was to remain on the statute book indefinitely, rather than expire. The Fenian threat led to the passage of similar legislation in Nova Scotia and Prince Edward Island.[119]

Conclusion

Firearm regulation clearly predates Confederation. Bans on the discharge of weapons in towns and cities sought to prevent shootings, fires, or nuisances. Legislators also passed measures to decrease the dangers of violence at polling places and at public meetings. They further limited firearm possession or use during times of real or potential tumult, such as immediately after the fall of New France, during the rebellions of 1837–8, in response to the canal riots of the mid-1840s, and when fears rose of potential threats from the United States. The state, however, usually imposed modest levels of regulation and made most measures temporary. Legislation almost never advocated permanent limitations on when and where guns could be carried, nor, certainly, for the kinds of measures that became contentious in the late twentieth century, such as the licensing of gun owners or the creation of a firearm registry.

Several factors explain the modest nature of firearm regulation in the pre-Confederation period. Even when circumstances called for gun control, politicians questioned their constitutional authority to impose strict measures, especially laws that disarmed men of property. In addition, legislators knew that the limited power of the state prevented more aggressive measures. Gun owners could easily hide their weapons. Even when the colonial state focused its resources to regulate guns for short periods, it rarely secured all arms. The failures to round up all weapons in post-Conquest New France or at violent canal sites demonstrates the perpetual challenge of enforcing gun laws.

Legislators also chose not to regulate firearms because British North Americans kept arms only when necessary, making gun possession far from ubiquitous in much of the pre-Confederation period. A combination of sufficient agricultural production, a decline in duelling, the creation of professional police forces, and less fear of Aboriginal Peoples dissuaded many people from keeping firearms. Country store records, low levels of firearm murders, and poorly armed militias and rebels provide evidence that British North Americans often lacked firearms. Given the paucity of weapons, guns generally posed few problems.

The technological limitations that made firearms less dangerous than later guns also mitigated the desire for more regulation. Muzzle-loaded weapons could kill, but a slow rate of fire, poor accuracy, and unreliability meant that they caused relatively little concern in normal circumstances. In the 1860s, breech-loading rifles began to appear in British North America, but these arms created excitement, not fear. Modern rifles became associated with manliness and promised a means of defending the colonies from the American behemoth. Advocates of modernizing the militia, establishing volunteer units, and creating rifle associations all claimed that trustworthy British men should develop rifle-shooting skills. Governments thus encouraged the ownership of rifles for defensive purposes – a policy that continued after Confederation.

2

"The government must disarm all the Indians": Controlling Firearms from Confederation to the Late Nineteenth Century

After Confederation the new national government started to think seriously about how to defend Canada against the United States. It thus amalgamated the colonies' militias and, with the assistance of provincial governments, supported shooting associations and encouraged rifle ownership by most men. The 1867 *British North America Act* divided legislative responsibility between the federal and provincial governments. Ottawa received jurisdiction over the criminal law, thus empowering the federal government to impose firearm regulations. The state's desire to encourage the use of rifles meant, however, that governments rarely passed laws affecting the possession or use of such guns by citizens deemed loyal. Rifles thus remained largely unregulated until the twentieth century. Legislators passed gun controls affecting only groups thought to threaten the state or its goals. Most often, these measures sought to disarm minority groups deemed to lack the full privileges of British citizenship, especially Irish-Catholic Canadians and Aboriginal Peoples.

While the state generally left long guns uncontrolled, Ottawa placed important limitations on the availability and use of pistols. Cheap, mass-produced revolvers appeared in Canada by the 1870s, sparking concerns that such weapons increased the number of shooting accidents, encouraged suicide, and led to murder. Canadians worried that young, working-class men carried pistols to demonstrate their manliness. Legislators responded to these concerns, but with trepidation.

Ottawa largely banned people from carrying revolvers and required retailers to keep records and to sell pistols only to people over fifteen years of age. Parliament did not enact stricter gun laws for several reasons. Politicians doubted the ability of law enforcement officials to implement strong firearm laws. Some believed that gun control would, in effect, only disarm the law abiding. In addition, a number of leading politicians, including John A. Macdonald and Edward Blake, suggested that British subjects possessed a right to possess weapons grounded in the English *Bill of Rights*. Ottawa thus refused to respond aggressively to the "pistol problem."

Rifle Shooting and the Militia after Confederation

Canadians interested in defending the new nation continued to encourage the civilian use of rifles. The first Canadian *Militia Act*, passed in 1868, provided for the creation of an active militia of 40,000. By 1869, 37,170 volunteers joined the militia, and a further 618,896 technically served in the reserve. Active militia members received training in rifle shooting, and an average of 20,000 men a year attended militia camp between 1875 and 1896. The federal government provided the active militia with weapons. Ottawa wanted to improve the quality of rifle shooting, and the 1868 *Militia Act* thus allowed the government to sanction the organization of rifle associations.[1]

The *Militia Act*'s reference to rifle associations hinted at the extent to which Ottawa encouraged rifle ownership and use by most men after Confederation. A national rifle-shooting body formed in 1868: the Dominion of Canada Rifle Association. The association held its first annual prize tournament that same year on Laprairie Common near Montreal, distributing $5,155 in prizes among the almost seven hundred competitors. The militia leadership played a large role in organizing the association, which became the first sports organization in Canada to receive federal funding in the form of annual grants. Over the next four decades, the federal government provided an average grant of $10,000 per year directly to the association. In addition, it purchased or rented lands for the association's rifle ranges, helped construct and maintain facilities, and provided ammunition either for free or at discounted prices. The federal government spent over $642,000 between 1868 and 1908 for the purchase, rent, construction, and repair of rifle ranges, and a further $708,000 to fund rifle-shooting competitions. In all, Ottawa provided more than $1.5 million to promote rifle shooting before 1908.

Figure 6: Rifle associations remained popular across Canada after Confederation. Here the Elbow River Rifle Club poses with their prized trophies in 1904.
Source: Glenbow Archives, NA-33-34

Provincial rifle-shooting associations also benefited from government largesse. For example, in 1876 the Ontario Rifle Association received $1,800 from the dominion, as well as $600 from the government of Ontario. In comparison, the association raised only $26 from fees.[2]

Elite Canadians strongly advocated popular rifle ownership and use. The executives of rifle associations typically included a "who's who" of local and national leaders. For example, New Brunswick Senator Amos Edwin Botsford served as the Dominion Rifle Association's first president. Vice-presidents included the Speaker of the House of Commons, lawyer James Cockburn. The governor general, Viscount Monck, acted as the association's honorary patron, and lieutenant governors, the minister of militia, and the premiers of the first four provinces, among others, became vice-patrons. Prominent merchants, public officials, and politicians also donated cash prizes. The Marquis of Lorne, Canada's governor general from 1878 to 1883, and a keen promoter of

Figure 7: Elite Canadians continued to encourage rifle shooting after Confederation. Here, the wife of Prime Minister John A. Macdonald opens the Dominion Rifle Association match in Ottawa in 1873.
Source: *Canadian Illustrated News* 8, no. 14 (4 October 1873): 212

rifle shooting, pressured merchants to donate prizes and money for competitions.[3]

Advocates of rifle shooting supported such associations for several reasons. Some continued to emphasize that rifle shooting encouraged Canadian manhood. Juxtaposed with domestic urban life, the rifle symbolized power and the outdoors.[4] Proponents also argued that such associations added to Canadian security. Rifle training could also encourage national unity in a country still in search of an identity. In 1886, for example, the *Military Gazette* suggested that rifle association meetings would "engender a kindly feeling between the various sections of the Dominion," and that this could "keep up and strengthen the territorial and political links by which we are united together."[5] Participation in the annual shooting competitions held by the English National Rifle Association at Wimbledon encouraged a sense of Canadian pride. In 1861, the association invited teams from British North America to compete in its matches. A Canadian national team first attended in 1872 with funds from the Dominion Rifle Association's federal grant, and Canadian shooters continued to participate for the next four decades. Newspapers closely followed the results of English competitions and celebrated the success of notable Canadian shooters.[6]

Canadians also took pride in the reputation Canadian riflemen developed in the United States as crack shots. In the late 1860s and early 1870s, several American commentators suggested that Canadian rifle associations had made Canadians better marksmen than Americans. The *New York Times*, for instance, asserted that the Canadian policy of providing long-range rifle ranges had "developed a large and formidable force for national defense." Canada had 45,000 trained marksmen among its volunteer forces, "while the United States has none."[7] The skill of Canadian marksmen became a common refrain in *Forest and Stream*, an American journal focused on hunting, fishing, and outdoor recreation. In 1873, it noted that Canadians had a "marked proficiency" in rifle shooting and would be "formidable rivals and hard to beat" in any shooting competition.[8] In 1875, it recalled how the appearance of Canadian riflemen a few years earlier "was talked about almost in bated breath, and with awe and reverence."[9] Interest in Canadian shooting led the *New York Times* and *Forest and Stream* to publish the results of Canadian competitions frequently.[10]

The reputation of Canadian riflemen caused American advocates of rifle shooting to a look to Canada for assistance in establishing the National Rifle Association. The NRA's founders expressed concern that Americans had allowed their shooting skills to deteriorate after the Civil War. New York state, and later the federal government, helped fund the NRA, representatives of which visited Ottawa and Toronto to collect information on organized Canadian rifle shooting. Canadian riflemen provided plans and drawings used to create the first NRA range, at Creedmore, New York, in 1872. American shooting enthusiasts acknowledged the important role Canadians played in establishing the NRA. According to *Forest and Stream*, Canadian rifle men "taught us practically our first rifle lessons," and the early success of the NRA was due to the willingness of Canadian shooters to assist Americans.[11] Canada acted as "our foster mother, and we, as her children in the rifle school, owe her a lasting debt of gratitude."[12] Through the 1870s, Canadians and Americans regularly attended each other's shooting events, and Canadian clubs challenged American associations, and vice versa, to competitions.[13]

The rifle-shooting movement boomed through the 1860s but lost popularity by the 1880s. Canadians continued to found associations, especially in the west, but many rifle groups struggled.[14] Associations had difficulty retaining paying members and became very reliant on government funding – they were unable to sustain themselves but for the efforts of politicians to arm Canada's citizens. Even the Dominion Rifle Association required financial assistance to continue its operations. In 1884, Adolphe Caron, the minister of militia, defended a two-thousand-dollar supplement to the eight-thousand-dollar grant to the Dominion Rifle Association on the ground that failure to provide the extra money would prevent the association from competing in England or force it to reduce the prizes awarded in shooting competitions so "as to destroy the association."[15]

Rifle-shooting associations faced several challenges by the 1880s. The declining fear of an American attack and the waning military enthusiasm sapped the drive to train men in rifles. Critics also questioned the value of government investment. The *Winnipeg Times* argued that no one "has yet been able to show what the country makes by sending riflemen to Wimbledon every year." "It is a pleasant jaunt for the lucky marksmen, no doubt," noted the *Times*, "but what public purpose does it serve?"[16] Some military men also questioned the investment. In his first annual report upon taking command of the militia, Major General Frederick Middleton expressed surprise at the independence of rifle associations (which he thought the Department of Militia should direct) and doubted the alleged benefits of shooting competitions. In his view, the "so-called good shots are so artificially trained, and fire under such exceptional advantages at fixed targets, much larger than the body of a man, and at known distances, that when brought into the field to fire at moving men, at unknown distances, who also fire back at them, their good shooting often ceases."[17]

The dangers of rifle shooting in, or close to, urban centres also caused concerns. When associations began to organize competitions in the early 1860s, they typically used sites the militia or volunteer units employed on the edges of cities and towns. As urban centres grew, businesses and homes surrounded shooting ranges, meaning that stray bullets could strike citizens, especially as rifles achieved longer effective ranges. The danger of rifle ranges in urban areas became apparent in Toronto in 1887 when a bullet fired from the Garrison Common struck and killed John Perley Macdonald, the seventeen-year-old son of the manager of Confederation Life. Macdonald was rowing a small boat near the range, when a bullet struck him. The incident unleashed a series of forceful calls that the range be moved. The Toronto Rifle Association and the city's volunteers, however, refused to relocate, and the debate over the Garrison Common range continued until a new location opened in 1893.[18]

Concerns with safety, and questions about the value of organized shooting, decreased interest in the rifle movement. In 1890, the *Winnipeg Tribune* noted the absence of a Manitoba team at the annual Dominion Rifle Association matches in Ottawa and suggested that rifle shooting "seems to be at a low ebb in Canada."[19] Liberal MP George Elliott Casey reported in 1892 that in "western Ontario interest in rifle-shooting has almost died out." He noted that only greatly increasing the funding to associations would stem this decline, since "the money obtainable is not sufficient to induce the men to come out, and in consequence rifle-shooting has greatly fallen off."[20] This decline would be short-lived, however. In the late 1890s, the emergence of a robust imperialist impulse would revitalize rifle shooting in Canada, as will be shown in chapter 3.

Regulating Rifles

State support for target shooting meant that governments made few efforts to regulate the ownership and use of rifles by loyal citizens. This remained the case even as advanced arms became affordable for more Canadians when American gun makers cut prices in response to competitive pressures during the 1870s and 1880s. The Winchester Company sharply reduced the list prices for its breech-loading repeating rifles between 1873 and 1885. The list price (in American dollars) for the company's Model 66 declined from forty-five dollars in 1874, to twenty-four dollars in 1880, and to sixteen dollars by 1885, while the list price for the Model 73 went from fifty to eighteen dollars in the same period. American gun makers, always in search of foreign markets, sought to sell these weapons in Canada. In 1887, for instance, the Winchester Repeating Arms Company had eighteen Canadian dealers.[21] For example, one Toronto retailer, Charles Stark, sold the Winchester repeating rifle, calling it a "superb and matchless weapon" that could "kill sixteen Fenians in as many seconds without reloading." High-volume sales had reduced the price of Winchesters to eighteen dollars for a rifle that held thirteen rounds and as little as twenty dollars for a sixteen-shot version. Stark also carried a Remington magazine rifle holding nine rounds that cost twenty-five dollars, while a seven-shot Spencer retailed for just fourteen dollars.[22]

While the state encouraged most Canadians to own modern rifles, Ottawa suppressed their use by people deemed dangerous. The pre-Confederation legislation meant to prevent unlawful training in the use of arms became the basis for a similar measure passed by the new Canadian Parliament in 1867. MP George-Étienne Cartier explained that the Fenian threat motivated the government. Like the pre-Confederation legislation, the new act prohibited meetings to train or drill, or be trained to use arms without lawful authority. Violators faced up to two years' imprisonment. Justices of the peace could also seize arms or ammunition kept for any unlawful purpose.[23]

The federal government also sought to control the supply of guns in what became western Canada. In 1867, Ottawa banned the importation of firearms and munitions of war, except from Britain, without permission. North-West Mounted Police enforced this restriction in the west. Following the Red River Rebellion of 1869, the dominion government established and armed the NWMP in 1873 as a means of extending state power in the west, controlling Aboriginal Peoples, and encouraging additional European settlement.[24] The "Mountie" subsequently became a popular symbol of Canadians' perceived adherence to law and order that stood in stark contrast to the dominant symbols of western settlement in the United States, including heavily armed sheriffs, cowboys, and soldiers. For instance, the gunfighter, according to Joseph Rosa, became the "New World's counterpart of the knights in armor and the Robin Hoods of the Old."[25] Canadian historians contest the popular image of the Mountie, instead emphasizing the paramilitary nature of the force and the role Mounties played in subduing and controlling Native Peoples. The weapons carried by the early Mounties add credence to this more critical interpretation. The federal government heavily armed the Mounties with revolvers and, at first, short Snider-Enfield rifles, then Winchester guns.[26]

European settlers heading west after Confederation often took shotguns or breech-loading repeating rifles. Gun sellers deemed the west a lucrative potential market and advertised firearms to settlers. Charles Stark, for instance, suggested that people moving west not take cash, but a stockpile of guns to sell or trade. According to Stark, settlers could use Winchester rifles "to kill bear, deer, and buffalos in the North-West, and as everybody is going, everybody should provide themselves with a Winchester."[27] Stark offered to mail guns to

Figure 8: The Dominion government used the heavily armed North-West
Mounted Police to enforce state policies on the prairies. This Calgary Mountie
displays his Ross rifle and revolver in about 1905 or 1906.
Source: Glenbow Archives, NA-2307-44

customers for one dollar to encourage orders. Such appeals bore fruit
for retailers, as Lawrence William Herchmer, the commissioner of the
Mounties, declared in 1887 that the Winchester rifle was "long the favourite arm with western prairie men."[28] Westerners owned weapons

to hunt food, to protect domesticated animals, and to defend themselves from feared attacks by Aboriginal Peoples. While residents of
eastern British North America expressed less concern with Aboriginal
Peoples by the 1840s, western settlers continued to fear Native Peoples.
Several infamous incidents fed European unease. Native People in
British Columbia killed a number of Hudson's Bay Company employees in the 1820s and 1840s, and in 1864 members of the Chilcotin tribe
killed eighteen white labourers in the interior of British Columbia.[29]
Fear of wild animals also encouraged western gun ownership. As late
as 1889, British Columbia Senator Thomas Robert McInnes claimed
that in his province, especially in its mining, lumbering, and hunting
areas, men "find it not only necessary to carry rifles" but "take pistols
along, for fear they may wound some savage animal and be attacked
in return."[30] Liberal MP William Mulock thus claimed in 1892 that in
the northwest, guns for self-defence were "almost as necessary a part
of a man's apparel as his hat or boots."[31]

Despite the tendency of white settlers to arm themselves, the federal
government's attempts to limit gun ownership in the west focused on
the possession of firearms by Aboriginal Peoples. Native Peoples in the
west had acquired gunpowder technology at a relatively early date,
thanks to European traders. The Canadian government also provided
some weapons in getting western tribes to sign treaties. For example, in
Treaty No. 7 signed between Ottawa and the Aboriginal Peoples residing in modern-day southern Alberta, the Canadian government promised to provide chiefs with Winchester rifles. Some Aboriginal Peoples
acquired such modern rifles, but many owned and used older arms.
In 1872, Ottawa estimated that the "Blackfoot people" numbered 2800
men, women, and children, and owned 105 rifles, 260 revolvers, and
436 flint guns. The "Blood tribe" of 2300 people possessed 141 rifles,
318 revolvers, and 202 flint guns. Of course Native Peoples preferred
modern rifles to flintlocks and sought to procure them.[32]

Many European Canadians, however, objected to the possession of
advanced weapons by Aboriginal Peoples. Politicians often claimed
that heavily armed Natives made the west a potentially dangerous
place. John Christian Schultz, a member of the House of Commons representing Lisgar, Manitoba, called on the Conservative government in
1879 to stop the flow of Winchester and other breech-loading rifles into
the northwest. Prime Minister John A. Macdonald, however, said that
the commissioner of the Mounties had not reported any large influx of
such weapons.[33]

Events in American territory buttressed the concern with Aboriginal Peoples armed with repeating rifles. George Custer lost the 1876 Battle of the Little Big Horn to Aboriginal People who possessed many modern rifles. Custer's men, in comparison, carried single-shot Springfields. Following the battle, Native leader Sitting Bull and his Sioux followers fled to Saskatchewan. The Mounties took possession of their firearms and ammunition meant for trading. Authorities allowed the Sioux to use guns for subsistence hunting only, and the Mounties issued permits approving the sale of firearms.[34] According to Desmond Morton, Custer's defeat "exercised a powerful influence on Canadian opinion, sustaining a popular image of the Métis and Indians as well-armed, eagle-eyed marksmen superbly mounted," when in fact most "were fortunate to have a single, worn-out shotgun."[35] Newspapers in the first half of the 1880s portrayed western Native Peoples as heavily armed, and the commissioner of the NWMP appealed to Ottawa for new rifles, in part because the force's arms were "inferior to that which most of the Indians (all of those in the southern district) are armed."[36]

Efforts to limit gun ownership among the western Aboriginal Peoples increased following the Northwest Rebellion of 1885. The destruction of the buffalo threatened the Native Peoples of the plains with starvation. Unable to secure adequate assistance from the Canadian Indian Department, some Aboriginal People advocated armed resistance. Metis leader Louis Riel encouraged Natives Peoples and the Metis to express their grievances. In 1884, many agreed to a "Revolutionary Bill of Rights," created a provisional government, and formed an armed force. The rebels defeated a small group of volunteers and Mounties at Duck Lake, but soon faced thousands of troops dispatched from the east. While some Aboriginals and Metis had modern repeating rifles, the majority possessed less-advanced weapons. The better-armed and numerically superior Canadian forces soon quashed the uprising.[37]

The rebellion sparked appeals to disarm western Aboriginal Peoples for the safety of white settlers. The Toronto *World* declared that "the Indians of the Northwest should be immediately disarmed, in order fully to secure settlers against danger and damage." "The fact is that no Indian should be allowed to have a rifle at all," concluded the *World*, since shotguns were sufficient to kill the small game left on the prairies.[38] Western papers agreed. The *Calgary Weekly Herald* believed that "if this country is to be made habitable for white men the government must disarm all the Indians."[39] Ottawa's policy of encouraging Aboriginal People to become farmers, rather than migratory hunters, also spurred

Figure 9: European Canadians expressed concern about the possession of
modern rifles by Aboriginal Peoples, such as this Blackfoot man (ca. 1889),
who exhibits a repeating rifle as a prized possession.
Source: Glenbow Archives, NA-2084-63

calls for disarmament. The *McLeod Gazette* noted that the government's goal was "to make the Indians self-supporting, and to do this they propose to make them a race of farmers." Before this could be done, the government had to confiscate "every gun," and the rebellion presented "an excellent excuse for putting this in practice."[40] The lieutenant governor of the North-West Territories, Edgar Dewdney, also supported this idea. He advocated confiscating the rifles and horses of the Aboriginal participants in the rebellion.[41]

The Conservative government of Prime Minister John A. Macdonald refused to completely disarm western Aboriginal Peoples, but passed legislation enabling it to place limitations on the possession or sale of guns in the North-West if necessary. Once proclaimed in any district of the North-West Territories, the act made it an offence to possess, sell, exchange, or barter "improved arms" (all weapons other than smooth-bore shotguns) or ammunition without the permission of the lieutenant governor. The focus on "improved arms" reflected the perceived potency of modern rifles. Selling arms without permission could lead to a prison term of up to six months and/or a fine of as much as two hundred dollars.[42]

If proclaimed, the act applied to people of all races, but the debates in Parliament made clear that the government's main goal was the disarmament of Aboriginal Peoples. Prime Minister Macdonald chose his words carefully, suggesting that Ottawa's objective was "to collect arms of precision" to prevent them falling into the "hands of certain classes" to "give satisfaction and confidence to the settlers." Macdonald generally disliked firearm regulation, and he thus pointed out that the act imposed temporary measures.[43] While Macdonald referred only to "certain classes," other MPs openly stated that the government sought the ability to disarm Aboriginal Peoples. Conservative Quebec MP Joseph Caron indicated that the "white people" of the northwest were "very anxious" to keep rifles "out of the hands of the Indians."[44] Liberal opposition MP John Fairbank agreed, announcing it was "right that the Indians should not be allowed to have military rifles," for the "Indian is a very different person with a Winchester in his hands from what he is without it." A well-armed Native person had a tendency to "become rather saucy," and thus "nothing would please the settler more than to find that rifles are no longer in the possession of the Indians."[45]

Opponents of the bill questioned whether it should apply to British subjects, not whether "Indians" should be disarmed. Several MPs argued that Canadians, as British subjects, had a right to bear arms. This belief fit well with the liberal principles dominant in the late nineteenth century, which emphasized individual liberty and property rights.[46] Liberal leader, lawyer, and liberal thinker Edward Blake made the case for white settlers' right to possess weapons: "The character of the white population is eminently one which fits them to be trusted with arms. That is the ordinary right of British citizens, secured to them in effect by the great charter; and it is secured to citizens of the American Republic by the constitution; and it ought not be taken away from settlers in the North-West, and the power should not be placed in the hands of the Executive to take away that right."[47]

Prominent Liberal MP, and future Supreme Court of Canada Justice, David Mills also raised this constitutional concern. He called the bill "very objectionable," for the British constitution held that it was "one of the rights of a British subject to have fire arms in his possession." It was "one of the provisions of the declaration of rights," he declared in referring to the English *Bill of Rights* of 1689. Mills, like Blake, even referenced the American Second Amendment as a source for his claim, arguing that the American constitution had simply copied the "fundamental privileges of British liberty."[48] While nineteenth-century liberalism emphasized formal equality between subjects, Mills voided the right of Aboriginal Peoples to possess arms by refusing them all the protections accorded by British justice. As noted in chapter 1, the *Bill of Rights* had placed important religious and class limitations on the right to possess arms. During the debate in the 1840s over legislation allowing the disarmament of canal workers, several legislators had noted this right but refused to extend it to the Irish because they lacked property – a key requirement of full citizenship in the 1840s. In the late nineteenth century, Canadian lawyers also denied the right to people disqualified as full citizens, including Natives. This position was consistent with the refusal to grant other rights of citizenship to Aboriginal Peoples. As E.A. Heaman points out, European Canadians often deemed Native persons "outside the liberal public sphere, devoid of such qualifications as literacy, property, even reasoning power."[49] Mills openly defined "Indians" as less than full citizens in debating the gun legislation. They did "not appreciate the principles of self-government" and "do not enjoy the full rights of citizens."[50]

While Canadians would largely forget the English constitutional argument against gun control by the early twentieth century, they would repeat other reservations expressed about the 1885 legislation. Critics, for example, doubted that the government could implement the act successfully. Historians correctly note that the mid- to late nineteenth century was a period of substantial growth in state power. The debates over the 1885 bill, however, display many politicians' acute awareness of Ottawa's limited ability to enforce some criminal laws. Several MPs suggested that the government could not implement the legislation among the scattered population of the northwest.[51] Liberal MP Richard Cartwright also foreshadowed the regional divisions over gun control that emerged in the twentieth century, noting the very different attitudes to firearms on the western frontier in comparison to those in the more established areas of Canada. In the "old settled country" the "use of arms is a luxury and arms are not required to be carried for the protection of personal property." But for isolated settlers in the west, a limit on the possession of arms appeared the "most pedantic piece of legislation."[52] The assumption: settlers needed modern rifles.

It does not appear that the federal government ever proclaimed the 1885 law. The fact that the act would have disarmed Europeans *and* Aboriginal Peoples probably prevented its use. The government likely also recognized that Aboriginal Peoples would resist any attempted disarmament. In addition, Prime Minister Macdonald later acknowledged the difficulty of preventing Aboriginal People from procuring modern rifles because of the long border with the United States.[53] The federal government instead took a less extreme step. In August 1885, Cabinet issued an Order in Council employing an 1884 amendment to the *Indian Act* to prohibit the sale or gift of ammunition to any Native person in the North-West Territories without the written permission of the superintendent general of Indian Affairs.[54] The government thus succeeded in targeting the use of weapons by Aboriginal Peoples, while leaving white settlers alone.

Nevertheless, these measures failed to quell the desire to limit the use of modern firearms by western Native People. Lieutenant Governor Dewdney wanted weapons, including rifles, less available to Native Peoples and suggested that they be prevented from taking them off reserves without permission.[55] NWMP Commissioner Herchmer also suggested that permitting Native People to travel off their reserves and to "carry arms (mostly of repeating pattern)" was "liable sooner of later to result in serious trouble, involving not only the cattle business in the West, but the settlers." If preventing Native People from acquiring repeating rifles proved impossible, he advocated that "they be compelled to leave them on their reserves."[56]

Ottawa's desire to make Aboriginal Peoples self-sufficient farmers, and the frontier less threatening for white settlers, motivated the government's gun-control policies in the northwest. The federal government's approach to firearms in the west stood in stark contrast to Ottawa's typical attitude towards the ownership and use of modern arms in the late nineteenth century. The national government promoted gun ownership and rifle practice by trusted subjects as a means of defending the new nation, encouraging unity, and buttressing masculinity. However, the 1885 legislation and Order in Council again reflected the willingness of authorities to limit firearm ownership and use by "suspicious" groups by denying them the rights of full citizenship.

The Modern Revolver

While Canadian legislators encouraged "British" men to own and use rifles, they expressed reservations about the increasing availability of another technologically advanced weapon: the modern revolver. Unlike rifles, which remained unregulated except during times of tumult, by 1892 Ottawa actively regulated the use and then the ownership of pistols.

Smooth-bore, muzzle-loaded pistols existed for several centuries but had important weaknesses. Most were single-shot weapons, although gun makers produced double-barrelled pistols, as well as "pepperbox" guns with several barrels. These guns lacked accuracy, even when fired by the best marksmen. A skilled soldier could hit a target from only ten yards. Balls could also slip out prior to discharge.[57] Pepperbox pistols had additional weaknesses: multiple short barrels made them heavy and even less accurate than single-shot pistols.[58]

Technological changes revolutionized pistols as much as long guns in the nineteenth century. The most important innovation was the creation of multi-shot revolvers. In Britain, Elisha Collier patented a flintlock revolver in 1818, and Samuel Colt patented an even more important innovation in 1835: the first successful "percussion revolver." This weapon had a revolving cylinder with several chambers. Into each chamber, the shooter loaded gunpowder and a ball (or a paper cartridge). In the rear of each chamber, the shooter placed percussion caps that, when struck, ignited the powder in the chamber. Colt also developed a mechanism that rotated the cylinder when the shooter cocked the gun with the hammer. Despite Colt's innovations, consumers found his revolvers heavy and expensive, and Colt's company went bankrupt in 1842, although he later reopened his business, which subsequently became a leading American handgun maker. His manufacturing techniques also helped usher in the "American system" of mass production, which, in time, allowed for the production of large numbers of cheap revolvers.[59]

Pistol design continued to improve in other ways. After Colt's patent expired in 1857, various American manufacturers, including Remington, Starr, Whitney, and Smith & Wesson, began making revolvers, often with innovations. Horace Smith and Daniel Wesson, for instance, produced the first revolver that fired metal cartridges without percussion caps. Smith & Wesson revolvers could thus be quickly loaded by inserting cartridges into the rear of each chamber. Other makers adopted this innovation, including Colt, which began manufacturing Peacemaker revolvers with self-contained metallic cartridges in 1872. Gun companies soon introduced two additional innovations. First, they developed "double action" revolvers that could be fired just by pulling the trigger, rather than by cocking the weapon and then pulling the trigger, thus allowing a faster rate of fire. The second innovation permitted quicker loading: Smith & Wesson developed guns with hinged frames in the 1870s, allowing the barrel and cylinder to be tipped forward.[60]

Early revolvers proved too expensive for mass consumption. Colt initially marketed beautifully crafted firearms as status symbols, not as weapons for average people. A few businesses began advertising revolvers in British North America in the late 1850s, although cost made these guns too expensive for most citizens.[61] English firms, for example, took out advertisements in Toronto marketing their pricey revolvers. Deane & Son of London offered a new revolver for seven pounds, ten shillings in 1859. In 1863, Quebec citizens could purchase a revolver for the smaller, but still substantial, sum of four pounds, four shillings. An Ottawa retailer offered a variety of revolvers in 1866, the least expensive of which sold for seven dollars.[62]

The price of revolvers declined substantially during the 1870s and 1880s. In part, lower prices resulted from the increased production of revolvers during the American Civil War. The end of the war left gun companies with excess manufacturing capacity, so they responded by mass producing new inexpensive guns for domestic and foreign civilian markets. As a result, by the 1890s, cheap weapons "offered firepower for the price of a man's shirt."[63] Revolvers also dropped in price in Canada. Retailers advertised revolvers in Winnipeg for as little as $1.50 in 1883. Toronto gun seller Charles Stark carried fifty different styles and makes of revolvers in 1882, some of which sold for as little as $1.00. Among the cheapest weapons were poorly made cast-iron guns, such as the "British bull-dog" revolver.[64]

Retailers and manufacturers aggressively marketed pistols in Canada. American manufacturers sometimes played on the fear of crime, suggesting that people needed revolvers in a modern, heavily armed society. Remington took this approach in 1866: "In these days of Housebreaking and Robbery, every House, Store, Bank and Office should have one of Remington's Revolvers."[65] Some Canadian retailers copied this approach, such as one Toronto company that claimed that a revolver in the house "gives a sense of security."[66] Businesses also emphasized the beauty of their guns in an effort to attach status to particular models. For example, Toronto gunsmith and gun seller William G. Rawbone stressed the beauty of a new revolver it nicknamed the Toronto Belle. Rawbone said that the "entire pistol is polished and nickeled in first-class style, and for smooth, easy working cannot be surpassed," offering it for the bargain price of $2.75.[67] Retailers also enticed buyers by displaying revolvers prominently in store windows.[68]

The number of revolvers in Canada in the nineteenth century is impossible to determine precisely, but the absence of domestic revolver manufacturers means that changes in the value of imported guns hints at the relative availability of firearms. For a couple of reasons, however, one must exhibit care with these statistics. First, government records valued *all* guns that entered Canada, not just pistols. Second, official figures undoubtedly underestimated the value of weapons entering the country since they failed to account for weapons brought illegally across the American border. Nevertheless, the available figures show substantial growth in gun imports. The total value of firearms imported into Canada for domestic consumption rose from $14,902 in 1869 to $102,583 in 1874. The value of imported guns then declined to $52,212 by 1879, before more than tripling to $188,326 in 1883.[69]

"A necessary part of a young man's outfit": The Pistol Problem

Susan Binnie's fine studies of state responses to social disorder show, as this work does, that gun regulation often stemmed from concerns with collective violence. However, her claim that gun regulation "did not reflect any popular or widely recognized demand for weapons control"[70] requires amendment. Import statistics, retail advertisements, and social commentary all suggest that cheap pistols became widely available in

Canada by the 1870s. The appearance of such weapons and the lack of government regulation led Canadians to express fear that revolvers encouraged shooting accidents, crime, and suicides. Such concerns ultimately spurred government action.

Canadians blamed revolvers for causing a perceived spike in gun accidents. British North Americans long suffered from occasional gun accidents. Muskets, for example, sometimes fired prematurely or simply exploded. The growing popularity of rifle shooting also resulted in users sometimes shooting each other or themselves by accident. The increased ownership of revolvers, however, especially among young urban men, sparked strong concerns about firearm accidents.

Occasionally, accidents occurred when women handled revolvers. In Saint John, New Brunswick, for example, a woman picked up a revolver and in a jocular fashion said, "Leona, I'll shot you." The gun went off and the bullet entered a thirteen-year-old girl's chest and lodged behind her shoulder blade.[71] Another incident occurred in Brockville, Ontario, in 1882, when Ida Quigg, aged twenty-two, accidentally shot herself with a Smith & Wesson revolver left on a dresser. She apparently caught the revolver while dusting, causing it to discharge into her stomach.[72]

More frequently, accidents involved young men who carelessly handled weapons. A few examples can illustrate this common problem. In 1881, nineteen-year-old George Merritt shot and killed himself while cleaning his revolver. Merritt had "displayed an intense fondness for firearms" and possessed several revolvers.[73] In Saint John in 1887, John Langan, aged twenty-one, received a fatal shot in the eye when he let his friend examine his revolver.[74] One of the "most unhappy fatalities that has occurred in Toronto for some time" took place in 1891 when a sixteen-year-old was sent to fetch a revolver. On his way back with the gun, a passing workman asked to examine it. The revolver went off, and a bullet entered the workman's brain.[75]

Children and youth proved especially prone to shooting themselves, or others, with revolvers. In the nineteenth century, legislators did not require the safe storage of revolvers or dictate that owners unload guns not in use. Nor did governments place any age restriction prior to 1892 regarding who could acquire a pistol. Not surprisingly, young people got their hands on guns, and, beginning in the late 1870s, newspapers included many stories of tragic gun accidents. For example, in Toronto in 1879, a thirteen-year-old had a revolver in a room he shared with his nine-year-old brother. When the younger child looked at the gun, it discharged a bullet that entered his face just below one of his eyes, lodging in his jaw.[76] When George Lyons, aged fifteen, tried to teach Arthur Mead, aged five, how to shoot a revolver, "Mead transferred one of the cartridges from the revolver to Lyon's left shoulder."[77] Such incidents appeared regularly in the press across the country.[78]

Revolvers also acted as the perfect tool to commit crimes because they offered substantial firepower in a small, concealable package. Criminals easily hid revolvers in pockets, especially since some tailors supplied men's trousers with a "pistol pocket." Senator Robert Read from Ontario complained in 1877 that there was "scarcely a pair of trowsers [sic] made at the present day which was not provided with a pistol pocket in which to conceal firearms."[79] The ability to fire several times in quick succession also made the revolver an especially useful tool for criminals. Shooters could fire multiple rounds to injure or kill several victims, or to ensure a target was dead. So, for example, when a young man in Hamilton sought revenge against the seducer of his sister, he fired four shots from a revolver, severing a leg artery in the alleged Casanova, killing him.[80] Ontario Liberal Senator Richard William Scott identified the importance of changing firearm technology in 1889, suggesting that the number of murders increased in Canada "simply from the facility which the revolver affords for taking life."[81] Newspaper accounts of burglaries and robberies also frequently mentioned criminals carrying revolvers, either to commit the crime or to defend themselves if discovered or pursued.[82]

The revolver also served as a perfect tool for suicides and murder-suicides. A person considering suicide could acquire a cheap revolver, then easily hide it until he or she made a final decision. In addition, revolvers' simple design meant that almost any depressed individual could easily load and fire a revolver into his or her mouth, temple, or chest. Incidents from across Canada illustrate that people of all walks of life used revolvers to commit suicide.[83]

Residents of British North America expressed little concern over modern pistols when reports first appeared of criminals employing revolvers in the late 1850s.[84] Even the prosecution of Patrick James Whelan for using a pistol to murder MP Thomas D'Arcy McGee in 1868 did not stir much concern over the dangers of revolvers. By the 1870s, however, Canadians suggested that revolvers constituted a growing danger. They, for instance, blamed revolvers for gun accidents. The *Globe* thus described an accidental shooting with a revolver in Brampton, Ontario, as one of those "sad events which results from the careless handling of firearms, and from which the public are being constantly warned."[85]

The alleged integration of revolvers as part of the culture of young men represented a special concern. Commentators suggested that many young men carried cheap, easily hidden, and deadly revolvers to demonstrate their manliness. Ontario Liberal Senator Billa Flint claimed in 1877 that the "youth of our land are fast training themselves in the use of firearms, and particularly pocket pistols." "Mere boys," he continued, "who could save a little money, used it for the purpose of obtaining pistols." Lawyer and Conservative Senator Alexander Campbell of Ontario also suggested that young men increasingly carried firearms. In the late 1850s, he had "hardly ever heard of young fellows carrying concealed weapons," but by 1877 it was "quite common." He blamed this trend on the idea of some young men that carrying a weapon "shows in some way their manliness." Liberal Senator David Reesor, also of Ontario, complained that a certain class of young men was "generally more anxious to possess their first revolver than their first watch," while Senator James Dever, a Liberal from New Brunswick, claimed that a pistol had become a key part of a young man's outfit.[86]

This was not an issue just in eastern Canada. Western cities also experienced problems with pistols. Winnipeg's mayor criticized the growing tendency of men to fire pistols on city streets in 1874, and the *Winnipeg Daily Free Press* suggested two years later that "pistol shooting by boys is becoming common."[87] By the late 1880s, cowboys in Calgary carried revolvers, and authorities prosecuted several men for firing pistols on the community's streets.[88] Young men in Britain and the United States, especially in urban centres, also armed themselves with revolvers in the last third of the nineteenth century. The phrase "God created men; Colonel Colt made them equal" became a widely heard refrain in the United States.[89]

Critics tried to mock the bravado young men exhibited when carrying a firearm. One writer suggested that the impregnability men felt when handling a gun encouraged shooting accidents. "What cowards women are when there is a gun or a pistol in their vicinity. They will 'O dear!' and 'O, don't!' and 'O, for mercy's sake!' and will tremble like a poplar leaf, even though the gun or pistol be without lock, stock, and barrel." "But a man, how different!," continued the writer, for he "will take up the weapon with a charming nonchalance, cock it, peer into the muzzle, and give a first-class job for either the doctor or undertaker."[90] The idea that carrying a weapon buttressed one's masculinity also came under attack. In his charge to a Toronto General Sessions grand jury in 1877, Judge Kenneth Mackenzie critiqued the view that carrying a firearm was a manly practice. "Nothing can be more at variance with true manliness and manhood," suggested Mackenzie, "than indulging in those cowardly practices of secreting offensive weapons and firearms on their person for purposes of mischief."[91] Such critics represented some of the first efforts to challenge the connection between masculinity and pistols, but the link proved difficult to break.

Canadians expressed special concern over the potentially deadly mixture of male bravado, pistols, and alcohol. Critics of revolvers suggested that men, especially young men, emboldened by alcohol, quickly took offence, drew revolvers, and opened fire. An 1881 incident involving a drunk man wounding another led the *Globe* to damn the common practice of carrying pistols and to assert that "no man ever draws a knife or a pistol on another unless" he is "in a passion or a state of intoxication."[92] A few years later, reports that police got drunk and fired off revolvers led the *McLeod Gazette* of Alberta to suggest that "this blazing away with a pistol whenever a man gets drunk, whether it be in the hands of a policeman or a citizen, is getting monotonous, and must be put down with a high hand."[93] Middle-class demands for temperance in the nineteenth century represented an effort to create a "hegemonic way of viewing the world" that emphasized industriousness and respectable lifestyles.[94] Commentators argued that young men endangered their futures when they mixed alcohol and guns. Pistols handled by drunken men snuffed out lives, at worst, or, at best, caused potentially serious injuries that limited the ability of young men to support themselves and contribute to society.

People concerned about revolvers also warned that Canadians had to treat guns differently from Americans. Many Canadians after the Civil War critiqued Americans' propensity to purchase and use revolvers and thus called on Parliament to better regulate pistols. Press accounts indicated that differences emerged in attitudes to gun ownership and use in Canada and the United States by the 1860s. In an 1866 article entitled "A Belligerent People," the Halifax *Citizen* suggested, "Our American cousins are rapidly becoming a people of firearms," and revolvers "abound everywhere" in the United States. "Their Press narrates," noted the *Citizen*,

as an ordinary item of news, the fact that a short time ago, an Indiana schoolmaster was about to punish a female scholar after the style in Cambridge,

Mass., when a chivalrous boy drew a revolver and threatened to shoot the master! The master then drew a revolver and shot at the boy, wounded him, and was the next moment himself wounded by a pistol ball! Master and scholars appear to have been abundantly provided with deadly weapons. Again, we are told that, recently, a man living at a village near Mobile, attempted to frighten some girls by wrapping a white cloth around his body and personating a ghost. All ran but one, who pulled out a revolver and fired six balls into the head and body! At the first shot the ghost fell dead, but she continued firing, two balls penetrating the forehead, and the other four the region of heart.[95]

Canadian newspapers frequently carried stories suggesting Americans had a tendency to commit mass murders with revolvers, to participate in bizarre gun fights, and to allow children to use pistols with disastrous results.[96] These stories reinforced Canadians' perception of themselves as comparatively law-abiding and peaceful, but also warned of the dangers of greater pistol ownership and use. By the end of the 1870s, the view that Americans were too fond of revolvers permeated political debates and the press in Canada. For example, in 1877 Senator Robert Barry Dickey of Nova Scotia claimed that young men in Canada had begun to carry and use pistols too freely, "a practice unfortunately too prevalent in the adjoining republic."[97] Fear of allowing Canada to adopt a gun culture similar to that of the United States thus helped motivate Canadian legislators to adopt new control measures.

Regulating Pistols to 1892

The growing concern with revolvers led to calls for government legislation. Prime Minister Macdonald's Conservatives, however, generally resisted efforts to regulate them. The Liberal government of Prime Minister Alexander Mackenzie (1874–8) and the Conservatives after Macdonald's death in 1891 proved more willing to pass important gun-control measures to limit the carrying of concealed weapons, to prevent children from shooting themselves or others, and to ensure that retailers kept records of revolver sales.

Prior to the late 1870s, Canadian gun legislation had limited scope and application. Various cities, as they had before Confederation, banned the discharge of firearms within city limits.[98] The federal government also limited gun possession and use in places and at times deemed dangerous to the established order. For example, in 1869 Ottawa passed legislation to deal with labour violence at large public works, modelling the 1869 act after the 1845 Province of Canada legislation. Cabinet could proclaim the statute's provisions in effect where a canal, railroad, or other public work was under construction. Once Cabinet proclaimed the act, officials could prohibit the sale of liquor and dictate that no employees of public works possess any firearm or a number of other kinds of weapons. Persons found carrying a banned weapon faced a fine of two to four dollars for each weapon. Violators who concealed arms faced larger potential fines, from forty to one hundred dollars. The act proved a weak tool, however. In 1870, Ottawa amended the legislation so that it could be employed *either* to prohibit the sale of alcohol *or* the possession of weapons. While the government employed the act to ban alcohol several times, Ottawa never proclaimed the firearm regulations, perhaps because the legislation banned *all* employees from carrying weapons.[99] This meant disarming men working in rural areas with wild animals, and, perhaps more importantly, disarming management as well as labour.

An 1869 law preventing individuals from carrying "offensive weapons" also illustrated the limitations of Canada's early gun laws. As noted in chapter 1, the British North American colonies passed similar measures before Confederation. The federal act stipulated a fine of between ten and forty dollars for anyone who carried "about his person any Bowie-knife, Dagger or Dirk, or any weapons called or known as Iron Knuckles, Skull-crackers or Slung Shot, or other offensive weapons of a like character."[100] To modern eyes, the provision against possessing "other offensive weapons" could prevent the public from carrying revolvers. However, the provision did not, in fact, include firearms, at least according to Prime Minister Macdonald, whose government passed the law.[101] In the House of Commons debate over the act, Liberal Alexander Mackenzie suggested that pistols be included in the list of weapons that the statute would ban Canadians from carrying. According to Mackenzie, for every "one injury inflicted by knives, 20 or 30 had resulted from pistols." Prime Minister Macdonald rejected this proposal, however. He generally opposed new gun laws during his long tenure as prime minister, and in debating the 1869 legislation he offered one of his favourite arguments: citizens needed arms to protect themselves from American criminals who crossed into Canada. From the United States flowed "lawless characters in the habit of carrying weapons." If it was "known that our people were prohibited by law from defending themselves, these parties might be encouraged to greater depredations," he suggested.[102] Macdonald added other arguments against gun regulation in subsequent debates.

The perception that revolvers posed a growing danger led to calls for stronger gun control. In 1871, the *Globe* damned pistols as "an unmitigated evil" and claimed that every boy had "pistol fever." The *Globe* thus advocated outlawing revolvers, or, at the least, appointing a board of examination to determine the "amount of sense necessary to make a person a safe custodian of a loaded pistol."[103] A Toronto magistrate lamented that Ottawa did not extend the law against carrying unlawful weapons to include revolvers. Prominent Conservative lawyer, politician, and judge Robert Harrison also advocated strongly for regulating revolvers, at least the possession of pistols by the less-respectable classes. Harrison had experience with such weapons, having purchased a revolver during the Fenian raids of 1866. He nevertheless criticized pistols as "too common in our country" and "much too indiscriminately used."[104] He continued to voice this view after his 1875 appointment as chief justice of the Ontario Court of Queen's Bench, telling a jury in 1876 that no citizen should carry a revolver. Harrison introduced a House of Commons bill in 1872 to add pistols to the offensive weapons list that the 1869 legislation banned people from carrying.[105] Although Harrison was a Conservative and a good friend of Prime Minister Macdonald, his bill failed to gain government support.

Despite powerful advocates of new laws, Ottawa refused to pass aggressive measures regulating pistols. Why? As already shown, Macdonald and others feared disarming Canadians in border areas. Opponents of regulating pistols also believed that new gun laws risked infringing upon the right of British subjects to bear arms found in the English *Bill of Rights*, and repeated by William Blackstone in his *Commentaries on the Laws of England*. Politicians had voiced a belief in such a right during debates in the Canadas in 1845 and would do so again in 1885. Parliamentary opponents of Harrison's 1872 amendment also used the language of the English *Bill of Rights*. Liberal lawyer Edward Blake, for instance, argued that it "struck him that very dangerous consequences to the liberty of the subject might ensue from the proposal." Prime Minister Macdonald politely discussed his friend Harrison's idea but ultimately rejected it, in part because of "the principle laid down in Blackstone of the right of parties to carry weapons in self-defence."[106] Macdonald restated the importance of the English constitutional right several times, suggesting its importance to his reluctance to regulate gun ownership during his long tenure as prime minister.

Passage of the first substantial regulation of revolvers had to wait until Macdonald's Conservatives lost power to Alexander Mackenzie's Liberals in 1874. The use of revolvers in episodes of collective violence contributed to the decision to pass legislation. Riots in Canada decreased in frequency during the 1860s, but through the 1870s the number of riots increased. Many stemmed from sectarian and ethnic tensions and the stress caused by the economic downturn of the 1870s. Militiamen suppressed workers during the Grand Trunk Railway Strike of 1876–7 and the Lachine Canal strikes of 1875 and 1877. The battle over French-language schools in New Brunswick led to the 1875 Caraquet Riot, in which several participants fired revolvers. Members of the Orange Order often battled French and Irish Catholics. Several riots sparked by public religious displays resulted in participants drawing and firing pistols. Catholic processions in Toronto led to the so-called Jubilee riots of 1875 in which rioters discharged revolvers. Rioters also brandished revolvers in Montreal in 1875 when a Catholic mob stopped the interment of Joseph Guibord in a Catholic cemetery.[107] Such incidents, unsurprisingly, caused widespread alarm.

Mackenzie's government passed two important pieces of gun regulation in 1877 and 1878. The initial push for a new gun law came from the Senate. Ontario Conservative Senator Robert Read, a distiller, farmer, and tanner, introduced a bill in 1877 to limit the use of revolvers. Like Harrison earlier, Read proposed adding pistols to the 1869 legislation banning the carrying of offensive weapons because of "the custom prevalent among the young men of the country of carrying concealed on their persons, pocket pistols, or revolvers."[108] Read also sought ways that Canada could avoid experiencing American levels of gun violence, noting ominously that pistols killed 312 people in the United States in the previous year.[109]

Liberal MP Edward Blake responded to this pressure by introducing legislation targeting pistol use. In 1872, he had opposed Harrison's bill as an infringement of individual liberty. Riots and the perceived spate of murders, accidents, and suicides using pistols, however, led him to make an exception. He told the Commons that "there could be no doubt that the practice of carrying fire-arms was becoming too common." Like others, he emphasized the dangers of armed working-class young men, suggesting that "the rowdy and reckless characters, and boys and young men" carried revolvers, thus indicating a strong concern with the mixture of pistols and masculinity. But he did not advocate banning revolvers. Instead, he crafted a law reserving the use of revolvers for respectable individuals. The bill's design in part reflected Blake's concern with enforceability; if Parliament prohibited everyone from carrying revolvers, then "reckless characters, who intended violence, would not care about the law, and would carry small concealed weapons; while the sober, law-abiding citizen would be unprotected." Blake also crafted his legislation to abide by the spirit of the *Bill of Rights* guarantee of arms to men "for their defence suitable to their condition." In 1885, the federal government would override the right because it deemed Aboriginal Peoples incapable of full citizenship (and thus unable to claim all the rights British justice afforded). The state in 1877 also refused to recognize the right for young, working-class men. Significantly, the government made this legislation permanent, unlike most previous gun controls. John A. Macdonald, now the leader of the opposition Conservatives, continued to oppose firearm legislation, although even he agreed with a proposed provision against pointing unloaded guns at people, for it was "grievous to read in the newspapers of persons carelessly, mischievously, and wantonly pointing firearms without knowing whether they were loaded or not, and destroying valuable lives."[110]

The 1877 act represented the first substantial effort to regulate pistols. It largely banned the carriage of pistols. The federal government dictated that a person found carrying a pistol or air gun (that is, a gun that used compressed air as a propellant) without reasonable cause to fear an assault or injury to himself, to his family, or to his property had to find sureties for keeping the peace for up to six months. If unable to find sureties, authorities could impose a jail term as long as thirty days. The act also provided that anyone arrested either on a warrant or while committing an offence and in possession of a pistol faced a fine of between twenty and fifty dollars, or up to three months in jail. Parliament also dictated that a person who carried a pistol with intent to do injury could receive a fine of between fifty and two hundred dollars, or go to jail for up to six months. With these provisions, the government clearly aimed to reduce the criminal use of revolvers. Ottawa also attempted to prevent accidents by dictating a fine of twenty to fifty dollars (or as many as thirty days in jail) for anyone who pointed any firearm, whether loaded or unloaded, without a lawful excuse. Parliament excused sailors, soldiers, volunteers, and police from the act when they carried loaded pistols while working.[111]

Dominion statistics show the extent to which authorities used the law against carrying unlawful weapons. Although these figures did

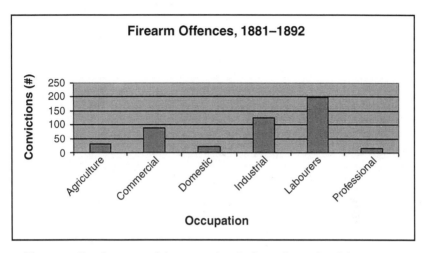

Figure 10: Employment of those convicted of carrying unlawful weapons, 1881–92.
Source: Canada, Criminal Statistics, 1881–1992, in *Sessional Papers*, 1883–93

not indicate whether the conviction was for carrying a firearm or some other unlawful weapon, between 1881 and 1892 the government reported 1,466 convictions for weapons offences – a substantial number, buttressing claims that many citizens carried weapons. Geographically, Ontario saw the most convictions by far, with just over 65 per cent, followed by Quebec (20.8 per cent), Manitoba (5.5 per cent), British Columbia (2.8 per cent), New Brunswick (2.7 per cent), Nova Scotia (2 per cent), the territories (0.8 per cent), and Prince Edward Island (0.3 per cent).[112] Ontario had a population just over 40 per cent larger than Quebec's between 1881 and 1891, so having more than three times as many convictions indicates that either Ontario had a greater problem with weapons or that heightened public concern led to more aggressive prosecution. Regardless of which explanation is correct, the high proportion of convictions from Ontario helps explain the many calls for legislative action that came from that province.

Federal crime statistics also provide information about many of those convicted between 1881 and 1892. These statistics are incomplete, because beginning in 1884 Ottawa tabulated detailed information only for those convicted of indictable firearm offences. Nevertheless the available evidence indicates that the vast majority (78.5 per cent) of those convicted resided in urban areas. Law enforcement also frequently charged working-class men; the dominion reported the employment of 478 of those convicted for the indictable offence of carrying unlawful weapons, and 97.1 per cent were industrial workers, labourers, domestics, or commercial employees. Professionals accounted for only 2.9 per cent.[113]

The 1877 legislation failed to solve the pistol problem, as riots in Montreal in 1877 and 1878 made apparent. Plans for the Orange Order to march on 12 July to commemorate the 1690 Battle of the Boyne sparked violence in 1877. High tensions led to cancelation of the procession, but 12 July failed to pass peacefully. On 11 July, a sixteen-year-old militiaman killed a Catholic labourer with a bayonet. The next day, Catholics attacked Protestants as they left church. Brawls broke out throughout the city, men brandished revolvers, and one young Orangeman, Thomas Hackett, received a fatal shot during a melee. Over the next few days, a number of rioters fired revolvers in different parts of the city.[114]

Montreal officials employed the 1877 act to help quell the violence. The city recorder prosecuted John Sheehan, whom authorities later charged for the murder of Hackett, for pointing a revolver at William Charles Patton. Later in July, the recorder convicted two other men of carrying revolvers. More sectarian violence marked the day of Hackett's funeral, with several men drawing revolvers and opening fire.[115] The Montreal *Daily Witness* thus called the 1877 legislation a "dead letter."[116] Many people feared that violence could repeat in 1878, and events substantiated such concerns. After roughly one hundred men gathered near Montreal's Wellington Bridge, one Catholic, John Colligan, died and others received gunshot injuries.[117]

The Montreal violence led to calls for stronger measures. "Prudence" wrote to the *Montreal Gazette* to complain about the "murderous attacks with pistols," which "for some time back have been of such frequent occurrence in the streets of Montreal and elsewhere in Canada." Prudence called on the government to stop the flow of revolvers into Canada.[118] Members of the Catholic clergy of Montreal asked for stronger gun laws, noting that so long as "bands of people, especially young men, can parade the streets by day and by night, having deadly weapons concealed on their persons and hatred in their hearts, there can be no security for the peace of the city, nor even for human life."[119]

The events in Montreal compelled Blake to act in Parliament. For nearly a year "the city had been the scene of frequent violent attacks" and "firearms had been used with the utmost recklessness." The existing laws did not allow police to search people for concealed weapons, and, in his view, lacked sufficient penalties. Thus the "lawless character might without apprehension carry his revolver," for he could "fairly presume that the law-abiding citizen, knowing it was a crime to carry a weapon, would not carry one, so that immunity and license to the lawless individual might result." Constitutional concerns once again shaped the legislation's details. He warned against interfering too strongly in the rights of subjects and thus decided against including a provision to ban weapons in homes, because such a measure "involved the exercise of the arbitrary right of searching, which was very liable to be abused" and would have "infringed to a certain extent upon the well-worn opinion that a man's house is his castle." Blake also stated that "under ordinary circumstances" the act "would deserve the term odious legislation."[120] This again reflected Blake's belief that men of property possessed a right to possess arms in normal circumstances.

Prime Minister Mackenzie supported Blake's legislation, though he, and others, expressed reservations about disarming citizens in proclaimed districts and the ability of authorities to implement the act successfully. The act "would require a strong force" and "would be very imperfectly executed."[121] The Speaker of the House of Commons, Timothy Warren Anglin of New Brunswick, worried that allowing people to keep guns in their homes would make the new law ineffectual. He advocated a stronger bill to disarm the whole population, except for "persons of known respectability," who could receive licences to have arms in their homes.[122]

Blake's bill combined provisions of the 1869 legislation against guns around public works with an imperial statute designed to prevent the possession of arms in Ireland. The new act allowed Cabinet to proclaim the statute's provisions operative in a district or districts as needed, and once proclaimed, the only people allowed to carry weapons were justices of the peace, members of the military while on duty, police officers, or a person licensed under the act. People could, however, keep guns in their own homes or businesses, thus reflecting the common view that men of means could possess and use arms to protect themselves and their property. Anyone who violated the ban faced a prison term of up to twelve months. Unlike the 1877 legislation, the new statute allowed for the search of persons suspected of carrying weapons. Justices of the peace could also issue search warrants for homes or businesses if they believed they contained guns kept for the purpose of being carried in a proclaimed district. The reluctance to pass an onerous piece of legislation meant that Parliament made the act temporary – it remained in effect until the end of the next session. Ottawa, however, renewed the statute several times, and it remained on the statute book until 1884. Cabinet proclaimed the act in effect in Montreal and the County of Hochelaga for six years, in Quebec City in 1879, and in Winnipeg in 1882.[123]

Once again, new legislation did not end calls for stronger gun control. Canadian law still allowed any person to buy a revolver and did not require retailers to keep records of gun sales. The calls for strengthening laws came from a multitude of sources. A Winnipeg grand jury pleaded in late 1878 that authorities had to "carry out with the utmost severity the law with respect to the carrying of firearms," for Winnipeg's citizens had a "floating population continually surrounding us," and thus "some action should be taken to limit this dangerous habit."[124] The *Toronto World* condemned the "great evil of carrying concealed firearms."[125] A Guelph hardware merchant declared in 1882 that "the law as to carrying revolvers seems to be defective" and recommended that purchasers be required to get permission from two magistrates, for, although he profited from selling guns, "the sale now is going on at an alarming and to a dangerous extent."[126] The Toronto *Globe* pressed hard for more aggressive laws, particularly after the murder of the newspaper's iconic founder, George Brown, in 1880.[127] The *Globe* had fired the shooter, George Bennett, for intemperance. When Bennett entered Brown's office to request a certificate stating that he had worked at the newspaper, an argument ensued, Bennett pulled a revolver and fired, striking Brown in the leg. At first, Brown's injury appeared slight, and Brown went home. The wound, however, became infected, and Brown developed a fever, became delirious, and died at the age of sixty-one.[128]

With Prime Minister Macdonald refusing to act, several senators attempted to amend Canada's gun laws in the late 1880s. Senator Robert Read continued to advocate for new legislation, introducing a bill in 1889, because one could "scarcely take up a paper" lacking "reports of loss of life from the use of the 'ready revolver.'" He lamented the propensity for men and youth to carry revolvers: "I notice that even boys carry them," and that "young men carry them to their daily labor." His measure, though, was not radical. He proposed that persons carrying offensive weapons receive a fine, rather than be forced to give a surety, in the hope that that this would alter people's attitudes towards car-

Figure 11: Shooting of George Brown. Following the death of Brown, his newspaper, the *Globe*, became a strong proponent of regulating pistols.
Source: *Canadian Illustrated News* 21, no. 15 (10 April 1880): 229

rying weapons.[129] The Senate passed a bill, but it died in the House of Commons. The Senate passed a similar measure in 1890, but the lower house again refused its support, and Read lamented that his bills were "slaughtered with the innocents in the Commons."[130]

The failure of Read's bills once again stemmed largely from the opposition of John A. Macdonald, who had become prime minister for the second time in October 1878. New gun laws had to wait until Macdonald's death in 1891.[131] After years of calls for stronger measures, Attorney General John S.D. Thompson finally included important new rules concerning firearms, especially pistols, in the first *Criminal Code*. According to Thompson, the *Criminal Code* sections dealing with firearms established severe penalties because it was "the only way to prevent the carrying of weapons for offensive purposes."[132] The *Code* thus dictated a punishment of up to five years for carrying an offensive weapon for a purpose dangerous to the public peace and made it a summary offence to possess any firearm if disguised.[133]

The *Criminal Code* incorporated four other important provisions. First, it raised the penalties for carrying a pistol without justification (although Canadians could still keep such a weapon in their home or business) to a fine of between five and twenty-five dollars and up to one month in jail. Second, the *Code* created a new system for identifying who could carry a revolver. Canadians at least sixteen years old could obtain a "certificate of exemption" valid for twelve months if they convinced a justice of the peace of their discretion and good character. Justices had to record such certificates and make a return of any issued. The certificate of exemption system marked a substantial increase in the state's supervision of pistol use but also reflected the continued belief that respectable men of good character could arm themselves. The third major innovation in the *Criminal Code* was a prohibition on the sale or gifting of pistols (or air guns) to anyone under the age of sixteen. This was the first time that Canada placed an age restriction on to whom guns could be sold. The fourth innovation was that gun sellers had to keep a record, including the date of the sale, the name of the purchaser, the maker's name, and any other mark identifying the gun. This represented the first time the government forced gun sellers to keep track of sales.[134]

In passing these measures, Canada took a more proactive approach to gun regulation than Britain. Britain also considered new gun controls in the late nineteenth century because of a perceived problem of revolvers. In 1870, the *Gun Licenses Act* imposed a fee on any who carried or used weapons outside of their home. Liberal governments in Britain proposed several bills in 1890s designed to stop gun violence. For example, Prime Minister William Gladstone's government introduced a bill in 1893 to restrict the ownership of pistols less than fifteen inches long, required pistol owners to be over eighteen years old, and identified legitimate retailers as those possessing a licence. The bill failed to become law, as did another introduced in 1895 that would have required identification marks on pistols, increased the licence fee for selling pistols to dissuade retailers from carrying cheap revolvers, and required pistol owners to get a licence annually. Not until the early twentieth century did Britain create important new gun controls.[135]

Conclusion

Canadian governments took very different approaches to rifles and pistols after 1867. Ottawa reorganized the militia and continued the pre-Confederation policy of encouraging the ownership and use of rifles by loyal subjects through financial support for rifle associations. The threat of attacks from the United States motivated these policies, as did a belief that rifle shooting stoked manly character and encouraged national unity. When Ottawa regulated long guns, it created measures designed only to disarm potential rebels or prevent them from training in the use of arms. The fear of particular groups, especially Fenians and Aboriginal and Metis resisters of western expansion, motivated the regulation of modern rifles.

In comparison, Ottawa enacted more aggressive legislation to regulate the use of pistols by all Canadians. It is difficult to determine the extent of the pistol problem in Canada before 1892 using statistical evidence, so one is left to rely on the comments of politicians, journalists, and legal professionals, prosecution statistics, and evidence of gun imports. Although all are imperfect sources, collectively they indicate that Canadians in the 1870s and 1880s, especially urban residents, dealt with the introduction of substantial numbers of cheap, mass-produced, and concealable pistols. Ottawa responded with legislation in the late 1870s and 1892 that represented the beginning of permanent regulation of handguns. This early legislation began to differentiate the firearm laws of Canada and the United States and became the cornerstone of a regulatory framework that, over time, encouraged a substantially lower level of pistol ownership in Canada than in the United States and also, perhaps, different attitudes to handguns in the two nations.

The firearm laws enacted in the late nineteenth century, however, should give pause to progressive Canadians who sometimes celebrate gun control as a pillar of Canadian identity. For many progressives, gun regulation has become a means of distinguishing Canada from the United States. But less than noble impulses motivated most gun-control measures in the quarter century after Confederation. Legislators, for instance, designed pistol laws to discourage young working-class men from carrying revolvers. Canadian politicians suggested that such men posed a serious threat to Canadian order, especially during periods of ethnic, religious, and class conflict. On the other hand, many parliamentarians believed that people of property had a constitutional right to possess arms. Legislators thus ensured that respectable citizens could defend their lives and property against the reckless.

3

"A rifle in the hands of every able-bodied man in the Dominion of Canada under proper auspices": Arming Britons and Disarming Immigrants from the Late Nineteenth Century to the Great War

From the 1890s to the Great War, a groundswell of support for the British Empire in English Canada deeply affected Canadian gun culture. Middle-class and elite urban men flocked to the forests to hunt, in part because hunting promoters suggested that good marksmanship would benefit Canada in future imperial conflicts. The same motivation helped renew interest in formal rifle shooting. The federal government fully supported the arming of trustworthy citizens. Ottawa thus boosted financial support for rifle associations, encouraged the cadet movement, and invested in domestic ammunition and firearm industries.

Most men had little practical need to own a rifle, but hunting and shooting became integral to their definition of masculinity. Gun manufacturers and retailers actively encouraged the perceived relationship between manhood and firearms. While guns had long served as useful tools for rural Canadians to hunt, kill pests, and protect property, in the late nineteenth century rifles became more than practical implements – they became desired consumer items that could allegedly inculcate manly character in hunters and target shooters. Business also aggressively attempted to expand the market for firearms by appealing to women shooters and redefining some weapons as toys and thus as acceptable and desirable consumer items for young people.

The place of firearms in the emerging Canadian consumer society created troubling policy questions. The pre-war period witnessed the birth of the regulatory state, as governments sought to shape individual behaviour and ameliorate some of the negative aspects of industrial society. The state tried to delineate distinctions between "safe" and "unsafe" weapons, while businesses pushed back by blurring the distinction in order to sell to the largest possible audience. In addition, the desire to protect wildlife for recreational hunters encouraged Ottawa and the provinces to pass game laws to limit the use of particular kinds of arms that placed animal populations at risk of complete destruction.

Government efforts to regulate gun use by young people evidenced the tension between business interests and state regulatory goals. Despite the efforts of retailers and manufacturers to market their guns as widely as possible, Ottawa deemed *some* weapons unsuited for youth under the age of sixteen, thus limiting the agency of a group deemed incapable of possessing the rights of full citizens. Efforts to shape gun use by immigrants represented a parallel gun-control story. High levels of immigration before the Great War fuelled concerns with firearm use by new Canadians, leading several provinces and Ottawa to enact laws to prevent the misuse of some kinds of dangerous weapons, especially pistols.

Recreational Hunting

In the late nineteenth and early twentieth centuries, an interconnected set of cultural attitudes concerning masculinity, modernity, and imperialism led many Canadians to take up hunting as a recreational activity. This interest in hunting by middle- and upper-class men affected gun control, for hunters (who had political clout) had little interest in regulating their own behaviour and, in fact, encouraged greater training in the use of rifles.

Hunting became entwined with imperialist sentiment in English Canada. As John MacKenzie notes, hunting served as "a mark of the fitness of the dominant race, a route to health, strength, and wealth, an emblem of imperial rule, and an allegory of human affairs."[1] Imperialists celebrated hunting for improving the martial skills of Canadians needed to help Britain in any future armed conflict. Men learned to track prey, subsist in natural settings, and, most importantly, shoot at moving targets. Deer, moose, bears, or rabbits would, in wartime, be replaced by enemy soldiers. Sport, especially hunting, was thus "ideal training for the manly game of war."[2] Military men regarded hunting as "essential training in the understanding of terrain, analysing the reactions of foe, courage, endurance, horsemanship and marksmanship."[3] The British Columbia provincial game warden made this point in his 1914 annual report, stating proudly that Canadian soldiers were "not mere target shots," for they could "do the shooting required of them," because there was "game in the country for men to shoot at."[4] The connection between hunting and imperialism would lead to efforts to expand access to firearms.

It was not just imperialism that encouraged hunting. A belief that many urban men and boys led sedentary lives that provided little opportunity for differentiation between the sexes also proved important. The sense of uncertainty created by the social adjustments of the late nineteenth century seemed to require a return to "core" cultural values, which, for many, meant socializing young people in how to be manly men.[5] The growth of recreational hunting reflected this belief. Middle-class, urban Canadians took cues from British gentlemen in advocating sport hunting as a respectable, manly activity. British hunters (and their Canadian counterparts) became part of a movement for outdoor, middle-class recreation at a time when reformers decried cities as unsanitary and rife with poverty. Urban residents thus sought out "pure" outdoor recreation. Hunting trips allowed men to create self-images in accordance with "bourgeois masculinity." Big game hunters, Tina Loo suggests, "defined themselves as skilled, self-reliant, self-controlled, chivalrous risk-takers."[6] As the size of the middle class grew, so did the pool of potential recreational hunters responding to a desire to demonstrate their manliness in the face of the modern industrial, urban world. These new hunters sometimes required instruction on the etiquette of hunting – rules that elite hunters had developed to ensure a "sporting" challenge to the hunt. So, for example, according to one sage, a "rabbit in motion affords a splendid opportunity for a display of marksmanship," but shooting a sitting rabbit was "pure murder."[7] Gun owners formed rod and gun clubs and trapshooting associations to practise shooting and to advocate for wildlife preservation to protect game.[8]

The growing interest in hunting led businesses to market guns and hunting gear to middle-class, urban hunters. Firearms thus became a commodity in the emerging Canadian consumer market. According to Keith Walden, businesses "tried to persuade individuals that personal identity depended not on geography, family background, religious values, occupation, or similar things, but on choices made among consumer goods found in the market-place."[9] Eaton's was a leader in the shift towards consumerism, a product of what David Monod calls the "retailing revolution" of the late nineteenth century that witnessed

Figure 12: Hunting became a popular recreational activity for middle- and upper-class men by the late nineteenth century. This group poses for a photograph in Okotoks, Alberta.

Source: Glenbow Archives, NA-2520-66

Figure 13: Gun clubs became popular in the early twentieth century. In this photograph, members of the Calgary Gun Club gather in front of their clubhouse in 1909.
Source: Glenbow Archives, PD-347-1-130

the emergence of "a national market, large-scale production, and mass merchandising."[10] Eaton's used large department stores, aggressive newspaper advertising, and mail order catalogues to take advantage of a growing demand for consumer goods. Guns promised profits to retailers such as Eaton's, which sought to sell firearms and related goods to hunters, target shooters, and children and youth.

Retailers branded middle-class hunters "sportsmen" in their advertisements, and they carried wide selections of firearms. American gun manufacturers actively marketed their guns far and wide. The Marlin Firearms Company of New Haven, Connecticut, for example, ran advertisements for its rifles in the *Twillingate Sun*, published on Newfoundland's north coast.[11] Businesses recognized that middle-class hunters represented a very profitable group, as they purchased a substantial amount of paraphernalia beyond guns and ammunition. As early as 1893, the H.P. Davies Company of Toronto announced to "sportsmen" that it possessed rifles, shooting coats, decoy ducks, and ammunition. The next year it added other hunting accoutrements, including flasks, knives, hats, caps, leggings, gun cases, game bags, shell bags, whistles, bird calls, and everything requisite "except the game."[12] In their desire to commune with nature, hunters heavily participated in modern consumer culture.

Urban sportsmen criticized rural subsistence hunters who continued to hunt for food or to supplement their income. Such hunters did not receive the "sportsmen" title because their inability to fully partake in the modern economy forced them to kill – they *had* to hunt. As well, recognition that big game hunters poured cash into local economies through money spent on provisions, guides, accommodation, and train travel led to efforts to prevent local residents from shooting the large animals preferred by sport hunters, such as bear and moose.[13] Native Peoples, in particular, received criticism for recklessly destroying wildlife. White hunters claimed that Aboriginal People, lacking awareness of the sportsman's creed, shot female animals, hunted out of season, or used "unsportsmanlike" methods. They killed out of a love of slaughter, many suggested. The image thus emerged of the "Indian as ecological menace."[14] Senator Mackenzie Bowell asserted in 1894 that Native Peoples in the northwest killed large numbers of caribou "often through sheer love of slaughter."[15] Some rural people resisted the transformation of wildlife into a commodity for recreational hunters. Farmers complained that "fish and game had been diminished as adjuncts to the farm economy," as they were "progressively transformed into forms of property controlled by alien state agents in the interest of nonresident recreations."[16] Hunters tramped across crop land in search of prey and risked life and property when they shot their high-powered rifles.

The desire to preserve game populations contributed to the passage of new legislation to protect wildlife. The advanced firearm, a potent symbol of modern industry and human mastery over the environment, risked destroying the animal resources that allowed men to escape the urban world through hunting. Legislators thus passed game laws that limited what, when, and how animals could be killed. The provinces had jurisdiction to regulate hunting within their boundaries, while the federal government legislated for the territories, and both levels of government tended to target subsistence hunters. Authorities, for example, used game acts to prosecute Native hunters. Some provinces also passed licensing laws in the early twentieth century. In the nineteenth

Figure 14: Modern weapons allowed for hunters to kill large quantities of
wildlife, thus leading to legislative efforts to preserve wildlife. In this 1926
image from Unity, Saskatchewan, hunters armed with repeating weapons
show off their haul from a morning and an evening shoot.
Source: Glenbow Archives, NC-37-143

century, legislators had sometimes required visitors to Canada to acquire a licence, but in the early twentieth century governments increasingly compelled residents and non-residents alike to acquire licences.
This helped governments regulate and keep track of the number of
animals hunted, and hunting regulations also allowed authorities to
take possession of weapons for violations of game acts (such as hunting
without a licence).[17]

Legislators used game laws to ban the use of specific types of weapons as hunting arms to preserve wildlife. Several provinces outlawed
hunters from employing huge "punt" guns or "swivel" guns that could
annihilate large numbers of birds.[18] Commercial waterfowl hunters often employed such weapons. Legislators also expressed concern over
newly designed "automatic" weapons that could quickly fire a large
number of rounds, and several provinces limited the use of automatic
guns as hunting weapons.[19] These measures constituted one form of

gun control that stirred relatively little public debate. Future intrusions into hunters' habits, however, would create a greater backlash.

Hunting Accidents

The growing interest in sport hunting, particularly among urban men, resulted in concerns that part-time, recreational hunters would accidentally shoot themselves or others. Technological improvements to rifles made amateur hunters more dangerous. Powerful hunting arms had longer effective ranges. Some gun makers celebrated the advantages of powerful hunting rifles. The Ross Rifle Company, for instance, boasted of the "low trajectory of the Ross Rifle,"[20] while Winchester bragged that its .401 calibre hunting rifle struck with a "force enough to topple over the biggest game – penetration enough to reach the innermost vital spot." "It hits like the hammer of Thor," suggested Winchester.[21]

However, rounds that missed game could travel considerable distances and hit people moving through forests and fields. According to the *Globe*, the modern rifle "with long range, flat trajectory and great power of penetration, has become a new danger" that was "greatly enhanced by the presence of a growing element whose eyes distort every moving or irregular object into a bear or deer."[22] The tendency of inexperienced hunters to handle such arms unsafely became a constant refrain by the mid-1890s. The *Twillingate Sun* of Newfoundland felt it necessary to publish "Hints for Handling Guns," which included obvious advice: "Never point a gun toward yourself or any other person."[23] The *Globe* complained in 1894 that the "usual quota of shotgun accidents has been reported" because of amateur hunters' lack of firearm knowledge. While the "backwoods man" understood how to handle guns, this could not "be expected in the amateur who goes out for a few days shooting in the fall and lays the gun away for a year." The result was "often a fatal accident."[24]

Concerns with accidents led some businesses to employ new marketing approaches to sell firearms. Some asserted the safety of their weapons. William M. Cooper of Toronto, for instance, called the Bullard Repeating Rifle the "strongest, safest and most perfect working Repeater in this country."[25] Toronto gun seller Charles Stark advertised a breech-loading shotgun by suggesting it was the "safest, the best shooting, the handsomest gun" ever offered at its price.[26] In 1891, Stark took a new approach, offering to provide life insurance to purchasers of his weapons. "The safest way to insure your life against shooting accidents is to use a Marlin Repeating Rifle," suggested Stark. However,

THE DUCK SHOOTING SEASON.

Figure 15: The attire of the hunters in this 1877 illustration demonstrates the middle-class nature of recreational hunting. The gentleman pointing his finger is perhaps warning the man on the left to avoid pointing the rifle at other people.
Source: Canadian Illustrated News 16, no. 14 (6 October 1877): 209

the "cheapest way to insure your life against every kind of accident is to buy a 'Cycle, Gun, Rifle, or Watch (amounting to $15 or over) at Stark's and get a $200 accident insurance policy free."[27] This approach was unusual but highlighted the efforts of business to reassure hunters of their safety.

Accidents led to appeals for legislation. In 1898, for instance, the *Toronto Star* reported on a gun accident that proved the necessity of restrictions on the "indiscriminate sale of firearms."[28] This was a minority position, however, as reflected in the inability of legislators to pass criminal law provisions designed to prosecute people who accidentally shot others. In 1908, the Conservative MP representing Huron West, Ontario, Edward Lewis, introduced a *Criminal Code* amendment to specifically punish homicides committed while hunting. He proposed that anyone who shot another person, even if the hunter believed the target was a deer, moose, or other animal, was guilty of an indictable offence and liable to two years' imprisonment. Lewis acknowledged that he targeted recreational hunters with his bill. Lewis failed in 1908, so he tried once more, unsuccessfully, in 1910. At least one province stepped in to fill the void. Saskatchewan dictated fines of between five hundred and one thousand dollars for any hunter who shot at or wounded another person by accident, even if the shooting did not constitute a crime under the *Criminal Code*. Further, Saskatchewan threatened to revoke the hunting licence of any hunter who shot at or wounded another by accident.[29]

By the early twentieth century, the popularity of hunting among urban men had grown immensely. Amateur hunters fled to the woods each fall to take part in an anti-modernist excursion that buttressed men's sense of masculinity. These urban hunters posed dangers to wildlife, themselves, and their hunting partners, and governments thus nibbled away at the right of hunters of use certain types of weapons. In general, however, politicians (many of whom actively hunted) did not connect the deleterious effects of recreational hunting with a need to create ambitious new gun controls.

"To become a nation of sharp-shooters": Rifle Shooting in Pre-war Canada

Imperialist sentiment also resulted in renewed interest in the militia and rifle shooting. Many Canadians increasingly equated militarism with patriotism and saw militia service as a means to express their love of country and empire. In the 1860s and 1870s, advocates of rifle shooting argued that Canadians needed shooting skills to stop invasions from the United States. After a lull in support for rifle shooting in the 1880s, Canadians renewed their interest in the 1890s. Various journalists, politicians, and militia leaders asserted that Canada could support

Britain effectively in future wars only if men developed rifle shooting acumen. Businessman and politician Sir Richard Cartwright made this point to the Dominion Rifle Association in 1897, noting that rifle shooting was "not merely a pastime, but might be the means of rendering material assistance to the empire."[30] Thus, according to the *Globe*, to "become a nation of sharp-shooters is a worthy ambition for Canadians to cherish."[31]

Canadians' modest military experience strengthened the desire for an armed citizenry. A key lesson taken from the Anglo-Boer War of 1899–1902 was that armies consisting of crack rifle shots would determine the outcomes of future conflicts. After war broke out in southern Africa between the British colonies of the Cape and Natal and the Boer republics of the Orange Free State and the Transvaal in 1899, Britain requested Canadian assistance. After intense debate, Canada obliged, sending its first hastily organized battalion of volunteers in October 1899. By the end of the conflict, 8,300 Canadians had enlisted. According to Desmond Morton, the eventual British victory and the relatively light casualties suffered by Canadian forces (only 242 died) "did much to encourage a naïve military enthusiasm in Canada."[32] An exaggerated belief in the importance of rifle shooting formed part of this naïvety. Newspapers consistently stressed rifle shooting in discussing the Boer War. The Edmonton *Bulletin*, for instance, suggested that the war showed that the "increase in the range and rapid fire of the weapons" meant that "drill is subordinated to marksmanship."[33] *Rod and Gun in Canada* made the same point more simply. The "great lesson of the South African war" was that "every Briton must know how to shoot."[34]

Another Boer War lesson also strengthened Canadians' interest in rifle shooting: that irregular troops – ordinary "citizen-soldiers" – could match the effectiveness of professional troops. The highly motivated Boer forces armed with German-made Mauser repeating rifles had shown themselves the equal of regular soldiers. A glorification of irregular soldiers was not entirely new. By the late nineteenth century, proponents of a "militia myth" in English Canada – especially in Ontario – credited Loyalist militias with defending British North America in the War of 1812. Irregular soldiers equalled regular soldiers *and* were better citizens. Rank and file soldiers lacked respectability, but amateur citizen-soldiers epitomized manliness, Christianity, and love of nation and empire. Further, press and politicians mythologized the role of Canadians in the Boer War by emphasizing the stereotype that Canadians knew how to ride, shoot, and live off the land.[35]

Figure 16: Many Canadians believed that the Boer War demonstrated that accurate shooting with the modern rifle was the most important skill for soldiers. This unnamed soldier of the 2nd Canadian Mounted Rifles fought in the Boer War.
Source: Glenbow Archives, NA-3378-11

These lessons made rifle training imperative. "What Canada needs most," *Rod and Gun* concluded, was "500,000 men of Anglo-Saxon and Celtic descent who could at short notice use their rifles to good effect."[36] Advocates of rifle shooting claimed that increased urbanization meant the loss of previous generations' shooting skills. Britain's enemy, the Boers, became, ironically, a model for modern citizen-soldiers. Canadians employed other models, however, making analogies between riflemen and the historic English longbowmen, and pointing to the Swiss requirement that every man practise with a rifle.[37]

Leading Canadian political figures again supported rifle shooting. In 1906, Governor General Earl Grey told the Dominion Rifle Association that every Briton must, as a responsibility to the empire, learn to fire a rifle accurately. Other strong supporters included the minister of militia under Prime Minister Wilfrid Laurier from 1896 to 1911, Frederick

Figure 17: By the early twentieth century, Canadians believed that citizen-soldiers, such as these Winnipeg members of the Canadian contingent serving in South Africa during the Boer War, were vital to defending Canada and the British Empire.
Source: Glenbow Archives, NA-5107-12

Borden, and his Conservative successor, Sam Hughes, who served as minister of militia from 1911 to 1916. Borden invested in rifle shooting, rebuilding ranges made dangerous by high-powered rifles. Hughes, a militant imperialist, long supported rifle practice as an inexpensive way to teach martial skills and provide trained men for the militia units when needed. In 1907, he became president of the Dominion Rifle Association, a position he used to press the government for more funding for rifle shooting.[38]

Increased federal support helped spur a growing interest in rifle shooting. Total defence spending increased from $1.6 million in 1898 to $11 million in 1914, and Ottawa used some of these funds to create a

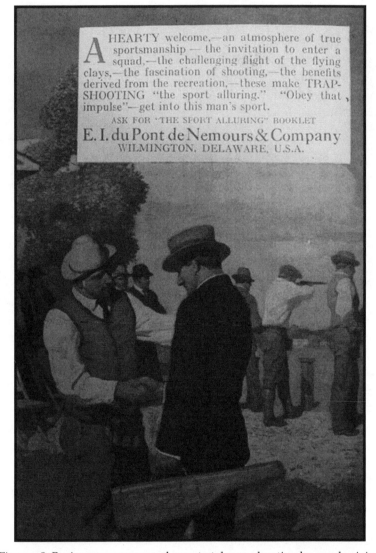

Figure 18: Businesses encouraged men to take up shooting by emphasizing
the manly nature of the hobby. For example, this American company
advertised in Canada by calling trapshooting a "man's sport" that offered
opportunities for comradeship and healthy living.
Source: Rod and Gun in Canada 18, no. 2 (July 1916), used by permission of the
Hagley Museum and Library

School of Musketry to teach target practice, armoury work, rifle range management, ammunition testing, and theory. The federal government also incorporated the Dominion Rifle Association in 1900 by an act of Parliament to strengthen the association's position. The dominion expected rifle associations would reciprocate by aiding in Canada's defence, if necessary. In announcing more funding for rifle associations at the meeting of the Dominion Rifle Association in 1901, Minister of Militia Borden thus stated that association members would "not simply be ornamental rifle shots" and would, "if necessity should demand," take "part and share in the defence of this country and of our flag."[39] Ottawa subsequently legislated that it could declare members of the Dominion Rifle Association (and other associations) militia for the defence of Canada.[40]

Imperialist sentiments, the lessons of the Boer War, powerful advocates, and government support thus renewed interest in rifle shooting prior to the Great War. Major rifle associations reported record numbers of shooters, and the number of rifle clubs grew substantially. In 1904, Canada had 291 civilian and military rifle associations with 22,935 members, but by 1914, the number of clubs had doubled to 583, and membership had more than doubled to 48,787. Interest in rifle shooting contributed to a substantial spike in gun imports into Canada. The value of gun imports for home consumption totalled $152,239 in 1892, dropped to $93,015 in 1897, then rapidly ascended, to $180,072 in 1901, $459,878 in 1904, and $900,031 in 1913. A growing percentage of these firearms came from the United States. In 1868, 64.1 per cent of firearms came from Britain, but by 1897 55.5 per cent of firearms entering Canada came from the United States – a figure that grew to 74 per cent by 1913. Not content with dominating the existing Canadian market in firearms, American companies spent considerable effort spurring the demand for guns by Canadian women and young people.[41]

Women and Rifle Shooting

Unlike during the first spurt of interest in rifle shooting during the 1860s and 1870s, the pre–Great War period witnessed the involvement of some women. In the first decade of the twentieth century, women formed their own shooting clubs or participated in competitions held by male-dominated associations. The Ladies Rifle Club of Charlottetown formed in 1905. The Hamilton Gun Club held its first "Ladies' Day" in 1905 and sixty women attended. A women's rifle club existed

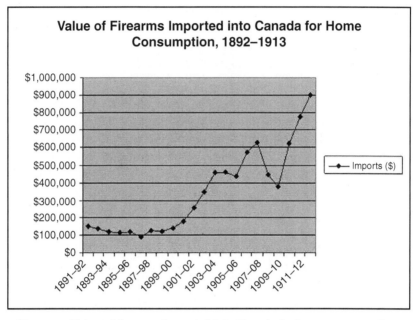

Figure 19: Value of firearms imported into Canada for home consumption, 1892–1913.

Source: Tables of the Trade and Navigation of the Dominion of Canada, in Canada, *Sessional Papers*, 1892–1914

in Vancouver by 1909, and Quebec City also developed a flourishing ladies' rifle club.[42] Women competed with the men at a Guelph Rifle Association shooting match in 1913, leading to the suggestion that "even Cupid will have to give up his absurd archery soon and take to the rifle."[43] In 1909, the Ladies' Rifle Association of Canada held its inaugural meeting in Toronto. The women in attendance received instruction and agreed to practise on a lawn during the summer.[44]

Given the connection between rifles and masculinity, the participation of women is at first surprising. However, women could take part if they dressed appropriately, used small-calibre weapons, and acted respectably. American models proved to Canadian women that shooting did not undermine femininity. Annie Oakley became famous performing target-shooting exploits in Wild West shows across North America, including in Canada.[45] Oakley possessed an ability to present "herself as a Victorian lady who also happened to be an expert markswomen."[46]

TORONTO WOMEN
LEARN TO SHOOT   JAMES PHOTO

Figure 20: Women expressed substantial interest in rifle shooting prior to, and in the early stages of, the Great War. Here several Toronto women learn to shoot, circa 1915.
Source: City of Toronto Archives, William James Family, fonds 1244, item 981

Middle-class Canadian women also emphasized Victorian qualities to make rifle shooting an acceptable activity, and the *Globe* defended female participants from the critique that they violated traditional gender norms. It noted in 1902 that the "average girl is afraid of firearms," but fortunately there were exceptions who took part in shooting and knew that "belonging to a rifle club need not and does not make a girl tomboyish."[47]

Women took up rifle shooting for several other reasons. The women who participated came largely from the respectable classes – women with leisure time accustomed to demonstrating acumen in areas traditionally dominated by men. There were also reputed health benefits: the *Toronto Star* believed it "excellent training for the eye and the nerve" that could be "indulged in by many women who find lawn

Figure 21: Most of the women involved in rifle shooting appear to have come from the middle class. They dressed as acceptable Victorian women to avoid criticism. Here Miss L. Ford practises shooting in Victoria, BC, 1900.
Source: Image H-02441 courtesy of the Royal BC Museum, British Columbia Archives

tennis or golf a form of exercise too strenuous for them."[48] Women, like men, also enjoyed the social aspects of shooting. Women interested in forming a rifle club in Charlottetown, for instance, met and fired at targets, then stopped for refreshments. A sense that women should know how to use firearms for self-protection also motivated some women. Women looking to defend themselves with guns gravitated to revolvers, and a there was a Toronto Women's Revolver Club by 1915.[49]

Businesses also encouraged women to use guns to expand the market for firearms. American companies urged Canadian women to shoot, often using advertisements that portrayed women handling weapons. In 1903, the Stevens Arms Company encouraged women to take up target shooting, noting that "there are no restrictions to this popular and fascinating sport, as old and young of both sexes can equally enjoy it."[50] Canadian companies made similar appeals. The Dominion Cartridge Company called shooting a healthy outdoor sport "for Men and Women" while portraying a well-dressed, middle-class couple carrying rifles.[51] Businesses pointed to some weapons as especially suited to women, especially air rifles and small .22-calibre guns. The Marlin Firearms Company pictured a female shooter in advertising its .22-calibre rifles.[52]

Women's use of guns thus reflected the extent to which firearms, especially rifles, became acceptable among the middle class. Some women, interested in demonstrating their capabilities vis-à-vis men, getting exercise, socializing, and defending themselves, sought to practise with rifles. Business also appealed to female shooters, believing them a valuable but untapped market.

Teachings Boys and Youth to Shoot

Business similarly sought to expand the market for firearms by encouraging young people to shoot. This strategy, combined with the interconnected set of cultural attitudes concerning masculinity, modernity, and imperialism, strongly encouraged young people to use firearms.

Instructing boys in military drill gained adherents as imperialist sentiments intensified in the 1890s. Proponents said exercise and participation in martial activities stemmed moral and physical decay and encouraged good character and thus combated youth delinquency. Many urban residents worried that boys loitered in the streets, made lewd remarks, spit tobacco, and violated middle-class ideals of proper behaviour. They thus sought to teach young people good posture, healthy living, and obedience to authority. Firearm training would create order by inculcating morality, manliness, and an ability to resist the evil temptations of the city.[53]

These attitudes led to efforts to train boys in the art of war. Boys' brigades represented an early effort to uplift youth in poor areas by blending recreation with military training. In Montreal, a boys' brigade enlisted young people who pledged abstinence and accepted military obedience. The group purchased rifles and drilled (although not all boys' brigades used firearms). Two other organizations proved even more important. First, the scouting movement begun by Robert Baden-Powell came to include rifle training in the early twentieth century. Baden-Powell published *Scouting for Boys* in Canada in 1908, and by

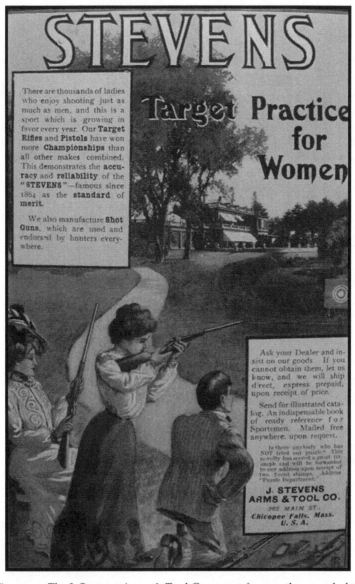

Figure 22: The J. Stevens Arms & Tool Company frequently appealed to
Canadian women as potential customers for its arms.
Source: *Rod and Gun in Canada* 5, no. 12 (May 1904), used with permission of
Savage Arms

1910 Canada had approximately 5000 Scouts – a figure that climbed to 13,565 by September 1914. As several historians have noted, scouting was an imperialist organization influenced by muscular Christianity, anti-modernist sentiments, and middle-class ideas of hunting. Generally catering to boys between the ages of eleven and fourteen, scouting sought to turn boys into good citizens and good soldiers by inculcating patriotism and imperialism.[54] Baden-Powell, in fact, suggested that scouting trained boys for war. He encouraged boys to shoot, writing in *Scouting for Boys*, "Every boy ought to learn to shoot and to obey orders, else he is no more good when war breaks out than an old woman."[55] Some Scouts practised target shooting in Montreal before the Great War, and the Canadian scouting movement awarded hundreds of marksmanship badges.[56]

The cadet movement proved even more important than Scouts in encouraging shooting. Canadian governments supported the cadets. In 1898, Ontario promised to grant fifty dollars to any school board having a cadet corps of at least twenty-five boys. Ottawa integrated the cadets into the militia system with the 1904 *Militia Act*, which allowed Ottawa to provide cadet corps with arms. Minister of Militia Frederick Borden then entered negotiations with the provinces to incorporate military training in schools as part of a national system so that every boy would learn to use a rifle. Borden's efforts received a boost from the establishment of the Lord Strathcona Trust, designed to encourage drilling, physical training, and shooting in public schools. The cadet movement picked up even more steam after Sam Hughes became minister of militia following the 1911 election. Hughes increased the federal budget for cadets from $93,000 in 1912 to $400,000 in 1913, and ordered several thousand .22-calibre Ross rifles for cadets. By 1914, the number of cadets had reached almost 45,000. This government stimulation resulted in greater interest in rifle shooting by boys, and the creation of a generation of young men ready to fight and die in the Great War.[57]

Gun retailers and manufacturers buttressed state efforts that encouraged young people to shoot, but this is not to say that businesses attempted to sell all kinds of weapons to boys and youth. In particular, businesses did not market pistols to young people, thus acknowledging the danger of such weapons. Retailers, however, widely sold pistols to the general public, with the result that some fell into young hands. While businesses deemed pistols too dangerous for young people, they aggressively marketed other types of arms to children and youth.

Figure 23: The state actively encouraged young people to develop skill with rifles prior to the Great War. In this 1912 photograph, the Calgary public school champion rifle shots stand with their awards.
Source: Glenbow Archives, PB-855-1

Canadian retailers made "toy pistols" widely available. These pistols took several forms. Some were small-calibre (.22-calibre) guns that fired blank cartridges. Others exploded a detonating wafer charged with a fulminating compound. Businesses sold these extremely cheap "toys" in the United States in the 1880s, often to celebrate the Fourth of July, and many Canadian retailers also offered such toy guns. For example, as early as 1869 one Halifax merchant advertised a "patent revolver for boys" as "quite a new and ingenious Toy, which can be fired fives times in succession."[58] By the end of the nineteenth century, many other retailers carried toy pistols. The Consolidated Stationery Company of Winnipeg, for example, advertised toy pistols as a means of celebrating Victoria Day, while Simpson's included a cap gun in its Christmas 1906 catalogue.[59]

Air rifles also appeared in the Canadian market. The air gun was long deemed an "assassin's weapon" because of its ability to fire almost silently. American companies, however, reshaped public opinion about such guns when they began to mass produce and market inexpensive air rifles. In 1888, the Plymouth Iron Windmill Company manufactured the first all-metal air gun. The company subsequently changed its name to the Daisy Manufacturing Company, began developing new models, including repeating air rifles, and slowly consolidated its market position. At first, businesses often advertised air guns as suitable for adult entertainment, rather than as children's toys. For example, in 1896 the Griffiths Corporation appealed to middle-class men and women, suggesting that air guns "furnish excellent amusement for lawn or parlor." The company's air guns sold for $1.00 and up.[60] This low price was typical. A new Daisy air rifle sold for just 99 cents in Saint John in 1896, while in 1913 one Edmonton retailer offered several models ranging in price from $1.10 to $1.98.[61] Youth could graduate from air rifles to more powerful arms, especially .22-calibre rifles. A number of companies produced such rifles, the small size of which encouraged the sense that young people could safely handle them. Like air rifles, such guns were inexpensive. Eaton's, for example, offered .22-calibre rifles for as little as $2.00 in 1899.[62]

Retailers often described or portrayed air rifles as toys. Eaton's employed this approach for a time, including air guns in the toy section of its 1892–3 Fall–Winter catalogue, while a Victoria retailer sold a variety of "military toys" in 1897, including Daisy air rifles, and Simpson's included air guns in the toy section of its 1906 Christmas catalogue.[63] Eaton's shifted air guns to the firearm section of its catalogue by 1902, although the primary market for the weapons remained boys, as evidenced, for instance, when Eaton's called the King air rifle "a splendid rifle for boys" in 1910.[64] Other retailers did not overtly claim the suitability of air rifles for boys, but advertised them beside toys, thus implicitly suggesting the appropriateness of air rifles for young people.

A number of businesses also suggested that young people could safely handle air rifles by offering them as compensation for selling products. This practice, according to Gary Cross, stemmed from toymakers' realization that "children had limited financial autonomy" but "unlimited desires."[65] In Ontario, boys could receive a free air rifle for selling twelve boxes of Dr Groves' Famous Stomach, Kidney, and Liver Pills. Businesses took out such advertisements in almost all parts of Canada, including in small-town newspapers, thus ensuring the avail-

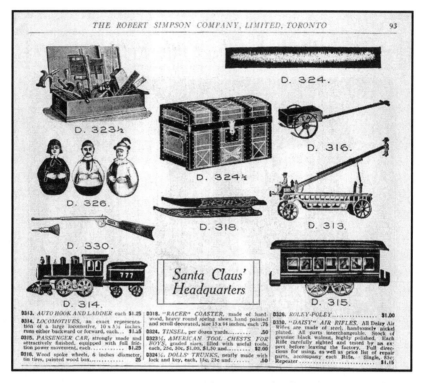

Figure 24: Like many other retailers, Simpson's in 1906 still placed air rifles amongst toys.
Source: *Simpson's Christmas Catalogue, 1906*, 93, LAC, http://www
.collectionscanada.gc.ca/mailorder/index-e.html, used with permission of
Sears Canada Inc.

ability of air rifles to boys and youth in smaller communities and rural areas. For example, a Toronto company offered a Daisy air rifle to boys in Wetaskiwin, Alberta who sold forty sets of greeting cards.[66]

Businesses also actively marketed .22-calibre rifles to boys and youth in the early twentieth century. While retailers did not call such arms "toys," they placed advertisements beside or amongst toys, or named and described the guns to appeal to young consumers. Eaton's, for instance, called the Stevens .22 Little Scout rifle a "splendid little rifle for boys or youths."[67] The Stevens Arms Company of Massachusetts consistently targeted youth in its Canadian advertisements. In 1902, the company portrayed boys shooting and recommended some of its models for "younger shooters."[68] The Canadian Ross Rifle Company also began to produce and market a .22-calibre "cadet" rifle, describing it as a "splendid arm for training boys or men" that was "perfectly safe."[69]

Companies sought to make firearms attractive consumer items for young people by emphasizing the beauty of their guns. C. Flood & Sons of Saint John described an air rifle as "the handsomest air rifle in the world,"[70] while a Winnipeg company offered a "genuine Steel, Black Walnut Air Rifle, handsomely nickelled [sic] and polished" to anyone who sold twelve Japanese silk fans.[71] Retailers also employed the ultimate symbol of the new consumerist mentality, Christmas, to sell air guns and .22-calibre rifles. Toronto's Charles Stark, for instance, suggested in 1904 that as a Christmas present nothing was "nicer for a boy than a small 22 caliber rifle,"[72] while in 1910 Eaton's listed air guns and small game rifles as desirable "Gifts for Lively Boys" at Christmas.[73] Gun manufacturers also enticed parents to purchase weapons for their children using Christmas. The Stevens Arms Company showed Santa Claus carrying a rifle and told parents that Santa would be speeding over rooftops "loaded down with Stevens Firearms for the youths of the land."[74] In employing the holiday season to market guns, retailers and manufacturers thus sought to take advantage of the burgeoning Canadian consumer culture.

Businesses also emphasized that owning or using a gun could transform boys into men. Given the cultural context in which many Canadians both celebrated imperialism and saw hunting and rifle shooting as antidotes to the deleterious effects of modern urban life, retailers advertised guns to boys with images and language that suggested using arms signified manliness and/or love of empire. The Stevens Arms Company emphasized the role of firearms in turning boys into men in blunt terms: "Make a man of your boy by giving him a 'Stevens'; he will surely appreciate it, and you will add to the education of your son."[75] Businesses promoted the role of guns in bringing together father and son, thus allowing for invaluable bonding and the transfer of wisdom regarding how to be a man. A common suggestion was that arming your son would instil in him manly qualities, such as independence, self-sufficiency, and an ability to protect personal property, all of which represented desirable characteristics in a liberal nation.[76]

By the early twentieth century, Canadian boys and youth had available to them a veritable arsenal of weapons. Mass produced and cheap, revolvers, toy pistols, air guns, and .22-calibre rifles found their way

Figure 25: Many retailers and gun manufacturers, including the J. Stevens Arms & Tool Company, employed the Christmas season to sell its firearms. *Source*: *Rod and Gun in Canada* 5, no. 7 (December 1903), used with permission of Savage Arms

Figure 26: Retailers drew upon widely held ideas concerning masculinity and imperialism to make weapons appealing to boys and youth. In this advertisement, a boy participates in a "war on cats" using an air rifle. *Source: Globe*, 2 February 1901

into the hands of young people from coast to coast. The accessibility of these weapons, however, led to various concerns, including fears of gun accidents, worries over environmental destruction, and apprehension about creating a generation of violent youth.

Accidents caused the most concern. Although quantification of the problem is impossible, weapons of all sorts clearly caused injuries and deaths. For example, cheap revolvers sometimes found their way into the hands of children, often with disastrous results. In reflecting on one accidental shooting, a coroner's jury in 1901 thus called attention "to the careless way in which the revolver and cartridges were left lying around where children could get access to them."[77] "Toy" pistols proved a concern as well, for such guns caused a substantial number of injuries and deaths in the United States and, to a lesser extent, in Canada. In 1880, the *Chicago Daily Tribune* damned the toy pistol as the "most prolific of all sources of accidents to children."[78] Reports from across the United States explain the *Daily Tribune's* assertion. In just one year, 1882, toy pistols led to the death of twenty-eight boys in several American cities. Fatalities occurred in a number of ways, but most stemmed from "lockjaw" (i.e., tetanus) acquired when boys stuffed gravel, slate pencils, or old nails down the barrel to create projectiles, then accidentally or intentionally shot themselves or others with these makeshift bullets. Even without such projectiles, some toy guns could burn or break the skin if fired at close range. The injuries and deaths caused by toy pistols led several American jurisdictions to ban the sale of such guns.[79]

Canadians noted accidents with toy pistols in the United States, Britain, and Canada and cautioned against the use of such guns.[80] After a youngster shot a toy pistol at another boy in British Columbia in 1880, the justice of the Victoria police court warned that such weapons could kill if fired at close range.[81] *Pleasant Hours*, a Methodist journal, declared in 1884 that "the toy pistol has been conceded to be a more dangerous weapon in the hand of the thoughtless boy than the real pistol."[82] Nova Scotia physician and senator William Johnston Almon said he had seen "a good many accidents happen from toy pistols," and he had "known children's eyes to be put out and severe wounds to be inflicted." Almon later told his fellow senators that he wanted to prohibit the sale of toy pistols because he had treated two boys who had injured themselves with toy pistols loaded with stones.[83]

Some Canadians also deemed .22-calibre rifles and air guns dangerous. Air rifles resulted in a spate of accidents, as one example can illustrate. In 1907, two boys in Toronto went down Dufferin Street with an air rifle. They came across a six-year-old boy and told him to raise his hands. The air rifle went off, striking the child in the eye.[84] Such accidents led the *Manitoba Morning Free Press* to criticize air guns as "exceedingly dangerous weapons in the hands of careless boys."[85] Many accidents also involved .22-calibre rifles. For example, in 1910 a thirteen-year-old Montreal boy stumbled, causing the discharge of his .22-calibre rifle, and the bullet lodged in the hip of his fourteen-year-old companion.[86] Such incidents led the *Cayley Hustler* of Alberta to complain about the frequency of accidents and to suggest that many

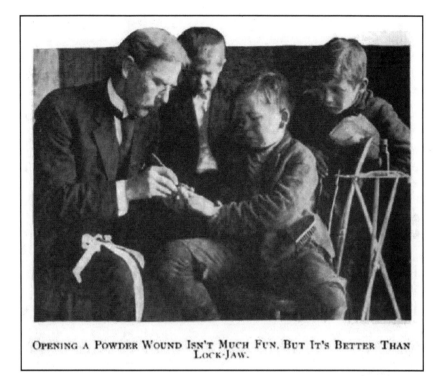

OPENING A POWDER WOUND ISN'T MUCH FUN, BUT IT'S BETTER THAN LOCK-JAW.

Figure 27: Toy pistols led to many expressions of concern in the United States and Canada because of the tendency of injuries to result in tetanus.
Source: C.H. Claudy and Clarence Maris, "The Deadly Toy Pistol," *Technical World Magazine* 11, no. 1 (March 1909): 480

men and boys lacked awareness of the dangers of guns, and "should be forbidden to handle a rifle at all for generally some one else is the victim of their ignorance."[87]

While accidents formed the major concern, some Canadians also worried that toy pistols encouraged boys to become too attached to real guns. The *Globe*, for example, believed that toy pistols contributed to the tendency of young men to arm themselves. It called toy pistols "suggestive playthings" that bred in children a desire to "handle the genuine article," and businesses were "thus directly answerable for many lamentable happenings."[88] A writer in Edmonton made a similar complaint in 1906. A young man condemned the use of realistic toy arms after a boy pretended to rob him: "Does it not seem altogether beyond belief that any man in his right senses, after all the warnings we have had in the shape of murders and accidents, should allow his son the possession of even a supposedly harmless air gun, knowing how one thing leads to another." "Firearms," he concluded, "and small boys have, or should have, no thing in common."[89]

Another complaint was that boys from cities took small rifles to suburban areas to shoot indiscriminately at animals and property. A newspaper from rural Ontario, the *Temiskaming Speaker*, discussed this problem in 1909 when it described an accident in which a man had been shot by a .22 rifle, presumably fired by a youth, while waiting on a railway platform. "Better to cut out the 'twenty two' and the 'air gun' entirely than have these accidents continue," concluded the *Speaker*.[90] A particular worry was that armed boys might destroy animal populations. As noted earlier, Canadians in the first decade of the twentieth century sought to preserve wildlife, and they deemed thoughtless boys to be part of the problem. In Victoria, for instance, the Society for the Prevention of Cruelty to Animals discouraged boys and youth from slaughtering birds.[91] Complaints from the suburban areas of Toronto led the *Star* to suggest in 1911 that the "annual invasion of the suburban districts by the city lad with his 22-calibre rifle has begun." The boy "shoots squirrels, chipmonks [*sic*], birds, and anything that comes before his eyes," lamented the *Star*.[92] Thus, while Canadians generally encouraged boys to shoot, some advocated the imposition of reasonable limits to this activity.

Social reformers in the pre-war period believed that the autonomy of young people had to be constrained in a rapidly changing social, cultural, and economic context. The result was, according to Cynthia Comacchio, the "expanded regulation of adolescence" with the purpose of "training the ideal, responsible, conscientious adult citizen."[93] As noted earlier, the goal of creating ideal citizens led to efforts to train young people to use firearms. Several provincial governments also enacted child protection legislation, established family courts, created evening curfews, and extended the period of compulsory schooling. In addition, the federal government passed the *Juvenile Delinquents Act* of 1908, which created the category of "juvenile" crime and empowered the state to deal aggressively with those deemed delinquent.[94] The concern that some boys had access to arms but lacked sufficient training or mental maturity, and the belief that young people might use guns for nefarious ends, led to efforts to regulate the availability of *some* weapons to *some* youth. The choices legislators made in framing these laws illuminates how they determined when youth had sufficient capacity to be entrusted safely with weapons, and how legislation sought to delineate boundaries between the problematic categories of "safe" and "unsafe" weapons and between "toys" and "firearms."

Some arms seemed easy to categorize as dangerous weapons. As noted in chapter 2, Parliament perceived revolvers to be so dangerous that in 1877 it largely banned people of all age from carrying such weapons.[95] Pressure to limit young people's access to pistols emerged in the Senate by the late 1880s, and in 1892 the first Canadian *Criminal Code* prohibited the sale or gift of pistols (and ammunition for such arms) to anyone under the age of sixteen. Those convicted faced a fine of up to fifty dollars. This was the first time that Ottawa placed an age restriction on who could purchase guns. The government's decision to impose an age restriction was a typical response to perceived social problems in this period, a time when legislators imposed or altered the minimum age at which youth could leave school to enter the workforce, or engage in sexual relations.[96] Ottawa thus created a demarcation line between youth and adulthood that sought to prevent the use of dangerous pistols by reckless young people.

The 1892 *Criminal Code* also prohibited the sale or gift of air guns to anyone under the age of sixteen, threatening a fifty-dollar fine for violators.[97] This provision reflected the traditional perception of air guns as sneaky, unmanly, and potentially dangerous. In 1892, Canadians had not yet widely accepted air rifles as toys. As air guns became defined as toys, however, children, youth, and adults would frequently disregard the law, as people saw little potential harm in young people owning a Daisy or a similar air gun.

The 1892 legislation contained important loopholes that reflected attitudes towards other weapons and the ability of adults to successfully supervise armed boys and youth. One important loophole was that Ottawa did not ban the *possession* of air guns or pistols by those under sixteen. Parliament therefore allowed parents or organizations to place such guns in the hands of young people. Nor did the law ban the sale of rifles to youth. The widespread support for training boys and youth in rifle shooting and the mesh of ideas concerning imperialism, hunting, and manliness meant that the state did not want to completely disarm young people. Parliament thus made no effort to regulate weapons deemed beneficial, and boys and youth continued to have free access to rifles until 1913.

Occasional voices spoke out in favour of new laws, or, at the very least, stricter enforcement of the 1892 legislation. The *Manitoba Morning Free Press*, for instance, complained that retailers disregarded the *Criminal Code* provisions banning the sale of some kinds of guns to boys under sixteen, while in 1898 a coroner's jury examining an accidental shooting deprecated the practice of letting young boys go out shooting and recommended a law forbidding children under sixteen from handling all kinds of firearms.[98] In making a case for new laws, some commentators asserted that weapons were *not* toys. The *Globe* suggested in 1913 that some people regarded a small-calibre rifle "as a toy" – an impression the *Globe* tried to correct: "Many fatalities have resulted from a failure to appreciate or consider the strength and efficiency of the various makes of 22-calibre rifles, and something should be done to dispel popular ignorance in this regard."[99]

Given the widespread encouragement of shooting by boys and youth, such calls often went unheeded, as a parliamentary debate stemming from rural objections to the policy of encouraging boys to shoot demonstrated. A few MPs expressed concerns that the attractiveness of military drill drew farm boys into cities. As well, a few parliamentarians warned against inculcating boys with militarism at too early an age. Advocates of teaching boys to shoot dismissed such claims by arguing that rifle practice created manly character and by drawing upon the rhetoric of imperialism. Sam Hughes asserted that wherever "you have a strong military spirit, you have more manhood in the youth of the country," while Frederick Borden quoted from literature suggesting that rifle training would improve boys' "health, strengthen their moral fibre and add to their professional, industrial or labour value when they are attained to manhood and entered on the serious business of their lives."[100] While accidents constituted a real concern, the perceived solution was to give boys *more* training in the use of arms, not less. For example, in a column devoted to women's issues, the *Victoria Daily Colonist* advised mothers to have children trained with firearms, for "a well-trained youngster will soon learn to be proud of the fact that he is trusted with a real gun."[101] Given the dominance of these attitudes, Ottawa took little action to prevent boys and youth from acquiring most weapons.

With Ottawa taking little action, people used by-laws and the civil justice system to shape young people's use of firearms. Municipal authorities sometimes employed local by-laws to charge youth who fired guns in highly populated areas, often after an errant shot harmed a bystander.[102] Gun accidents involving children also led individuals to seek remedies in the civil courts, with mixed results. In 1910, the Divisional Court of the Ontario High Court of Justice held merchants liable after they sold an air gun to a thirteen-year-old boy, who then promptly struck the daughter of a neighbour in the eye while attempting to shoot a bird.[103] In another case, from 1911, a twelve-year-old boy accidentally shot another twelve-year-old in the eye when they were out shooting together in Smiths Falls, Ontario. The father of the injured boy sought compensation through a negligence claim against the shooter's father, who, according to the claimant, loaned the gun to his son. The trial court found in favour of the plaintiff, but the Divisional Court of the Ontario High Court of Justice reversed the lower court decision on the ground that the injured boy was bright and knowledgeable about guns and had been contributorily negligent when he walked in front of the gun before it went off.[104]

Several provinces passed legislation regulating the purchase of air guns. In 1911, Ontario required purchasers to acquire a certificate issued under s.118 of the *Criminal Code* (which, under the *Criminal Code*, was needed to carry a handgun) or a permit from a police official. Other provinces soon passed similar legislation, including Manitoba and Saskatchewan in 1912, and British Columbia in 1913.[105] The certificate requirement for buying an air gun caused some consternation. Toronto Deputy Chief William Stark lauded the measure, however, because the "supply of guns and air rifles to boys will be stopped." In his view, there were "altogether too many air rifles in the hands of careless boys. They are very dangerous, and very mischievous. No living thing, bird or squirrel, or anything else, is safe within the city limits, or the suburbs."[106]

The federal government finally acted in 1913. Ottawa made it an offence for anyone to sell any kind of firearm to a minor under sixteen, or to sell or give a pistol or air rifle to anyone under sixteen. Once again, there were important loopholes. Ottawa did not ban the possession of weapons by boys under sixteen – just the sale and/or gift of weapons – and thus allowed for parents or organizations to provide rifles to young people to hunt or to target shoot as part of an organized group.[107]

The period of the late nineteenth and early twentieth centuries was a key time in the formation of a relationship between young people and firearms. Imperialist sentiments led to efforts to encourage boys and youth to use rifles. Anti-modernist concerns also helped promote the use of guns, as many Canadians believed firearms could instil masculinity in a generation whose urban environment risked making them effeminate. The mass production and skilled marketing of inexpensive firearms further cemented the connections between guns and young people. Businesses redefined some arms – in particular air rifles – as toys, while cleverly marketing small-calibre rifles to youth, although Canadians debated whether such arms were guns or toys. Despite widespread support for encouraging the use of firearms by boys and youth, the perceived spike in accidents caused by pistols, toy guns, air guns, and small rifles eventually led to modest action. Ironically, the very factors that led Canadians to train young people to use guns, such as industrialization and urbanization, made it necessary to regulate weapons through state mechanisms and organizations like the Scouts and the cadet movement.

Industrial Arms Manufacturing in Canada

The government efforts to encourage rifle shooting by men and young people before the Great War illustrate the state's interest in arming, not disarming, most Canadians. The support given to domestic production of ammunition and firearms before 1914 also is evidence of the federal government's desire to encourage gun ownership. Nineteenth-century states required access to gunpowder and weapons for their armies. Unlike the American and British governments, which sponsored gun manufacturing, Canada did not underwrite large-scale domestic production of firearms in the nineteenth century; instead, Ottawa imported arms, placing no customs duties on weapons for the militia.[108]

While Canada initially relied on imported rifles, Ottawa eventually encouraged the domestic production of ammunition. Establishing such an industry, however, was no easy task, given the competition from American companies. The leading cartridge maker in the United States, Winchester, produced one million cartridges per day by 1875. The Conservative minister of militia from 1880 to 1892, Adolphe-Philippe Caron, nevertheless urged domestic production, since it would allow Canada to access fresh ammunition as needed, rather than stockpile imported rounds. Governments commonly established a high tariff wall to protect domestic industry in the late nineteenth century, and Canada levelled a 30 per cent duty on imported ammunition in 1881, raising it to 35 per cent by 1890 to encourage Canadians to produce gunpowder and cartridges.[109]

An ammunition cartridge factory in Quebec began production in the

Figure 28: The Dominion Cartridge Company appealed to Canadians'
sense of nationalism to sell its ammunition, asking consumers to
"Support Home Industry."
Source: *Rod and Gun in Canada* 5, no. 10 (March 1904)

early 1880s, but the firm faced substantial challenges. Rifle shooters initially complained about the quality of the ammunition. Also, despite the
high tariff wall, the company, which became known as the Dominion
Cartridge Company, struggled to compete with American manufacturers. In 1883, several leading American producers formed the Ammunition Manufacturers Association. The association, which survived until
1907, sought to establish ammunition prices that guaranteed a level of
profits. Despite these challenges, the Canadian ammunition industry
achieved some success. The minister of militia reported proudly in
1903 that production in 1904 would reach over two million rounds.[110]
Some of this output went to the Canadian military, but the Dominion
Cartridge Company also developed a domestic civilian market behind
the tariff wall by selling to hunters and target shooters. It appealed to

nationalist sentiments and pocketbooks, advertising its ammunition as "Made in Canada" that sold at a *"less-the-duty price."*[111]

Ottawa eventually also threw its support behind a firearm manufacturing enterprise: the Ross Rifle Company. While Canada had a long history of small-scale gun production by skilled artisans, Canadians had not participated in the industrialization of the firearm industry that reshaped American and European arms manufacturing. Canadian gunsmiths faced so much competition from foreign gun makers that they mostly became merchants for foreign manufacturers. After Minister of Militia Frederick Borden failed to convince the British government to allow Canada to manufacture the Lee-Enfield rifle, the Liberal government threw its support behind a plan of Sir Charles Ross, a Scottish promoter, to manufacture a Canadian-made firearm.[112] The Ross rifle became one prong of Laurier's attempts to encourage domestic manufacturing, although providing sustainable employment was not the government's only motivation, for, as Desmond Morton concludes, the Ross rifle was a "manifestation of military nationalism."[113] The dominion initially ordered 62,000 rifles. The company also sought to develop a civilian market, using the advantage of a 30 per cent tariff wall to compete with foreign guns. The Ross Rifle Company thus began producing hunting rifles, target guns, and weapons for the youth market.[114]

Canadians initially celebrated the erection of the Ross factory in Quebec City as an indication of the nation's economic and military development. The *Globe*, for example, declared that the factory would produce a "distinctly Canadian arm of great excellence," using "all the latest and most modern machinery."[115] The Ross rifle's excellent record as a target shooting rifle encouraged this sense of pride. In 1909, competitors using the Ross rifle took half of the first prizes at the English National Rifle Association annual competition. Shooters with Ross rifles won the highest prize, the King's Prize, in 1911 and 1913.[116] Sam Hughes thus declared the rifle had "made a name for itself as superior to every other."[117] The *Calgary Daily Herald* also trumpeted these feats, congratulating the company and declaring the rifle "Canada's National Arm."[118] The Ross Rifle Company then employed these successes to market its guns, suggesting that the Ross rifle was "recognized to be the best British military target rifle" and that wins in England represented "an Unparalleled Feat."[119]

The Ross rifle, however, proved a disaster on the battlefields of the Great War. It weighed a pound heavier than the British Lee-Enfield rifle, and, more importantly, had a delicate design that frequently

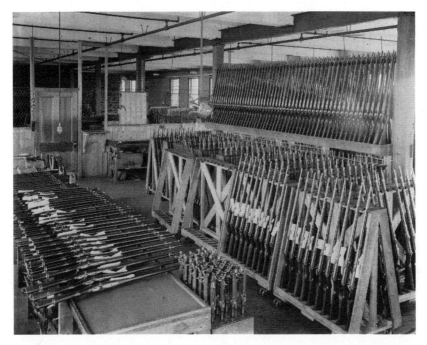

Figure 29: Many Canadians expressed pride at the establishment of the
Ross Rifle Company, at least until the poor performance of the company's
guns in the Great War. The interior of the Ross Rifle factory hints at the size of
the business.
Source: LAC, PA-107378

jammed. There had been signs of this; for example, the North-West
Mounted Police had discarded its Ross rifles because of their inability
to withstand rough usage. Canadian servicemen took the weapon to
war in 1914, but after a long public debate, Ottawa withdrew the gun
from service in 1916.[120]

The Great War both destroyed Canadians' faith in their home-grown
weapon and proved incorrect the lessons drawn from the Boer War.
The First World War undermined the perceived importance of citizen-
soldiers skilled in long-range rifle fire. Machine guns and heavy artillery allowed enemies to maul or destroy entire regiments filled with
crack shots. In the interwar period, governments thus gave less encouragement for rifle shooting. The cost of ammunition and the price

Figure 30: The Great War demonstrated the importance of the machine gun and the overstated role of accurate rifle shooting. Members of the machine gun section of the 50th Battalion, Canadian Expeditionary Force, pose with their machine gun in 1917.
Source: Glenbow Archives, NA-4025-24

of high-tech target rifles also drove many recreational shooters from the sport during the Depression.[121] Hunters chose to join rod and gun clubs, rather than rifle shooting associations. "What Ails Rifle Shooting?," the *Globe* thus asked in 1930 in noting that many rifle associations had disappeared.[122] In early 1938, 184 active military and civilian rifle shooting associations existed, in comparison to 583 in 1914.[123] This important shift meant that the state withdrew much of its support after decades of enticing men to use modern rifles. It also meant that, in the future, hunters' groups would prove the most powerful organizations representing the interests of gun owners.

"Disarming the foreigners ... is the only way to render them harmless": Immigration and Gun Control

The popularity of recreational hunting and the state encouragement of rifle shooting meant governments passed relatively little legislation designed to limit the ownership and use of long guns in the two decades before the First World War. The increased regulation of handguns, however, represented an exception to the generally modest system of gun control. Canadians expressed fear about the immigrants flowing into the nation from continental Europe. Like youth, immigrants allegedly lacked mature "British" instincts for the proper use of guns, and thus the state sought to control their use of arms.

As noted in chapter 2, in 1892 the federal government had required most people who wanted to carry a pistol to acquire a "certificate of exemption." Canadians at least sixteen years old could obtain a certificate valid for twelve months if they could convince a justice of the peace of the applicant's discretion and good character. The legislation also required that businesses record the date of the sale, the name of the purchaser, the pistol's manufacturer, and any other mark allowing for the gun's identification.[124]

The 1892 legislation failed to solve the perceived pistol problem. In fact, the introduction of new kinds of handguns stoked public concerns further. In 1893, Ludwig Loewe & Company of Germany developed a commercial handgun that held ammunition in the gun's handle. Upon firing, the barrel and breechblock slid back along the top of the frame, the pistol expelled the spent cartridge, a new round entered the firing chamber, and the gun was cocked. Other gun makers soon copied this basic design, including John M. Browning. These improved guns entered the Canadian marketplace by the early twentieth century.[125] Eaton's, for instance, sold the Savage automatic pistol, which, according to Eaton's, could carry ten rounds of ammunition and was the "most powerful, accurate and rapid fire pistol invented."[126] These guns so unsettled police that the Chief Constables' Association called for a prohibition on automatic pistols in 1912.[127]

The wide availability and inexpensive price tag of many pistols continued to trouble gun control advocates. Eaton's, for example, offered a variety of revolvers for sale in its 1899 catalogue, some for as little as $1.75.[128] Second-hand stores also sold revolvers. In 1902, a coroner's jury in Kingston called attention to the numerous second-hand stores selling guns after a fifteen-year-old boy bought a used revolver and then shot a fourteen-year-old girl at school, while in 1909 a resident of Toronto appealed for new guns laws to stop the "open manner in which fire arms are allowed to be displayed in shops and sold over bargain counters."[129]

Many Canadians continued to see pistols, unlike rifles, as a great evil. Newspapers reported numerous accidents, suicides, and murders com-

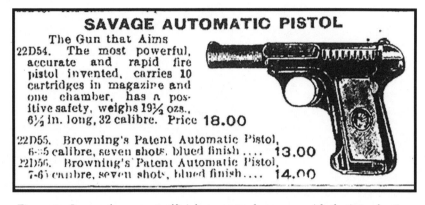

Figure 31: Law enforcement officials expressed concern with the introduction of "automatic" pistols into Canada, such as the Savage automatic pistol carried by Eaton's department store.
Source: *T. Eaton Co. Fall/Winter 1910–11 Catalogue* (Winnipeg ed.), AO, F229-2-0-11, used with permission of Sears Canada

mitted with handguns. The press pleaded with citizens to stop carrying handguns and even questioned the propriety of producing such arms. The pistol was "at once so dangerous, and so generally useless that it should be outlawed," concluded the *Toronto Star*, for it did "much evil and little good."[130] Charles Allan Stuart of the Supreme Court of Alberta also heavily criticized the availability of handguns in Canada. "It is beyond my understanding why a revolver is allowed to be sold," he mused. "There ought to be a law passed to do away with such things," he suggested.[131] The *Globe* expressed concern as well, suggesting that "the unguarded revolver has more victims to its discredit than smallpox or any of the infectious diseases." It thus made an appeal: "Let moral and social reformers consider the revolver."[132] The reference to moral and social reformers was telling, indicating that some Canadians believed that the regulation of pistols should become part of the broader effort to regulate society more closely.[133]

Social reformers expressed apprehension about new immigrants' supposed tendency to use pistols. Legislators supporting new gun laws in the late 1870s to the early 1890s had often feared young urban men and Aboriginal Peoples. The bogeyman for legislators in the early twentieth century changed with the influx into Canada of many southern and eastern European immigrants. Ottawa would have preferred "British" immigrants but reluctantly admitted settlers from places outside the British Isles, northern Europe, and the United States. These less "desirable" immigrants from eastern Europe (such as Russians and Poles), and, especially, southern Europe (such as Italians and Greeks) came to Canada in large numbers. The 1910 to 1913 period witnessed especially heavy rates of immigration, with the number of immigrants peaking at over four hundred thousand in 1913. The government hoped that many of the newcomers would establish agricultural communities in the west, and some did, but others instead moved into urban centres, where they worked in factories or helped construct streetcar lines and sewage systems. Other immigrants worked in railway construction or found employment in the resource sector, such as lumbering and mining.[134]

Many established Canadians suggested that the new immigrants possessed cultural predispositions to violence, including gun violence, and occasional reports of riots involving immigrants armed with pistols stoked such concerns.[135] Newspapers in Toronto and Montreal warned about immigrants armed with guns, often invoking ethnic clichés in asserting the propensity of some immigrants to use weapons. The *Toronto Star*, for instance, stated that recent immigrants "have had to be fined to teach them that they must not practice revolver shooting on Sunday." "As we have no Czars and Grand Dukes to assassinate," suggested the *Star*, it was "really not as indispensably necessary that a resident should know how to shoot straight as it seems to be in Russia."[136]

Established Canadians perceived Italian immigrants as especially prone to using guns. Between 1901 and 1914, approximately 119,000 Italians came to Canada. Agents, or *padroni*, brought many migratory workers, forcing employees to complete dangerous and poorly paid labour in railway construction and mining operations. Other Italians earned wages in Canada's growing cities, especially Toronto and Montreal, working in construction, manufacturing, and urban infrastructure sectors. Many established Canadians viewed these working-class Italians with suspicion and voiced the widely believed view that "hot-blooded" Italians committed violent acts with knives or guns. Newspapers thus made sure to point out the Italian ethnicity of defendants involved in shooting incidents.[137] The *Montreal Gazette* lamented in 1911 that the "Italian with a revolver has added another to the somewhat long list of murders for which his countrymen in this city are responsible."[138] The press also publicized allegations that the Italians constructing railroads in Ontario possessed guns. In 1905, "An Actual

Settler" from Heaslip, Ontario, said every Italian on the Temiskaming and Northern Ontario Railway line had a rifle or shotgun "inseparable from him." The settler thus hoped that in the "interest of the settler and law and order," the "whole of the foreign element should be disarmed."[139]

The *Montreal Herald* connected the problems of allegedly inherent violent Italians and widely available pistols. It referred to the "murder mills" of Montreal – second-hand stores with windows packed with revolvers, automatic pistols, rifles, and daggers. The paper claimed that Italians usually bought used revolvers, which could be purchased at numerous second-hand stores for an average price of two dollars.[140] The perceived importance of the issue led the *Herald* to publish cartoons criticizing the availability of weapons. One cartoon showed two immigrants looking at a sign that read, "NEWLY ARRIVED MIGRANTS. Notice.—In order that you may feel thoroughly at home in Montreal the authorities permit the sale to you openly of revolvers, knives, etc. Thus you are enabled to settle your differences in your native way without the trouble of going to law. If you kill anyone it is murder and if you are caught you will be hung. But it is quite easy not to be caught so do not let that worry you."[141]

The *Herald* again attacked the sale of revolvers in another cartoon entitled "Accessory Before the Fact." The cartoonist showed a man purchasing a second-hand weapon. The store owner asked his customer why he wanted a gun. "I want to kill a man who took my girl," was the reply. "Tut! Tut!," chided the retailer, "don't you know that is very wicked?" This did not, however, stop him from offering a gun for sale, since the owner declared, "We have them all the way from a dollar and a half and up."[142]

Canadians also expressed apprehension about Japanese and Chinese immigrants possessing arms. The 1907 Vancouver race riot stoked fears that Asian immigrants might use guns against white Canadians. The riot began when a mob attacked Vancouver's Chinatown following a meeting of the Asiatic Exclusion League. Some Japanese purchased firearms to fend off attackers, and white British Columbians expressed alarm after newspapers reported large weapons purchases by "asiatics." The Japanese demonstration of martial prowess in the Russian-Japanese War of 1904–5 made this especially concerning. Many Canadians drew from the war an impression that "asiatics" were a militaristic "race." Local officials thus responded to the 1907 riot by trying to stop the sale of firearms to "Orientals."[143]

Figure 32: In this cartoon, the *Montreal Herald* expresses its belief that
immigrants were prone to misusing firearms.
Source: *Montreal Herald*, 23 June 1911

Animosity towards Asian workers helped motivate a 1913 British
Columbia game law amendment. The amendment required hunters to
acquire a licence to carry a firearm for hunting in British Columbia.
Provincial Game Warden Bryan Williams explained the motivations

Figure 33: As this 1911 cartoon illustrates, the *Montreal Herald* criticized the availability of firearms before the Great War.
Source: *Montreal Herald*, 24 January 1911

for the gun licence system. Gun licences, he reasoned, would decrease the number of accidents, raise revenue for game preservation, and dissuade men unaccustomed to firearms from renting or borrowing guns. However, the province's primary motivation was to restrict gun use by "foreign elements." Williams suggested that the number of men carrying firearms in the province had "increased enormously, and a great proportion of this increase consist of a bad foreign element who have no knowledge or respect for any Game Laws." These foreigners were "scattered throughout the Province in construction and other Camps, and with the amount of railways being built, are rapidly clearing out the Country, not only of Game and Fish, but of everyother [sic] wild living thing." "Japanese, Chinese, hindoos etc," would "kill anything at any time of the year if they can with impunity."[144] The British Columbia *Game Act* did not explicitly ban foreigners from acquiring and using guns. Instead, the legislature sought to disarm foreign workers by instituting differential licence fees. *Both* residents and non-residents had to acquire licences. However, people who had not resided in the province for six months (meaning many temporary foreign workers) had to pay much larger licence fees.[145] This measure demonstrated how legislatures could surreptitiously pass gun controls targeting specific groups.

Concerns with armed immigrants before the Great War resulted in a massive increase in the number of prosecutions for carrying unlawful weapons. There were just 68 prosecutions in 1893, but 1085 in 1913, and the prosecution of many immigrants contributed to this spike. From 1892 to 1899, only 6.6 per cent of those convicted (for whom the government reported birthplace information) came from outside the British Empire or the United States. In comparison, between 1910 and 1913, 40.2 per cent of those convicted originated from outside the British Empire and the United States.[146]

These prosecutions did not end calls for new legal measures. "Disarming the foreigners," declared the *Globe*, was "the only way to render them harmless."[147] Justice James Emile Pierre Prendergast of the Manitoba Court of King's Bench also appealed for new legislation in 1911, because foreigners quickly turned to pistols. While it had "not been the custom for Canadians to carry firearms," Canada had "thousands of immigrants arriving" introducing "a custom from which we have been free in the past. These people are indulging in the foolish practice of carrying firearms."[148] The commissioner of the Royal Northwest Mounted Police reported the discovery of automatic pistols on many newly arrived immigrants and suggested that authorities should confiscate all such weapons at ports of entry. Law enforcement, however, felt powerless to disarm immigrants. In 1911, for example, the Montreal chief of police wanted to round up suspicious Italians to check them for concealed knives and revolvers but concluded that he lacked the necessary authority.[149]

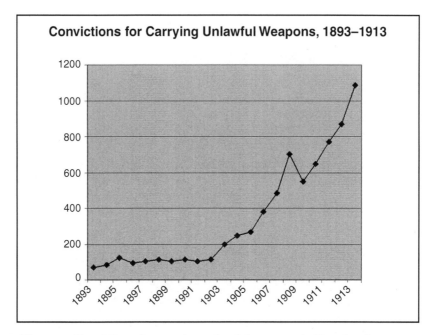

Figure 34. Convictions for carrying unlawful weapons in Canada, 1893–1913.
Source: Canada, *Sessional Papers*, 1893–1914

Canadians interested in new gun-control legislation had foreign models to study and consider. Many Americans became concerned with immigrants' use of guns and agitated for legislation before the First World War. The most famous American act, New York's 1911 Sullivan law, placed strict limitations on carrying deadly weapons and on the sale of guns. The Sullivan law required urban residents to acquire a permit to possess concealable firearms and forced businesses to sell pistols only to persons who presented valid permits. Retailers had to keep records of gun sales. Canadian gun-control advocates could also look to Britain, where parliamentarians wrestled with the challenges of pistols in the two decades before the First World War. Britain passed the *Pistols Act* in 1903, which restricted the purchase of a pistol – defined as a weapon with a barrel less than nine inches – to anyone over eighteen and not drunk or insane. Parliament also required handgun purchasers to have a gun or game licence, or, if a householder, indicate that he or she intended to use the gun within the home. The act contained some obvious loopholes. Manufacturers produced weapons with barrels longer than nine inches to avoid the *Pistol Act*'s requirements. The legislation also left unregulated the sale of second-hand pistols between individuals. Also, anyone could purchase a gun licence at a Post Office for ten shillings, so the licence really amounted only to a tax.[150]

Ontario responded first to concerns with armed immigrants. In 1907, Ontario banned labourers working on the construction of railways or other public works from possessing firearms under its game act.[151] This failed to solve the perceived problem, and when an Italian labourer shot and killed his foreman at a Canadian Northern Railway construction camp in 1910, the *Globe* declared that the situation was "becoming dangerous."[152] The newspaper alleged that thousands of Italians working in railway construction gangs often carried firearms.

Canadian MPs introduced bills designed to prevent the possession of arms by foreigners. Conservative MP Edward Lewis, a lawyer representing Huron West in Ontario, strongly advocated such legislation, introducing bills in 1908 and 1909 to limit gun ownership by southern European immigrants. He proposed requiring that all immigrants at ports of entry be searched for dangerous concealed weapons and that Canada deport immigrants found with a concealed weapon within two years of arriving. Lewis expressed particular concern with the availability of weapons in second-hand and hardware stores, complaining that new immigrants arrived and immediately saw "exposed for sale in the second-hand stores, hardware stores and others, rows of revolvers."[153] This led immigrants to infer the necessity of a knife or gun in Canada. Lewis thus proposed banning pawnshops and second-hand stores from exhibiting guns in windows. Lewis also suggested requiring anyone wanting to purchase a handgun to get a permit from a police magistrate, justice of the peace, or chief of police. The existing law necessitated a "certificate of exemption" for those wanting to carry such a weapon, but not a permit to buy a handgun. Officials would have the discretion to refuse permits to applicants who seemed dangerous. Hardware stores and hunting publications opposed these proposed gun laws. In the end, the Liberal government banned the sale or exposure for sale of several kinds of dangerous weapons, including bowie knives, daggers, dirks, metal knuckles, or skull crackers (though not handguns). It also increased the penalty for carrying offensive weapons.[154]

This measure did not end complaints about armed immigrants, leading Lewis to again introduce a bill in Parliament in early 1911 that con-

Figure 35: Hardware merchants often resisted new gun controls in the
early twentieth century because firearms formed an important part of their
business. The Musson and Ross hardware store in Wainwright, Alberta,
offered rifles for sale, as can be seen in this picture of their stock in 1914
(the guns are on the left).
Source: Glenbow Archives, NA-2835-4

tained many of the same provisions of his previous efforts. His measure
also had a class element, as Lewis said the bill proposed permitting authorities to search every "vagrant, or loose, idle, or disorderly person"
for offensive weapons. In advocating for his bill, Lewis warned that
violence in Canada had started to trend toward American levels, thus
evidencing the continued importance of developments in the United
States for Canadian gun-control debates. He also blamed immigrants
for misusing firearms, attributing crime "principally to the great importation of foreigners, and, secondly, to the fact that crime has not
been punished with the vigour which formerly characterized the authorities." He criticized Italians as tending to carry concealed weapons
and to use them "upon slight provocation."[155] However, the Liberal

government of Prime Minister Laurier, which had overseen the influx of immigrants, refused to pass Lewis's bill.

With Ottawa refusing to legislate, several provinces tried to disarm immigrants. Ontario acted first, passing *The Offensive Weapons Act* in 1911. The act required the purchaser of a pistol to have acquired a certificate issued under s.118 of the *Criminal Code* (which was needed to carry a handgun), or a permit from the superintendent of the Ontario Provincial Police or a local chief constable. Retailers who sold handguns to a person lacking a permit faced fines of between twenty-five and two hundred dollars, or imprisonment for as long as six months. Ontario also required retailers to keep detailed records of pistols sold, including the date of sale, name of gun maker, the weapon's serial number, and information about the purchaser. Police could inspect these records at any time. Further, the act allowed Ontario police to search for and seize any weapons carried illegally and required police to report when they found foreigners with illegal weapons to the minister of the interior "with the view towards deporting such person under the Immigration Act."[156] Several provinces soon followed Ontario's lead: Manitoba and Saskatchewan in 1912, and British Columbia in 1913, passed statutes modelled on Ontario's.[157]

Soon after Laurier's Liberals lost power to Robert Borden and the Conservative Party in 1911, the new government passed a measure similar to these provincial acts. The Chief Constables' Association had lobbied for amendments to the nation's gun laws, suggesting that Ottawa should copy Ontario's legislation.[158] The *Canada Law Journal* also declared the existing laws insufficient, asserting that no person should carry a pistol any more than he should have "a bottle of prussic acid, arsenic, or other deadly drug."[159] In introducing the bill, Minister of Justice Charles Joseph Doherty emphasized that high rates of immigration necessitated action: the stream of immigrants contained "a larger proportion of persons with regard to whom it is unsafe and certainly undesirable that the procuring of weapons" should "be as easy as it is under present conditions."[160]

The 1913 federal legislation made several important changes to Canada's gun laws. First, it increased penalties substantially, providing sanctions of up to one hundred dollars or three months in jail. Authorities could impose these penalties on anyone who carried a pistol that could be concealed on the person without a permit (a Form 76 permit). The government eliminated the right of citizens to carry a weapon simply because they had a reasonable cause to fear an assault. Who could possess a Form 76 permit? "Upon sufficient cause being shown," a member of the Royal Northwest Mounted Police, commissioner of the Dominion Police, or certain other police officials could grant a permit valid for up to twelve months if the official felt satisfied with the applicant's "discretion and good character." The act also restricted who could purchase a pistol, since retailers could sell a pistol only to someone possessing a permit. The new act also included extensive search-and-seizure provisions that allowed police to search any person they suspected of carrying a weapon, and then to seize that weapon if carried without a permit.[161]

The act included exemptions allowing for the possessions of handguns in homes and businesses. These exemptions reflected the extent to which legislators continued to target immigrants and the poor, not men of property. In 1914, Alphonse Verville, a plumber and Quebec Labour MP, criticized the exception allowing for guns at workplaces and introduced a bill to prevent businesses from employing men who carried arms. He complained of the bloodshed that stained Buckingham, Quebec, in 1906, when a company employed armed men, ostensibly to protect its property. The company's real motivation, Verville suggested, was "to enforce its impositions on the discontented workmen."[162] His bill would have allowed provincial attorneys general to decide whether people could be armed on work premises. Verville introduced the measure on behalf of the Trades and Labour Congress, which had long supported such a law. In 1907, for example, the Trades of Labour Congress had sought legislation to prohibit the carrying of firearms by private detective agents. Verville's bill, however, did not become law.[163]

Conclusion

In the three decades before the Great War, Canadian governments strongly encouraged loyal men (and even boys and youth) to use modern rifles. Imperialist sentiments helped drive this trend. Canadians interested in supporting Britain believed that conflicts such as the Boer War demonstrated the importance of training citizen-soldiers as expert rifle shots. The concern with modernity also played a role. Men living sedentary lives in an increasingly urbanized and industrialized environment supposed that rifle training could buttress their sense of masculinity. Ottawa thus supported ammunition and rifle manufacturing in Canada, funded rifle associations, and encouraged shooting by cadets and school children. Business also helped arm Canada by taking advantage of the new culture of consumerism to aggressively market advanced firearms. Retailers and manufacturers encouraged ownership by emphasizing the beauty and safety of firearms and the connection between firearms and masculinity. Businesses helped define some arms, in particular air rifles, as toys. While retailers and manufacturers backed away from calling other guns – such as small-calibre rifles – toys, they still declared such weapons suitable for youth.

Despite widespread support for encouraging rifle use, governments took important legislative steps to reduce access to *some* weapons for *some* people. The perceived spike in accidents caused by pistols, toy guns, air guns, and small rifles eventually led to limits on gun sales to young people. The massive influx of immigrants in the late nineteenth and early twentieth centuries also resulted in provincial and federal efforts to regulate firearms, especially pistols. Gun laws in the pre–Great War period thus again demonstrated the thesis that unease with the presence and activities of certain ethnic, racial, demographic, or class groups often motivated firearm regulation. The perceived face of the bogeyman changed, but the public's association of gun violence with a handful of particular groups at any one time remained constant.

Because legislators focused on the use of arms by minority groups, few Canadians offered much resistance to stronger gun control. Some leading Canadian lawyers and politicians, including John A. Macdonald and Edward Blake, had suggested in the nineteenth century that firearm laws violated the constitutional right of British subjects to arm themselves. Politicians rarely cited that right after 1900, but legislators usually made sure to include exemptions allowing gun possession in homes and places of business, thus providing men of means with the ability to defend themselves, their family, and their property.

4

"Hysterical legislation": Suppressing Gun Ownership from the First to the Second World Wars

The desire to suppress gun ownership and use by specific ethnic or class groups only intensified with the onset of the Great War in 1914. During the conflict, Canada sought to control firearms owned by "enemy aliens." In the immediate aftermath of the war, fear of Bolsheviks led Ottawa to enact a new, temporary gun-licensing program. Leaders' worries about the potential dangers of armed, desperate men in the Depression, and "fifth column" activities in the Second World War resulted in further legislation.

Canadian gun-control efforts from the Great War to the Second World War represented the beginnings of an important shift in state policy towards firearms. As shown in previous chapters, governments had long encouraged men (and youth) to own and use rifles. By the end of the First World War, however, the state lost much of its interest in arming average citizens. Ottawa did not necessarily discourage gun use by men deemed loyal, but it abandoned the goal of arming and training entire generations with modern rifles. Instead, Canadians expressed concern that portrayals of firearm use in American movies, radio programs, and dime novels encouraged youth to adopt a violent gun culture. This resulted in a modest effort to discourage boys and youth from using arms.

Gun control in the 1914 to 1945 period also evidenced a growing, though not yet mature, belief in the ability of the state to regulate firearms successfully. During the First World War, Ottawa attempted to disarm *all* enemy aliens. After the war, the federal government briefly attempted to license the vast majority of gun owners. By the middle of the Depression, Ottawa forced *all* pistol owners to register their handguns. During the Second World War, Canada required, for the first time, that *all* firearms be registered. While the federal government made some of these measures, including the Second World War registry, temporary, the passage of these laws hinted that the Canadian state felt increasingly confident in its ability to regulate firearms more closely. At the same time, governments defended their right to arm police, reflecting a belief that the state had reserved for itself the ability to possess pistols in public spaces.

Gun Control during and after the Great War

The outbreak of war in Europe in 1914 led to efforts to disarm enemy aliens. As shown in chapter 3, Canadians had frequently suggested that southern and eastern Europeans tended to use guns maliciously. With the Austro-Hungarian Empire aligned with Germany against Britain and France, the concern with recent European immigrants did not abate. In 1914, more than five hundred thousand people lived in Canada who originally had been born in, or had roots to, Germany or Austria-Hungary. Of these, roughly one hundred thousand still held citizenship in one of these enemy powers. Their presence led to fears of sabotage. As a result, Ottawa required 80,000 enemy aliens to register and placed over 8,500 in internment camps.[1]

The federal government also sought to disarm enemy aliens with an Order in Council issued in September 1914 under the authority of the *War Measures Act*. Ottawa banned the possession of firearms, ammunition, and gunpowder by enemy aliens, who had ten days after the order's publication to deliver their arms and ammunition to a justice of the peace or the Royal Northwest Mounted Police (RNWMP). Authorities issued receipts for the firearms and ammunition. If law enforcement "reasonably suspected" that an enemy alien possessed arms or ammunition, then officials could, without a warrant, search for and seize these goods. Failure to surrender guns and ammunition could result in a fine of up to five hundred dollars or as many as three months in jail. The government also banned the sale or transfer of guns to enemy aliens, threatening violators with fines (of up to one hundred dollars) or imprisonment (one month in jail).[2] Ottawa thus kept up a long tradition of temporarily disarming groups that the government deemed suspicious.

Authorities enforced the ban on enemy aliens possessing weapons. Many enemy aliens voluntarily handed in firearms. To find resisters, the Mounties sent spies into communities with large enemy alien populations to collect information on who might pose a security risk. The government also investigated tips from local residents.[3] Evidence underpinning investigations sometimes proved flimsy, such as when a search took place after an officer overheard two men on a train mention that a large number of Germans in the Lacardaire area of Saskatchewan possessed arms. The investigation found "not one iota of truth in the report."[4] Sometimes the police acted too aggressively in seeking out arms from enemy aliens, with the result that they took guns from naturalized citizens of the United States or Canada. Authorities, for example, confiscated the shotgun of Valentine Gottinger, and imposed a ten-dollar fine. Six months later the government returned the gun, when Gottinger proved he was a naturalized citizen.[5]

When detected with illegal weapons, enemy aliens reacted in various ways. Some claimed ignorance of the law – an often plausible claim, given that many lived in rural communities and lacked fluency in English. One can speculate, for instance, that Frank Gajdosik, a twenty-three-year old of Austrian birth who had left Canada in October 1914 to work in Montana, was ignorant of the law when he returned to Canada in April 1915. After an officer seized two firearms from Gajdosik's trunk, Gajdosik plead guilty, received a $5.00 fine, and had to pay government legal expenses totalling an additional $12.40. A few enemy aliens actively resisted. For example, in Saskatchewan Andrew Koch sold his rifle after hearing of the order, rather than hand the gun to authorities. Some falsely claimed to own no firearms; they hid their weapons or simply kept quiet in the hope the government would not confiscate their guns if they avoided trouble.[6] A few even expressed their displeasure to authorities. The RNWMP reported that H.M. Stuhr had no intention of giving up his guns and planned to "make trouble" if the police attempted to seize his arms. He was, however, only indignant when the police eventually took his rifle, shotgun, and revolver.[7]

Many of the enemy aliens from whom the police took arms posed little threat. For instance, the RNWMP took a Mauser rifle and shotgun from Frank Hagn, an enemy alien with one eye, a deformed shoulder, a pregnant wife, and eleven children.[8] As well, many of the confiscated arms were either small-calibre weapons or in various states of disrepair. For example, the Mounties confiscated a .22-calibre rifle in Yorkton, Saskatchewan, described to be in "very bad condition, being worn out and rusty." It was "broken at the stock and wrapped with wire" and was "impossible to clean" without spending a large amount of time.[9] Most of the arms confiscated came from relatively new immigrants, and so the fines imposed, while usually small, undoubtedly caused some hardships. Those convicted of selling weapons to enemy aliens sometimes faced high fines as well.[10]

The concern with possible enemies within continued after the war's conclusion. Canadians worried less about "fifth column" and more about ideological dissension. The 1917 Bolshevik Revolution led to criticisms of the activities of "radicals" suspected of wanting to undermine the war effort or even to overthrow the government. The founding of the Communist International in March 1919 further strengthened worries about political radicalism. While the left consisted of a complex amalgam of groups with often widely divergent ideas, many Canadians lumped them together and viewed them suspiciously. Security officials worried about their inability to identify people holding "communist" or "Bolshevik" views. Alleged radicals could blend into the population, such that security officials "began to see the population as a whole as the primary object of attention."[11]

The difficulty many military veterans experienced when reintegrating into civilian life worsened the perceived security situation. Returning soldiers faced high levels of unemployment and vented their frustration at immigrants. Some veterans called for stronger efforts to keep guns out of the hands of aliens. For example, in August 1918 a group of veterans in Toronto agreed to a set of resolutions, including demands for the return of all aliens to their home countries (or that Canada draft them into the Canadian Expeditionary Force), the internment of enemy aliens, and the disarmament of all aliens, "it being a well known fact that the majority are in possession of firearms."[12]

The labour troubles in Winnipeg in 1919 strengthened concerns over security. Labour radicalism had grown in the west during the war, and in May 1919 the Winnipeg Trades and Labour Council called a general strike, which thirty thousand workers soon joined. Labour stoppages in support of the Winnipeg workers broke out across the country. The Mounties eventually dispersed a demonstration in Winnipeg by firing shots into the crowd, killing two. Police later claimed to find shell casings from weapons allegedly possessed by strikers, but gunfire injured no police, and historians generally agree that the strikers did not shoot at the police. Following the strike, Ottawa made protesting more difficult and banned groups that aimed to achieve governmental, industrial,

THE SORT OF "EQUIPMENT" FOUND ON MANY ALIENS

Figure 36: The concern with armed aliens continued after the Great War. In a 1919 exposé, the *Globe* warned that many aliens carried arms illegally.
Source: *Globe*, 14 June 1919

or economic change. Some Canadians also called for limits on the possession of firearms by aliens. A number of Ontario municipalities made this demand, while the *Globe* appealed for needed new gun controls because many aliens had found loopholes in existing firearm legislation.[13]

The acting minister of justice in Prime Minister Robert Borden's Union government, Arthur Meighen, responded with gun legislation in 1919 limiting aliens' ability to own and use firearms. He claimed there was an "alarming propensity of revolvers" in Canada, and thus it was "high time" the government ensured "weapons were not being concealed, not by tens or scores, or even hundreds, but by thousands, upon thousands of people." These were "nearly all" held by aliens.[14] He thus proposed banning aliens from having any kind of firearm unless they had a licence.

Opponents criticized Meighen's attempt to single out aliens. Several MPs suggested the government risked overreacting and made liberal arguments that the law should treat aliens and British subjects equally (Canadians technically remained British subjects until 1946). Liberal MP Samuel William Jacobs from Quebec, for instance, called the bill "hysterical legislation." He believed that the law should apply to everyone or no one, for a British subject could "do as much damage with a revolver as an alien." Andrew Ross McMaster, another Liberal MP from Quebec, similarly opposed the "idea that there should be one law for the alien and one law for the British subject." He admitted the dangers of carrying revolvers but said it was "the glory of British countries wherever the British flag floats that underneath its folds all those who conduct themselves peacefully are treated in the same manner."[15] Opponents of the proposed law thus claimed equality as too important for the state to sweep aside.

The government responded to opposition arguments by claiming many aliens, by carrying deadly weapons and committing crimes, obviated the state's obligation to provide equal treatment. Meighen also defended the differential treatment by admitting the state's inability to carry out more ambitious, universal gun laws. To compel all citizens to acquire licences, he said, "would be a very burdensome matter."[16] Despite the objections of opposition MPs, Borden's Union government possessed a comfortable majority in the Commons and passed the new gun law. Legislation in 1913 had required that a person possessing a pistol have a Form 76 permit. With the 1919 legislation, the government required aliens to have such a permit to possess any firearm.[17]

The government passed even stronger controls in 1920. Parliament stipulated that *all* Canadians had to acquire a Form 76 permit for almost all guns in their possession. This applied to owners of rifles as well as pistols and thus represented a substantial increase in state supervision of gun ownership. The only exception was that the federal government did not require British subjects to get a permit for shotguns already in their possession, which, Ottawa felt, farmers often owned and posed less danger if a political insurrection occurred.[18]

The federal government took this drastic step because of continued fears of upheaval. Justice Minister Charles Joseph Doherty warned that police reports and information from military authorities suggested that "in certain localities at different periods there was what looked like an extraordinary movement in the acquisition of firearms." The leader of the government in the Senate, Albertan lawyer James Lougheed, stated explicitly that the government sought to prevent armed uprisings. He claimed that "in case of a threatened riot or rising a great number of rifles might be imported," and "if every British subject is entitled to have a rifle without a permit the accumulation of those rifles might precipitate a great deal of trouble and difficulty." The government had thus grown suspicious of British subjects as well as foreigners. Ordinary Canadians, Lougheed warned ominously, were "human, and under certain conditions their minds are inflamed just the same as those persons of other nationalities."[19]

The government's sudden concern with British subjects in part reflected unease with the return of thousands of unhappy soldiers, many of whom brought home handguns as war trophies. Authorities did not know how many pistols entered Canada as war souvenirs, although in 1933 the federal minister of justice estimated the number at 250,000.[20] This influx of weapons appeared especially dangerous because some veterans had embraced radical ideas while in Europe. Politicians also considered the mental state of some veterans. In 1920, Conservative Senator Patrick Charles Murphy, a physician from Prince Edward Island, suggested that veterans "subject to shell-shock" were "apt to use those weapons" they brought home. This was "all the more important for the returned soldier, because he knows how to shoot," added Quebec Liberal Senator Raoul Dandurand.[21]

Fully implementing the 1920 act would have required a substantial government effort, but it appears Ottawa initially hoped to employ the law only selectively. Senator Lougheed indicated that Ottawa intended to devote few resources to ensuring that all Canadians applied for permits, unless an insurrection took place, it which case it was "well to have upon the statute book a law such as this, so that at a critical time we may enforce it."[22] The 1920 act nonetheless represented Ottawa's first effort to regulate the possession of rifles by all Canadians. Previous governments regulated long guns only at times of feared insurrection, but left hunters and target shooters alone. The 1920 legislation constituted an attempt at near-universal firearm regulation.

The enactment of a law that could affect "average" gun owners caused opposition in and outside Parliament. Critics questioned several aspects of the legislation. MPs complained the act cast suspicion too broadly, for many law-abiding British subjects would be forced to acquire permits. Charles Gavan Power, a Liberal MP from Quebec, for example, claimed the government excessively feared insurrection. The government had "got it into their heads that Bolshevism or some other 'ism' is rampant in the country."[23] Hunters and target shooters took umbrage at the inference that they were criminals. "Subscriber" deemed revolvers offensive weapons, but "to classify a rifle as an offensive weapon" was "somewhat far-fetched." The law "appears to place us all in the light of either being actually criminals, or of probably becoming criminals."[24] Others argued the law would disarm only the law-abiding. W.G. Rankin of North Bay, Ontario, for instance, believed the new law a "splendid concession in favor of the criminal class," for highwayman and burglars could attack victims lacking any defence.[25]

The law's possible application to most gun owners also opened up regional tensions and rural-versus-urban divisions. For example, "C.A.P." from Winnipeg offered a westerner's perspective on the need for weapons. In his view, people living on the frontier were "at the mercy of the coyote," and their "existence is sometimes threatened by timber wolves, cougars, grizzlies, or polar bears." Such people had an "urgent need of a trustworthy weapon," but the 1920 law would delay the purchase of ordinary hunting guns.[26] The *Toronto Star* admitted that the law seemed geared to urban conditions. "This law is a sweeping one," it declared, as it represented "a law of general disarmament." Urban crime necessitated the law, but in "many parts of the country" citizens would regard it "as a serious interference with individual rights." "A fact not sufficiently considered by those who make laws," the *Star* complained, "is the wide difference between urban and rural conditions."[27]

The fear that many Canadians might advocate radical views quickly subsided, and in 1921 the government repealed the requirement that British subjects acquire permits for their long guns, although they still needed permits for handguns carried outside the home or place of business, or for any handguns purchased. According to Justice Minister Doherty, critics of the 1920 act felt it "operated too rigorously" and subjected citizens to "unnecessary annoyance."[28] Ottawa, however, continued to require that aliens acquire a permit, and, just to be safe, the federal government allowed for a quick response to threats to the state. The 1921 legislation empowered the government to restrict weapons "in the public interest." By proclamation, Cabinet could forbid for indefinite periods the possession of any firearm without a permit. Also, the government reserved the right to forbid the sale of any firearm to someone without a permit.[29] These measures were more in line with Ottawa's traditional gun-control approach of restricting access to firearms at specific times and places.

Continuing Concerns with Pistols

While fear of a serious threat to the state subsided by the early 1920s, Canadians remained concerned about the availability of handguns. Popular pressure slowly mounted for yet stronger government regulation. In 1920, Senator John Waterhouse Daniel, a Conservative doctor from New Brunswick, claimed, rather absurdly, that there existed "hardly a house in the whole Dominion of Canada in which there is not a revolver."[30] Conservative MP Thomas Langton Church, a former mayor of Toronto, complained about men carrying arms: "We are gradually getting like Chicago, where it is very popular for people to carry pistols in their hip pockets."[31] Several leading newspapers, including the *Globe*, *Toronto Star*, *Montreal Gazette*, *Ottawa Journal*, *Calgary Daily Herald*, and *Vancouver Sun*, published appeals to ban, or limit access to, pistols. Judicial and law enforcement officials also called for action. The Chief Constables' Association discussed the problem of pistols several times in the 1920s.[32] Justice James Hyndman of the Alberta Supreme Court disapproved the large number of shooting cases before the courts and suggested that "some people think it a trifling matter to carry firearms about with them." He warned, however, that Alberta courts would "look with stern disapproval on the practice of carrying dangerous weapons."[33] An increase in the number of homicides in Canada in the second half of the 1920s helps explain the concern: the homicide rate increased from 1.3 murders per hundred thousand Canadians in 1926 to 2.1 murders per hundred thousand in 1930.[34]

Despite appeals for new gun controls, Ottawa took no action between 1921 and 1933.[35] Napoléon Antoine Belcourt, a lawyer representing Ottawa in the Senate, became the leading parliamentary proponent for new gun laws during the 1920s. He declared as early as 1920 that he did not see why anybody should have a pistol. Belcourt introduced several gun control bills in the Senate between 1926 and 1930 that received substantial support from police. The Senate supported his bills, but the House of Commons refused to approve the measures. Various MPs suggested Belcourt's proposals criminalized the law-abiding, expanded the role of government too aggressively, and threatened to punish veterans in possession of war souvenirs. Gun manufacturers, hardware stores, and hunting groups also opposed more gun regulation in the 1920s. The Hardware Merchants' Association of Canada, for instance, objected to regulating hunting rifles, claiming that restrictions would damage the lucrative hunting tourism trade.[36] Belcourt grew increasingly frustrated, warning in 1930 that "in the republic to the south of us, the revolver is master," and that in the United States it was "admitted generally that the situation is hopeless." He believed that if Parliament failed to act, "we shall find before many years have elapsed that we shall no longer be able to cope with it."[37] Parliament eventually passed legislation to better regulate handguns, but Belcourt would not live to see it – he died in 1932.

Police and Guns

I cannot get it. Can you understand it?
They wing the citizen, miss the bandit.
Why can't they pot gunmen on the run?
It seems to me the law's a goose.
It shoots the man without a gun.
And lets the man with gun go loose.[38]

While Ottawa toyed with laws meant to regulate most gun owners, governments settled the question of whether state actors – the police – should be armed. A traditional reluctance to arm police stemmed from the belief that law enforcement would kill bystanders or suspects eventually proved innocent, that criminals would freely use guns if faced by armed police, and that Canada should copy British precedents of unarmed police.[39] In 1911, the *Montreal Gazette* noted that British law enforcement usually lacked arms, while the "opposition to the use of military weapons in civilian duty is practically unknown in continental Europe."[40] As late as 1913, the *Canada Law Journal* declared revolvers "not safe even in the hands of the police." Pistols "should only be entrusted to men of proved discretion, and only in cases of extreme necessity."[41]

Such reticence to arm police prevailed throughout much of the Anglo-American world. While many individual police armed themselves, authorities often debated for several decades whether to make handguns standard equipment. In London, for example, resistance to allowing police to carry firearms meant that the London Metropolitan Police carried truncheons in the mid-nineteenth century, although some inspectors carried pistols. So did some mounted police in rural areas. During the Fenian scare of 1867–8, the London police received revolvers, but they stored them unless needed. In New York City, the police did not issue firearms, but by the 1850s most of New York's police armed themselves without formal authorization. Not until the 1890s did New York issue standardized revolvers to the police department.[42]

Canada experienced similar experimentation with arming police, such as in Hamilton, which initially emphasized physical strength in preventing crime and apprehending criminals. The city's police nevertheless often carried privately owned guns while on duty until prohibited from doing so in the late 1870s. The death of a constable subduing a burglar in 1884 led to a reconsideration of this policy. Constables received guns when on night patrol, but this proved a temporary measure, and the police later lost the privilege of carrying guns, although some officers possessed concealed weapons anyway. The death of a constable in 1904 resolved the issue in favour of arming police. The Hamilton police received Colt revolvers.[43]

Other Canadian police forces adopted pistols as standard equipment. Some Toronto police used revolvers in the 1880s, and Henry James Grasett made arming patrolmen one of his first acts when he became chief constable in 1886. Winnipeg police received revolvers in 1911. Other forces had to wait. Halifax, for instance, delayed arming its constables: in the 1920s, the city's force owned a handful of revolvers for emergencies, although, as in other places, constables sometimes carried their own personal weapons. Halifax finally received handguns as standard equipment in the early 1970s. The Royal Newfoundland Constabulary did not regularly carry side arms until the late 1990s.[44]

While municipal police sometimes worked unarmed, federal and provincial police forces usually received firearms early in their existence. In 1868, future Dominion Police commissioner, Gilbert Mc-Micken, asked the attorney general of Canada that the new Dominion Police "be furnished with revolvers." While he had previously received six Colt revolvers for the force, he believed the Dominion Police required fourteen.[45] The North-West Mounted Police had rifles and revolvers from its inception. The provincial police forces established in Saskatchewan and Alberta after the Mounties withdrew from many of their previous duties also armed constables with pistols, while keeping a handful of heavier weapons at headquarters to deal with especially dangerous criminals.[46]

By the interwar period, Canadians generally accepted armed police but still debated how freely law enforcement should use handguns. The 1892 *Criminal Code* included limits on the force police could employ. A police officer "in lawfully proceeding to arrest a person" could, if the person fled to avoid arrest, use such force as necessary to prevent escape, "unless such escape can be prevented by reasonable means in a less violent manner."[47] The *Code* included no specific guidelines for

Figure 37: A gun belonging to the BC Provincial Police, ca. 1940.
Source: Image B-06147, courtesy of Royal BC Museum, BC Archives

the appropriate use of firearms by police, and several incidents in the 1920s and early 1930s stirred a debate regarding how quickly police should draw and fire weapons. One prominent incident was the 1928 shooting of Albert Samson in Toronto. Samson had refused to stop a car when ordered, leading a constable to open fire, killing Samson. The *Toronto Star* criticized the police: "The man who is running away is not at the moment a menace." While trying to escape showed "disrespect for the police," that was "not a capital offence."[48] The chief justice of the High Court Division of the Supreme Court of Ontario, Richard Meredith, criticized police who fired on people accused of committing trifling offences and called for a full investigation into the Samson incident. Meredith told Minister of Justice Ernest Lapointe that it "requires a great stretch of imagination to hold that petty police officials have power to kill unarmed and unresisting persons, without trial, for petty offences only suspected," when the death sentence "after trial and conviction of the vilest offense, is not executed until the Governor-General has considered the case and in effect confirmed the sentence."[49] Senator George Lynch-Staunton became a vocal critic of police gun use. For several years, he complained about police shooting fleeing suspects and sought, unsuccessfully, criminal law amendments to limit the right of police to use firearms. While a few peace officers found themselves charged criminally or civilly because of their actions, in most cases courts granted police considerable latitude in the discharge of their weapons. For example, the officer accused of manslaughter for shooting Samson received an acquittal.[50]

Law enforcement officials and associations defended the arming of police and argued for latitude in how police used weapons. The Chief Constables' Association, for instance, criticized Lynch-Staunton's efforts. The Samson shooting led the Toronto chief constable to assert the impossibility of developing hard and fast rules to evaluate the appropriateness of police use of revolvers. The debate subsided during the Depression, as Canadians, worried about social disorder and crime, lost interest in disarming police.[51] Law enforcement thus cemented their right to pistols at the same time that the state would tighten regulations on privately owned handguns.

Guns and Young People in the Interwar Period

While governments invested in police firearms, they spent less effort encouraging young people to use weapons in the interwar period. As discussed in chapter 3, governments actively encouraged children to shoot prior to the Great War. In the interwar period, however, the decline in imperial sentiment, the sense that weapons such as machine guns and heavy artillery would win future wars, and a belief that Canada faced no imminent war meant that interest waned in rifle shooting in schools by the early 1930s. Some youth, however, still practised with rifles in cadets, the scouting movement, and some schools.[52]

Despite the *Criminal Code* limitations on selling guns to people under sixteen, boys and youth continued to acquire firearms. Businesses persisted in marketing air guns and .22-calibre rifles to young people by connecting weapons with masculinity, individualism, and nationalism. Firearm retailers, however, often employed different cultural symbols to establish these connections. After 1918, retailers drew upon the popular cowboy craze to market toy arms and air guns to children and youth. Eaton's carried a sixty-shot repeating air rifle endorsed by Buck Jones, a star of Hollywood cowboy films, while Nerlich & Co. of Toronto sold cap guns endorsed by Gene Autry, and "cosmic" guns, including Buck Rogers pistols.[53]

Critics again complained about the negative effects of firearm use by young people. Many Canadians believed young people were prone to

Figure 38: Canadian retailers in the interwar period, such as Nerlich & Co., advertised toy guns endorsed by stars of American cowboy films.
Source: Nerlich & Co. General Catalogue, Season 1938–1939, LAC, http://www .collectionscanada.gc.ca/mailorder/index-e.html

accidentally shooting themselves or others.[54] Between 1921 and 1939, 2,851 Canadians died from accidental gunshot wounds. This figure included 269 children under the age of ten (9.4 per cent of the total), and another 921 between the ages of ten and nineteen (32.3 per cent). Rural and urban residents complained that boys and youth also caused property damage or shot animals with air guns or .22-calibre rifles. In Cardston, Alberta, for example, a local paper blasted boys for shooting power line insulators, plunging the community into darkness. Cardston residents also accused boys of striking livestock with .22s, and several landowners responded by requiring that people ask permission before entering their property with firearms.[55] In the same period, Chief A.G. Shute of Edmonton drew attention to the "serious matter of young children with firearms" and questioned why parents believed it a "manly thing for a boy of tender years to have a .22 rifle."[56] Such statements reflected worries about youth delinquency in the interwar period, a time when Canadians wanted to shape boys into "social citizens" who honoured democracy, law, and work.[57] The wanton destruction of property and livestock indicated a lack of respect for these key touchstones of good social citizenship.

A desire to prevent young people from adopting perceived American attitudes towards guns partly drove worries about delinquent Canadian youth. American movies, crime novels, and magazines aroused criticism. Films often portrayed, and to some extent celebrated, western gunslingers, as well as criminals such as Al Capone, John Dillinger, "Machine Gun" Kelly, and Bonnie Parker and Clyde Barrow. Canadians expressed concern that impressionable boys and youth would copy the behaviour of these famous figures. The Kitchener police chief, for instance, believed boys played with guns because they read "too many dime novels dealing with the exploits of Jesse James and like characters."[58] Such views led to appeals to limit young people's exposure to violence in pop culture. The Sault Star concluded that the "movie revolver" was "out of place in Canada and should be suppressed," for portrayals of such arms conveyed "to impressionable people a wrong conception of law and order under the British flag."[59] Chief Inspector George Guthrie of the Toronto Police captured the result of these cultural trends: "To the youthful criminal," the use of firearms "seems to be a necessity." "Life, to these young bandits," Guthrie lamented, "is seemingly of little concern."[60]

Concerned citizens responded with efforts to ban portrayals of gunplay. Eight provinces had censorship boards by 1915, and some censors in the immediate post-war period disapproved of movies that included gunfights. The Ontario film censor also required the painting out of images of pistols in motion picture advertising. Even before this order, pictures of pistols in posters had often been obscured.[61] In the late 1930s, Ontario Liberal MP William Robert Gladstone proposed banning the publication of crime magazines with covers depicting people pointing guns, for these magazines tended "to educate growing boys to think that there is nothing wrong about pointing a gun at a person, and as a result we see boys playing at bandit and hold-ups."[62] The government refused to support the idea, however, since boys could always just open up magazines to see similar pictures. Gladstone made another such effort, unsuccessfully, in 1945.[63] While Gladstone's proposals failed to result in action, they suggested the existence of some public concern.

Ottawa responded to worries over armed youth with *Criminal Code* amendments to spur the enforcement of age restrictions on gun sales. In 1933, Ottawa removed the requirement for a permit to purchase an air gun, perhaps reflecting the view that air rifles posed less danger than other arms needing a permit, such as pistols. Ottawa also lowered the age requirement for purchasing a firearm or air rifle from sixteen to twelve. MPs noted that Canadians had widely disregarded the age restriction on gun sales. Alfred Speakman, a United Farmers of Alberta MP, doubted whether there existed "any law more honoured in the breach than this."[64] The government hoped that reducing the age would increase enforcement, but the change failed to achieve this effect. The *Vancouver Sun*'s 1936 appeal that parents prevent boys of seven or eight from using air guns evidenced the law's failure, and the *Globe* noted that officials rarely laid charges for selling air guns to boys. The *Globe* thus called for tougher laws. Appeals led to modest action. In 1938, the federal government again raised the age young people could buy guns (from twelve to fourteen).[65] Such legislative tinkering did not appease everyone, and after the Second World War an increasing gulf emerged between those who advocated training young people to shoot and those who believed boys and youth were incapable of safely handling firearms.

New Gun Laws in the Depression

The debate over young people's use of firearms constituted just one part of a larger discussion about gun control in the Depression decade, when Ottawa took important action. Several factors contributed to the federal government's decision to institute new gun controls in the Depression. Fear of social disorder was again important. Initial hopes that the economic downturn would be short evaporated by the early 1930s. Prime Minister R.B. Bennett established relief camps in 1932 to house and employ the many single, unemployed men travelling across the country in search of work. These camps would busy men who represented a potentially dangerous group in the eyes of the government. The work camps, however, undermined Ottawa's goal of suppressing political dissension, for the Communist Party found the camps fruitful locations to recruit members, even though Bennett banned the Communist Party in 1931 and imprisoned several of its leaders. Despite attempts to suppress dissent, Ottawa became concerned that political radicals would arm themselves.

Fear of increased criminal activity also motivated new efforts to regulate firearms. The number of people found guilty of indictable offence grew substantially during the Depression. In 1926, the government reported 185 convictions for indictable offences per hundred thousand Canadians. The rate increased to 279 per hundred thousand in 1930, and to 427 per hundred thousand in 1939.[66] The rise resulted from more criminal activity or stricter law enforcement (or both), but whatever explains the increase, Canadians felt more susceptible to criminals during the 1930s. Politicians expressed fear that desperate men might commit robberies and hold-ups with firearms. Senator (and former prime minister) Arthur Meighen, for example, believed that the carrying of concealed weapons became "more and more general with the spread of banditry and robbery."[67] The *Calgary Daily Herald* connected easy access to firearms with crime in 1933: "There is no doubt that the epidemic of armed holdups in recent months has been inspired by the laxity of the law controlling the sale and possession of death-dealing weapons."[68] At times, Canadians blamed the irrational choices of "bad" men for crime; at other times, however, legislators recognized that hunger and hardship drove men (and sometimes women) to committing gun crimes. MP Angus MacInnis, an independent labour MP representing a Vancouver riding, suggested the latter, for he believed some people committed crimes with guns because "the pressure of circumstances drives them to that extreme."[69]

Particularly frightening crimes often motivated gun control, and this held true in the Depression. In 1933, a burglar murdered a young Toronto patrician. John Copp, a twenty-two-year-old University of Toronto medical student and football star, suffered a fatal gunshot after the burglar entered his father's home.[70] Notables at the funeral included Mayor William Stewart and a large number of city council members, provincial and federal government representatives, and university officials, as well as thousands of grieving citizens. A prominent resident of Toronto, the director of the Royal Ontario Museum of Archeology, Professor C.T. Currelly, claimed that the Copp shooting "has had an

effect on the University of Toronto such as I have not known before."[71]
The murder led to a campaign to disarm people in possession of firearms illegally and to calls for stricter gun control.[72]

Fear of dissent and crime thus motivated appeals that Ottawa prohibit the importation, manufacture, and sale of pistols. Ottawa received letters and petitions from individuals, municipal governments, and boards of trade and various other societies, while newspapers issued numerous editorials demanding limits on access to handguns.[73] For the first time, women's groups also appealed for gun control. The Toronto Women's Liberal Association advocated a prohibition on the manufacture, importation, or possession of firearms, except for "legal protective requirements."[74] The National Council of Women also requested Bennett impose stringent gun-control measures. Canadian police in the 1930s, including the Chief Constables' Association of Canada, continued to support stronger gun laws, including the registration of handguns.[75] The proposal to register pistols reflected a growing confidence in the ability of the state to regulate firearms – never before had there been substantial public support for permanently registering an entire category of weapons.

The fact that criminals could conceal pistols made such guns especially troublesome. Innovations making other firearms concealable motivated additional appeals for new gun controls. So-called sawed-off shotguns concerned parliamentarians. The sawed-off shotgun was a modified version of a standard shotgun, produced by literally sawing off a regular shotgun's barrel to only a few inches in length. Shortening the barrel decreased the weapon's range but created one advantage: the gun became concealable. Canadians objected to these weapons in the mid-1920s. In 1926, for example, Sir Henry Drayton, a lawyer and Conservative MP from Ontario, said the "sawed-off shot-gun and the revolver" were "the two things which are really dangerous." Later, in 1933, Liberal MP Thomas Reid of British Columbia declared that many bandits carried sawed-off shotguns, for they could "be easily concealed under the coat." Parliamentarians typically associated sawed-off shotguns with criminal activities. As Manitoba Liberal MP John Power Howden suggested in 1933, "Anyone who has a sawed-off shotgun under his coat means business." "He is a criminal," Howden declared.[76]

The British and Americans expressed similar concern about dangerous guns in the 1930s and passed new firearm laws. Britain enacted legislation in 1933 increasing the punishment for using guns to commit crimes and making it an offence for anyone to employ a firearm, or imitation gun, to resist arrest. In 1936, Britain regulated shotguns with barrels less than twenty inches long, created complex regulations for gun dealers, and allowed chief constables to add conditions to firearm certificates. In the United States, the American Bar Association recommended that pistol manufacturers produce guns only for government and official use. The American Revolver Association opposed such proposals and instead produced a model *Uniform Firearms Act* that states could adopt to regulate handguns. Its proposals included a forty-eight-hour waiting period and a requirement that police examine applications for gun purchases to prevent firearm ownership by drug addicts, minors, or criminals. In the 1920s, at least seventeen states passed major gun legislation, often based on the model statute. Washington also became more involved in regulating firearms during the Depression, passing the *National Firearms Act* in 1934. Congress responded to concerns with violence, including gang violence associated with prohibition. As well, an assassination attempt on President Franklin Roosevelt spurred action. The *National Firearms Act* regulated several classes of dangerous weapons, including sawed-off shotguns and automatic weapons. Furthermore, Congress imposed taxes on these weapons to discourage their production and purchase. Washington passed another major piece of legislation in 1938, which established licensing and record-keeping procedures for those who sold firearms in interstate commerce.[77]

Canada had several advantages over the United States in controlling dangerous weapons. First and foremost, as of 1933, no pistol manufacturers operated in Canada, meaning there was no domestic manufacturing industry to lobby against gun control. Also, the importation of pistols meant that, theoretically, Ottawa could stop such weapons from entering the country. The federal government had long banned the importation of handguns under the *Customs Act* except under a permit granted by the minister of national revenue.[78] Canada had other advantages, including the existence of a national police force and the absence of constitutional barriers to gun control measures. Nevertheless, some people suggested that new laws would not solve the perceived problem with pistols. The attorney general of Ontario, William Price, told Prime Minister Bennett in early 1934 that in "a new country like Canada" it was "pretty difficult to take firearms away from the populace" and that it seemed to him "almost an impossible task to guarantee that the people of the underworld, or those who are anti-social, would never be able to get a revolver."[79]

Despite such doubts about the effectiveness of gun control, Bennett's Conservative government passed several important laws that, in some respects, went beyond the British and American measures. Bennett shared the popular concern with revolvers, suggesting that the pistol problem was a "matter of gravest importance" and that "something must be done."[80] His government thus introduced two major pieces of gun legislation, one in 1933 and one in 1934, to reduce the use of pistols and other concealable weapons. The 1933 act increased the potential punishment for people who carried a pistol or other concealable firearm outside of their home or business without a Form 76 permit. As well, it made carrying a pistol or concealable weapon in any vehicle a crime. Ottawa increased the potential punishment for violations of these rules to up to five years. To combat the criminal use of firearms, Parliament also dictated the addition of two years to the sentence of people guilty of committing a criminal offence if a pistol was used. In addition, for the first time, the government required pistol retailers to acquire a permit, hoping this would decrease the number of second-hand stores selling handguns.[81]

While the *Winnipeg Free Press* noted that the 1933 act imposed "drastic changes," the legislation failed to solve the pistol problem,[82] so Bennett's government passed even stronger legislation in 1934. The most important provision required the registration of all pistols, either with the RCMP or with someone authorized by the provincial attorneys general. The registration recorded the name, address, and occupation of the owner, the planned use of the gun, and a full description of the weapon. Previous to this measure, Canadians needed a permit to carry or purchase a pistol. The 1934 law, however, essentially meant the government could attach every pistol to a specific owner. Ottawa thus imposed the first permanent gun registry in Canada, albeit for only one type of weapon.[83]

The registration of pistols proceeded slowly but surely. The large number of weapons in circulation surprised some officials and led to some hiccups. In St Catharines, Ontario, local officials ran out of registration forms because of the quantity of guns. In Winnipeg, the registration bureau extended hours and days of operation because so many owners sought to register pistols.[84] The RCMP played a major role in the registration, creating a central bureau for registering handguns, which contained 85,607 records after just one year. The Mounties reported that the public assisted "in a praiseworthy manner," thus suggesting that the law generated little public resistance.[85] The number of registrations increased to 160,653 by 1937, when the RCMP indicated that the "bulk of the work is practically completed."[86] By 1940, the number of pistols registered had reached almost two hundred thousand.

The registry generally garnered public praise. The *Winnipeg Free Press*, for instance, declared it would help curtail crime. The widespread popular support for regulating pistols prevented any outcry against the measure inside or outside Parliament. The Dominion of Canada Rifle Association noted the legislative change in its official publication, *Canadian Marksman*, but did not disparage the measure.[87] Law enforcement also lauded the registry's benefits. The RCMP claimed in 1938 that "the results obtained from registration are proving of increasing value and far beyond expectation."[88] The RCMP highlighted incidents in which the registry allowed for the return of stolen guns and for the identification of criminals. The Mounties also emphasized that provincial and municipal police forces frequently employed the registry.[89]

Legislation passed by the Liberal government of Prime Minister Mackenzie King after his 1935 election victory further tightened laws regulating dangerous weapons. To prevent the use of short rifles, his government banned the possession of a rifle with a barrel of less than twenty inches in length without a permit. In 1938, Parliament also banned the destruction of serial numbers on pistols and other concealable guns. To get all pistols registered, Ottawa further required a "general registration" of handguns in 1939, then every five years thereafter. The federal government also sought to reduce gun crimes by dictating that extra jail time for committing an offence with any kind of weapon would be added at the end of the original sentence.[90]

The creation of the handgun registry indicated the Canadian state's growing confidence in its ability to regulate firearms using national institutions such as the RCMP. Neither Britain nor the United States introduced such a program in this period, despite the existence of similar concerns with pistols. The handgun registry proved uncontroversial when introduced and remained so in the future – no sustained effort to have it eliminated ever emerged. Such would not be the case for an even more ambitious gun registry in the future.

Firearms in the Second World War

The Canadian state again demonstrated its expanding confidence to impose gun control during the Second World War. The outbreak of war in 1939 meant a rapid militarization of Canadian society and industry. Over one million Canadians would serve in the armed forces, and, even more so than in the First World War, Canada acted as an arms plant. Canada produced a range of weapons, from Bren guns to Lee-Enfield rifles. Canada also manufactured more than 4.6 billion rounds of small arms ammunition, but even this level of production proved insufficient, leading Ottawa to ration ammunition to the public. As well, the military found itself short of pistols. The Wartime Prices and Trade Board thus banned the sale of .38-, .45-, and .455-calibre pistols to the public without board approval. The Department of National Defence also used the handgun registry to identify gun owners who might sell or donate weapons to the armed forces. Many gun owners obliged.[91]

War led to renewed efforts to control firearms. Convictions for carrying unlawful weapons spiked. In 1935, there were 513 convictions for carrying unlawful weapons – a figure that jumped to 1086 in 1940 (before quickly dropping back to pre-war levels). War also led to several new gun regulations, framed as Orders in Council under the authority of the *War Measures Act*. As in the First World War, the state viewed enemy aliens suspiciously, and in October 1939 Ottawa prohibited enemy aliens from possessing any kind of firearm or ammunition. Aliens again had to deliver their guns to a law enforcement official with the understanding that authorities would return the arms after hostilities ended. Failure to deliver weapons could result in a fine of up to five hundred dollars or to imprisonment for up to three months. In June 1940, Ottawa strengthened this law by requiring German or Italian aliens *and* all persons of German or Italian ancestry who had become naturalized British subjects since 1 September 1929 to hand over weapons.[92] This measure was stronger than the law during the First World War, which had not required naturalized citizens to surrender guns. The RCMP declared the regulations forbidding alien gun ownership "rigidly enforced," and by March 1941 the Mounties held 13,133 firearms owned by enemy aliens or naturalized citizens from Germany or Italy.[93]

Resistance to these measures led the government to soften the regulations. Some naturalized residents complained, as did foreigners who made their living as trappers and guides. As a result, Ottawa made its policies more flexible in January 1940, allowing aliens of "unquestioned loyalty to Canada" to have firearms if granted an exemption certificate. By the end of March 1941, authorities had issued 4,657 resident alien gun permits to applicants requiring a weapon for sporting purposes, to make a living, or to protect farms and gardens against animal pests.

As well, from July 1940 to March 1941, officials granted 9,016 permits to foreign visitors to Canada. This figure rose to 14,180 by March 1942, but decreased to 9,759 in 1943 because of a decline in sport hunting tourism. By the end of the war, authorities issued approximately 60,000 permits to non-resident aliens visiting Canada.[94]

The desire to control firearms during the war also led Ottawa to take a dramatic new step: it introduced a national gun registry for all weapons. In September 1940, Ottawa required all gun owners to register their rifles and shotguns (in addition to the pistols and concealable weapons previously registered). Those who failed to register faced potential fines and/or imprisonment. The system created a national reporting system, in which the commissioner of the RCMP received a copy of every registration certificate.[95]

The public expressed little dissatisfaction with the 1940 registration. Concerns with enemies within motivated most Canadians to accept a registry. To quiet any potential opponents and to ensure compliance, the government substantially increased the potential penalty for failing to register rifles and shotguns to a five-hundred-dollar fine (up from fifty dollars) and as long as two years in jail (up from thirty days). The government designed the gun registry as a temporary measure, which probably prevented more resistance. Ottawa destroyed the registry's records after the war.[96]

The registration of all firearms, a massive undertaking, taxed the RCMP's resources. In 1941, the RCMP declared that the registry had "caused an enormous amount of work."[97] The government printed two million registration certificates. In the program's first year, Canadians registered 1,447,065 rifles and shotguns, yet the process remained incomplete. By March 1943, this figure increased to approximately 1,650,000, and in 1945 the RCMP reported 1,727,868 registered rifles and shotguns, as well as 222,053 pistols, for a total of 1,949,921 registered arms. The lack of serial numbers on some guns, especially .22-calibre rifles, proved troubling, leading the Chief Constables' Association of Canada to request that Parliament require every firearm manufactured to bear a serial number.[98]

The gun registration scheme of the Second World War reflected the growth of state power. The war led to unprecedented efforts to quantify Canadian society, and wartime fears created an environment that permitted government initiatives to accumulate previously "private" data. These programs included fingerprinting about 20 per cent of all Canadians by 1947. Gun registration provided another prime example.

Figure 39: Cst. J.S. Ferguson of the Royal Canadian Mounted Police operates
a sorting machine in the Firearms Registration Branch at the RCMP
headquarters.
Source: National Film Board of Canada / LAC, PA-145022

According to Larry Hannant, the registry "helped condition Canadians
to relinquish voluntarily information that was useful to the state and
its political police."[99] The RCMP used the advanced technology of IBM
tabulation machines to process the registry.[100]

At the end of the war, Ottawa returned impounded weapons, although it continued to require aliens to obtain permits until 1950. Re-

turning thousands of weapons proved a large task and, in the end, the government failed to locate many owners and eventually destroyed unclaimed guns. Peacetime also resulted in new concerns about the prevalence of firearms. The press produced ominous stories suggesting a spike in illegal gun sales, that criminals desired to steal pistols, and that factory workers had stolen guns from arms plants. The tendency of many servicemen to bring pistols into Canada as war souvenirs also created worry. The RCMP even warned that some veterans returned with fully automatic (or "sub-machine" guns), which the force concluded could easily fall into criminal hands.[101] After a spate of gun accidents in the fall of 1945, Liberal MP Robert Gladstone wondered if the government could protect citizens "from the dangers arising out of the flood of weapons going about the country."[102] Ottawa proved better prepared for the influx of guns than it had in 1918–19. The Department of National Defence prohibited the possession of enemy weapons. Many soldiers violated this prohibition, but police still required the registration of any pistols brought into Canada. By March 1946, authorities registered at least 30,000 handgun war souvenirs. This influx contributed to a spike in the number of registered weapons in Canada, from 222,053 in 1945 to 310,910 by 1948. State efforts to control weapons after the war also resulted in another temporary increase in the number of convictions for carrying unlawful weapons, from a wartime low of 451 in 1943 to 1250 in 1946, before declining to half that number by the early 1950s.[103]

Conclusion

The gun-control measures adopted from the Great War to the Second World War frequently stemmed from a desire to limit firearm ownership or use by potentially disloyal subjects. The identity of the groups changed somewhat in the period, however. Armed enemy aliens from Germany and Austria-Hungary motivated legislation in the Great War. During the Second World War, the government turned its attention to the possession of firearms by Germans, Italians, and Japanese in Canada. There is little concrete evidence to prove that members of any of these groups actually sought to carry out sustained "fifth column" activities, but widespread suspicion led Ottawa to act. After the First World War, fear of Bolsheviks led to legislation targeting gun ownership by aliens. In the Depression, the prospect of social disorder resulted in new firearm laws that controlled the ownership and use of

Figure 40: German handguns were among the war souvenirs Canadian servicemen brought back to Canada. Major F.G. Dalton of Royal Canadian Regiment shows German Luger pistols to the disarmament expert Sergeant O. Sweethy.
Source: Alexander M. Stirton / Canada, Department of National Defence / LAC, PA-151929

handguns by men made desperate by unemployment. Such targeting of gun ownership by groups deemed suspicious was, of course, nothing new.

The 1914 to 1945 period was significant, however, for it represented a period of change, not just continuity, in Canadian gun laws. Municipal, provincial, and federal governments concluded that police should carry handguns. Ottawa also began to flex the growing muscles of the state, making sustained efforts to regulate pistols. Public support for the control of such weapons, especially during the uncertainty of the Depression, meant no outcry met the creation of a handgun registry. The licensing provisions passed immediately after the Great War and the firearm registry established in the Second World War further exemplified this increased state confidence. These laws sought, if sometimes temporarily, to regulate all guns and their owners more seriously. Rather than modestly target gun possession by specific ethnic groups, Ottawa demonstrated its emerging belief that the state could regulate firearm ownership amongst the general public. The government nevertheless often pulled back because of worries over the limits of state power and the belief that ordinary gun owners did not require supervision in times without tumult. The mixture of permanent and temporary gun laws thus made the First World War to Second World War period a transitional one in state approaches to private firearm ownership. While governments deemed some weapons dangerous, and thus in need of regulation, politicians deemed hunting rifles safe for most Canadians. After the Second World War, attitudes to hunting rifles shifted, with the result that long guns also came under greater levels of government control.

5

Angry White Men: Resistance to Gun Control in Canada, 1946–1980

The gun-control issue largely disappeared from public debate for more than twenty years after the end of the Second World War. The limitations on carrying concealable weapons and the creation of the handgun registry in the 1930s helped defuse fears about pistols. The popularity of hunting and a decline in popular concern with specific ethnic groups also made gun control recede as a political and social issue. This quiet period ended abruptly in the late 1960s when increased rates of violent crime, several infamous shootings, and renewed fears that Canadians risked adopting American gun culture spurred legislative action. Changing attitudes towards hunting arms also motivated calls for new laws. For the first time, many urban Canadians concluded that hunting rifles required regulation. The federal government, unlike in the past, felt capable of successfully implementing legislation governing ordinary long guns. The Liberal government of Prime Minister Pierre Trudeau thus introduced ambitious new legislation.

Efforts to create new firearm laws sparked a furious response, however. In the past, groups facing gun controls usually lacked the political clout to successfully oppose legislation. Hunters, target shooters, and gun collectors, on the other hand, formed a powerful constituency. Firearm owners responded to proposed legislation with a barrage of arguments, many underpinned by a sense that governments intended to interfere with individual liberty. Firearm owners linked gun control to popular concern over the growth of the regulatory state, and they asserted a strongly held belief in a vaguely defined right to possess arms. They feared that the state would confiscate privately held arms. Gun owners also felt insulted that the state considered them potentially dangerous. Feelings of working-class disempowerment and western alienation became entwined in the gun-control debate, amplifying the rhetoric of firearm owners. The ferocity of the resistance to Ottawa's legislative proposals made the 1970s debate over gun control among the most heated in Canadian history. In the end, gun-control opponents forced Prime Minister Pierre Trudeau's government to pass relatively weak regulations that generally left average gun owners alone.

Post-war Legislative Tinkering

Consensus defined Canadian political life in the two decades after the Second World War. The dominant federal political parties – the Progressive Conservatives and the Liberals – frequently offered similar platforms. Both parties tended to extend the benefits of the social welfare state, combat discrimination, and pursue economic policies to expand the middle class. Personality, not policy, often determined which party held power.[1] In this consensus period, gun regulation largely receded as a political issue. Canadians expressed concern with gun accidents, the difficulties of registering all handguns, and the criminal use of weapons, but little panic about any of these dangers. Ottawa tinkered with firearm laws, introducing minor revisions to the *Criminal Code* to address the availability of "unsafe" weapons, not hunting arms.

Pistols remained in the category of unsafe weapons. Canadians possessed a growing number of registered handguns in the post-war period. In 1945, the registry included 222,053 firearms. This figure rose to 359,324 in 1955, and to 530,567 by 1968,[2] and the increase caused apprehension. For example, the federal leader of the Progressive Conservative Party in 1950, George Drew, a lawyer from Ontario, supported making hunting rifles and shotguns widely available, but, in advocating for the stronger regulation of handguns, said pistols were "in an entirely different category." "It is only within a limited field," Drew concluded, "that they may be regarded as competitive or sporting weapons."[3] Drew offered a typical categorization of safe and unsafe weapons in the 1950s. In the 1970s, however, gun-control advocates contested this division.

The concern with handguns led Ottawa to establish criminal penalties for people who misused imitation firearms. Criminals had for many years occasionally employed toy handguns. In 1947, the Ontario Court of Appeal ruled that an imitation gun used in a hold-up was not an "offensive weapon" within the meaning of the *Criminal Code*.[4] Parliament responded by redefining armed robbery to include being armed with an offensive weapon "or imitation thereof."[5] This failed to solve the problem, as evidenced by a spate of hold-ups with toy pistols in Vancouver in 1948, which led the city's chief constable to appeal for a ban on the manufacture and sale of toy guns.[6] In 1951, Ottawa broadened the definition of offensive weapon to include "anything that is designed to be used as a weapon" and "anything that a person uses or intends to use as a weapon, whether or not it is designed to be used as a weapon."[7] In 1959, Parliament further limited the use of fake guns by explicitly adding imitation weapons to the list of offensive weapons banned if carried for a purpose dangerous to the public peace or for the purpose of committing an offence.[8]

Ottawa passed several other reforms to prevent possession of unsafe weapons. In 1951, the federal government required anyone who found a firearm believed lost or stolen to report the weapon or deliver it to the police. Ottawa also added automatic weapons to the list of guns requiring registration, dictating that owners had to register weapons that could be fired "in rapid succession during one pressure of the trigger."[9] The government included automatic weapons on the request of the Canadian Association of Chiefs of Police, which regarded such guns "as much more dangerous weapons" than pistols.[10] In 1960, Ottawa banned the possession of rifles with a barrel less than twenty inches in length with a butt or stock that could be folded, telescoped, or shortened. The federal government took this action after selling 2800 surplus military Hornet rifles to arms dealers. These short rifles had collapsible stocks, with the result that people could hide them under overcoats. The government repossessed the weapons and reimbursed owners. A final reform to note: Ottawa required the commissioner of the RCMP to maintain a central registry of every firearm registration certificate issued under federal gun laws. Previously, there had been a co-operative effort to centralize record-keeping, but Ottawa had not required centralization.[11]

Provincial Hunting Legislation

While the federal government only tinkered with firearm laws before the late 1960s, the provinces substantially increased supervision of hunters' gun use. Calculating the number of active hunters at any one time is challenging. Hunting licences provide one means of gauging changing levels of participation, but comparisons between provinces are difficult because jurisdictions had different categories of licences. Nevertheless, it appears that the number of Canadian hunters increased substantially in the 1950s and 1960s, before levelling off in the 1970s. A sample of game licences from several provinces illustrates the growth in the number of men who took to the woods. In 1946, for instance, Newfoundland sold 3,845 big-game licences, but by 1960 it sold 15,386 – an increase of 300 per cent at a time when Newfoundland's population increased by just 36 per cent. In British Columbia, the number of licensed hunters grew from 67,396 in 1950 to 153,424 in 1970. This 128 per cent increase surpassed the province's 88 per cent population growth. A similar jump occurred in Ontario, where the number of resident hunting licences grew from 219,916 in 1946 to 621,942 in 1966 (a 183 per cent spike at a time when the province's population increased 70 per cent). The growth in hunting stemmed from the post-war economic expansion that gave more men the time and money to take part. Inexpensive war-surplus rifles and new highways also allowed widespread participation. A similar boom in hunting occurred in the United States after the Second World War. Returning American veterans trained in the use of arms spent pent-up financial resources on guns and hunting paraphernalia, egged on by marketers who used the increased interest in firearms generated by film and television portrayals of the old west to capture consumers' imaginations.[12] The large number of Canadian men who took up hunting would prove significant, for it made hunters' groups extremely influential in gun control debates in the 1970s and beyond.

Ever since the emergence of recreational hunting as a popular pastime for middle-class men in the late nineteenth century, Canadians had expressed concern with hunting accidents. Urban men who put down tools, bookkeeping pencils, and doctors' stethoscopes to pick up hunting rifles failed to inspire a sense of safety. Concern only grew as the number of hunters (and firearm accidents) increased in the post-war period. Canada experienced an increase in accidental firearm deaths, from 92 (including 79 men and 13 women) in 1944 to a post-war high of 216 (202 men and 14 women) in 1960. This represented a 50 per cent increase in the number of accidental gun deaths per capita (from 0.8 to 1.2 per hundred thousand).[13]

The government reaction to hunting accidents was similar to the response to automobile accidents after the Second World War. According to Christopher Dummitt, automobiles represented "modern control over the environment" but also called for an "equally modern system of control." Rather than take control of the technology itself – the automobile – safety advocates called for a "greater system of personal control and called on Canadians to adopt a whole new modernist mindset based on risk-management principles."[14] Provinces seeking to reduce gun accidents took a similar route, creating safety programs to shape appropriate male behaviour by encouraging, or requiring, training in safe firearm usage. At first, some provinces employed voluntary hunter-safety campaigns. For example, in the late 1950s the Nova Scotia Department of Lands and Forests enlisted the help of rifle clubs for the department's Safe Hunting Campaign. The clubs opened their premises to the public and supplied instructors to demonstrate safe hunting practices. Nova Scotia also used radio, television, and newspaper advertisements to stress gun safety in the home and in the woods.[15]

Over time, a number of provinces transitioned from voluntary to mandatory safety programs. Ontario, for instance, began a voluntary hunter-safety training course for new hunters in the late 1950s but eventually made it mandatory. New hunters under twenty years of age had to complete a firearm safety course to receive a licence, while hunters older than twenty had to provide proof of experience or pass a hunting-licence examination. By the mid-1970s, a patchwork of provincial laws required varying levels of training. Quebec required all hunters to complete a firearm-handling safety course. Manitoba, on the other hand, only required hunters under nineteen to receive firearm-safety training, while British Columbia made gun training compulsory for all people who had not previously hunted, regardless of age.[16]

Hunters' groups did not resist these measures and, in fact, often strongly advocated for such courses. In Ontario, for instance, the Ontario Federation of Anglers and Hunters led the effort to increase hunter safety. Supporters credited these provincial programs with substantially reducing the number of gun accidents involving hunters. In Ontario, the number of hunting-accident deaths dropped precipitously, from thirty-six in 1960 to just eight in 1970. National statistics also show the decline in accidental firearm deaths. From the peak postwar accidental death rate of 1.2 per hundred thousand Canadians in 1960, the rate gradually fell – to 0.5 in 1972, and to just 0.2 per hundred thousand in 1982.[17]

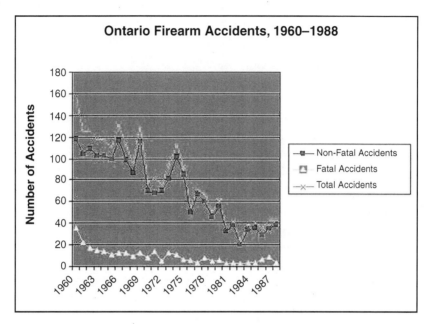

Figure 41: Ontario firearm accidents, 1960–88.
Sources: Ontario, Department of Lands and Forests, *A Statistical Reference of Lands and Forests Administration, 1968*; Ontario, Department of Lands and Forests, *Statistics* (1970–2); Ontario, Ministry of Natural Resources, *Statistics* (1973–88)

Gun Control in the 1960s

The post-war lull in debates over gun control ended by the late 1960s when an increasing number of journalists, politicians, police officials, judges, and social commentators suggested Ottawa pass more aggressive firearm laws. The federal government began to consider new gun regulations in the early 1960s. John Diefenbaker (prime minister from 1957 to 1963) had long advocated for stronger gun laws; for instance, he asked the Liberal government in 1945 to restrict access to revolvers. In 1960, his government created an informal committee to examine Canada's firearm laws consisting of representatives from the Department of Justice, the Department of National Revenue, the RCMP, and the Canadian Association of Chiefs of Police. The committee ceased its work in 1963, and its recommendations led to no legislation. Word of the committee's existence, however, created apprehension amongst some gun owners, who worried that Ottawa intended to impose new firearm controls. Rod and gun clubs sent numerous letters defending the private use of guns for sport, and these appeals helped dissuade government action, even after Montreal experienced several high-profile gun crimes.[18]

The minority Liberal governments of Prime Minister Lester Pearson (1963–8) avoided new firearm laws, although pressure mounted for action in Canada, as elsewhere. The assassinations of President John F. Kennedy in 1963, and Martin Luther King and Robert Kennedy in 1968, fed a growing unease about public order. In the United States, the assassinations led Congress to pass a new federal gun-control bill in 1968. Grounded in Washington's right to regulate interstate commerce, the new act made mail-order gun purchases more difficult, raised the fee on federal gun-dealer licences, and limited foreign and interstate gun traffic to legitimate importers, dealers, and manufacturers. The British Parliament also acted in this period. Following the murder of three police officers in 1966, Britain introduced a certificate system for shotguns in 1967.[19]

The next Liberal prime minster, Pierre Trudeau, proved bolder than Pearson, introducing new gun-control measures in 1969. These gun provisions constituted one part of a massive criminal law omnibus bill that, among other things, decriminalized homosexuality and weakened restrictions on lotteries. In introducing the legislation, Minister of Justice John Turner asserted that Canada's gun laws required amendment; however, he also recognized that the bill might prove controversial. His goal was "to achieve controls which will discourage and penalize the criminal and the criminally careless, which will remove lethal weapons from the irresponsible or mentally ill," which would "help to foster social attitudes against violence" and would "leave the avenue open for responsible people to engage in legitimate sport and hobbies involving firearms." Turner hoped to defuse potential opponents, but the challenges of passing the legislation became immediately apparent. He noted the impossibility of preventing all criminals from getting weapons, even if the government tried to take all guns out of circulation. This comment led an unidentified member of the Commons to shout out a warning: "You would have a revolution."[20]

This kind of emotional reaction to legislation regulating "ordinary" gun owners led the federal government to offer relatively modest proposals in 1969. It nevertheless received several thousand letters from concerned gun owners. To allay their fears, Turner met with well-established interest groups, including the Dominion of Canada Rifle Association, the Shooting Federation of Canada, the Canadian Wildlife Federation, and the Ontario Revolver Association.[21] Turner took their advice on some issues, and the executive director of the Canadian Wildlife Federation reported that meetings with government officials had resulted in "a broad measure of agreement on almost all of the points raised for discussion."[22] This give-and-take between government and established firearm groups meant that the gun-owning public expressed only muted opposition.

Parliament designed the legislation to keep firearms away from those deemed potentially dangerous. Ottawa again altered the minimum age for purchasing firearms, raising it from fourteen to sixteen. Those under sixteen could attain an underage permit, although youth under fourteen could receive a permit only if they lived in prescribed areas and could show they needed a gun to hunt for food or support their family. Parliament also banned the sale of a firearm to anyone the seller knew (or had good reason to know) was of unsound mind. Further, Ottawa permitted judges to make an order prohibiting people convicted of an offence with a weapon from carrying or possessing a firearm or ammunition for up to five years. The legislation also created a new system for categorizing firearms. "Unrestricted" weapons included "safe" firearms, meaning hunting rifles and shotguns. The "restricted" category consisted of guns deemed somewhat dangerous – weapons fired with one hand, guns that could be fired in rapid succession with one press of the trigger, weapons less than twenty-six inches in length, and arms not normally used for hunting or sporting activities declared restricted by the federal Cabinet. Possessing a restricted weapon without a permit could result in a jail term of up to two years. Individuals who wished to possess restricted weapons outside of their home or business needed a permit issued for prescribed reasons and for limited periods of time. The "prohibited" category was to include especially dangerous arms not classified as "restricted" and not commonly used for hunting or sporting purposes, which the federal Cabinet declared prohibited. Possessing a prohibited weapon could lead to imprisonment for up to five years.[23] In sum, the 1969 legislation empowered the government to ban especially dangerous weapons, to closely regulate handguns, and to limit access to firearms by the young, the mentally ill, or those who had shown themselves willing to use weapons in criminal activity. It left recreational shooters and hunters largely alone.

While Ottawa created a framework to closely regulate dangerous weapons, the Liberal government proved reluctant to use the act's provisions to full effect. By 1975, Cabinet had declared only one make of arm "prohibited." Sawed-off shotguns and rifles (which had previously been banned) became "restricted" weapons under the 1969 law. Also, the act made fully automatic guns restricted, rather than prohibited, weapons.[24] Gun groups' lack of resistance to the legislation is thus unsurprising. The vast majority of Canada's hunters, target shooters, and gun collectors experienced no deleterious effects. At the same time, however, the legislation raised the antennae of some gun owners, who began to watch Ottawa more closely in case politicians proposed stricter regulations in the future.

Gun Control in the 1970s

The 1969 *Criminal Code* amendments did not stop calls for stronger firearm regulations. In fact, several events energized gun-control advocates in the early to mid-1970s. The actions of the Front de libération du Québec (FLQ) led to complaints about the availability of firearms. The FLQ raided several armouries and retail stores to acquire weapons as part of its effort to secure Quebec independence. Opponents of the organization also accused it of purchasing guns legally to use in terror activities. MP Eldon Wooliams of Calgary South thus asked the government if it planned to declare semi-automatic M-1 rifles prohibited weapons to prevent kidnappers from purchasing such guns.[25] The *Globe and Mail* questioned why anyone, even at the height of the FLQ crisis, could walk into a war-surplus store in Montreal and leave with a semi-automatic rifle: "It is one of the idiosyncrasies of Canadians that we take much more care in regulating the sale of a bottle of wine than we do the sale of deadly weapons."[26]

Increasing rates of violent crime in the 1960s and 1970s also motivated advocates of stronger gun controls. The number of crimes of violence reported by police grew from 44,026 in 1962 (237 per hundred thousand people) to 135,424 in 1975 (585 per hundred thousand). The number of homicides experienced a similar spike, from 253 in 1964 (1.31 per hundred thousand) to 701 in 1975 (3.03 per hundred thousand). Gun-control advocates expressed worry that the rate of firearm-related crimes increased even faster than the rate of crime not involving firearms in the first half of the 1970s. Non-firearm murders increased by 14 per cent between 1970 and 1974, but murders involving guns increased 46 per cent in the same period. On a per capita basis, the number of homicides involving firearms more than doubled between 1966 (0.49 homicides per hundred thousand) and 1974 (1.18 per hundred thousand). Other crimes involving firearms also jumped. The number of non-firearm robberies in Canada increased 11 per cent from 1974 to 1975), but robberies involving firearms grew by 53 per cent. A spike in suicides involving firearms (from 609 in 1966, or 3 per hundred thousand, to 1021, or 4.5 per hundred thousand in 1974) also aggravated the concern with guns.[27]

The civil disobedience and crime in urban areas motivated new legislation. Progressive Conservative MP Marcel Lambert, representing Edmonton West, warned of growing gun violence in Canadian cities: "Our major metropolitan centres have become more and more the locale for crimes of violence. There is increased use of guns in Toronto today. We hear of people standing on the street, a car pulling up, and immediately there is fire from an automatic weapon. It is a gangland crime. The city of Montreal is replete with such crimes. The easiest thing in many of our major cities today is to get hold of a gun or a knife and use them."[28] Many leading newspapers also suggested that Canadian cities faced a growing gun problem and called for action.[29] Concern with guns in urban centres was not new. But, by 1971, with roughly three-quarters of the country residing in towns and cities, a larger percentage of Canadians worried about urban gun crime. A Toronto grand jury identified Canada's growing urban population as a rationale for stringent gun controls. The jurors noted that opponents of regulating firearms emphasized the negative effects on rural citizens but asserted that "Canada is now an urbanized country with the vast majority of the population living at close quarters in the cities and towns."[30] Urban Canadians, such as these grand jurors, would prove the strongest proponents of gun control in the 1970s.

The dangers of mixing firearms with illegal drug use also motivated advocates for new firearm laws. The popularity of drugs such as marijuana and LSD in the late 1960s counterculture resulted in a spike in the number of drug charges. Drug-related convictions increased from 337 in 1964 to 30,485 in 1974. Gun-control proponents connected drugs with crime and suggested that people committed gun crimes while under the influence or to steal to feed their addiction.[31]

Infamous crimes, as in the past, motivated demands for gun control. Key incidents included the murder of two Toronto constables in 1973, and two police officers near Moncton, New Brunswick, in 1974. Crimes involving young people proved especially influential in encouraging legislative action. In May 1975, a thirteen-year-old boy armed with a .22-calibre rifle briefly held three teachers and more than one hundred children hostage at a Scarborough, Ontario, school. Soon after, Michael Slobodian, a sixteen-year-old student at Brampton's Centennial Secondary School, went home for lunch and returned with two rifles hidden in a guitar case. He killed a teacher, fatally wounded a student, and injured thirteen others before killing himself. Then, in October 1975, eighteen-year-old Robert Poulin took a sawed-off shotgun to Ottawa's St Pius X High School. He killed one student, injured several others, then committed suicide. The Brampton and Ottawa school shootings became important symbols for those wanting to revise Canada's gun laws. The parents of John Slinger, the seventeen-year-old student victim in Brampton, appealed to the government for new gun control laws and held a high-profile meeting with Solicitor General Warren Allmand. The public began to pressure the government through petitions following the school violence. Twenty-five thousand people from the Brampton area signed a petition in support of more effective gun regulation, while over seven thousand Ottawa high school students signed a petition calling for restrictions on the availability of firearms. In addition, Vancouver's Maggie Burtinshaw circulated a petition that garnered 10,000 signatures after a thirteen-year-old, who had broken into a department store to steal guns and ammunition, killed her son.[32]

The school shooting incidents all involved hunting weapons, not handguns. This fact stimulated a new argument in the first half of the 1970s: that *all* guns, including hunting rifles and shotguns, posed dangers and thus required regulation. A growing number of Canadians expressed unease that the government left such guns largely uncontrolled. British Columbia NDP MP Stuart Leggatt, for example, noted in 1973 that half of the firearm murders in Canada involved hunting rifles. "Yet a rifle," he complained, was "something one can buy without restriction in any department store. Persons of unsound mind, persons with serious criminal records, have ready access to weapons."[33] The idea that governments should regulate hunting rifles represented a radical departure and would prove contentious.

Canadians also noted the gun crime ravaging the United States and argued that Ottawa should limit access to all firearms to prevent increased violence in Canada. Critics of the American situation often focused on the dangers of small, cheap pistols – "Saturday night specials." Canadian newspapers detailed the reluctance of the United States Con-

"Sorry — the law requires a prescription for tranquilizers."

Figure 42: As this cartoon suggests, Canadians in the 1970s expressed concern about the ease with which people could buy ordinary hunting weapons.
Source: Edd Uluschak, *Edmonton Journal*, 19 August 1975

gress to pass new gun controls, despite numerous assassinations and a high murder rate. Proponents of firearm regulation suggested that strong gun control differentiated Canada from the United States and that even tougher laws would ensure that the distinction continued.[34] This argument proved popular in the 1970s – a time when many Canadians expressed concern about the "Americanization" of Canadian culture and industry.

The National Rifle Association (NRA) became the bogeyman for Canadians worried about the Americanization of Canadian gun culture. The NRA grew by leaps and bounds after the Second World War when millions of demobilized American soldiers returned home with an interest in firearms and hunting. The influx of ex-military personnel drove the NRA away from its traditional emphasis on target shooting and instead focused it on serving its hunting constituents. According to one authority, the NRA shifted from a "quasi-governmental league devoted to military preparedness to a truly national group catering to the needs of sportsmen carrying guns."[35] It had long participated in some lobbying activities, but by the late 1960s the NRA found itself divided between an older generation wanting it to remain a staid hunters' organization, and younger radicals who gradually took control and made the NRA into an activist group devoted to stymying new gun-control initiatives. By the mid-1970s, the NRA had over one million dues-paying members and employed a full-time staff of 250 in Washington.[36]

Gun-control advocates worried about the NRA's potential influence in Canada. Some MPs suggested that NRA publications might entice Canadians into adopting American attitudes towards firearms.[37] Several politicians also condemned the NRA as a front for the American firearm-manufacturing industry. Critics laid the failure to pass new gun control measures in the United States, despite popular support for gun laws, at the NRA's feet. Liberal Senator Frederick William Rowe from Newfoundland offered a typical complaint about the NRA in 1974 when he argued that "the most potent single lobby in the United States today is the National Rifle Association," a group that spent "hundreds of millions of dollars, not to convey the truth to the people of the United States, and inferentially to Canada, but to distort the truth."[38] Canadian politicians thus painted the NRA as an anti-democratic lobbying organization and warned against allowing gun groups similar power in shaping domestic firearm policy.

Warren Allmand became a leading Liberal Party advocate for stricter gun controls. A Montreal-born lawyer elected to the House of Commons in 1965, Allmand first expressed interest in toughening firearm regulations while a backbencher. He tirelessly advocated new gun laws, seeking to closely regulate *all* Canadian gun owners and to limit access to *all* weapons, included hunting arms. In 1971, for example, he proposed permitting only government stores to sell guns, requiring Canadians to apply for permission to buy a gun, imposing a waiting period for gun purchases, and dictating that gun-purchase applications be made public to allow other citizens to object. Further, Allmand advocated requiring gun owners to complete an annual report of their firearm use and to report on the condition of their weapons. When gun owners no longer needed their firearms, Ottawa would force them to return their guns to a government-run agency. Allmand also suggested prohibiting handguns, short rifles, and automatic weapons. Allmand was a backbencher when he made these radical proposals but soon found himself better placed to effect change. He entered cabinet as solicitor general in late 1972 and continued to advocate new gun controls. Allmand was not alone in pursuing this goal, as other proponents of new firearm regulation introduced private member's bills in 1973, 1974, and 1975 – none of which, however, became law.[39]

Bill C-83 (1976)

Despite substantial pressure for legislative action, the Liberal government generally resisted introducing new measures. A 1972 ban on carrying offensive weapons onto an airplane without consent designed to prevent hijacking represented one exception.[40] The reluctance to introduce new gun controls stemmed from the Liberal Party's disunity on the issue. Otto Lang strongly opposed firearm regulation within the Cabinet. A former dean of law at the University of Saskatchewan, Lang entered the Commons in 1968 representing the Saskatchewan riding of Saskatoon-Humboldt and served as minister of justice from 1972 until September 1975. He consistently opposed new gun laws as minister of justice. In 1973, for instance, he critiqued proposals for firearm legislation because gun controls "most certainly interfere with the ordinary activities of a lot of law-abiding citizens, whereas in no way are they certain to interfere with the activities of criminals."[41] He claimed no deep philosophical position against gun control; he simply believed that more regulation would accomplish little.

Legislation thus had to wait until Lang moved out of the justice portfolio, and in a 1975 Cabinet shuffle Prime Minister Trudeau replaced Lang with Vancouver Centre MP Ron Basford. Basford shared Allmand's belief that Canada required stronger gun laws. Allmand and Basford serving, respectively, as solicitor general and minister of justice set the stage for government action. The federal Liberals could also count on the support of the Progressive Conservative government of Canada's largest province. In 1974, an NDP opposition member produced a semi-automatic .22-calibre rifle in the Assembly to emphasize the danger of firearms. The Ontario solicitor general, George Kerr, sympathized with gun-control advocates, and he announced in July 1975 that Ontario would introduce provincial legislation if Ottawa failed to act. Ontario Attorney General Roy McMurtry also supported stronger firearm legislation, and Premier Bill Davis ultimately made gun control part of the Progressive Conservative Party platform in the 1975 provincial election.[42]

The federal government hired two academics to study the potential benefits and drawbacks of new gun controls. Criminologist William Du Perron first produced a report, but the government never released his 1974 findings, allegedly because Du Perron doubted the benefits of intensifying gun controls. Ottawa subsequently commissioned a second study by Martin Friedland, dean of the University of Toronto's Faculty of Law. Friedland made several recommendations. He advocated making sawed-off shotguns and fully automatic arms prohibited weapons and further suggested that the government limit the permissible rationales for getting a handgun permit. In addition, he recommended the creation of a new category of firearms, "controlled" weapons, to include all rifles, shotguns, and air guns. This recommendation reflected the emerging sense that long guns posed a substantial problem. Anyone wanting to purchase or use a controlled weapon would have to attain a licence by passing a competency test. However, Friedland did not propose making the licensing provision retroactive. That is, Ottawa would not require Canadians who already owned, but did not use, a gun to acquire a licence, only those who planned to use their weapon or buy a firearm. He rejected more ambitious state efforts at regulation; for example, he dismissed the idea of registering all guns because of the cost, administrative difficulty, modest benefits, and tendency to "criminalize" citizens who failed to register their arms.[43]

Ottawa held meetings with provincial attorneys general in 1975 to gauge the level of provincial support for stronger gun laws. It also sought to determine the number of firearms in Canada so that legislators and bureaucrats could better estimate the potential cost and administrative complexities of implementing new legislation. The existing weapons registry provided Ottawa with the number of pistols and other registered weapons in circulation. But the federal government, according to the Research Branch of the Library of Parliament, had "no way of establishing how many firearms there are in the country."[44] The Firearms Registration Section of the RCMP estimated in 1975 that Canadians possessed 8,919,312 rifles and shotguns, although it concluded that this figure was "probably conservative."[45] In August 1976 Statistics Canada estimated that almost 2.5 million Canadians owned guns, a majority of whom reported themselves as active shooters – roughly 1,527,000 used a gun in the previous twelve months. The survey also suggested that private citizens possessed 5,303,000 firearms, but Statistics Canada noted that "a precise count or estimate of the *total number of firearms* in Canada is virtually impossible." The number of all guns could be as high as ten million, and probably ranged between seven and eight million. The considerable inaccuracy of these estimates posed problems for the federal government, which needed good figures to determine the cost of regulating weapons more closely.[46]

Despite such uncertainty, the federal government included new gun provisions in a 1976 omnibus criminal-law amendment bill (Bill C-83) known as the "peace and security" package. Ottawa proposed increased penalties for unlawful weapons use. The bill also included provisions requiring more careful weapon storage and an ambitious licensing system for gun owners (although not a system of registering firearms). Friedland had suggested that people be required to get a licence only if they planned to use or purchase a gun. The government, however, proposed forcing *all* gun owners to get a licence, even if they owned, but did not use, a firearm. This licensing proposal became controversial, but Cabinet initially seemed unaware that it might draw the ire of gun owners. Other provisions also caused controversy. For example, Ottawa proposed requiring each licence applicant to find two suitable guarantors to attest to the applicant's suitability. Also, the bill permitted officials to refuse licences to individuals deemed unstable or potentially dangerous.[47]

Minister of Justice Basford attempted, unsuccessfully, to head off potential criticisms, emphasizing that rising levels of crime necessitated the bill and suggesting that the government sought to avoid "undue interference with legitimate ownership and use of common firearms."[48] The Liberals seemed well placed to pass Bill C-83. The party had won a majority in 1974, and public opinion polls indicated that a majority of Canadians supported stiffer firearm controls. As well, many prominent newspapers supported the bill, while Canada's leading police organization, the Canadian Association of Chiefs of Police, approved of most aspects of the proposed legislation. But despite such support, the Liberals faced substantial parliamentary opposition. Rural New Democratic Party MPs criticized the new gun control, and the party as a whole opposed other aspects of the omnibus bill, including changes to the government's ability to wiretap telephones.[49] The Progressive Conservatives expressed even more hostility. Former prime minister John

Diefenbaker called the licensing scheme a "preposterous bureaucratic plan which cannot work."[50] But opposition parties in a majority government cannot stop government action. The concerted efforts of gun owners, however, would prevent the passage of Bill C-83.

The Canadian "Gun Lobby"

Firearm owners organized themselves to resist Bill C-83. Hunters, target shooters, and firearm collectors together formed a large and powerful political constituency, and passing gun regulations thus proved difficult. Analysing the opposition to gun control provides an opportunity to contribute to the Canadian literature on social movements, in particular how organizations representing white, working-class, and middle-class men employed legal arguments. Most scholars of post–Second World War Canadian social movements focus on highly educated "progressive" groups, such as the Canadian Civil Liberties Association. Few studies have focused on how "conservative" groups used the language of rights to resist government regulation.[51]

Not only white men opposed the Liberal gun legislation. Aboriginal and Metis organizations also voiced displeasure, including the National Indian Brotherhood. The Native Council of Canada (representing approximately 750,000 non-status Indians and Metis) threatened to tell its members to disregard Bill C-83 and sought to have the government exempt its membership from the legislation. The Council for Yukon Indians also expressed its dismay, for it believed that Bill C-83 would end Native Peoples' traditional lifestyle and interfere with their right to hunt.[52] Native groups would remain opposed to new gun controls. In 1977, the National Indian Brotherhood expressed opposition to proposed federal gun-control legislation on several grounds. "Firearms were a well-established means of hunting at the time the treaties were signed," suggested the Brotherhood, and thus to "take those means away today is to restrict the main means of hunting and is tantamount to removing the right to hunt." The Brotherhood also believed that limitations on gun use by young people would prevent the transfer of hunting skills between generations. As well, it suggested that federal gun control failed to recognize communal ideas of ownership. The Brotherhood provided an example in which several adults living in the same house assumed that all household goods were "more or less available to all of them, with some qualification for need, seniority or other factors which they have worked out within their own customs." How would local law-enforcement officials, wondered the Brotherhood, determine to whom a gun belonged?[53]

Non-Native westerners became leading opponents of Bill C-83. The western provinces had some of the highest rates of per capita gun ownership in Canada. According to a Statistics Canada study, only 11.5 per cent of Quebec residents owned a firearm, while 22 per cent of those living on the prairies had a gun. The national average was 302 guns per thousand Canadians fifteen years of age and older, while Prairie residents possessed 490 firearms per thousand people, with the Atlantic region (410) not far behind. British Columbia also reported gun ownership above the national average (373), while Ontario (257) and Quebec (190) had the lowest levels.[54] The lower levels of firearm ownership in "central" Canada fed fears in the west that the wishes of Ontario and Quebec would shape firearm policies. Bob Scammell, chair of the legislation committee of the Alberta Fish & Game Association, expressed westerners' unease with legislation emanating from Ottawa: "We in the west are quite convinced that made-in-the-east firearms legislation has very little application to conditions as they exist in other parts of the country."[55] Feelings of western alienation ran high in the 1970s, and Prime Minister Trudeau struggled to gain western Canadian support, in part because westerners perceived him as a member of the eastern elite. Gun control became another issue stoking the disconnect between eastern and western interests.

No single organization represented all gun owners. The most important groups fell into three categories: hunters' associations, shooting clubs, and collectors' organizations. Hunters expressed interest in protecting the use of hunting rifles and shotguns. There were numerous such groups in Canada, most prominently the Canadian Wildlife Federation (CWF) – an umbrella organization for its provincial affiliates. Shooters' organizations, such as the Dominion of Canada Rifle Association and the Shooting Federation of Canada, focused on protecting access to handguns as well as long guns. Collectors often accumulated long guns and handguns, as well as vintage and automatic weapons. Organizations representing collectors included the Canadian Black Powder Association, the Lower Canada Arms Collectors' Association, and the Canadian Guild of Antique Arms Collectors.

Firearm owners had difficulty speaking with one voice. The interests of hunting, collecting, and shooting groups often diverged. Owners of handguns and automatic weapons, for instance, often suspected that hunters' organizations, such as the CWF, would defend only the use of hunting rifles. The modest size of the Canadian gun-manufacturing industry made forming a unified Canadian gun lobby difficult. In the United States, major firearm makers contributed heavily to the NRA. Some Canadian companies occasionally lobbied politicians to shape or limit new gun controls. In addition, in 1973 a new group formed to speak for firearm and ammunition manufacturers: the Canadian Sporting Arms & Ammunition Association, which consisted mostly of Canadian subsidiaries of American companies such as Remington and Winchester. The association claimed that Canada's arms-manufacturing industry directly employed 1500 people, mostly in Quebec and Ontario, and as many as 25,000 more in retail sales and arms repair. It estimated the annual value of the retail sales at $77 million for sporting arms, ammunition, gun accessories, and repairs.[56] These figures, while impressive, proved too small to sway most political figures. The Canadian arms industry thus possessed a smaller voice in the debate over gun control than its American counterpart.

The lack of a national organization representing all Canadian gun owners led to efforts to create one. In 1972, Firearms and Responsible Ownership (FARO) formed in Alberta. FARO resulted from the efforts of one man, Bill Jones, whom *Maclean's* described as a "brash, outspoken man" with a personal arsenal of forty weapons.[57] Jones hoped to lead a national organization, but the group grew slowly. It had approximately 270 members in 1972 and constantly appealed for funds. Jones spent his own money on FARO, slowly selling off pieces of his farm when donations and membership fees proved insufficient to continue the fight against firearm legislation. By 1976 FARO claimed 20,000 members through individual memberships and affiliated gun clubs. Although relatively small, FARO always punched bigger than its weight. FARO met with MPs to advocate against new legislation, and gave testimony before parliamentary committees.[58] The *Globe and Mail* thus called FARO "one of the most active and vocal pro-gun lobbies in the country."[59] Because Albertans became some of the fiercest opponents of firearm regulation, the province hosted other, less successful advocacy groups, such as Responsible Alberta Gun Owners (RAGO).[60]

Some of the older, more established organizations mistrusted radical upstarts like FARO. Despite this uneasiness, the belief that law makers intended to target gun ownership led the CWF, the Shooting Federation of Canada, and FARO to form an important, if short-lived, umbrella organization, which called itself the Canadian Association for

Sensible Arms Legislation (CASAL) to demonstrate to the public that it opposed only intrusive government interventions. Of course, critics said the name belied the group's true intent. The *Ottawa Citizen* called the moniker a misnomer, while the *Globe and Mail* suggested that "MPs will do us all a great service if they pay only as much heed to CASAL as its arguments deserve: None."[61] The founding groups nevertheless hoped CASAL could help stop Bill C-83 and, if necessary, assist governments in preparing more palatable firearm legislation. Other organizations received invitations to participate, including the Dominion of Canada Rifle Association, the Canadian Trappers Federation, the Canadian Guild of Antique Arms Collectors, and RAGO.[62] The decision to join forces surprised gun owners accustomed to disunity. *Canadian Handgun* thus called CASAL's establishment "the most momentous occurrence in the history of the shooting sports."[63]

A former police officer, Leonard Nicholson, became a potent spokesman for CASAL. Nicholson enlisted in the RCMP in 1923. After briefly serving in both the New Brunswick and Nova Scotia provincial police forces, he returned to the RCMP in 1931, eventually serving as RCMP commissioner from 1951 to 1959. Nicholson consistently opposed new gun controls in the 1970s. He often spoke for the CWF while serving as a CWF director and the chair of its Firearms Legislation Committee. Described in the *Ottawa Citizen* as "one of the best law enforcement officers the world has ever known,"[64] Nicholson studied gun legislation closely and produced an influential CWF policy paper frequently referenced positively by gun-control opponents. As a well-respected former police officer, Nicholson's presence proved vital to the gun lobby. He legitimated opposition to firearm regulation.[65]

The groups making up CASAL tried to suppress their differences. A consistent tension resulted from some organizations' view that governments should never ban any class of weapons, because prohibiting, for example, automatic firearms would establish a precedent allowing the government to outlaw other kinds of guns, such as semi-automatics and pistols. CASAL initially smoothed over differences, agreeing to several recommendations in an effort to portray itself as a thoughtful and responsible body. CASAL recommended requiring gun owners to carry documentation proving their qualifications to use a firearm off their property but suggested easily obtained documents would suffice, such as a hunting, trapping, or guide licence, a provincial gun-carrying certificate, evidence that the bearer had passed a firearms safety course, or proof of membership in an approved shooting or collectors' club.

CASAL also advocated making criminal records available to check the backgrounds of safety course applicants. The organization further urged stiffer penalties for criminals who used an offensive weapon. CASAL thus suggested gun control that left average firearm owners largely alone but imposed harsher sentences for criminals.[66]

Gun groups employed a variety of methods to stop new firearm legislation. Some, such as the Canadian Sporting Arms & Ammunition Association, preferred quiet lobbying pressure. It had a full-time executive secretary in Ottawa, and its representatives met with the minister of justice and other government officials to press its case that gun control would harm Canadian industry. Most opponents of new gun legislation, however, took a more public, vocal stance. They called mass meetings, sent delegations, took out advertisements, and circulated petitions. Various groups also organized letter-writing campaigns to Parliament. To amplify the effect of these letters, associations gave advice to working-class gun owners, urging them to avoid sounding unreasonable or threatening. The British Columbia Federation of Shooting Sports, for example, told its members to use "*your own words and phrases*," and to be "*polite and brief.*" The Ontario Arms Collectors' Association similarly requested that members contact their MP, but intoned "BE POLITE."[67] Gun owners responded to letter-writing appeals by sending a massive amount of correspondence to the offices of parliamentarians and to local and national news outlets. Canadians fiercely debated the abolition of capital punishment in 1976, yet the number of gun-control letters sent to Parliament swamped the death-penalty correspondence.[68] Progressive Conservative MP Lloyd Crouse of Nova Scotia claimed he received more mail regarding Bill C-83 than any other issue in his almost nineteen years as an MP. The reaction to the bill was "almost violent," he reported.[69]

Opponents of gun control recognized that only political pressure could prevent government action. Organizations thus contacted MPs to threaten electoral defeat. The Dominion of Canada Rifle Association, for example, asked its members to tell every MP that if he or she supported Bill C-83 then "you will work towards his defeat in the next federal election, as well as at the riding level."[70] Groups claimed to represent millions of gun owners to emphasize their political clout. To make this pressure as effective as possible, the CWF spearheaded an effort to identify the positions taken by members of Parliament on gun control. The CWF shared this information with other organizations, many of which encouraged gun owners to join political riding associations to vote against candidates supporting regulation. For instance, FARO encouraged its members to do this: "JOIN THE POLITICAL PARTY OF YOUR CHOICE – AT THE RIDING LEVEL!!! JOIN NOW!!! IT IS IMPERATIVE THAT YOU ACT *BEFORE* WE LOSE THE POTEN-TIAL!!!" "REMEMBER," FARO told its members, "a person cannot get elected if he cannot get nominated."[71]

Nicholson, Jones, and other gun-group representatives voiced their opposition in every available public forum. They appeared on radio and television programs and prepared opinion pieces for newspapers. Leading gun-control opponents also spoke frequently at public meetings, which generated considerable local press coverage.[72] Liberal MPs sometimes attended these meetings to defend the government's proposals but typically received hostile receptions. For instance, the crowd at a public meeting in Scarborough booed Solicitor General Warren Allmand, and one gun owner pushed forward during a break to declare, "You're scaring us to death with this, man."[73]

Gun groups had a much bigger voice than the small and relatively ineffectual organizations supporting firearm regulation. The National Firearms Safety Association, an ad hoc organization formed in 1975, promoted gun control but it lacked a strong organizational structure. It ran its operations out of a loaned office, had no paid employees, and could not even afford a telephone. It claimed to have three thousand members, which was a modest number, given that there was only one such organization.[74]

Gun groups offered a variety of arguments to oppose Bill C-83. Most doubted that it would reduce the criminal use of firearms or stop school shootings. The BC Federation of Wildlife thus called Bill C-83 "a massive con job being perpetrated on the public to give the impression that the government is actually taking some positive action."[75] Others argued that Bill C-83 would in fact increase crime. The president of the Quebec Rifle Association claimed that if the law disarmed Canadians, then "the small but never eradicated criminal and subversive element will have an 'open hunting season.'"[76] Gun groups encouraged Ottawa to leave ordinary gun owners alone and spend more time and effort enforcing existing laws. For instance, they complained that the courts failed to give stiff sentences to criminals who used guns. Canadian firearm owners also imported slogans from the American gun-control debate. By the mid-1970s, the phrase "Guns don't kill people; people kill people" had appeared in Canada, as had another slogan: "When guns are outlawed, only outlaws will have guns."[77]

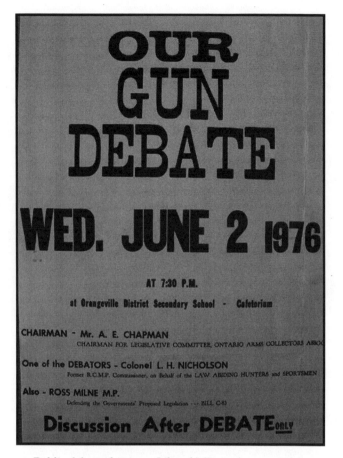

Figure 43: Public debates between Liberal MPs and gun control opponents often became heated. This poster advertises a debate between Leonard Nicholson and Liberal MP Ross Milne in Orangeville, Ontario.
Source: LAC, MG31, E54, vol. 9, file 3

Critics of firearm regulation also invoked international examples, frequently pointing to the failures of regulatory efforts in Britain, and especially the United States. Detroit, New York, Chicago, and Massachusetts served as illustrations of jurisdictions in which stiff gun laws had proved ineffective. Gun-control opponents also cited international examples, especially Switzerland and Israel, which combined high lev-

Figure 44: Gun-control opponents frequently argued that the federal
government should punish criminals more severely, rather than regulate
average gun owners. Opponents made that point clearly at this public
meeting held to oppose Trudeau's legislation in 1976. Seated left to right are
Leonard Nicholson, Bill Jones, and the owner of a local sporting goods store,
Steve Thompson.
Source: Orangeville Citizen, 9 June 1976

els of gun ownership and low levels of crime, to show that Ottawa need
not pass new legislation.[78]

Gun groups uniformly opposed a national firearm registry. Ottawa
had *not* actually proposed a registry, but opponents of firearm control
intentionally or unintentionally conflated the licensing of owners with
arms registration. Gun organizations condemned a national registration as expensive and impossible to implement. The Shooting Federation of Canada, for instance, said that gun registration would lead more
people to disregard the law; rather than register, owners would "lose"
their guns.[79]

Many gun owners worried that Bill C-83 represented the first step
towards the confiscation of all weapons. Handgun owners, aware of

the long history of state efforts to control pistols, consistently expressed this belief. *Canadian Handgun*, the voice of the Ontario Handgun Association, warned in 1968 that every gun owner should oppose gun controls. Otherwise, "you will have only yourself to blame when the police come knocking at your door to confiscate your newly-prohibited rifles and shotguns."[80] Gun owners' groups stoked the fear of confiscation in the debate in the 1970s. FARO consistently asserted that the Liberals wanted to confiscate all firearms.[81] In 1976, RAGO provided alarmist information sheets for customers of sporting goods stores: "THIS MAY WELL BE YOUR LAST ENJOYABLE HUNTING SEASON!!!!!!!" Bill C-83 was an "extremely repressive bill with open provision for future confiscation of many types of firearms and ammunition."[82] Such comments reflected gun owners' deep distrust of the Canadian political elite.

Even if the government refrained from confiscating weapons, many gun owners believed Ottawa would hassle hunters, collectors, and shooters with new regulations until they gave up their weapons. The Shooting Federation of Canada argued that the federal government used a "law and order" pretext to achieve the Liberal government's "real intent of banning guns, through extensive bureaucracy if not through direct legislation."[83] A related argument was that costly firearm licence fees would lead working-class gun owners to disarm. Excessive government regulation and fees would, in effect, dissuade gun owners from keeping weapons.[84]

Firearm organizations also often emphasized the urban-versus-rural divide in an effort to disparage gun-control advocates and to stoke the anger of gun owners. Hunting organizations before the Second World War tended to cater to middle-class and elite hunters. They had, as noted in chapter 3, sought to preserve game animals for recreational hunters, sometimes angering rural residents in the process. In comparison, organizations opposed to firearm regulation in the 1970s generally espoused working-class, rural concerns. Gun groups sought to protect firearm ownership from perceived assaults by urban, elitist politicians they believed wanted new legislation. Bert Bush of the Ontario Handgun Association thus referred to politicians who supported gun control as "pussy willies,"[85] while a director of the British Columbia Wildlife Federation took aim at the "city-boy Ron Basford and his cringing colleagues in Ottawa."[86] FARO complained that most proposed gun controls were "gut reactions by Parliamentarians to small, vocal, rather paranoid urban pressure groups."[87] Such comments suggested that gun control advocates lacked the qualities of "real" men, including patriotism, self-reliance, courage, family togetherness, a willingness to defend one's home, and good sportsmanship. Statistics Canada estimated that men comprised the vast majority of firearm owners (95 per cent) – a fact reflected in the overwhelming role that men played in the battles against legislation and the gendered language employed in the debate.[88]

Hunters, especially working-class hunters, chaffed at suggestions that more genteel pursuits could serve as appropriate outlets for men to express their masculinity, and instead asserted their respectability. The publisher of *Out of Doors* magazine, Daniel Thomey, called Canadian hunters the "honest hard-working backbone of this democracy, the people who have a solid moral sense." Thomey offered an image of hunters as rugged individuals, as "men" in juxtaposition to weak urbanites.[89] *Out of Doors* magazine offered patches declaring, "Proud to be a hunter and I will defend that right."[90] Other gun owners noted that respectable, middle-class Canadians traditionally participated in recreational hunting. A Toronto hunter thus claimed his lineage from "a long line of farmers, school teachers, preachers and other professions, most of whom to my knowledge have owned guns and who have hunted." There were "no murderers among my ancestors."[91] Such assertions reflected the desire to defend the connections between gun ownership, good citizenship, and masculinity.

Gun owners expressed anger over particular provisions in Bill C-83 that suggested Ottawa doubted their respectability. Firearm owners, for instance, complained about the bill's requirement that a licence applicant find two guarantors to sign his or her application. Critics assumed that the government would stipulate that appropriate guarantors worked in an approved list of professions, such as law, medicine, or the ministry. Gun owners perceived this a slap in the face – why should working-class hunters have to get the signatures of social "superiors" who likely knew nothing of hunting or firearms? Daniel Thomey, for example, declared there was "no way in this world that I will degrade myself by seeking a guarantee from two so-called 'better' people as to my moral character to own a firearm."[92] The enforcement provisions in Bill C-83 accentuated class antagonism. Working-class firearm owners complained that gun proposals made them feel as though they were the criminals. The federal government's concurrent effort to abolish the death penalty aggravated this perception – gun owners claimed the abolition of capital punishment reflected Ottawa's willingness to coddle criminals, while at the same time threatening law-abiding, working-class firearm owners.[93]

Hunters also felt the sting of criticisms by environmentalists and animal rights advocates in the 1970s. Bert Bush of the Ontario Handgun Association claimed, "I'm afraid to hunt deer anymore." "Everyone thinks I'm the dirty guy with the black hat who killed Bambi's mother," he explained.[94] A controversial CBS documentary entitled *Guns of Autumn* showing hunters committing atrocities against wildlife made FARO despondent, for it believed the program deliberately portrayed American hunters (and, by extension, Canadian hunters) as "callous beasts with no feelings, whose only interest in hunting is blood and gore." *Guns of Autumn* constituted part of a "joining of forces" in America "between the anti-hunting and pure anti-gun factions." "By cleverly and deceitfully portraying the American hunter as a brute," FARO continued, critics of hunting "move ever closer to their real purpose of making hunting less of a 'socially acceptable' activity."[95] FARO warned that Canadian hunters would soon face the same kind of attacks.

While Canadian firearm owners feared the influence of American environmental concerns, they pined for an opportunity to claim a right to their weapons. This led some gun groups to hope that Canada would constitutionally entrench a right to bear arms. For example, the Manitoba Association of Gun Owners called for an amendment to the 1960 Canadian *Bill of Rights* that would guarantee unhampered ownership and use of firearms by law-abiding citizens.[96] By requesting such an amendment, the Manitoba association implicitly admitted that Canadians lacked a right to possess firearms. Many gun owners' groups, however, refused to admit the absence of a right to arms in Canada.

Because Canada lacked a written constitutional guarantee to firearm possession, firearm owners attempted to claim a "right" on a variety of grounds. They seemed unaware of the limited right to arms found in the English *Bill of Rights*, instead arguing, rather vaguely, that English constitutional traditions and/or the common law ground a right to have weapons. The Firearms Legislation Committee of the British Columbia Federation of Shooting Sports, for instance, asserted boldly that the "private possession of arms has always been synonymous with freedom." The "English Common Law (from the 12th century)" guaranteed the right of men to bear arms, but Bill C-83 "would deny that *right*," and establish it as a "bureaucratic privilege."[97]

Many groups objecting to firearm regulation made their claims in traditional liberal terms – emphasizing "freedom from" government intervention. They variously argued that gun laws violated an individual's right to personal property, privacy, and equal treatment under the law. RAGO, for instance, called C-83 an "extremely repressive bill," that would "severely restrict your enjoyment of personal property and privacy."[98] Still other opponents ground a right to own guns in Canadians' historic use of arms. They believed citizens possessed a kind of "customary" right handed down from previous generations. The Ontario Federation of Anglers and Hunters made such a claim: "Unencumbered private ownership of firearms" was a "tradition deeply rooted in our Canadian heritage and is a right far too basic and elemental to risk its loss through misdirected, ill-advised and fundamentally unworkable laws."[99] Leonard Nicholson offered a similar analysis. He did not claim a right to bear arms, but he bristled when the government said Parliament granted the "privilege" to possess a weapon. "Citizens have owned and used firearms in Canada ever since the country was settled," Nicholson suggested. "Does a custom such as this, extending over hundreds of years require Parliamentary sanction and if so when was it given[?]"[100]

Casting firearm ownership as a right allowed gun groups to assert that regulation constituted a serious step towards despotism. A past president of the Shooting Federation of Canada, D.L. Aiton, suggested that history taught that the "most serious and final obstacle to a totalitarian dictator has always been the ability of a citizenry to rise to its own defense. Tyrants have had, therefore, to devise ways and means of removing all arms from their intended subjects before taking actual control. In this world today the most menacing force is that of the Communist conspiracy which actively promotes gun registration and confiscation."[101] Aiton then offered historic examples of confiscation efforts, including gun-control policies in Nazi Germany. Armed citizenry equalled a free citizenry, argued Aiton: "The Communist conspiracy or any other tyrant has never been able, or dared, to take over a single country in which people were armed."[102] Aiton's argument that gun control advocates held a communist position, while seemingly an extreme view, resonated with other firearm owners. A sporting goods store in Orangeville, Ontario, for example, handed out flyers claiming to lay out the "Communist Rules for Revolution," which included finding a pretext to register all firearms "with a view to confiscating them and leaving the population helpless."[103] A few politicians also expressed this fear. In November 1976, the Alberta Social Credit Party passed a resolution against gun control after one former MLA declared

that "Karl Marx's manifesto said one of the first objectives of any so-
cialist government is to implement gun control."[104] Several MPs also
opposed new firearm legislation because, as the MP for Parry Sound–
Muskoka reminded the Commons, "one of the first things that a communist government does when it takes over a country is to outlaw the
ownership of guns."[105] While seemingly fanciful, such beliefs spread
easily in the firearms community.

Gun owners found evidence for this fear in the growth of state regulatory activity in Canada. After the Second World War, Liberal and
Progressive Conservative governments expanded the social safety net.
The 1960s witnessed "frenetic activity in public-policy formation"[106]
leading to the creation of vast new programs, but by the late 1960s
some Canadians sensed that the federal Cabinet had lost control of the
burgeoning bureaucracy. In the 1970s, the oil crisis and inflation undermined the post-war confidence that the state could continue creating new social programs. Resentment towards taxation grew, while
attacks on "bureaucrats," "red tape," and "big government" gained
strength. The opposition to gun control reflected the shifting public
opinion about the government's role. In discussing Bill C-83, Nova
Scotia MP Elmer MacKay suggested that Canadians resented bureaucrats and feared firearm regulations would "interfere with something
they consider pretty basic, owning a gun."[107] Another Progressive
Conservative MP, Don Mazankowski, representing Vegreville, Alberta, saw gun control as just another way for government to expand
its role at the expense of individual liberty: "We have had a wage and
price control program which started out to be selective and has now
become universal, with the threat of becoming permanent. We have
seen a move away from the free market economy. We have more and
more government intervention, more regimentation, more inspectors
and more statistics. We have growing confrontation between business
and government, government and labour, and we have an increasing
tendency towards individual Canadians becoming numbers rather
than individuals. We have more licences, more permits, more bureaucracy, and more cost."[108]

Gun groups also claimed that firearm laws unnecessarily interfered
in the lives with average citizens. The Firearms Legislation Committee
of the BC Federation of Shooting Sports asserted that Bill C-83 constituted just part of the Liberal government's broader agenda to rapidly
increase its "control of many facets of everyday life," such as "control
of the media, wage and price controls, unlimited wiretapping, search

and seizure without warrant, and the open ended procedure by order in council." These developments "very strongly suggest the concept of a totalitarian state."[109] Such arguments reflected the blowback from decades of an expanding welfare state. While the activist Liberal government sought to improve people's lives, critics argued that regulation (including gun control) interfered with working-class people's liberty.

The government's proposal to use Orders in Council to fill out the skeletal legislative framework of Bill C-83 also caused alarm. Gun-control opponents called this undemocratic and suggested it made abiding by the law difficult. The British Columbia Federation of Shooting Sports claimed it was "purely law by decree and the law abiding citizen could be deemed a criminal overnight simply through not being aware of what changes and/or new regulations had been made."[110] The British Columbia Wildlife Federation offered a similar argument: "We are concerned that these powers are the beginning of the removal of Government from the control of Parliament."[111] The federal government's willingness to flesh out gun controls with regulations and Orders in Council therefore magnified the perceived threat to individual liberty.

Gun owners thus offered sustained and emotional resistance to Bill C-83. The intense feelings expressed often struck observers as overwrought. Proponents of new firearm laws made analogies between automobile licences and firearm licences and wondered why the latter proved so contentious. For many gun owners, the answer was obvious. White, rural, working-class men felt increasingly disempowered in Canadian society. Gun control became a focal point for all this group deemed awry in society: government bureaucracy, high taxes, social policy shaped by eastern elites, and less emphasis on values such as individual responsibility.

The Government's Response

The lobbying efforts and arguments of firearm owners proved extremely effective, and politicians advocating gun control expressed surprise at the forcefulness of the opposition. The Liberals responded by limiting the length of the parliamentary debate on Bill C-83 – a move that gun groups deemed further proof of the Trudeau government's tyranny. The Liberals also introduced amendments meant to placate firearm owners, such as lowering the age at which a minor could acquire a licence and providing free permits for people living in designated areas who hunted or trapped to support their family. These minor amendments did not quell the opposition, however, and when Parliament adjourned for the summer in 1976 the Liberals shelved Bill C-83 before third reading. When the House of Common reconvened in the fall, the government ended the parliamentary session adjourned for the summer. This meant that Bill C-83 died on the order paper. The bill had proven too divisive for the Liberal Party, which was bleeding popular support. In September 1976, a Gallup poll placed Liberal electoral support at only 29 per cent. Following the Bill C-83 debacle, Trudeau replaced Warren Allmand as solicitor general with Francis Fox.[112]

Despite receiving a bloody nose, the Liberal Party, or at least a contingent of the party, remained interested in pursuing stronger gun controls. As if on cue, a new shooting incident stiffened the backbone of Liberal Party members who desired new measures. In September 1976, the Clarke Institute for Psychiatry in Toronto discharged Ernest Lamourandire. He promptly purchased a rifle, climbed to the top of a building, and shot at strangers on the streets below. He injured five people before turning the weapon on himself. "Cash and carry and kill," lamented the *Globe and Mail* after the incident, which, the paper declared, proved the need for tough new firearm measures. The shooting should "silence all opponents of gun control," it wrote hopefully, if incorrectly.[113]

The ferocity of the opposition to Bill C-83 led the Liberals to debate whether to make a second attempt at passing new gun controls. With the Liberal caucus divided, Justice Minister Basford had to argue in Cabinet for the wisdom of pursuing new measures. The government ultimately decided to strike an informal committee of Liberal MPs from eastern and western Canada and from urban and rural areas to produce an amended bill that could satisfy the caucus.[114] The result was a watered-down bill, C-51, that the government could pass with less resistance. As historians Tom Traves and John Saywell conclude, Bill C-51 was "obviously a compromise designed to win approval from the anti-regulation lobby."[115] Justice Minister Basford said as much in the Commons, assuring Parliament that the government had consulted more broadly than it had in drafting Bill C-83. Responding to the major complaints voiced in 1976, Basford promised that the new bill involved "the least possible interference in the lives of responsible Canadians." The government sought to zero in on "those gun owners or would-be owners who might be dangerous to themselves or others if they have access to a firearm."[116]

The new bill contained some of the same provisions as Bill C-83. The government again proposed stiffer sentences for the criminal use of guns, tighter regulations of firearm businesses and dealers, expanded powers for police to seize arms, and penalties for careless storage and use of weapons. Bill C-51, however, contained very different provisions for screening present and new gun owners. The government had proposed in Bill C-83 to set up a licensing system to screen all gun owners, requiring even long-time hunters to obtain a licence, but with Bill C-51, Ottawa planned to require new gun owners only to acquire a Firearms Acquisition Certificate. A certificate, valid for five years, allowed for the purchase of an unlimited number of rifles and shotguns, and the government would not force purchasers to state a reason for applying for a certificate. Also, Ottawa dropped the requirement that applicants find guarantors to support their application.[117] The Liberals thus designed Bill C-51 to avoid angering existing gun owners while targeting the criminal use of arms.

In an effort to defuse opposition, the government also met with gun owners' groups. Minister of Justice Basford sat down with CASAL representatives, and even Prime Minister Trudeau met with the Canadian Wildlife Federation. The government incorporated some of their suggestions. Minister of Justice Basford, for instance, acknowledged that the government removed the requirement for guarantors because of gun owners' opposition. Basford spent considerable time convincing gun owners to ease their opposition. He gave interviews to journals read by firearm owners and delivered speeches to groups that had opposed Bill C-83. Basford consistently tried to emphasize points of agreement and to clear up popular misconceptions, such as that the government wanted to register all weapons. He also took the Liberal Party's message onto the airwaves, speaking on various television programs. Most of the mainstream gun owners' groups eventually concluded that their efforts had made the proposed federal legislation palatable, if not perfect, and thus requested the government amend rather than abandon the bill.[118]

Not all gun groups took such a constructive position, however. Radicals remained incensed. A federal Order in Council issued in March 1977 that placed the AR-15 rifle on the restricted list of firearms helped spur new resistance. The semi-automatic AR-15 was a civilian variant of the standard issue American Army rifle. Gun owners complained that the Order in Council failed to distinguish between the automatic military version and the semi-automatic civilian model and suggested

Figure 45: To appease gun owners, Prime Minister Trudeau (third from left) and Minister of Justice Ron Basford (third from right) met with Canadian Wildlife Federation representatives.

Source: Robert Lewis, "The Hidden Persuaders," *Maclean's*, 13 June 1977, 40b, used with permission of the Canadian Wildlife Federation

Figure 46: The sale of semi-automatic military-style weapons drew the attention of gun-control advocates. This 1976 advertisement shows several semi-automatic weapons for sale, including the AR-15 and the Ruger Mini-14, the weapon used in the 1989 Montreal Massacre.
Source: *Canada Gunsport*, 7 July 1976

that Ottawa restricted the AR-15 because of its appearance rather than its capabilities. The Order in Council also reaffirmed the belief that the Liberals acted undemocratically and might employ executive orders to disarm Canadians. Reports that only a small fraction of Orders in Council appeared in the *Canada Gazette* furthered the sense that rule by executive edict would leave gun owners in the dark about the state of gun laws.[119]

The divisions between the mainstream and radical gun owners' groups became public in June 1977 when CASAL presented a brief before the Parliamentary Justice and Legal Affairs Committee considering Bill C-51. CASAL experienced a lengthy and contentious internal debate about the association's stand on Bill C-51. Eventually, members agreed that the CASAL brief should endorse the CWF recommendations already before the committee and add a few other points that did not involve any matter of principle. At the committee hearing, however, three of the most strident opponents of proposed legislation represented CASAL: Michael Martinoff, Burt Bush, and Bill Jones. The CASAL representatives, according to Nicholson, "super-imposed their own views both as to the general tenor of the Brief and on specific points."[120] Martinoff delivered most of CASAL's testimony. Unfortunately for CASAL, several members of the committee found him unprepared, contradictory, antagonistic, and unwilling to compromise. In his introductory remarks, Martinoff chose not to summarize CASAL's position; instead, he presented his own views as those of the entire organization and expressed his personal frustration with the actions of government officials. Unlike some advocates for gun owners, Martinoff seemed unaware of the potential dangers of appearing less than respectable. He, for instance, expressed anger about the decision to make the AR-15 a restricted weapon and declared his intentions to disregard the law. MPs thus felt free to disparage the CASAL representatives. Mike Landers, a Liberal from New Brunswick, told Martinoff that he "would rather be in the woods with Elmer Fudd than with you."[121] Liberal MP Simma Holt proved especially critical. Unlike the friendly gun-club crowds to which Martinoff often spoke, Holt questioned basic claims of gun control opponents, including the belief that Canadians had a "right" to arms:

Mrs Holt: You mentioned infringement on your rights and your civil liberties of having to purchase a licence. I think you referred to the common law and all those nice principles. Can you tell me if you feel it is an infringement on your rights to have to have a licence to drive a car – which is another dangerous sort of weapon too?

Mr Martinoff: I am very glad you raised that point. I understand that all the criminals using firearms in Canada last year killed under 1,500 people, but impaired drivers killed about 4,000.

Mrs Holt: I am not asking you that. I admit that the car is a dangerous weapon in the hands of an incompetent or a drunk, and so is a gun a dangerous weapon in the hands of an incompetent or drunk. I know some pretty sleezy [*sic*] people who are not all that sane – even some in the gun clubs are not all that sane. I want to know if you think it is an infringement of a

person's rights to have to buy a licence for a car. That is not a very complicated question, is it?

Mr Martinoff: Well, if the government would introduce a requirement of an
alcohol acquisition certificate to prevent incompetence [*sic*] from drinking
before driving their cars, I think the government would then be treating
drivers and drinkers on a par with firearm owners. But I do not see any
great rush to introduce an alcohol acquisition certificate, even though impaired driving, as a social problem, is far more serious than the misuse of
firearms by criminals.

Mrs Holt: But you cannot drive a car without a licence.

Mr Martinoff: But you can buy alcohol and drive impaired without a licence to
buy alcohol.

Mrs Holt: You cannot drive a car without a licence. Is that an infringement
of your civil liberties? Do you not understand English? I am asking you a
simple question and you are evading because you have no answer.[122]

The poor CASAL presentation, according to the organization's secretary, was "nothing short of a catastrophe" that destroyed the group's
credibility.[123] The CWF disassociated itself from the CASAL brief.
Nicholson had resigned from the steering committee of CASAL prior
to CASAL's appearance before the Justice and Legal Affairs Committee
and he later rejected the idea of taking part in any further attempts to
pressure the government.[124]

The split in CASAL was important, although not determinative, to
the passage of Bill C-51. While Martin Friedland suggests that CASAL's
fracture might "have been the turning point in the debate,"[125] the legislation was already widely accepted by most gun groups, largely
because their earlier lobbying efforts had proved so effective. The legislation, after all, reflected the views of mainstream groups like the CWF.
Ron Basford confirmed the important role of the gun organizations in
shaping the eventual legislation. After Nicholson had appealed for additional amendments to Bill C-51, Basford suggested that the CWF had
no reason to complain. "You must admit, in all fairness," he told Nicholson, "that the government acceded to a number of different opinions," with the result that the legislation was "palatable to the majority
of Canadians."[126]

Implementation of Bill C-51

After the passage of Bill C-51, Ottawa launched a public relations program to ensure support and compliance. The federal government took out advertisements in major Canadian newspapers and sent brochures explaining key aspects of the new law to approximately fifteen thousand firearms businesses across Canada. The federal and provincial governments also entered financial agreements that reimbursed the provinces for the costs of administering the new law.[127]

Some problems nevertheless emerged in implementing the legislation. Ottawa never proclaimed the requirement that FAC applicants complete a firearm safety course or test, because the federal government failed to secure provincial consent. The federal government also experienced challenges when it widened the definition of restricted weapons on 1 January 1978. All semi-automatic weapons less that twenty-six inches in overall length, or with barrels less than 18.5 inches, became restricted. This made as many as 100,000 weapons restricted. The owners of these re-categorized weapons, however, proved reluctant to register. By March 1978, fewer than 1 per cent of people owning these firearms had registered. This low compliance rate led Ottawa to implement an "amnesty" program in November 1978. People with unwanted guns could hand them to authorities. Also, owners of restricted weapons could register late without penalty. In total, authorities received approximately 47,000 arms during the amnesty.[128]

While many gun owners remained apprehensive about the intentions of the federal government, Ottawa never tried to limit firearm ownership using the 1978 law. Authorities denied few FAC applications: 0.39 per cent in 1979, 0.52 per cent in 1980, and 0.60 per cent in 1981. Moreover, half of the rejected FAC applicants who launched appeals were successful. In an apparent effort to pacify opponents of gun regulation prior to the 1979 federal election, the Liberal government announced plans to create a National Advisory Council on Firearms to include representatives from all concerned constituencies, including the police, provincial and territorial firearms officers, conservation groups, competitive shooting associations, hunters' organizations, Native Peoples, the medical community, the media, and the business world. The Advisory Council would ensure that the government heard a diverse set of views before introducing new firearm regulations. Ottawa also promised to conduct a major research study to evaluate the effectiveness of the 1977 act.[129]

Efforts to placate firearm owners did not stop the work of a new organization opposed to gun control. In November 1977 representatives of several groups met in Calgary, agreeing to establish a new organi-

Figure 47: This federal firearm amnesty poster was distributed to publicize the amnesty and to inform gun owners of the classification system for firearms. *Source*: LAC, MG26, C-55, vol. 6, file 11.

zation, the National Firearms Association. Bill Jones, the driving force behind FARO, became the association's first president. Formally established in 1978, the group hoped to become a Canadian version of the NRA. Unlike many of the more established groups, the National Firearms Association sought to repeal Bill C-51. It aimed for a membership of three hundred thousand but struggled to reach this lofty goal.[130]

Conclusion

The battle over gun control from the late 1960s until the late 1970s represented an important shift in the history of Canadian firearm regulation. For the first time, Parliament considered regulating the vast majority of firearm owners in a meaningful way. While, in the past, governments had regulated the use of arms by minority groups such as Irish immigrants, Aboriginal Peoples, or alleged Bolsheviks, Ottawa designed bills in the 1970s to shape how working-class white men used "average" guns. To a great extent, this explains the ferocity of the resistance. The fights in the 1970s also established the parameters of future, highly polarized gun control debates. Rural Canadians disparaged urban Canadians. Working-class gun owners complained about white-collar elites, and proponents of smaller government criticized advocates of greater state regulation.

The 1970s gun-control debate scarred the Liberal Party. In January 1978, Ron Basford announced that he would not run in the next federal election – a decision, gun groups suggested, forced upon him by the large number of firearm owners who had joined his riding association.[131] In the 1979 federal election, the Liberals suffered defeat for the first time since 1963. The Progressive Conservative Party, led by a westerner, Joe Clark, took the reins of power, but could secure only a minority government. Western Canadians rejected the Liberals en masse because of a range of Liberal policy positions, including its gun control program. The Liberals went from thirteen seats to just three in the four western provinces. Many firearm owners celebrated the defeat of Trudeau and the Liberal Party, and claimed some responsibility for the result. The National Firearms Association, for instance, asserted the instrumental role of gun owners in forcing long-time advocates of firearm controls, such as Basford and NDP MP Stuart Leggatt, to retire from federal politics before the election. Rather ironically, the association also took credit for the defeat of Liberal MP Otto Lang, who had opposed new weapons laws but apparently belonged to the wrong party. National Firearms Association president Bill Jones made sure to point out that Clark's government "owes a debt to thousands of gun owners across Canada" and indicated that "the NFA intends to call in those debts."[132] The Progressive Conservatives, however, controlled

Parliament for less than nine months and made few amendments to Canada's firearm laws.[133] Gun owners nevertheless remained hopeful that the Progressive Conservative Party would eventually rescind the 1977 law. They would ultimately be disappointed, and many would, in time, shift their allegiance to a radical conservative party more willing to fight for the "rights" of gun owners.

6

Flexing the Liberal State's Muscles: The Montreal Massacre and the 1995 *Firearms Act*, 1980–2006

The polarizing debates over firearm regulation in the 1970s dissuaded all major political parties from pursuing gun controls during the 1980s. It would take a momentous event to stir the political will to pursue new measures. Canada's most infamous mass-shooting – the 1989 murder of fourteen female students at the École Polytechnique in Montreal – provided the necessary impetus. The political response to the "Montreal Massacre" culminated in the passage of the 1995 *Firearms Act*, which, among other measures, created a registry of all firearms.

When Canadians renewed their debate over firearms, gun groups again stood opposed. They employed the successful tactics and arguments of the 1970s, claiming, for example, that regulations violated individual liberty. The Liberal Party nevertheless passed the ambitious *Firearms Act* because of important contextual differences between the 1970s and 1990s. First, women and women's groups emerged as leading advocates of stronger gun laws in the 1990s. Women helped organize support for firearm laws, confronted the association between guns and masculinity, and argued forcefully that hunting arms posed special dangers to women. Second, the 1993 federal election smashed the traditional party system, empowering the Liberal Party to pursue new firearm legislation. During the 1980s, the three national political parties avoided tackling gun control to avoid fracturing party unity. Leaders attempted to hold together diverse caucuses that included MPs from across the country and from urban and rural ridings. The near-total destruction of the Progressive Conservative and New Democratic parties in 1993 and the concurrent rise of the regionally based and more ideo-logically homogeneous Reform and Bloc Québécois parties opened a policy window for legislative action by Liberal gun-control proponents. Finally, the growing confidence of the state to implement regulatory programs allowed for the passage of new firearm laws. In the 1970s, Ottawa had dismissed calls for a national long-gun registry as too expensive and difficult to enforce, but political leaders and bureaucrats in the 1990s believed the state finally possessed sufficient power to impose such a program.

The federal government, however, proved over-confident. Gun owners' fierce resistance, technological challenges, lack of provincial support, and bureaucratic foul-ups made the long-gun registry expensive and unpopular. The courts supported Ottawa's claim that it possessed jurisdiction to pass the *Firearms Act*, but public opinion for the government's policy withered. Critics redefined firearm regulation as a problem of public waste and mismanagement, rather than as a public safety issue. Despite a decrease in the 1990s in the percentage of citizens who hunted and owned firearms, and a decline in the misuse of arms, fewer and fewer Canadians supported the long-gun registry, placing its future in serious doubt.

Gun Control in the 1980s

Canadian political leaders happily abandoned the gun-control issue during the 1980s. Pierre Trudeau's Liberal Party expressed little interest in pursuing new measures after winning another majority government in 1980. The 1976 and 1977 bills had divided the party, opening up cleavages between rural and urban MPs and representatives from eastern and western Canada. The Liberals instead seemed content to commission reports concluding that Bill C-51 had modestly improved public safety, and to produce materials, including a National Film Board production, designed to encourage firearm safety.[1] The potential political dangers of gun control also discouraged the other national parties. The Progressive Conservative Party and the New Democratic Party, like the Liberals, had rural and urban members in Parliament, and, in the case of the Progressive Conservatives, MPs from all regions of the country. A new debate over firearms risked stressing the cohesiveness of these diverse caucuses.

The gun-control issue, however, did not disappear completely. The media frequently reported on the high rate of gun crime in the United

"...*Cross yer heart an' hope to die, you ain't gonna use this on no presidents or people...*"

Figure 48: As they had for decades, many Canadians in the 1980s expressed disbelief that the United States refused to implement stronger gun controls. This *Winnipeg Free Press* cartoon appeared soon after the attempted assassination of President Ronald Reagan.
Source: *Winnipeg Free Press*, 1 April 1981, used with permission of the *Winnipeg Free Press*.

States and the unwillingness of Congress and President Ronald Reagan (even after he survived an assassin's bullet) to enact stronger firearm regulations.[2] This coverage emphasized the perceived differences between Canadian and American gun culture and regulation, and motivated appeals for new laws to cement these distinctions. Newspapers occasionally ran columns or editorials calling for greater gun control. The Canadian Association of Chiefs of Police also voted unanimously in 1986 to ask Ottawa to stop the growth in privately owned firearms, expressing particular concern with restricted weapons, the number of which grew steadily, from 750,000 in 1980 to 980,986 in 1990.[3]

Several members of Parliament also introduced private member's bills to either strengthen or weaken the legislation passed in the 1970s. The competing goals of proposals often demonstrated the internal fractures over gun control within the major political parties. NDP MP and lawyer Svend Robinson advocated stronger gun laws: he proposed requiring the acquisition of a certificate to purchase any firearm, the registration of all arms, and the imposition of a "cooling off" period for weapon purchases. Another proposal, by MP Jim Fulton, evidenced the disunity of the NDP caucus. Fulton sought to weaken regulations: he called on the government to eliminate the FAC requirement established by Bill C-51 for rural and northern residents. Robinson represented a suburban Vancouver riding (Burnaby), while Fulton served as MP for Skeena, a largely rural riding in northern British Columbia. Progressive Conservative MPs also offered divergent proposals. Progressive Conservative MP Blaine Thacker, a lawyer representing the Alberta riding of Lethbridge-Foothills, proposed eliminating the FAC procedure and replacing it with a firearms-proficiency test administered by hunting associations and shooting clubs. Thacker thus sought to ensure that potential gun owners knew how to handle arms, but to dispense with the screening process used to identify individuals unsuited to owning weapons.[4] On the other hand, Alan Redway, a Progressive Conservative Toronto MP and lawyer, asked for tougher gun controls, arguing that the public's right to protection "overrides the rights of the hunters, target shooters, gun collectors and professionals."[5] Tensions even appeared in the Liberal Party. Former solicitor general Warren Allmand introduced bills that would require all gun owners to acquire a Firearms Acquisition Certificate. Some of these bills thus indicated some interest in passing new legislation, but with their divided caucuses, party leaders expressed satisfaction with the status quo.[6]

Although political party leaders expressed little desire to reignite the gun-control debate, firearm owners continued to fear greater state regulation. Gun groups complained about the bills introduced by backbench MPs and criticized Ottawa whenever new Orders in Council reclassified additional weapons as restricted.[7] Just the suggestion of new firearm legislation allowed Trudeau's opponents to stoke fears of government oppression. For instance, Progressive Conservative MP William Vankoughnet from Ontario, in discussing possible gun controls, claimed that Trudeau had "relished the taste of repression" when his government employed the *War Measures Act* in 1970, and he had "been trying one way or another ever since to recapture that taste."[8]

While Trudeau avoided the issue during the 1980s, the Progressive Conservative government of Brian Mulroney that came to power in a 1984 election landslide considered some modest proposals. Public opinion polls showed broad support for stronger gun laws. As well, the murder of three people in 1984 at the Quebec National Assembly by a man armed with a stolen automatic weapon demonstrated the danger of military-style arms. Police groups continued to press for stronger gun laws, in particular for limiting access to automatic weapons converted to semi-automatics. Law enforcement worried that criminals could again make such guns fire as automatics. Mulroney's government responded by announcing plans in 1989 to ban the importation of fully automatic weapons converted to fire only as semi-automatics.[9] Events in Montreal later in 1989, however, intervened before Ottawa acted.

The Montreal Massacre

The lull in the debate over gun control ended in late 1989. On 6 December 1989, twenty-five-year-old Marc Lépine entered the École Polytechnique, an engineering school affiliated with the University of Montreal, and systematically shot twenty-eight people before killing himself. He carried a legally obtained, American-made semi-automatic, a Ruger Mini-14. Lépine first entered a classroom and divided male and female students. He declared, "I am fighting feminism" and proceeded to shoot all nine women in the classroom, killing six. He then travelled through the school, shooting people he came across in corridors, the cafeteria, and in another classroom. By the end of his rampage, Lépine had killed fourteen women and injured ten other women and four men. The entire incident lasted no more than twenty minutes. His suicide note made his motivations clear – he blamed feminists for ruining his life.[10]

While Canada had experienced other mass murders, the Montreal Massacre dwarfed them in scope, symbolic importance, and publicity. Lépine's motivation multiplied the horror of the event. The murders dominated the national media over the ensuing week. Quebec's National Assembly declared a three-day period of mourning, and in Montreal a candle-light vigil for the victims attracted five thousand people. The shooting also led to annual commemorations across Canada at which people both remember the lives lost and appeal for action to stop violence against women.[11]

The murders in Montreal led almost immediately to calls for stricter gun control. Opposition MPs urged the Progressive Conservative government to act, and Warren Allmand introduced another bill in Parliament.[12] Opinion polls suggested that calls for new controls found a receptive electorate. An Angus Reid poll conducted in December 1989 indicated that 72 per cent of Canadians wanted to make it more difficult for people to purchase deadly weapons. A 1991 Gallup poll reported that 79 per cent supported stricter gun controls, 17 per cent wanted the existing laws retained, and just 2 per cent desired less restrictive regulations. Media outlets discussed gun-control issues at length and often called for legislative action. The *Globe and Mail* pleaded for a complete ban on automatic and semi-automatic weapons, except for those required by the police.[13] "No one can properly claim that Marc Lepine would still have murdered every one of those young women," concluded a writer on the editorial page of the *Winnipeg Free Press*, "if he had been unable to get his hands on a weapon specifically designed for multiple killing."[14] A report that the store clerk who sold Lépine his rifle thought Lépine "didn't appear any crazier than anybody else" encouraged the sense that Canadian law made guns too accessible.[15] Parliament also received numerous petitions demanding stricter gun control. Students at the École Polytechnique circulated a petition calling for a ban on the private ownership of semi-automatic guns. It eventually garnered half a million signatures.[16]

The Montreal Massacre significantly altered the nature of the Canadian gun-control debate. For the first time, advocates of stronger regulations created a powerful advocacy group. Following the massacre, Heidi Rathjen, an École Polytechnique student, and Wendy Cukier, a Ryerson business professor, formed Canadians for Gun Control. This group soon merged with another organization to form the Coalition for Gun Control, with Cukier as president. The group became extremely prominent, and Rathjen and Cukier began to comment frequently on firearm legislation.[17] As noted in chapter 5, there had been no powerful gun-control advocacy group in the 1970s, meaning that hunting, shooting, and collectors' organizations commanded the attention of the public unopposed. The Coalition for Gun Control became a professional, well-financed group with thousands of members. By 1994, it had a $200,000 budget and used the practices of a professional lobby group, such as meetings with parliamentarians, giving testimony before government committees, organizing letter-writing campaigns, issuing press releases, and appearing on radio and television news programs. Its calls for more stringent gun control eventually received the support of organizations that included the Canadian Association of Chiefs

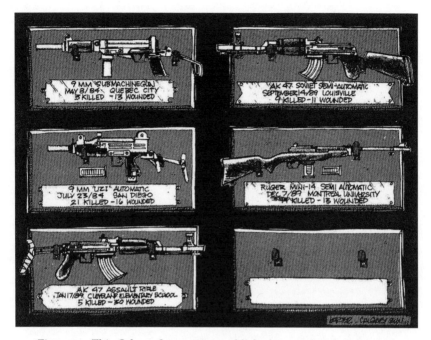

Figure 49: This *Calgary Sun* cartoon published soon after the Montreal
Massacre catalogues the use of automatic and semi-automatic weapons in
various murders and leaves a space for the next atrocity.
Source: *Calgary Sun*, 10 December 1989, used with permission of Sun Media
Corporation

of Police, the Canadian Police Association, the Canada Safety Council,
the Canadian Association of Emergency Physicians, the Trauma Association of Canada, the United Church of Canada, the Canadian Bar
Association, and the Federation of Canadian Municipalities. By early
1995, the coalition claimed the endorsement of 320 organizations for its
gun-control position.[18]

The prominent roles played by Cukier and Rathjen reflected the vital
place of women in the 1990s gun-control debate. Other women also
called for stricter firearm regulations, including Suzanne Laplante-
Edward, the mother of one of the victims in Montreal, and Priscilla de
Villiers, who advocated for stronger gun control after a man armed with
a legally owned rifle murdered her daughter in 1991. Female MPs from
several political parties also asserted that firearm regulation constituted

Figure 50: Women became leading proponents of new gun-control legislation after the Montreal Massacre. Here, Priscilla de Villiers and Wendy Cukier join other gun-control proponents on Parliament Hill.
Source: Fred Chartrand, Canadian Press

an important women's issue. In addition, several women's groups lent their support to the cause, including the Canadian Advisory Council on the Status of Women. Advocates of gun control pointed to the many female victims of gun murders – 806 women died in homicides involving firearms between 1980 and 1993.[19] Women challenged the cultural link between masculinity and firearms. Quebec Progressive Conservative MP Pierrette Venne blasted her male colleagues for refusing to regulate "phallic symbols."[20] The Canadian Advisory Council of the Status of Women criticized the notion that "guns are a natural part of masculinity" and claimed that deference to this idea silenced women's voices in discussions of firearm regulation. The Status of Women questioned why the government consulted gun owners in how best to regulate firearms, noting that the state did not ask substance abusers for their wisdom on regulating drugs, or tobacco manufacturers about how to control cigarettes.[21] Over time, other women's organizations – including the YWCA, the Canadian Federation of University Women, and the Alberta Council of Women's Shelters – expressed support for new gun laws in the hope that strong firearm regulation would help prevent violence against women.

Some gun owners chafed at the role women took in the debate over firearm laws in the 1990s. A huge majority of gun owners in Canada continued to be men and the gendered nature of the debate often bubbled to the surface.[22] Many hunters, shooters, and collectors dismissed the urban women who led the fight for stricter gun control. In the 1970s, firearm enthusiasts had often disparaged advocates of firearm regulation as effeminate city dwellers. This continued in the 1990s, but now there were actual, not just figurative, "women" to criticize. Groups representing gun owners found galling the success of women like Rathjen and Cukier in garnering public support. A researcher for the Canadian Firearms Action Council complained about the positive press Rathjen and Cukier received. "They're two women – that's it," he said. "Just two women who believe in a Utopian world in which banning all handguns will solve all crimes."[23] The executive manager of the Ontario Handgun Association took aim at the effort to make gun control a women's issue, claiming the Coalition for Gun Control had "used every trick in the book to push the issue out of the realm of reality into emotional hysteria" and was "successful in turning the whole gun control issue into a symbol of violence against women," such that "woe betide any M.P. who spoke against it."[24] The critique that the Coalition for Gun Control used fear to stoke support was ironic, given that gun groups had for years stirred the anxiety of owners with claims that Ottawa wanted to confiscate firearms. Opponents of gun regulation often refused to recognize the argument (made clear to many by the Montreal Massacre) that combining modern weapons with a masculine ideal valuing power and violence might pose special dangers to women.

Despite widespread calls for stronger gun control immediately after the Montreal Massacre, the Progressive Conservative government resisted introducing new measures. The party had ingratiated itself with firearm owners in the 1970s by opposing Trudeau's gun control bills and it hoped not to alienate this vocal part of its political base. Justice Minister Doug Lewis thus proposed only to proceed with the government's earlier promise to stop the importation of automatic weapons converted to semi-automatics. This measure, however, would not prevent the ownership of arms manufactured as semi-automatic weapons, including the Mini-14 used in Montreal, as several commentators pointed out. Liberal MP John Manley, a lawyer representing an

Figure 51: Three days after the Montreal Massacre, the *Globe and Mail*
published this cartoon, which suggested the dangers of integrating gun
ownership with popular conceptions of masculinity.
Source: Brian Gable, *Globe and Mail*, 9 December 1989

Ottawa riding, sought to keep up the pressure on the government by
introducing a private member's bill requiring a FAC for each firearm,
an increase in the age limit for acquiring a FAC, and higher FAC fees.[25]
The Montreal Massacre clearly motivated new legislation, but other developments also contributed to the government's willingness to pass
stronger gun controls, such as the confrontation at Kahnawake and
Kahnesatake in the summer of 1990 caused by the City of Oka's plan
to develop a private golf course and new housing on land used by Aboriginal Peoples. A police officer died in an exchange of gunfire with
the Mohawk resisting the development.

The Mulroney government finally acted in June 1990, when the
new federal justice minister, Kim Campbell, introduced Bill C-80. Gun
groups were primed to criticize Campbell and her proposed legislation.
As a well-educated woman representing an urban riding, Campbell
perfectly represented the gun-control advocates hated by firearm owners. She also expressed beliefs anathema to gun owners, suggesting,
for example, that the Liberals' 1978 legislation had reduced the num-

ber of deaths and injuries from firearms. The bill Campbell introduced proposed banning automatic weapons converted to semi-automatics and establishing stronger screening procedures to identify potentially unstable gun owners. In addition, the government planned to prohibit large-capacity magazines. Gun-control proponents, however, condemned these proposals as inadequate.[26]

The Progressives Conservative government nevertheless proved unable to pass even these modest proposals because of the opposition of gun owners. *Canadian Handgun* offered a response typical of many hunters, target shooters, and collectors. It referred to the bill as a "piece of garbage Ms Campbell is trying to force down our throats."[27] As they had in the 1970s, gun groups came together to fight the proposed legislation, forming Safeguard: Canadians for Responsible Gun Laws – an umbrella organization that mounted an advertising campaign against Bill C-80. Several groups opposed to new firearm regulation appeared before the parliamentary committee considering the bill, much to the consternation of some family members of Montreal Massacre victims, whom the committee did not initially invite to give evidence.[28] The opposition of gun owners forced Campbell to reassure "the legitimate gun owners of Canada" that the government did not intend "to prohibit or confiscate large numbers of commonly used firearms." But despite such assurances, the government's proposals split the Conservative caucus, with many rural MPs opposing the bill. For example, Geoff Wilson, a Progressive Conservative MP representing Swift Current, Saskatchewan, lashed out at urban Canadians because he was "tired of these nonsensical references to Montreal," and he wondered if Bill C-80 was a "Toronto-style bill."[29] On the other hand, many women and urban Progressive Conservative MPs supported Bill C-80 and even called for its strengthening. MP Pierrette Venne advocated for the legislation and criticized efforts by her fellow Progressive Conservative MPs to water down the legislation in committee. Another Conservative MP, Toronto's Barbara Greene, openly mocked a fellow member of caucus for arguing for the necessity of large-capacity magazines. With the caucus split, the government sent the bill to committee, where it died when the session of Parliament ended in late 1990.[30]

The death of Bill C-80 led gun-control advocates to condemn the Progressive Conservatives as unwilling to protect women. The Mulroney government responded with a new bill, Bill C-17, in 1991. "Gun control works," declared Justice Minister Campbell.[31] After the failure of Bill C-80, Prime Minister Mulroney enforced party discipline on Bill C-17

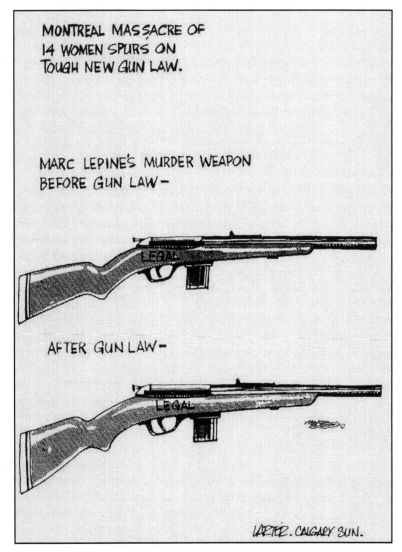

Figure 52: The failure of Prime Minister Brian Mulroney's gun-control legislation to ban the kind of weapon used in the Montreal Massacre became a common criticism. The *Calgary Sun* notes in 1990 that proposed federal legislation would not have stopped Marc Lépine from buying his weapon. *Source*: *Calgary Sun*, 28 June 1990, used with permission of Sun Media Corporation

to quiet restless rural MPs. Gun-control opponents in the Progressive Conservative caucus, however, helped shape the legislation. Rural MPs wanted assurances that the government could not prohibit models of weapons without the approval of the House of Commons. The legislation thus included a provision allowing twenty MPs or fifteen Senators to stop the prohibition of certain models of weapons or kinds of ammunition. If a sufficient number of MPs or Senators objected, all of Parliament had to vote on the regulations banning the arms or ammunition. On final reading, Bill C-17 passed in the House of Commons by a 189 to 14 margin. Many MPs, however, skipped the vote rather than be forced to support the bill.[32]

Bill C-17 altered Canada's firearm laws in several important ways. To prevent mass murders, Ottawa moved about two hundred gun models to the lists of restricted and prohibited weapons and placed limits on the size of magazines. The government designed other measures to prevent accidents, limit crimes of passion, and prevent theft. Ottawa required gun owners to store firearms and ammunition separately, keep weapons in inoperable condition, and hide and lock guns during transport. As well, the government raised the minimum age to acquire a firearm from sixteen to eighteen and imposed a twenty-eight-day waiting period for the issuing of a gun permit. Further, the legislation required a FAC applicant to provide the names of two references and complete a course or test in the safe handling and use of firearms. The government also granted firearms officers the authority to interview neighbours, social workers, spouses, and dependants before issuing a FAC. Further, the Progressive Conservatives declared a gun amnesty period, during which time Canadians in possession of illegal weapons could turn them in without penalty.[33]

These provisions displeased opponents *and* advocates of gun control. Many proponents hoped for even stronger legislation. The president of the Canadian Association of Chiefs of Police welcomed the law but noted that it "did not meet all of the concerns raised by the CACP."[34] The government's decision to include provisions placating gun groups disappointed the CACP. For example, Ottawa allowed existing owners of automatics to retain their arms through a "grandfather" clause, despite the opposition of the CACP. Critics also complained that Mulroney's government refused to ban semi-automatic weapons, such as the Mini-14 used in Montreal. On the other hand, the decision of their reputed ally, the Progressive Conservatives, to pass new firearm laws again outraged many firearm owners. Gun groups, hunting organizations, and collectors chose to fight the legislation using many of the tactics employed in the 1970s. The National Firearms Association, for example, organized a letter-writing campaign. As in the 1970s, gun groups also encouraged gun owners to join political parties, employed the language of civil liberties, and warned that Ottawa planned to confiscate whole classes of arms. The advocacy efforts of gun-control proponents and the memory of the Montreal Massacre, however, ensured the passage of the 1991 legislation.[35]

1993 Federal Election

In the 1993 federal election, the Liberals led by Jean Chrétien won 177 of 295 seats in the House of Commons, thus ending nine years of Progressive Conservative government. The 1993 election, however, was not just any election, for it witnessed important shifts in voting patterns that transformed the Canadian party system and set the stage for the passage of new gun controls. Since the Second World War, Liberals, Progressive Conservatives, and the NDP had fought national campaigns. The Liberals and Progressive Conservatives sought to form a government, while the NDP hoped to hold the balance of power in minority situations. Parties generally presented moderate policy platforms and, according to Stephen Clarkson, "operated under a general agreement about the legitimacy of the welfare state, official bilingualism, and equalization between regions."[36] In the 1993 election, however, voters fled Kim Campbell's Progressive Conservatives, which elected just two MPs, and reduced the NDP to a rump of just eight seats. Many of the Progressive Conservative and NDP candidates fell to candidates of two new parties, the western-based Reform Party and the Bloc Québécois, which ran candidates only in Quebec. The Reform Party won fifty-two seats, and the Bloc, with fifty-four MPs, became the Official Opposition.

This radical change in the party system had important ramifications for gun control. Canada's national parties traditionally offered middle-of-the-road firearm policies that appealed to urban, elite, and eastern voters, *and* avoided alienating western, rural, and working-class voters. The 1993 election, however, elevated two regional parties – the Bloc and Reform parties – that adopted gun-control positions appealing to their distinct geographic bases. The Bloc proved a consistent supporter of new gun laws because the Montreal Massacre had burnished support for firearm regulation in Quebec, and because the party's ideological orientation favoured state intervention on social policy. The Reform Party, on the other hand, strongly opposed gun control. Party members exhibited a distrust of experts and an ideological persuasion against state regulation. Reformers also critiqued "wasteful" public spending and called for the repeal or privatization of various government programs. This neoliberal ideology provided rich nectar to attract gun owners angered by the firearm policies of the Liberals and Progressive Conservatives. By the early 1990s, firearm groups increasingly saw the Reform Party, under the leadership of Preston Manning, as their only trustworthy political partner.[37] Gun owners lauded the comments of Reform MPs, such as Alberta's Deborah Grey, who declared that new firearm laws did "little in the way of protecting the average citizen" and "seriously undermines the freedom of the law abiding individual."[38] In formulating a policy on firearms, Reform struck a committee that included gun owners. The party concluded that firearm regulations penalized working people and that stiff sentences offered the real answer to gun crime. Several firearm organizations threw their support behind the Reform Party and even claimed a role in the devastation of the Progressive Conservative Party in the 1993 election.[39]

The Liberals remained the last "national" party standing, but it owed victory largely to Ontario and Quebec voters. The party thus shaped policies to please its base of support. The Liberals believed that Ontario voters would at least tolerate more intensive firearm regulation, while in Quebec, where the Liberals and Bloc vied for support, voters would embrace muscular controls. The Liberals further hoped that gun-control regulation could become an important wedge issue, driving home to moderate citizens that the Reform Party was a radical, right-wing, rural party that failed to advocate mainstream values. While gun groups spoke loudly, firearm owners represented a minority of Canadians, and the Liberals, sensing that many of these voters had wedded themselves to the Reform Party, did not fear losing their support. Liberal strategists also believed that strong measures would bolster the party's perceived "public safety" record at a time when the Reform Party sought to define itself as the party of law and order. Moreover, even if Liberal backbenchers rebelled against new gun controls, the firm support of the Bloc for firearm regulation gave the Liberals breathing room in the House of Commons.[40] Perhaps most importantly, Prime Minister Chrétien was no fan of firearms. He later admitted that he "never liked guns and have never bought one. I'm afraid of them, in fact, and don't really find much sport in killing birds or animals."[41] His opinion was vital, given the centralization of political power in the Prime Minister's Office during the Chrétien years.

The Liberals felt secure that additional gun-control measures would garner substantial public support. Firearm regulation remained a high-profile issue in Quebec, where in 1992 a Concordia mechanical engineering professor, Valery Fabrikant, killed four of his colleagues with a handgun. The incident spurred more calls for legislative action, including a petition signed by two hundred thousand pleading for the government to ban private ownership of handguns. The killing of twenty-three-year-old Georgina Leimonis at an upscale Toronto café in 1994 by a man armed with a sawed-off shotgun also resulted in gun-control appeals. Ontario Premier Bob Rae then demanded a handgun ban following the death of a Toronto police officer. Public opinion polls continued to show support for new firearm controls. A 1994 Gallup poll indicated that 83 per cent of Canadians favoured the registration of all guns, and a Gallup poll asking the same question found a smaller percentage, but still a majority (64 per cent) in favour in 1995. Even Alberta voters, according to a poll conducted for the provincial government, supported tougher gun laws. A concern with firearms smuggled from the United States also motivated gun control, especially in Quebec and Ontario. In addition, proponents of stronger gun controls noted that *even* the United States had passed new measures. In 1993, President Bill Clinton signed into law the Brady Bill, which required background checks on individuals wanting to purchase a firearm and established a five-day waiting period for authorities to complete background checks.[42]

1995 *Firearms Act*

The Liberals moved forward with ambitious gun-control measures in 1994, even though the party's 1993 election platform had barely mentioned firearm regulation. At the Liberals' 1994 policy convention a resolution won approval that called for stronger regulation of handguns, a ban on the private ownership of assault weapons, more restrictive rules for the purchase of ammunition, measures to limit gun smuggling, and harsher sentences for people who used guns in criminal activity. The convention also supported the creation of a national firearm registry.[43] With support from the party's base, Prime Minister Chrétien announced that his government would introduce new legislation.

The new minister of justice, Allan Rock, took the lead on the issue, but (like Kim Campbell) his views and background made him a target

ANTI-GUN NUT,
ALLAN ROCK, STALKS
COMMON SENSE
ON A SEEK AND
DESTROY MISSION...

Figure 53: Justice Minister Allan Rock became the target of critics of the
Firearms Act. As a leading Toronto lawyer, he buttressed the sense that urban
elites shaped Liberal gun policies. Here the *Winnipeg Free Press* describes Rock
as an "anti-gun nut."
Source: *Winnipeg Free Press*, 9 June 1995, used with permission of the
Winnipeg Free Press

for gun-control opponents. Rock was a prominent attorney in Toronto
before he won the Etobicoke Centre riding in 1993. He made no secret
of his desire to lower the level of gun ownership in Canada and raised
the possibility of prohibiting the private ownership of handguns. He
even believed that the government should consider banning private
ownership of all firearms in urban areas and admitted that he arrived
in Ottawa "with the firm belief that the only people in this country
who should have guns are police officers and soldiers."[44] Such statements proved controversial. Reform MPs and gun groups portrayed
Rock as the epitome of the Liberal's alleged big-city, elitist leadership.
MP Lee Morrison, a farmer and geologist representing a Saskatchewan
riding, attacked Rock's "patronizing view that gun owners need to be
protected from themselves," and he hoped that Canadians opposed to
firearm controls would send "a clear message against statism," such
that Rock would rethink "his elitist prejudices."[45]

Rock eventually released details of a very ambitious gun-control bill in which he proposed requiring all gun owners, not just new firearm owners, to get a new licence – a Firearm Possession Certificate. Other details included stiffer penalties for using a firearm to commit a crime, a requirement that handgun owners justify possession of their weapons every five years, and a ban of many models of handguns and assault rifles. The plan's centrepiece, however, was a national firearm registry obliging all gun owners to register every arm in their possession.[46]

Justice Minister Rock argued that stronger gun controls would preserve and strengthen the Canadian tradition of civility and prevent Canada from developing an American-style gun culture. Further, he emphasized that firearm regulations would protect women, noting that a woman was shot to death in Canada every six days. In an effort to mollify opposition, Rock met with over 150 national and regional organizations representing firearm owners. These meetings, he claimed, helped shape the eventual government policy. For example, firearm owners felt stigmatized because the federal government placed gun laws in the *Criminal Code*, so Ottawa responded by proposing to collect all relevant laws into a new *Firearms Act*. As well, Rock noted that the government abandoned early proposals to create urban gun-free zones and to ban all handguns after consultations with groups representing hunters, collectors, and target shooters.[47]

The gun registry became the most controversial of the government's proposals, despite powerful supporters. The Coalition for Gun Control and the Canadian Advisory Council on the Status of Women both supported the registry. Police organizations, including the Canadian Association of Chiefs of Police and the Canadian Police Association, also expressed support. The government stated several potential benefits of a registry. It would allow law enforcement to ensure that people ordered by a court to surrender their weapons because of, for example, a record of spousal abuse, did in fact surrender all their guns. The registry would also allow the federal government to track the approximately 375,000 firearms that entered Canada every year. Finally, the Liberals hoped the registry system would encourage gun owners to more carefully abide by safe storage requirements.[48]

The ambitiousness of the planned gun law, introduced in the House of Commons in February 1995 as Bill C-68, reflected the state's growing confidence in its ability to regulate millions of gun owners. In the past, governments rejected proposals for a national gun registry because of the problems of cost, administrative complexity, and potential non-compliance. While Ottawa focused on cost-cutting and deficit fighting in the mid-1990s, the government nevertheless felt that the civil service possessed sufficient resources and expertise to implement a national firearm registry. Advanced information technology, including a national computer system, and, eventually an online registration system, would ease the registration of millions of guns. To ensure compliance, Bill C-68 made possession of an unregistered firearm a criminal offence and threatened large penalties.

The federal government exhibited this confidence despite lacking key information on the extent of gun ownership and the effectiveness of previous firearm laws. In 1993, the federal auditor general deemed existing analyses of Canadian gun laws deficient and recommended that the government collect more data. The auditor general criticized the methodology and questioned the conclusions of a private-sector report commissioned to evaluate the 1977 firearm laws. Moreover, the auditor general condemned the Mulroney government's decision to pass legislation without the data necessary to evaluate the law's potential success. The auditor general thus called on Parliament to embark on a serious evaluation of the effectiveness of Canada's firearm laws. When pressed in Parliament on whether he intended to follow the auditor general's recommendation, Justice Minister Rock simply asserted that the federal government constantly reviewed gun-control provisions and that the Department of Justice had commissioned studies. Ottawa also lacked good estimates of the number of guns requiring registration. The Department of Justice estimated the presence of six million guns based on a 1991 poll. Some gun groups, in comparison, claimed the real figure surpassed twenty million. The number had important ramifications, since only an accurate estimate of the number of firearms would allow the government to gauge compliance with the registry and to estimate the program's cost.[49]

Despite government efforts to mollify gun owners, firearm groups fiercely opposed Bill C-68. Opponents employed many of the same tactics they used against the Liberals in the 1970s and the Progressive Conservatives in the early 1990s. They started letter-writing campaigns, circulated petitions, held rallies, and threatened to join political parties to oppose politicians supporting gun control. A September 1994 rally on Parliament Hill called "Fed Up" drew approximately ten thousand people.[50] Especially fierce opposition to the proposed legislation emerged in the west, which continued to report some of the highest levels of gun ownership in the country. Many westerners still distrusted

Figure 54: The media initially portrayed as unreasonable the resistance of
gun owners to the registration requirements of the *Firearms Act*. This 1994
Globe and Mail editorial cartoon makes such a point.
Source: Brian Gable, *Globe and Mail*, 2 Dec. 1994

the Liberal Party, which, some believed, intended to take guns the same
way Trudeau's Liberal government had allegedly tried rob western oil
riches under the National Energy Program. *Globe and Mail* columnist
John Barber thus declared that "Bill-68 is shaping up as the National
Energy Program of the 1990s."[51]

The registration proposal proved especially contentious, for it again
stoked fears that the state secretly sought to confiscate firearms. As had
occurred in the 1970s, organizations representing firearm owners made
analogies between modern arms control and the policies of Nazi Germany and Stalinist Russia.[52] Many firearm owners also continued to
claim gun ownership as a right, not a privilege. The arguments used
to ground this claim changed somewhat between the 1970s and 1990s,
however. Gun groups in the 1990s rediscovered the right to bear arms
found in the English *Bill of Rights* and repeated by Blackstone. References to the English right became a relatively common refrain in and
outside of Parliament. Saskatchewan MP Lee Morrison, for instance,
noted that the "greatest of all British jurists pointed out in his commen-

taries that without the auxiliary right to have arms, the absolute rights to life, security of person, liberty and property are illusory."[53]

The harsh sentences the Liberals proposed for non-compliance with the *Firearms Act* fed concern with government repression. Morrison, for instance, complained that a farmer who failed to register a single-shot .22 rifle could go to jail. "The inmates really have taken over the asylum," he argued.[54] The proposal that violators of the registration requirements receive a criminal record also aggravated gun owners. Ottawa believed that making failure to register a criminal offence would ensure compliance. If the government made violation a regulatory offence akin to a motor vehicle infraction, many gun owners, Ottawa feared, would simply refuse to register. This was a real concern, given that several leading public officials, including the Alberta minister of justice, warned of non-compliance.[55]

Other parts of Bill C-68 drew fire, especially provisions to empower the police. Bill C-68 proposed allowing police to enter private homes and businesses at a reasonable time of day without a warrant if the police officer suspected, with reason, that a firearm (even if legally possessed) was in the residence. The proposal thus allowed for police to search any private home with a registered weapon. If the resident refused entry, the police could get a warrant based solely on the ground that the resident had refused the search. These search provisions raised the ire of gun owners, *and* several civil liberties organizations. The Canadian Civil Liberties Association criticized the bill's search provisions (although it approved of the general goal of strengthening Canadian gun laws). The Canadian Bar Association, which had favoured gun-control bills since the 1970s, also expressed concern with the search-and-seizure provisions, as well as the mandatory minimum sentences included in the bill. For groups worried about civil liberties, the state's expanding confidence to regulate arms posed potential dangers.[56]

The cost of the proposed law also emerged as a concern. The conservative Fraser Institute claimed that the registry would cost at least half a billion dollars and perhaps as much as a billion. The complaints of museums with extensive collections of firearms requiring registration received widespread media attention. The Canadian Museum Association asked Ottawa to exempt antique firearms and reproductions from the registry to prevent museums from incurring substantial costs. Calgary's Glenbow Museum estimated that registering the arms in its collections would cost $9,000, while the Canadian War Museum believed its registration fees could total $180,000.[57]

In Parliament, the Liberals faced criticism from both opponents and advocates of stronger legislation. The Reform Party opposed Bill C-68, calling instead for tougher sanctions for criminals who used guns. On the other hand, the Bloc Québécois deemed the *Firearms Act* too weak. Political pressure created some dissension in the Liberal caucus, especially amongst rural, backbench MPs. On second reading, three Liberal MPs from rural Ontario voted against the bill, and two others abstained. The Reform Party stood uniformly opposed, except for MP Stephen Harper, who voted for the bill because, he said, a majority of people in his Calgary riding supported the legislation. Eight of nine members of the NDP caucus also voted against the bill because of the NDP's concern with losing traditional support in rural parts of western Canada. However, with the votes of the Bloc Québécois, the bill passed easily on second reading by a 173 to 53 margin.[58]

Prime Minister Chrétien sought to preserve party unity on Bill C-68. He thus punished the three Liberals who voted against the bill on second reading – they lost their seats on parliamentary committees. The government also sought to ensure unity by introducing a number of amendments in response to critics of the legislation. The government decreased the potential punishment for non-compliance (the maximum jail time for possession of an unregistered gun fell to six months), although possession of an unregistered gun remained a criminal offence. In addition, the Liberals altered the search proposals so that police would need a warrant to search the premises of any person possessing fewer than ten registered guns. The government also sought to fast-track the legislation to prevent opposition from shifting public opinion against Bill C-68, limiting the time the Justice Committee had to study the proposed legislation before sending it back to the Commons for third reading. On third reading, the bill again passed by a healthy margin: 192–63. Nine Liberal MPs opposed Bill C-68 and eight of nine NDP MPs again voted against the bill. The Bloc, however, unanimously supported the legislation, and three members of the Reform caucus from urban ridings also voted in favour. Some Progressive Conservative senators threatened to stop the bill, but the Senate ultimately approved Bill C-68 by a wide margin: 64–28. The legislation then received royal assent on 5 December 1995 – not coincidentally on the eve of the sixth anniversary of the Montreal Massacre.[59]

The *Firearms Act* created a complex array of regulations. It required all gun owners to acquire a licence to possess or acquire a firearm by 1 January 2001. Safety checks of applicants would ensure public safety.

Spouses and common-law partners who had lived with a licence applicant in the previous two years would receive notice of the application. Ottawa also required new firearm licence applicants to pass the Canadian Safety Firearms Test. Further, the act included *Criminal Code* amendments providing for stricter penalties for certain serious crimes involving firearms. As well, all .25- and .32-calibre handguns, as well as those with a short barrel (105 millimetres or less) became prohibited weapons. And, most controversially, the federal government required gun owners to register all of their firearms by 1 January 2003. Governments needed time to prepare for the act's implementation. As a result, the *Firearms Act* would come into force on 1 December 1998.[60]

Implementation of the *Firearms Act*

Ottawa created the bureaucratic tools needed to enforce the *Firearms Act*. It established a new administrative unit, the Canadian Firearms Centre, to carry out the program, and built centralized processing sites in Montreal and Miramichi, New Brunswick, to process licences and registrations. The federal government also established call centres in Miramichi, Montreal, and Victoria.[61] Opposition to the *Firearms Act*, however, did not dissipate once the government began to implement the legislation. Native organizations, gun and hunters' groups, and some of the provinces sought the amendment or repeal of the legislation before it came fully into effect.

Groups representing Native Peoples opposed several aspects of the *Firearms Act*, which required Aboriginal Peoples to get a licence and register their arms, but did not force them to pay fees. As they had in the 1970s, Native Peoples complained that the legislation violated treaty rights and interfered with traditional hunting practices. The Assembly of First Nations threatened to launch a legal challenge if the federal government refused to exempt Aboriginal Canadians from the legislation. The federal government responded by consulting with Native groups, then crafting a distinct system of regulations appropriate for Native communities: the *Aboriginal Peoples of Canada Adaptations Regulations*. Ottawa granted elders in Aboriginal communities a role in screening firearm licence applicants and allowed Aboriginal children under twelve to obtain a permit to participate in traditional hunts. As well, some Native People could informally show that they possessed an understanding of firearm laws and safety guidelines, rather than complete a regular safety course.[62]

Gun owners' groups and hunting organizations continued to seek the repeal or amendment of the *Firearms Act*. New organizations appeared to fight the legislation, such as the Canadian Institute for Legislative Action, which modelled itself after (and possibly received support from) the National Rifle Association. Older groups also continued to resist Ottawa. The National Firearms Association emerged as the most influential gun association in Canada by the mid-1990s. In 1994, it claimed to represent over one hundred thousand Canadians and had a $310,000 budget.[63] Led by its president, David Tomlinson, the NFA worked tirelessly against the *Firearms Act*. Described by the *Globe and Mail* as an "intensely angry Alberta-based organization,"[64] the NFA voiced the radical stances that first appeared in the 1970s, such as the view that Canadians had a "right" to guns and that widespread private gun ownership prevented government tyranny. In the 1997 federal election, the NFA threw its support behind the Reform Party and warned that the *Firearms Act* would lead to firearm confiscation. The association launched a "Give a Loonie to Save a Gun" campaign, asking gun owners to donate a dollar to the Reform Party for every gun they owned. The NFA also organized an "Operation Elimination" campaign to defeat targeted Liberal MPs. These efforts proved somewhat effective in rural parts of the country, such as in rural Saskatchewan, where gun control emerged as an important political issue in the 1997 election, and all but one Liberal MP in Saskatchewan went down to defeat.[65]

Gun owners again tried to create an umbrella organization to voice their concerns. In the 1970s, the short-lived Canadian Association for Sensible Arms Legislation had proved effective for a time. A similar short-lived organization, Safeguard, had emerged in the late 1980s. The *Firearms Act* spurred another effort to create such an organization: the Coalition of Responsible Firearms Owners and Sportsmen (CORFOS).[66]

Gun groups again used a variety of means to argue their case. In the fall of 1998, just before the government began phasing in licensing and registration provisions, a rally of between eight and ten thousand people protested on Parliament Hill.[67] A new tactic to resist firearm legislation emerged: the enlistment of academic support to criticize government policy. In the 1970s, gun-control opponents had fumed when academic commentators produced studies supporting firearm regulation, for such reports gave government action credence and gun owners felt unable to respond in similar terms. In the 1990s, however, the Fraser Institute supported research concluding that the *Firearms Act* would prove ineffective and expensive. It developed a relationship with Gary Mauser, a Simon Fraser University business professor. An American-born academic and gun owner with a PhD in psychology from the University of California, Mauser began writing on gun control in the 1990s, publishing work in a number of leading academic journals. His stature as a full professor at a reputable university made him a powerful voice criticizing gun laws. MPs opposed to firearm laws referenced his work, as did gun groups, some of which funded his research (although they usually laundered this funding through a think tank). For example, Mauser conducted a 1995 survey for the Fraser Institute partly funded by the Ontario Handgun Association. In 1997, the right-wing Mackenzie Institute published another study with funding provided by the Ontario Handgun Association.[68] The media at times mocked Mauser's work. For example, he produced a report based on a survey suggesting that Canadians used arms approximately sixty thousand times a year to defend themselves from animals and people.[69] *Globe and Mail* columnist Michael Valpy pointed out that the poll's sample size was "strikingly small" and that the study was published by the "relentlessly silly Fraser Institute."[70] Overall, however, Mauser's academic credentials meant that he influenced the public debate. Gun-control opponents and the media often cited his work. While Mauser had the biggest impact, a handful of other academics also expressed reservations about the wisdom of the gun registry.[71]

Critics of the *Firearms Act* alleged that it failed its core purpose: to stop gun violence. In its 1997 party platform, the Liberal Party trumpeted the *Firearms Act*'s passage, calling the new law "one of the toughest in the Western world."[72] This reflected the view that Canada had "achieved" gun control. This claim, however, proved a double-edged sword for the Liberals. Once gun control was "achieved," opponents of the *Firearms Act* could use every crime involving a firearm as evidence that regulation, especially the registry, was ineffective. In April 1996, Mark Chahal used two legally purchased handguns to kill his estranged wife, eight members of her family, and then himself in Vernon, British Columbia. This horrific incident became evidence of the state's limited ability to keep arms away from dangerous individuals. Chahal's wife had complained to the police of abusive treatment but had refused to help the police investigate. The RCMP suggested that it had to grant a gun permit when only marginal doubt existed about the applicant's suitability to have a firearm.[73] "How do you legislate a maniac?," asked the manager of Chahal's gun club.[74] Similarly, some gun-control opponents cited Jim Roszko's murder of four RCMP con-

Figure 55: Several thousand opponents of the federal firearm registry gather on Parliament Hill in 1998. Their posters reflect the beliefs common to gun owners, including that registration was the first step towards confiscation.
Source: Tom Hanson, Canadian Press

stables in Mayerthorpe, Alberta, in 2005 as demonstrating the futility of federal firearm laws.[75] What good was a gun registry, critics charged, if it could not prevent such violence?

The unwillingness of a vocal minority of gun owners to register their weapons also undermined the perceived effectiveness of the *Firearms Act*. The continued belief that registration presaged confiscation was the primary motivation for non-compliance. Members of a group called the Law-Abiding Unregistered Firearms Association advocated resisting the *Firearms Act* through non-compliance. This was a new tactic, for gun groups in the 1970s had fought new legislation, but once Parliament acted, they encouraged members to abide by the law, often providing information on how to comply even as they continued to grouse. Canadians unwilling to register their arms gained confidence that authorities would not prosecute. Several provinces, including British Columbia, Nova Scotia, Ontario, Alberta, Saskatchewan, and Manitoba, announced they would not charge individuals for failing to register firearms.[76] These provinces had important constituencies of hunters and/or ideologically conservative governments opposed to state intervention. The decision of these provinces left the duty to prosecute to the federal government.

Despite efforts to discourage compliance, a large majority acquired licences and registered their arms. Many, however, waited until very close to the December deadline. This caused a backlog and forced the federal government to issue almost five hundred thousand temporary licences. By July 2003, approximately 2.1 million of Canada's estimated 2.3 million gun owners had acquired a licence, and the government reported the registration of 6.3 million of the estimated 7.9 million long guns, suggesting a substantial level of compliance. Critics of the *Firearms Act*, however, alleged that Ottawa reduced its estimate of the number of gun owners from 3.3 million to 2.3 million to inflate the reported compliance rate. The Canadian Firearms Centre claimed that the reduction stemmed from the decision of up to one-third of gun owners to sell their weapons or hand them over to family members because they did not want to obtain a licence.[77] Many Canadians thus disarmed themselves rather than comply with the law. This result was not completely unexpected, for gun groups since the 1970s had argued that bureaucratic red tape would disarm Canadians almost as effectively as confiscation.

A declining interest in hunting by the 1990s also encouraged many Canadian to give up their firearms. Immediately after the Second World

War, working-class and middle-class men hunted for recreation. In the 1970s and early 1980s, male baby boomers, many of whom had hunted with their fathers in the 1950s and 1960s and possessed sufficient money and leisure time, also became active hunters. The number of provincial hunting licences in most provinces spiked in the two decades after the Second World War, then stagnated by the mid-1960s, before increasing again in the 1980s, as the number of deer hunters in Ontario illustrates. In 1980, 80,280 deer hunters killed 9,150 deer in the province. Eight years later, 136,500 deer hunters harvested 41,260 deer. By the 1990s, however, many middle-class and elite urban men began to abandon hunting. Fewer urban men owned a gun, or, if they did, used it less often or not at all. These changes occurred throughout Canada. In New Brunswick, for instance, the number of residents over the age of fifteen who hunted decreased from 20 per cent in 1981 to 12 per cent in 1997. A similar decrease occurred in Manitoba, where the proportion of adults who participated in recreational hunting dropped from approximately 20 per cent in the mid 1970s to about 10 per cent by the early 1990s. Gun ownership by young people in Canada also declined substantially. Survey data suggested that the number of firearm owners under the age of thirty-five declined by 39 per cent between 1991 and 2000. By the turn of the century, a majority of Canadian gun owners (61 per cent by 2001) reported using their firearms very infrequently (once a year or less) or never.[78] For such gun owners, giving up a rarely used firearm posed little hardship.

The *Firearms Reference*

Some firearm owners, unable to stop the Liberal Party through the electoral process, decided to challenge the legality of Canada's gun laws. The 1977 gun legislation had led to calls for court cases. However, most early challenges to the *Criminal Code* firearm provisions failed. In *R. v. Northcott*, for example, the British Columbia Provincial Court dismissed a federalism challenge to the FAC procedure.[79] In 1985, the Supreme Court of Canada, in a unanimous ruling, found constitutional the 1977 provisions imposing additional penalties for committing a crime with a firearm. The Ontario Court of Appeal, in 1990, upheld the *Criminal Code* requirement that judges impose a minimum five-year prohibition on firearm use for people convicted of an indictable offence involving violence for which the offender could be imprisoned for ten years or more.[80]

The above cases cropped up largely in ordinary criminal cases, but a few strident gun owners and groups also pursued legal challenges. Michael Martinoff, who had strongly opposed Trudeau's gun legislation, became involved in several cases. Martinoff owned dozens of restricted weapons as well as many other unrestricted arms. In 1987, he applied for a permit to carry a restricted weapon on two grounds. First, he claimed to need to carry a restricted firearm when he photographed wildlife, as he feared bear attacks. Second, he wished to carry a restricted weapon for use in a lawful occupation – as a gun instructor. When refused, Martinoff argued that the *Criminal Code* gun control provisions violated the *Charter* and constituted an unconstitutional encroachment by the federal government on provincial jurisdiction. The British Columbia Court of Appeal held against Martinoff. The court dismissed his constitutional arguments and concluded that officials correctly exercised their power to refuse him a permit to carry restricted firearms. This decision failed to discourage Martinoff.[81] In 1989, a customs officer at the Canadian-American border stopped Martinoff, who was legally transporting a shipment of firearms. Customs found Martinoff's personal handgun in the vehicle's glove compartment, and authorities charged him with possessing a restricted weapon at a place other than at one to which he was entitled. The case again went to the British Columbia Court of Appeal, which concluded that Martinoff should have been convicted.[82] Mulroney's legislation led to further legal proceedings. In 1993, the Supreme Court of Canada determined whether the police could seize semi-automatic weapons that could be easily converted into fully automatic arms. The Court concluded that the federal government could classify such guns as prohibited weapons. The Ontario Handgun Association also unsuccessfully challenged the prohibition on high-capacity magazines.[83]

Some gun groups had called for a federalism challenge to Canadian gun laws since the 1970s, and the enactment of the *Firearms Act* finally sparked an organized effort to find the federal government's legislation unconstitutional. Alberta announced in September 1996 that it would launch a constitutional challenge to the *Firearms Act*, taking the form of a reference to the Alberta Court of Appeal in 1997. Several other jurisdictions supported the challenge as interveners: Saskatchewan, Manitoba, Ontario, the Northwest Territories, and the Yukon. Two groups opposed to gun control also secured intervener status: the Shooting Federation of Canada and the Alberta Fish and Game Association. Ottawa defended the legislation and received the support of several interveners, including the Coalition for Gun Control, the Canadian Association of Chiefs of Police, the cities of Toronto and Montreal, and the Alberta Council of Women's Shelters.

The opponents of the *Firearms Act* argued that Ottawa lacked the jurisdiction to regulate "ordinary" firearms such as hunting rifles and shotguns. The "pith and substance" of the *Firearms Act* was the regulation of property and civil rights – a provincial area of jurisdiction. Ottawa argued in response that the *Firearms Act* fell within the federal jurisdiction over the criminal law and/or Ottawa's residual authority to regulate for the peace, order, and good government of Canada. Given the existing federalism jurisprudence, Ottawa offered the stronger set of arguments, such that legal scholars suggested that the case had little merit. This failed to deter opponents of the *Firearms Act*, however, likely because political purposes motivated them to undertake the doomed case – provincial leaders could emphasize their resistance through the courts.[84]

The Alberta Court of Appeal upheld the constitutionality of the *Firearms Act* by a close margin of three to two, the majority noting that both the federal and provincial governments could regulate guns for different purposes, and the irrelevance of the act's effectiveness to its constitutional characterization. Chief Justice Catherine Fraser found that Parliament's purpose in enacting the legislation was to enhance public safety by reducing gun crime, preventing suicides, and limiting the number of firearm accidents. While the act's provisions entailed the regulation of property, this was the means of the law, not its end, she concluded. The act's pith and substance was protecting public safety from the misuse of firearms, and the legislation thus fell within the federal criminal law power. The two justices who dissented defined the purpose of the law broadly: as regulating all aspects of the possession and use of firearms. The minority concluded that the *Firearms Act* represented a colourable intrusion into the provincial jurisdiction over property and civil rights and was an invalid exercise of Parliament's jurisdiction over criminal law or its peace, order, and good government authority.[85]

Defeated at the Court of Appeal, Alberta appealed to the Supreme Court of Canada. Alberta's position received additional support, as New Brunswick and Nova Scotia also joined the legal challenge. Three organizations representing gun owners intervened on the side of Alberta: the Coalition of Responsible Firearm Owners and Sportsmen, the Law-Abiding Unregistered Firearms Association, and the Shooting Federation of Canada. As well, the Federation of Saskatchewan

Indian Nations intervened, but only made argument regarding how the *Firearms Act* deleteriously affected Aboriginal rights. On the other hand, several groups and municipalities again intervened on behalf of the federal position. The cities of Winnipeg, Montreal, and Toronto argued for the *Firearms Act*'s validity, as did the Canadian Association of Chiefs of Police, the Canadian Pediatric Society, the Canadian Association for Adolescent Health, the Alberta Council of Women's Shelters, the Fondation des victimes du 6 décembre contre la violence, Canadians Against Violence Everywhere Advocating for its Termination (CAVEAT), and the Coalition for Gun Control.

The Supreme Court, in a unanimous decision, found the *Firearms Act* constitutional. In its short and anonymous reasons, the Court concluded that the legislation fell within the federal jurisdiction over the criminal law. The pith and substance of the legislation – controlling access to firearms through the use of penalties and prohibitions – was directed at public safety. Any intrusion into provincial jurisdiction over property and civil rights was minor enough to not upset the balance of federalism. The Court disposed of the argument that the *Firearms Act* would prove ineffective because of non-compliance, noting that Parliament was the best judge of whether a law would achieve its desired purpose. The Court also noted that its decision did not prevent provinces from regulating firearms.[86]

The Supreme Court's judgment destroyed gun owners' hope that they could defeat firearm legislation in the courts. A few ardent critics of the *Firearms Act* continued to suggest that a legal challenge employing the *Charter of Rights* might succeed, but most believed such an effort would fail.[87] The Supreme Court did not comment in the *Firearms Reference* on whether Ottawa's legislation violated the *Charter*, although in a later case, *R. v. Wile*, the Court hinted at its view. In *Wile*, a Nova Scotia man pled guilty to unlawfully producing cannabis. At sentencing, the Crown sought a mandatory firearm prohibition, which the defendant contested as "cruel and unusual punishment" in violation of s.12 of the *Charter*. After losing at the Nova Scotia Court of Appeal, the defendant went to the Supreme Court, which dismissed his appeal, and, in doing so, dismissed the idea that gun ownership was a right. Justice Louise Charron held that the "state interest in reducing the misuse of weapons is valid and important" and that "possession and use of firearms is not a right or freedom guaranteed under the *Charter*, but a privilege."[88] The courtroom losses led some gun owners and groups to conclude that only electoral success by a party opposed to regulating ordinary firearms could roll back Canada's gun laws.

Cost Overruns

In the ensuing political attacks on the *Firearms Act*, critics increasingly focused on the cost overruns of the gun registry. As seen in chapter 5, the potential expense of ambitious new firearm laws had worried policymakers, gun owners, and many members of the public since the 1970s. Police officials, for example, long opposed a registry because of the time and money needed to implement it. In 1973, the Canadian Association of Chiefs of Police warned that proposals to register all firearms should be "approached with extreme caution," for the cost would "be staggering."[89] Time proved the association prescient. In comparison to previous governments, Chrétien's administration expressed confidence that the state could successfully implement licensing and registration requirements at minimal cost. In February 1995, Minister of Justice Rock estimated the registry would cost $85 million but that fees would recoup much of this figure.[90] Ottawa, however, badly underestimated the program's expense.

Warnings about the cost of implementing the *Firearms Act* appeared soon after establishment of the Canadian Firearms Centre. The conservative *National Post* reported in May 1999 that 621 civil servants administered the program and that the federal government intended to hire at least an additional 184. Such reports angered gun owners who had long warned about the expense of ambitious firearm laws and who feared that a large, faceless bureaucracy would evaluate Canadians' right to possess a weapon. Budget overruns soon defined how Canadians perceived the *Firearms Act*. In 2002, the federal auditor general, Sheila Fraser, confirmed media reports of the program's ballooning price tag. In an extremely critical report, she revealed that by 2002 Ottawa had spent $688 million, and recovered just $59 million in fees. Moreover, Fraser concluded the total cost of the registry would reach $1 billion by 2005. The auditor general detailed some of the factors contributing to the cost overruns, including poor planning, a lack of bureaucratic leadership, and program restructuring. In addition, Ottawa misjudged the complexity and cost of the information technology systems needed. Gun owners added to the high cost in several ways. First, popular opposition led several provincial governments to refuse to participate in the registry, thus requiring the federal government to spend additional funds to manage the program. Second, to encourage reluctant gun owners to comply with the *Firearms Act*, Ottawa reduced or waived licensing and registration fees, decreasing the revenue meant to off-

Figure 56: Opponents of the *Firearms Act* portrayed it as a boondoggle. Focus on the cost of gun control drew public attention away from the possible benefits of the registry for law enforcement. Here, Prime Minister Jean Chrétien walks past a sign criticizing gun control as he heads to his campaign bus in Victoria, BC, in November 2000.
Source: Paul Chiasson, Canadian Press

Figure 57: The Reform Party made repeal of the long-gun registry a key part of its platform. Reform Party leader Preston Manning addresses gun-control opponents with former justice critic Jack Ramsay at a demonstration on Parliament Hill in 1998.
Source: Fred Chartrand, Canadian Press

set the program's expenses. Third, firearm owners completed close to half of all licence applications incorrectly, causing additional expense. Fourth, the opposition forced Ottawa to make expensive revisions to forms and to spend millions on advertising to encourage registration.[91]

The cost overruns proved extremely important in shifting public attitudes towards the firearm registry, which, as the perceived centrepiece of the Liberal gun-control regime, also changed the popular view of firearm regulation in general. Opinion polls conducted during the 1970s, 1980s, and 1990s had demonstrated broad support for increased firearm regulation. Infamous shootings, including school shootings in 1999 at Columbine, Colorado, and Tabor, Alberta, buttressed public support. In 1999, for example, a solid majority of Canadians expressed support for the gun registry: 76 per cent. Another poll, from 2001, showed that 61 per cent wanted even stricter firearm laws, while only 6 per cent advocated weaker regulations.[92] This kind of support had motivated the Chrétien government to employ gun control as a wedge issue with the Reform Party.

In the end, however, the gun-control strategy backfired on the Liberals. The expense of the new regulatory program allowed the Reform Party, and its later Alliance Party and Conservative Party variations, to recast gun control as a fiscal issue – as an issue of government waste – rather than as a public safety question. In 2003, the president of the Canadian Resource Centre for Victims of Crime captured the frustration of gun-control advocates who criticized the transformation of firearm regulation into a financial issue: "I'm alarmed the voices of victims of gun violence are being drowned out by the controversy of the costs of the firearms program."[93] While only a minority of Canadians wanted freer access to arms, a majority opposed perceived government mismanagement and waste. By 2004, 52 per cent favoured scrapping the registry, while only 43 per cent wanted it retained.[94] When Conservative Stephen Harper became prime minister in 2006 with a minority government, he took advantage of this shift in support and promised to kill the program.

Conclusion

From the 1990s to the early twenty-first century, gun control, more so than in any previous period, became a polarizing gender, social, cultural, economic, and political issue. The Montreal Massacre awakened many Canadians to the dangers of firearms for women. Women's groups thus strongly supported greater regulation in the hope of decreasing violence against women *and* cracking the cultural link between masculinity and firearms. Gun owners responded by defending the integral place of firearms in their definition of manhood. For westerners and rural Canadians, gun control came to represent their perceived disempowerment at the hands of eastern, urban elites. Residents of Canada's cities, on the other hand, increasingly believed firearms unnecessary and dangerous. Progressive Canadians lamented the firearm registry's expense but argued that the program encouraged responsibility with guns and might decrease violent crime. Fiscal conservatives suggested that the registry again showed the inability of the state to administer complex programs cost effectively. Politicians of various ideological persuasions grabbed hold of particular strands of the debate to rationalize their party platforms on guns and to drive wedges into the electorate. This politicization of the issue led many citizens to adopt strongly polarized positions on gun regulation, despite the long history and complex nature of the relationship between Canadians and firearms.

The national gun registry is significant in the history of Canadian state formation in two ways. First, Prime Minister Chrétien's decision to establish a registry reflected a belief that the state finally possessed the financial resources, human expertise, and technological tools to successfully implement a policy long deemed too challenging for even the national government. It thus represented the increased confidence of the state to impose its will on citizens. Second, the cost overruns and administrative failures of the registry damaged public faith in the ability of Ottawa to carry out large-scale regulatory programs. Canada felt the influence of the neoliberal critique of government that swept across many western democracies in the 1980s and 1990s based on the belief that the market, not the state, should order society. This ideological persuasion led to the privatization of several Canadian Crown corporations and the implementation of free trade agreements. Neoliberals found social policy a tougher nut to crack. Government-funded health care, the Canadian Pension Plan, and the Old Age Security program, to chose a few examples, proved relatively immune to attempts to limit the state's role, in large measure because many citizens incorporated such programs into their definition of Canada as a caring, civilized nation. Gun control was both a social *and* economic issue, and this fuelled the intensity of the debate. When it was cast as an issue of social progressivism, a majority of Canadians favoured regulating firearms, but when defined as an economic issue, gun control seemed less worth the cost.

Conclusion

In the 2006 federal election, the governing Liberal Party and the opposition Conservative Party staked starkly different positions on gun control. Liberal Prime Minister Paul Martin defended the long-gun registry and even proposed a ban on most handguns. The financial legacy of the registry shaped the public response to Martin's handgun proposal. The *Winnipeg Free Press* criticized the plan, reminding readers that the *Firearms Act* "proved expensive for all taxpayers – more than $1 billion spent on it with no discernible benefit."[1] The plan did not survive the election, as the Liberals fell from power for the first time since 1993, and Conservative Party leader Stephen Harper became prime minister in a minority government. His party, an amalgamation of the Progressive Conservative and Alliance (formerly Reform) Party had promised during the election to axe the registry. Opponents of the program had to wait, however, as a majority of MPs wanted the registry to be retained. As a temporary solution, the Harper government declared an amnesty for rifle and shotgun owners who failed to register their arms. After a second minority win in 2008, critics of the registry failed again to get a bill to kill the program through the Commons. Helping the Conservatives' cause was the presence of a female member of their caucus, Manitoba MP Candice Hoeppner, who proved a vocal opponent of the registry, and who introduced private member legislation to have it eliminated. Since the Montreal Massacre, women's groups had urged gun control, but Hoeppner's public stance allowed the Conservatives to claim that their opposition to the registry did not represent a lack of concern with women's safety. Her gender cloaked the fact that the registry's destruction would represent a substantial defeat for women's groups that had lobbied hard for the program.

The Conservative Party again attacked the registry in the 2011 election campaign. Various groups, including the Canadian Association of Chiefs of Police and the Coalition for Gun Control, sought to stir public support for the program. Police, for instance, argued that the registry encouraged gun-owner accountability, allowed police to determine if homes possessed weapons before entry, and made it easier to track arms used in criminal activity. Others claimed that the legal regime developed since the late 1970s had contributed to a reduction in gun violence, and thus the government should retain the registry. The homicide rate fell in 2010 to its lowest rate in forty-four years (1.62 homicides per hundred thousand people). The number of homicides involving firearms in 2010 (0.5 per hundred thousand) stood at less than half of its 1970s peak (1.18 per hundred thousand in 1974). In addition, the number of robberies involving firearms dropped, from 9,040 in 1981 (36.4 per hundred thousand) to just 3,671 in 2006 (11.3 per hundred thousand). The Conservative Party nevertheless announced it would eliminate the registry when it secured a majority government in 2011. The Conservatives complained about the program's high cost, questioned its effectiveness, and alleged that it harassed legitimate gun owners unnecessarily.[2]

Politicians and journalists in the early twentieth-first-century debate rarely remarked on the long and complex history of gun control. They failed to dispel a popular misconception that firearm regulation began in Canada after the Montreal Massacre. State efforts to regulate guns, in fact, predate Confederation. Early settlers brought firearms and provided them to allied Aboriginal Peoples. The ownership of firearms by colonials and even Aboriginal Peoples caused little alarm in much of the pre-Confederation period. Inhabitants of British North America employed muzzle-loaded, smooth-bore muskets and single-shot pistols to hunt and to protect themselves and their property. Levels of firearm ownership, however, changed over time and differed between places before Confederation. Interest in gun ownership waned in areas and at times that agricultural production rose, fear of Aboriginal People declined, duelling fell out of fashion, and worries over imperial wars subsided. Authorities in British North America nevertheless sought to shape gun ownership and use. They regulated firearm use in urban settings and during periods of high tension, such as elections, and passed legislation allowing for the disarming of groups deemed potentially dangerous. Fear of Aboriginal Peoples, French Canadians, and Irish canal workers led governments to restrict the free use of arms, or, in some cases, to place limits on gun ownership. That racial, ethnic, and class factors motivated regulation is of course not an especially surprising conclusion. Most social historians would expect it. The concern with particular groups is important, however, as the nature of the perceived "problem" shaped the regulatory framework. Much of the early regulation was temporary – the state sought to limit gun use or ownership by particular groups during times of real or imagined tumult.

The state eventually regulated firearms in a more sustained way. Improvements in the design and production of firearms in the nineteenth century, including the industrial manufacture of revolvers and magazine, breech-loading rifles, helped motivate legislators to pass more aggressive legislation. These weapons posed greater dangers than older pistols and muskets. They fired more rapidly, more accurately, and at longer ranges, and became relatively inexpensive with the establishment of modern arms factories. Easily smuggled and concealed, and produced in massive volumes in the United States, handguns proved an especially difficult problem to solve for Canadian legislators. In a series of legislative initiatives, however, Ottawa placed limits on the carrying and use of pistols. In 1877, the federal government required people carrying handguns to have reasonable cause to fear an assault or injury to themselves, their family, or their property. The 1892 *Criminal Code* dictated that persons wishing to carry a pistol acquire a "certificate of exemption." Amendments in 1913 increased penalties and required a permit to purchase a pistol. Other significant measures included the creation of a handgun registry in the 1930s, the decision to classify pistols as "restricted" weapons in the late 1960s, and the prohibition of some handguns in the 1990s. These laws collectively kept levels of per capita handgun ownership much lower in Canada than in the United States. The United States has approximately ten times Canada's population, but over sixty times as many handguns.[3]

While authorities consistently sought to decrease the public's use of handguns, they only reluctantly regulated modern rifles. Pressure to act built slowly, however. Frequent gun accidents involving rifles, as well as the destruction of wildlife, led to appeals for stronger gun control. Ottawa responded by limiting the sale of weapons to young people in the late nineteenth and early twentieth centuries. The provinces limited the kinds of weapons hunters could employ, and eventually developed firearm safety courses. By the late 1960s, a spike in gun violence, concern with public disorder, and fear of replicating American gun culture led to more aggressive government action. Infamous crimes proved especially powerful symbols for advocates of the stronger regulation of modern rifles. School shootings in the 1970s and the 1989 Montreal Massacre hardened public support for new measures to increase state control over "long guns." The Montreal Massacre became particularly important, for it led women's groups to focus on the gun-control issue. They charged that the availability of firearms increased the propensity of men to commit acts of violence against girlfriends, spouses, and perfect strangers. Licensing requirements and the long-gun registry represented ambitious efforts in the late twentieth century to more intensely regulate long guns.

Although modern rifles posed substantial dangers, a number of factors long mitigated the desire to strengthen gun control. Perhaps most importantly, for much of Canadian history the state sought to arm, not disarm, most male citizens. Pre-Confederation militia systems typically required inhabitants to drill and shoot and sometimes own a weapon. After Confederation, Canadians interested in defending the new nation against an American invasion or in supporting Britain in future imperial wars encouraged men to own firearms and become accurate shooters. Drawing inspiration from models as distinct as Boer sharpshooters and historic English archers, imperialists deemed expertise with the rifle an invaluable skill for Canadian men. This resulted in waves of interest in target shooting and in government support for rifle associations, domestic manufacturing of arms and ammunition, and the training of children and youth in military drill and shooting. The state's hope of creating citizen-soldiers who owned and trained with rifles began to wane only after the Great War demonstrated that the rifleman failed to dominate the modern battlefield.

The nexus established between firearms and masculinity also encouraged support for using rifles (and discouraged gun-control efforts). While firearms had long served as useful tools in settler communities, by the late nineteenth century guns became more than practical instruments. They became symbols of manhood at a time when an increasing percentage of Canadian men lived in industrializing cities. Many middle-class social commentators at the turn of the twentieth century said too many men lived in urban environments that encouraged sedentary, unmanly lives. They advocated rifle shooting and recreational hunting as solutions to such problems of modernity. For the men who flocked to shooting ranges or forests, the modern rifle represented personal power at a time when many felt disempowered by, and dislocated in, the modern world.

Business encouraged this connection between masculinity and firearms. Gun manufacturers and retailers sold weapons by emphasizing that ownership made average men into "sportsmen." Businesses emphasized the beauty and power of their weapons to make them consumer goods. They used stock images of soldiers and cowboys to convince men that gun ownership represented rugged individualism and love for empire and/or nation. Businesses also sought to expand the market for firearms by creating and advertising small-calibre weapons and air guns for women, children, and youth. Manufacturers and retailers sought to define such weapons as "safe" and suggested that firearms offered tickets to manhood for boys and youth. Many of the women who took up rifle shooting or hunting in the early twentieth century did not seek to challenge the connection between firearms and masculinity, but wanted to carve a niche for themselves as proper Victorian women capable to keeping up with men. Not until the 1989 Montreal Massacre would women's groups consistently connect gun control to the issue of women's safety. The suggestion that the relatively free access to firearms made male violence worse against girlfriends, spouses, and perfect strangers became a common refrain after 1989.

The gradually increasing power of the state eventually allowed greater levels of gun control. For much of Canadian history, politicians noted the difficulty of enforcing firearm regulations. Governments simply lacked the necessary administrative and policing capabilities to implement and supervise strong firearm laws. In time, the creation of professional police forces helped empower the state to carry out gun laws in a relatively systematic way. Technological improvements in data processing also permitted the creation of more ambitious state regulatory initiatives. The gun registry established temporarily in the Second World War used the most modern "computing" equipment available, while Ottawa could envision the registry created by the 1995 *Firearms Act* as potentially cost effective only with computers and the Internet. At times, governments proved overconfident. Despite the substantial size of the federal bureaucracy by the 1990s, Prime Minister Jean Chrétien's government introduced a long-gun registry with only a vague sense of the number of guns to be processed, the administrative complexity of a registry, or an accurate accounting of the program's cost. Those failings, more than the actual benefits or weaknesses of the registry as an instrument of securing public safety, doomed the program.

The perception that gun ownership is a right also slowed the passage of new firearm laws. Some nineteenth-century politicians refused to regulate guns because of their wish to avoid violating the rights of Englishmen. Figures such as John A. Macdonald, Edward Blake, and David Mills believed that "British justice" entailed a right to possess arms for men of property grounded in the English *Bill of Rights*. In the twentieth century, the nature of the rights claim changed. Canadians largely forgot about the English constitutional right to bear arms. Instead, gun owners opposed regulation by claiming that gun control violated individual, liberal rights. After the First World War, for example, opponents of firearm laws that targeted aliens argued that any such law should apply to everyone, or no one. By the 1960s, and especially the 1970s, gun owners spoke of a right to possess a gun, although they could only vaguely identify the source and scope of the alleged right. Gun owners claimed a right based on allusions to English traditions, the rights to privacy and property, and a "customary" right grounded in historic usage. Aboriginal Peoples also opposed laws that threatened their right to hunt and their communal conception of property ownership. Gun control became an especially heated topic by the 1970s, because it symbolized the dangers of an expanding state for individual liberty. Firearm owners connected gun control to the problems of an expanding government bureaucracy, interventionist economic and social policies, and high taxes. Gun owners thus voiced a powerful neoliberal critique of the interventionist state. Many rural, northern, and western citizens charged, often correctly, that federal firearm policy reflected the concerns of citizens of Canada's major cities. This added regional- and urban-versus-rural dimensions to the debates over gun control and made firearm regulation an especially divisive political issue.

The combination of neoliberal political ideology, regional bitterness, well-organized lobby groups, the urban-versus-rural divide, and competing conceptions of masculinity explain the ferocious resistance to gun control since the 1970s. Before that time, Canadians cast little suspicion on hunters. As recently as the 1960s, white male gun owners considered themselves among the pillars of Canadian society. Many were veterans of the Second World War or the sons of veterans. These white, working-class and middle-class hunters were accustomed to politicians courting them during elections. As urban middle- and upper-class men abandoned recreational hunting (having long since given up target shooting), hunting, shooting, and gun collecting remained of interest mostly to working-class, often rural, men. The withering of the gun community deprived hunters of an important part of their former coalition when Canadians debated the regulation of private firearm ownership in the late twentieth century. Gun owners lashed out at urban residents, calling them effeminate and elitist. Ironically, even though gun owners declined as a percentage of the general population, such arguments proved remarkably effective. Firearm owners tapped effectively into anti-state sentiments, questioned government waste, employed popular conceptions of masculinity, and stoked an inaccurate belief that all rural men traditionally possessed arms. The result was the destruction of the long-gun registry.

Notes

Introduction

1 Jean Chrétien, *My Years as Prime Minister* (Toronto: Vintage Canada, 2008), 208.

2 Ron Briley, Review of *Bowling for Columbine*, *Journal of American History* 90, no. 3 (2003): 1144–6; Brian D. Johnson, "Staring Down the Barrel of a Gun," *Maclean's*, 21 October 2002, 34; Dana Thompson, "Americans and Guns," *Newsweek International*, 3 June 2002, 62.

3 Susan Binnie, "Maintaining Order on the Pacific Railway: The Peace Preservation Act, 1869–85," in *Canadian State Trials*, vol. 3, *Political Trials and Security Measures, 1840–1914*, ed. Barry Wright and Susan Binnie, 204–56 (Toronto: University of Toronto Press and the Osgoode Society, 2009); Susan W.S. Binnie, "The Blake Act of 1878: A Legislative Solution to Urban Violence in Post-Confederation Canada," in *Law, Society, and the State: Essays in Modern Legal History*, ed. Louis A. Knafla and Susan W.S. Binnie, 215–42 (Toronto: University of Toronto Press, 1995); Martin L. Friedland, "Gun Control: The Options," *Criminal Law Quarterly* 18 (1975–6): 29–71; Gérald Pelletier, "Le Code criminel canadien, 1892–1939: Le contrôle des armes à feu," *Crime, Histoire & Sociétés* 6, no. 2 (2002): 51–79.

4 For examples, see Philip C. Stenning, "Guns & the Law," *Beaver* 80, no. 6 (2000–1): 6–7; Samuel A. Bottomley, "Parliament, Politics and Policy: Gun Control in Canada, 1867–2003" (PhD diss., Carleton University, 2004); Canadian Shooting Sports Association, "'For Their Own Good': Firearms

Control in Canada, 1867–1945," and "'For Their Own Good': Firearms Control in Canada, 1946–1977," http://www.cdnshootingsports.org/; Ruth Bleasdale, "Class Conflict on the Canals of Upper Canada in the 1840s," *Labour / Le Travailleur* 7 (1981): 9–39.

5 Joyce Lee Malcolm, *To Keep and Bear Arms: The Origins of an Anglo-American Right* (Cambridge, MA: Harvard University Press, 1994); Joyce Lee Malcolm, *Guns and Violence: The English Experience* (Cambridge, MA: Harvard University Press, 2002); Lois G. Schwoerer, "To Hold and Bear Arms: The English Perspective," in *The Second Amendment in Law and History: Historians and Constitutional Scholars on the Right to Bear Arms*, ed. Carl T. Bogus, 207–27 (New York: New Press, 2000).

6 For a discussion of the historiography concerning the second amendment, see Carl T. Bogus, "The History and Politics of Second Amendment Scholarship: A Primer," in Bogus, *Second Amendment in Law and History*, 1–15. For an overview of the legal debate over the second amendment, see Mark V. Tushnet, *Out of Range: Why the Constitution Can't End the Battle over Guns* (Oxford: Oxford University Press, 2007).

7 Robert H. Churchill, "Gun Regulation, the Police Power, and the Right to Keep Arms in Early America: The Legal Context of the Second Amendment," *Law and History Review* 25, no. 1 (2007): 139–75. For examples of such an approach, see H. Richard Uviller and William G. Merkel, *The Militia and the Right to Arms, Or, How the Second Amendment Fell Silent* (Durham, NC: Duke University Press, 2002); David Thomas Konig, "The Second Amendment: A Missing Transatlantic Context for the Historical Meaning of 'the Right of the People to Keep and Bear Arms,'" *Law & History Review* 22 (2004): 119–59.

8 Michael A. Bellesiles, *Arming America: The Origins of a National Gun Culture* (New York: Alfred A. Knopf, 2000). On the scandal, see Peter Charles Hoffer, *Past Imperfect: Facts, Fictions, Fraud – American History from Bancroft and Parkman to Ambrose, Bellesiles, Ellis and Goodwin* (New York: Public Affairs, 2004); James Lindgren, "Fall from Grace: Arming America and the Bellesiles Scandal," *Yale Law Journal* 111, no. 8 (2002): 2195–249; Clayton E. Cramer, "Why Footnotes Matter: Checking Arming America's Claims," *Plagiary* 1, no. 11 (1996): 1–31. For discussions of how Bellesiles might have approached his topic differently, see James Lindgren and Justin Lee Heather, "Counting Guns in Early America," *William & Mary Law Review* 43, no. 5 (2002): 1777–842; Gloria L. Main, "Many Things Forgotten: The Use of Probate Records in Arming America," *William & Mary Quarterly* 3rd ser., 59, no. 1 (2002): 211–16; Randolph Roth, "Counting Guns: What Social Science Historians Know and Could Learn about Gun Ownership, Gun

Culture, and Gun Violence in the United States," *Social Science History* 26, no. 4 (2002): 699–708.

9 Friedland, "Gun Control," 40.

10 The early historiography on Canadian state formation emphasized the growing power of the state in the mid- to late nineteenth century. See Allan Greer and Ian Radforth, eds., *Colonial Leviathan: State Formation in Mid-Nineteenth-Century Canada* (Toronto: University of Toronto Press, 1992); Bruce Curtis, *True Government by Choice Men?: Inspection, Education, and State Formation in Canada West* (Toronto: University of Toronto Press, 1992); J.I. Little, *State and Society in Transition: The Politics of Institutional Reform in the Eastern Townships, 1838–1852* (Montreal and Kingston: McGill-Queen's University Press, 1997); Bruce Curtis, *The Politics of Population: State Formation, Statistics, and the Census of Canada, 1840–1875* (Toronto: University of Toronto Press, 2001). More recent work, however, has sought to temper the perceived ability of the state to regulate the lives of citizens. See, for example, George D. Perry, "'The Grand Regulator': State Schooling and the Normal-School Idea in Nova Scotia, 1838–1855," *Acadiensis* 32, no. 2 (2003): 60–83.

11 For discussions of the importance of liberalism, see Ian McKay, "The Liberal Order Framework: A Prospectus for a Reconnaissance of Canadian History," *Canadian Historical Review* 81 (2000): 616–45; Ian McKay, *Rebels, Reds, Radicals: Rethinking Canada's Left History* (Toronto: Between the Lines, 2005), 49–80; Jean-François Constant and Michel Ducharme, eds., *Liberalism and Hegemony: Debating the Canadian Liberal Revolution* (Toronto: University of Toronto Press, 2009).

12 Wendy Cukier and Victor W. Sidel, *The Global Gun Epidemic: From Saturday Night Specials to AK-47s* (Westport, CT: Praeger Security International, 2006), 111–12; David B. Kopel, *The Samurai, the Mountie, and the Cowboy: Should America Adopt the Gun Controls of Other Democracies?* (Buffalo, NY: Prometheus Books, 1992).

13 The terms Canadians used to describe handguns changed over time. *Pistol* originally described muzzle-loaded weapons, but later came to refer to all kinds of handguns. *Revolver* referred to a gun with a rotating cylinder that could carry several rounds of ammunition. *Handgun* did not come into common parlance until the twentieth century.

1: Regulating Firearms before Confederation

1 Studies that have considered constitutional liberties in British North America, although not the right to bear arms, include Michel Ducharme,

Le concept de liberté au Canada à l'époque des Révolutions atlantiques (1776–1838) (Montreal and Kingston: McGill-Queen's University Press, 2009); Robert L. Fraser, "'All the Privileges Which Englishmen Possess': Order, Rights, and Constitutionalism in Upper Canada," in *Provincial Justice: Upper Canadian Legal Portraits from the Dictionary of Canadian Biography*, ed. Robert L. Fraser, xxi–xcii (Toronto: University of Toronto Press and the Osgoode Society, 1992); Jeffrey L. McNairn, *The Capacity to Judge: Public Opinion and Deliberative Democracy in Upper Canada, 1791–1854* (Toronto: University of Toronto Press, 2000); Paul Romney, "From Constitutionalism to Legalism: Trial by Jury, Responsible Government, and the Rule of Law in the Canadian Political Culture," *Law & History Review* 7, no. 1 (1989): 120–74.

2 Joyce Lee Malcolm, *Guns and Violence: The English Experience* (Cambridge, MA: Harvard University Press, 2002), 132.

3 Lee Kennett and James LaVerne Anderson, *The Gun in America: The Origins of a National Dilemma* (Westport, CT: Greenwood, 1975), 37.

4 Max Boot, *War Made New: Weapons, Warriors, and the Making of the Modern World* (New York: Gotham Books, 2006), 85; W.Y. Carman, *A History of Firearms from Earliest Times to 1914* (London: Routledge & Kegan Paul, 1955), 100–4; Robert Held, *The Age of Firearms* (London: Cassell, 1957), 20–59, 79–90; Kennett and Anderson, *Gun in America*, 36. The development of percussion caps in the first half of the nineteenth century enabled muzzle-loading guns to fire more reliably in bad weather. The percussion cap was a small cylinder with one closed end containing a small amount of explosive material. The percussion cap was placed over a hollow metal "nipple" at the rear of the gun barrel. When struck by the gun's hammer, the explosive in the percussion cap ignited, sending flame through the nipple to the main powder charge.

5 Carman, *History of Firearms*, 100–4; Boot, *War Made New*, 86; David Hackett Fischer, *Champlain's Dream* (New York: Simon & Schuster, 2008), 269, 616–19; Desmond Morton, *A Military History of Canada*, 5th ed. (Toronto: McClelland & Stewart, 2007), 1.

6 Brian J. Given, *A Most Pernicious Thing: Gun Trading and Native Warfare in the Early Contact Period* (Ottawa: Carleton University Press, 1994), 111–13; Hans Rollmann, "'So Fond of the Pleasure to Shoot': The Sale of Firearms to Inuit on Labrador's North Coast in the Late Eighteenth Century," *Newfoundland and Labrador Studies* 26, no. 1 (2011): 5–24; Louise Dechêne, *Habitants and Merchants in Seventeenth-Century Montreal*, trans. Liana Vardi (Montreal and Kingston: McGill-Queen's University Press, 1992), 80–1; Bruce Vandervort, *Indian Wars of Mexico, Canada and the United States,*

1812–1900 (New York: Routledge, 2006), 45; Laura Peers, *The Ojibwa of Western Canada, 1780–1870* (Winnipeg: University of Manitoba Press, 1994), 11–12; J.R. Miller, *Skyscrapers Hide the Heavens: A History of Indian–White Relations in Canada*, 3rd ed. (Toronto: University of Toronto Press, 2000), 61; Joyce E. Chaplin, *Subject Matter: Technology, the Body, and Science on the Anglo-American Frontier, 1500–1676* (Cambridge, MA: Harvard University Press, 2001), 80–1.

7 Given, *Most Pernicious Thing*, 56, 59; Morton, *Military History of Canada*, 3; S. James Gooding, *The Canadian Gunsmiths, 1608–1900* (West Hill, ON: Museum Restoration Service, 1962), 3, 25–6; Russell Bouchard, "The Trade Gun in New France, 1690–1760," *Canadian Journal of Arms Collecting* 15, no. 1 (1977), 3–12; Vandervort, *Indian Wars of Mexico, Canada and the United States*, 44; Dechêne, *Habitants and Merchants*, 79–81; Gilles Havard, *The Great Peace of Montreal of 1701: French–Native Diplomacy in the Seventeenth Century*, trans. Phyllis Aronoff and Howard Scott (Montreal and Kingston: McGill-Queen's University Press, 2001), 32–3.

8 Gooding, *Canadian Gunsmiths*, 8; S. James Gooding, *Trade Guns of the Hudson's Bay Company, 1670–1970* (Bloomfield, ON: Museum Restoration Service, 2003), 19; Arthur J. Ray, *Indians in the Fur Trade: Their Role as Trappers, Hunters, and Middlemen in the Lands Southwest of Hudson's Bay, 1660–1870* (Toronto: University of Toronto Press, 1974), 72–9; Miller, *Skyscrapers Hide the Heavens*, 157–8; Sarah Carter, *Aboriginal People and Colonizers of Western Canada to 1900* (Toronto: University of Toronto Press, 1999), 87.

9 Morton, *Military History of Canada*, 19. Also see W.J. Eccles, "The French Forces in North America during the Seven Years' War," in *Reappraisals in Canadian History: Pre-Confederation*, ed. C.M. Wallace and R.M. Bray (Scarborough, ON: Prentice Hall Allyn and Bacon Canada, 1999), 124.

10 Louise Dechêne, *Le peuple, l'état et la guerre au Canada sous le régime français* (Montreal: Boréal, 2008), 100, 128–9, 310; Paul-Louis Martin, *La chasse au Québec* (Montreal: Boreal, 1990), 21–49; Jay Cassel, "The Militia Legend: Canadians at War, 1665–1760," in *Canadian Military History since the 17th Century*, ed. Yves Tremblay, 59–67 (Ottawa: Department of National Defence, 2001); Russell Bouchard, *Les armes à feu en Nouvelle-France* (Sillery, QC: Septentrion, 1999); Allan Greer, *Peasant, Lord, and Merchant: Rural Society in Three Quebec Parishes, 1740–1840* (Toronto: University of Toronto Press, 1985), 6; Given, *Most Pernicious Thing*, 37–8; Eccles, "French Forces in North America," 124; Morton, *Military History of Canada*, 9–10.

11 David Calverley, "'When the Need for It No Longer Existed': Declining Wildlife and Native Hunting Rights in Ontario, 1791–1898," in *The Culture*

of Hunting in Canada, ed. Jean Manore and Dale G. Miner (Vancouver: UBC Press, 2007), 107; Thomas Radcliff, *Authentic Letters from Upper Canada: Including an Account of Canadian Field Sports by Thomas William McGrath* (Toronto: Macmillan, 1833), 106. On the propensity of pioneers to supplement their diet through hunting, also see Robert Leslie Jones, *History of Agriculture in Ontario, 1613–1880* (Toronto: University of Toronto Press, 1946), 77–8.

12 Jeffrey L. McNairn, "Meaning and Markets: Hunting, Economic Development and British Imperialism in Maritime Travel Narratives to 1870," *Acadiensis* 34 (2004): 23.

13 Catharine Parr Traill, *The Canadian Settler's Guide* (Toronto: McClelland and Stewart, 1969), 155.

14 Douglas McCalla, "Upper Canadians and Their Guns: An Exploration via Country Store Accounts (1808–61)," *Ontario History* 97, no. 2 (2005), 123, 136. In Newfoundland, sealers used large-calibre sealing guns known as "long-toms" to shoot adult seals before the advent of more advanced rifles. These unwieldy arms had little other use. James E. Candow, *Of Men and Seals: A History of the Land Newfoundland Seal Hunt* (Ottawa: Canadian Parks Service, 1989), 34; G. Hamilton May, "The Newfoundland Sealing Gun," *Canadian Journal of Arms Collecting* 4, no. 1 (1966): 18–21.

15 N.E.S. Griffiths, *From Migrant to Acadian: A North American Border People, 1604–1755* (Montreal and Kingston: McGill-Queen's University Press, 2005), 174–5.

16 McNairn, "Meaning and Markets," 14; Julian Gwyn, "The Mi'kmaq, Poor Settlers, and the Nova Scotia Fur Trade, 1783–1853," *Journal of the Canadian Historical Association* n.s. 14 (2003): 65–91.

17 George Colpitts, *Game in the Garden: A Human History of Wildlife in Western Canada to 1940* (Vancouver: UBC Press, 2002), 75, 78–9, 86–93.

18 Miller, *Skyscrapers Hide the Heavens*, 103–24; L.S.F. Upton, *Micmacs and Colonists: Indian–White Relations in the Maritimes, 1713–1867* (Vancouver: UBC Press, 1979); Ralph Pastore, "The Collapse of the Beothuk World," *Acadiensis* 19, no. 1 (1989): 52–71; Peter S. Schmalz, *The Ojibwa of Southern Ontario* (Toronto: University of Toronto Press, 1991); Donald B. Smith, *Sacred Feathers: The Reverend Peter Jones (Kahkewaquonaby) and the Mississauga Indians* (Toronto: University of Toronto Press, 1987).

19 Donald Fyson, *Magistrates, Police, and People: Everyday Criminal Justice in Quebec and Lower Canada, 1764–1837* (Toronto: University of Toronto Press and the Osgoode Society, 2006), 136–83; Allan Greer, "The Birth of the Police in Canada," in *Colonial Leviathan: State Formation in Mid-Nineteenth-Century Canada*, ed. Allan Greer and Ian Radforth, 17–49 (Toronto: Uni-

versity of Toronto Press, 1992); Greg Marquis, *Policing Canada's Century: A History of the Canadian Association of Chiefs of Police* (Toronto: University of Toronto Press, 1993), 27–39; Michael McCulloch, "'Most Assuredly Perpetual Motion': Police and Policing in Quebec City, 1838–58," *Urban History Review* 19, no. 2 (1990): 100–13; Nicholas Rogers, "Serving Toronto the Good: The Development of the City Police Force, 1834–1884," in *Forging a Consensus: Historical Essays on Toronto*, ed. Victor L. Russell, 116–40 (Toronto: University of Toronto Press, 1984); Greg Marquis, "'A Machine of Oppression under the Guise of the Law': The Saint John Police Establishment, 1860–1890," *Acadiensis* 16 (1986): 58–77; Philip Girard, "The Rise and Fall of Urban Justice in Halifax, 1815–1886," *Nova Scotia Historical Review* 8 (1988): 57–71; Greg Marquis, "State, Community, and Petty Justice in Halifax, Nova Scotia, 1815–67," in *Violent Crime in North America*, ed. Louis A. Knafla, 1–29 (Westport, CT: Praeger, 2003); Greg Marquis, "Enforcing the Law: The Charlottetown Police Force," in *Gaslights, Epidemics and Vagabond Cows: Charlottetown in the Victorian Era*, ed. Douglas Baldwin and Thomas Spira, 86–102 (Charlottetown, PEI: Ragweed, 1988).

20 Ute Frevert, *Men of Honour: A Social and Cultural History of the Duel*, trans. Anthony Williams (Cambridge, UK: Polity, 1995); Dick Steward, *Duels and the Roots of Violence in Missouri* (Columbia: University of Missouri Press, 2000); Donna Andrew, "The Code of Honour and Its Critics: The Opposition to Duelling in England, 1700–1850," *Social History* 5 (1980): 409–34; Antony E. Simpson, "Dandelions on the Field of Honor: Duelling, the Middle Classes, and the Law in Nineteenth-Century England," *Criminal Justice History* 9 (1988): 99–155.

21 Pistols, however, also increased the mortality rate from duelling. At least 15 per cent of participants in duels in England died in the 1785 to 1850 period. Richard Hopton, *Pistols at Dawn: A History of Duelling* (London: Portrait, 2007), 209–11; V.G. Kiernan, *The Duel in European History: Honour and the Reign of Aristocracy* (Oxford: Oxford University Press, 1988), 144–5; Simpson, "Dandelions on the Field of Honor," 106–7, 110–12.

22 Cecilia Morgan, "'In Search of the Phantom Misnamed Honour': Duelling in Upper Canada," *Canadian Historical Review* 76, no. 4 (1995): 553.

23 Morgan, "In Search of the Phantom Misnamed Honour"; Hugh A. Halliday, *Murder among Gentlemen: A History of Duelling in Canada* (Toronto: Robin Brass Studio, 1999), 151–76; Joseph C. Chapman, "Gentlemen, Scoundrels, and Poltroons: Honour, Violence, and the Duel in Nineteenth-Century British North America" (MA thesis, Dalhousie University, 1994); Jean-François Mathieu, "Le Duel au Canada, pratique et discours, 1646–1888" (MA thesis, Université de Montréal, 2005).

24 Robert H. Churchill, "Gun Regulation, the Police Power, and the Right to Keep Arms in Early America: The Legal Context of the Second Amendment," *Law and History Review* 25, no. 1 (2007), 144–45; Lois Schwoerer, *"No Standing Armies!": The Antiarmy Ideology in Seventeenth-Century England* (Baltimore, MD: Johns Hopkins University Press, 1974), 14–15.

25 Churchill, "Gun Regulation, the Police Power, and the Right to Keep Arms," 145–6; Joseph Plimsoll Edwards, "The Militia of Nova Scotia, 1749–1867," *Collections of the Nova Scotia Historical Society* 17 (1913): 63–109; David Facey-Crowther, *The New Brunswick Militia, 1787–1867* (Fredericton: New Brunswick Historical Society and New Ireland Press, 1990), 3, 6–7; *An Act for Establishing a Militia …*, S.N.B. 1787, c.1; *An Act for the establishing and regulating a Militia*, S.P.E.I. 1780, c.1.

26 *An Ordinance for regulating the militia of the province of Quebec …* (1777), articles 1, 5, and *An Ordinance for better regulating the Militia …* (1787), articles 1, 4, in Arthur G. Doughty, *Report of the Public Archives for the Years 1914 and 1915* (Ottawa: King's Printer, 1916), 68, 70, 180–1; *An Act for the better Regulation of the Militia …*, S.L.C. 1803, c.1, s.7; *Abstract of the Militia Act at present in force …* (Quebec: P.E. Desbarats, 1821), 10, 14, 16; J.L. Little, *Loyalties in Conflict: A Canadian Borderland in War and Rebellion, 1812–1840* (Toronto: University of Toronto Press, 2008), 12; Fernand Ouellet, "Officiers de milice et structure sociale au Québec (1660–1815)," *Histoire sociale / Social History* 12 (1979), 51–2; Christian Dessureault and Roch Legault, "Évolution organisationnelle et sociale de la milice sédentaire canadienne: le cas du bataillon de Saint-Hyacinthe, 1808–1830," *Journal of the Canadian Historical Association* n.s. 8 (1997): 87–112.

27 *An Act for the better Regulation of the Militia …*, S.U.C. 1793, c.1; *An Act to explain, amend, and reduce … the several Laws … for the Raising and Training the Militia of this Province*, S.U.C. 1808, c.1, ss.3, 14.

28 *An Act for the establishing and regulating a Militia*, S.P.E.I. 1780, c.1, s.27.

29 Quoted in David Webber, *A Thousand Young Men: The Colonial Volunteer Militia of Prince Edward Island, 1775–1874* (Charlottetown: Prince Edward Island Museum and Heritage Foundation, 1990), 36, 43.

30 Morton, *Military History of Canada*, 50; Facey-Crowther, *New Brunswick Militia*, 7, 32, 41.

31 Thomas C. Haliburton, *An Historical and Statistical Account of Nova-Scotia, in Two Volumes* (Halifax: C.H. Belcher, 1829), 2:297; Facey-Crowther, *New Brunswick Militia*, 74. Haliburton did suggest, however, that Nova Scotians called for militia service were "familiar with the use of the gun, and on average are better marksmen than European soldiers."

32 *British Colonist* (Halifax), 11 February 1851.

33 Roger Sarty, *Guardian of the Gulf: Sydney, Cape Breton, and the Atlantic Wars* (Toronto: University of Toronto Press, 2002), 65.

34 Robert Gourlay, *Statistical Account of Upper Canada with a View to a Grand System of Emigration* (London: Simpkins & Marshall Stationers, 1822), 1:230; George Sheppard, *Plunder, Profit, and Paroles: A Social History of the War of 1812 in Upper Canada* (Montreal and Kingston: McGill-Queen's University Press, 1994), 40–99; J.L. Granatstein, *Canada's Army: Waging War and Keeping the Peace* (Toronto: University of Toronto Press, 2004), 3–23; George Sheppard, "'Deeds Speak': Militiamen, Medals, and the Invented Traditions of 1812," *Ontario History* 82 (1990): 207–32; Morton, *Military History of Canada*, 54.

35 Lower Canada, House of Assembly, *Report of the special committee, to whom was referred that part of His Excellency's speech which referred to the organization of the militia* (Quebec: Neilson and Cowan, 1829), appendices [Canadian Institute for Historical Microreproductions (CIHM) no. 63940]. In 1833, one rough estimate of the number of Lower Canada militiamen who possessed hunting weapons was twenty-five thousand. Allan Greer, *The Patriots and the People: The Rebellion of 1837 in Rural Lower Canada* (Toronto: University of Toronto Press, 1993), 101; Luc Lépine, "La malice du district de Montréal, 1787–1829: essai d'histoire socio-militaire" (PhD diss., Université du Québec à Montréal, 2005), 215–22.

36 Quoted in Little, *Loyalties in Conflict*, 41, 46.

37 *Report of the special committee … referred to the organization of the militia*, 10.

38 Morton, *Military History of Canada*, 86.

39 Ibid.; Granatstein, *Canada's Army*, 18–19; Greer, *Patriots and the People*, 101.

40 Greer, *Patriots and the People*, 307; Colin Read and Ronald J. Stagg, eds., *The Rebellion of 1837 in Upper Canada: A Collection of Documents* (Toronto: Champlain Society, 1985), xlii, 121; Granatstein, *Canada's Army*, 15; *Journal of the House of Assembly of Upper Canada, 1837–8*, 16; Elinor Kyte Senoir, *Redcoats and Patriotes: The Rebellion in Lower Canada, 1837–38* (Stittsville, ON: Canada's Wings, in collaboration with the Canadian War Museum, National Museum of Man, and National Museums of Canada, 1985), 69, 71, 82, 108, 122, 129, 189; John Dickinson and Brian Young, *A Short History of Quebec*, 4th ed. (Montreal and Kingston: McGill-Queen's University Press, 2008), 166; Jean-Marie Fecteau, "'This Ultimate Resource': Martial Law and State Repression in Lower Canada, 1837–8," in *Canadian State Trials*, vol. 2, *Rebellion and Invasion in the Canadas, 1837–1839*, ed. F. Murray Greenwood and Barry Wright (Toronto: University of Toronto Press and the Osgoode Society, 2002), 227–8.

41 "Shooting a Man," *Globe*, 24 July 1857, 3.

42 Jim Phillips, "Women, Crime and Criminal Justice in Early Halifax, 1750–1800," in *Essays in the History of Canadian Law*, vol. 5, *Crime and Criminal Justice*, ed. Jim Phillips, Tina Loo, and Susan Lewthwaite, 74–206 (Toronto: University of Toronto Press, 1994); Donald Fyson, "Blows and Scratches, Swords and Guns: Violence between Men as Material Reality and Lived Experience in Early Nineteenth-Century Lower Canada" (paper delivered at the 78th annual meeting of the Canadian Historical Association, Sherbrooke, QC, June 1999).

43 For example, in the early nineteenth century, New York banned the discharge of arms in the city as part of its fire code. William J. Novak, *The People's Welfare: Law & Regulation in Nineteenth-Century America* (Chapel Hill: University of North Carolina Press, 1996), 57.

44 *An Act to prevent unnecessary firing off Guns ...*, S.N.S. 1758, c.25; *An Act in addition to ... An Act to prevent unnecessary firing off Guns ...*, S.N.S. 1769, c.3; *An Act for extending ... An Act to prevent unnecessary firing off Guns ...*, S.N.S. 1793, c.12; *An Act for extending ... An Act to prevent unnecessary firing off Guns ...*, S.N.S. 1807, c.21; R.S.N.S. 1859, c.100; *An Act to prevent the unnecessary Firing off Guns ...*, S.P.E.I. 1790, c.4.

45 *An Act to prevent the unnecessary discharging of Guns ...*, S.N. 1835, c.9.

46 For relevant Montreal by-laws, see *Quebec Gazette*, 12 June 1777; *Quebec Gazette*, 22 May 1783; *Quebec Gazette*, 25 February 1790; *Rules and Regulations of Police for the City and Suburbs of Montreal* (Montreal: James Brown, 1810), article 15; *Rules and Regulations of Police, For the City and Suburbs of Montreal* (Montreal: James Lane, 1817), article 11; *Collection des ordonnances et règlements de police en force dans la cité de Montréal* (Montreal: L. Perrault, 1843), 63; Charles Glackmeyer, *The Charter and By-laws of the City of Montreal together with Miscellaneous Acts of the Legislature Relating to the City* (Montreal: John Lovell, 1865), 302; *The By-Laws of the City of Montreal; with an Appendix* (Montreal: John Lovell, 1865), 78. For Quebec City by-laws, see *Quebec Gazette*, 1 June 1802; *Rules and Regulations of Police: With Abstracts of Divers Ordinances and Statutes Relating Thereto* (Quebec: John Neilson, 1811); *Laws and Regulations for the Government of the City of Quebec* (Quebec: Bureau & Marcotte, 1850), 1:142; Mathias Chouinard, *Règlements du Conseil de ville de la cité de Québec* (Quebec: L.-J. Demers, 1901), 212. For Trois-Rivières, see *Quebec Gazette*, 29 September 1791. Thanks to Donald Fyson for sharing these sources on the local regulation of firearms in Lower Canada.

47 Legislators empowered local governments to place limits on the firing of guns. For examples, see *An Act to establish a Board of Police in the Town of Belleville*, S.U.C. 1834, c.24, s.19; *An Act to define the Limits of the Town*

of London, in the District of London, and to establish a Board of Police therein,
S.U.C. 1840, c.31, s.21.

48 *By-Laws and the Rules of Order of the City of Hamilton* (Hamilton, ON: Christian Advocate Office, 1854), 43.

49 *By-Laws of the City of Toronto, of Practical Utility and General Application ...*
(Toronto: Henry Rowsell, 1870), 46; Mathias Chouinard, *Règlements du Conseil de ville de la ville de la cité de Québec* (Quebec: L.-J. Demers, 1901), 60.
Also see "By-Law," *Perth Courier*, 18 April 1851. In 1862, Lévis stipulated
a fine of four dollars for any person caught firing a gun in the community.
"Corporation of the Town of Levis," *Quebec Mercury*, 15 March 1862. Brandon, Manitoba, banned firing guns in the city by 1885. "Sunday Observance," *Brandon Sun Weekly*, 25 June 1885, 1.

50 *An Act to provide for the Freedom of Elections ...*, S.C. 1842, c.1, ss.27, 34, 37;
W.C. Keele, *The Provincial Justice, or Magistrate's Manual ...*, 2nd ed. (Toronto: H. & W. Rowsell, 1843), 242. The penalties changed over time. See *An Act ... to amend, consolidate, and reduce into one Act, the several Statutory provisions ... for the regulation of Elections*, S.C. 1849, c.27, s.52; *An Act respecting Elections of Members of the Legislature*, C.S.C. 1859, c.6, ss.74, 77, 80. Prince Edward Island banned people from carrying "offensive weapons" to or from polling places on elections days. *An Act to consolidate and improve the Laws for the Election of Members to serve in the General Assembly*, S.P.E.I. 1848, c.21, s.23. Nova Scotia banned threats of violence to intimidate on election days. *An Act to prevent Corrupt Practices at Elections*, S.N.S. 1861, c.19, s.5.

51 *An Act to provide for the calling and orderly holding of Public Meetings ...*, S.C. 1843, c.7, ss.15–16, 18; W.C. Keele, *The Provincial Justice, or Magistrate's Manual ...*, 4th ed. (Toronto: Henry Rowsell, 1858), 684–5; W.C. Keele, *The Provincial Justice, or Magistrate's Manual ...*, 5th ed. (Toronto: Henry Rowsell, 1864), 685–6.

52 John Mack Faragher, *A Great and Noble Scheme: The Tragic Story of the Expulsion of the French Acadians from Their American Homeland* (New York: W.W. Norton, 2005), 314.

53 W.J. Eccles, *The French in North America, 1500–1783*, rev. ed. (East Lansing, MI: Michigan State University Press, 1998), 234; McCulloch, "Battle of Sillery," 24.

54 Proclamation by Robert Monkton (22 September 1759), in Arthur G. Doughty, *Report of the Public Archives for the Year 1918* (Ottawa: King's Printer, 1920), 33.

55 Order to all Captains of militia on the South Shore regarding the laying down their arms, and taking the oath of fidelity (21 September 1760); Proclamation of General Jeffery Amherst (22 September 1760); Order to

inhabitants of Trois-Rivières to lay down arms, and take oath of Fidelity
(22 September 1760); Order to Captains of Militia to send to Government
House, all guns in their charge (16 October 1760), in Doughty, *Report of the
Public Archives for the Year 1918*, 73, 75, 199, 201, 217, 348, 350; Alfred Leroy
Burt, *The Old Province of Quebec*, vol. 1, *1760–1778* (Toronto: McClelland
and Stewart, 1968), 15–16, 24; Marcel Trudel, *Le Régime militaire dans le
Gouvernement des Trois-Rivières, 1760–1764* (Trois-Rivières, QC: Éditions du
bien public, 1952), 36–9.

56 Letter to Captains of Militia, sending them hunting licences (4 July 1761),
in Doughty, *Report of the Public Archives for the Year 1918*, 245; Burt, *Old
Province of Quebec*, 23, 37.

57 Doughty, *Report of the Public Archives for the Year 1918*, 350, 353–5; Trudel,
Le Régime militaire, 39–40.

58 Orders and proclamations of Murray for 6 July 1761, 28 July 1761, and 13
March 1762, les bibliothèques, Université de Montréal, http://calypso.bib.
umontreal.ca/cdm4/index_murray.php?CISOROOT=/_murray.

59 Letter to Captain of Militia at Yamaska to return surplus guns (6 March
1762), in Doughty, *Report of the Public Archives for the Year 1918*, 267, 269.

60 Order that the Inhabitants of Batiscan, and Rivière Batiscan, be required
to surrender their arms (28 March 1764), in Doughty, *Report of the Public
Archives for the Year 1918*, 335. The confiscation of arms may explain the
very small inventory of guns and firearm supplies at Samuel Jacobs's
store at St Denis, as detailed by Allan Greer. His business served a rural
constituency, and Jacobs attempted to stock everything that rural customers required. However, guns accounted for no more that 0.4 per cent of
the store's inventory in June 1775, and no more than 0.1 per cent in 1786.
Greer, *Peasant, Lord, and Merchant*, 155–6.

61 *An Ordinance for regulating the militia of the province of Quebec … (1777)*, article 1, in Doughty, *Report of the Public Archives for the Years 1914 and 1915*,
69; Hilda Neatby, *Quebec: The Revolutionary Age, 1760–1791* (Toronto: Mc-
Clelland and Stewart, 1966), 163.

62 *Act to prevent the unlawful training of persons to the use of Arms …*, S.U.C.
1838, c.11, s.6; Rainer Baehre, "Trying the Rebels: Emergency Legislation
and the Colonial Executive's Overall Legal Strategy in the Upper Canadian Rebellion," in Greenwood and Wright, *Canadian State Trials*, 2:47.

63 *An Ordinance to authorize the Seizing and Detaining for a limited time of Gunpowder, Arms, Weapons, Lead, and Munitions of War*, in *Ordinances made
and passed by the Administrator of the Government, and Special Council for the
Affairs of the Province of Lower Canada*, vol. 3, c.2 (Quebec: John Charlton
Fisher and William Kemble, 1838), 22; *An Ordinance to continue … a certain*

*Ordinance, relative to the seizing and detaining for a limited time of Gunpowder
...,* and *An Ordinance to render permanent certain Ordinances ...,* in *Ordinances made and passed by his Excellency the Governor General, and Special Council
for the affairs of the Province of Lower Canada,* vol. 5, c.2, 16 (Quebec: John
Charlton Fisher and William Kemble, 1839), 10, 58.

An 1845 volume of the revised acts and ordinances of Lower Canada incorporated the legislation. *The Revised Acts and Ordinances of Lower-Canada*
(Montreal: S. Derbishire and G. Desbarats, 1845), 176. In 1860, a draft version of the consolidated statutes also had the 1838 ordinance, although the
compilers questioned whether the act should be included, writing, "Query
whether this ordinance can apply now." *An Act respecting Arms and Munitions of War,* in *The Consolidated States for Lower Canada,* draft report (Quebec: Stewart Derbishire and George Desbarats, 1860), 55. The answer was
apparently in the affirmative, as the ordinance appeared in the final version of the consolidated statutes for Lower Canada published in 1861. *An
Act respecting Arms and Munitions of War,* C.S.L.C. 1860, c.8.

64 *An Act to prevent the Training of Persons to the Use of Arms ...,* 60 Geo. III, c.1
(1819) (U.K.); *An Act to authorise Justices of the Peace, in certain disturbed Coun-
ties, to seize and detain Arms collected or kept for purposes dangerous to the Public
Peace ...,* 1 Geo. IV, c.2 (1819) (U.K.); Colin Greenwood, *Firearms Control:
A Study of Armed Crime and Firearms Control in England and Wales* (London:
Routledge & Kegan Paul, 1972), 14–17; Malcolm, *Guns and Violence,* 95–9.

65 Bryan D. Palmer, "Labour Protest and Organization in Nineteenth-
Century Canada, 1820–1890," *Labour / Le Travail* 20 (1987): 61–83; Peter
Way, *Common Labour: Workers and the Digging of North American Canals,
1780–1860* (Cambridge, UK: Cambridge University Press, 1993), 205–6,
231–53; Bryan D. Palmer, *Working-Class Experience: Rethinking the History
of Canadian Labour, 1800–1991,* 2nd ed. (Toronto: McClelland & Stewart,
1992), 60–3.

66 H.C. Pentland, "The Lachine Strike of 1843," *Canadian Historical Review* 29
(1948): 263–4. For numerous examples of labourers stealing weapons to
arm themselves in 1844, see *Journals of the Legislative Assembly of the Province of Canada, 1844–1845,* Appendix Y. Also see E. Gibbs, ed., *Debates of
the Legislative Assembly of United Canada, 1841–1867,* vol. 6, pt 2 (Montreal:
Centre d'Étude du Québec, 1978), 1512. Taking guns from locals during
times of upheaval was not uncommon. In Bytown in 1849, rioters procured
guns from merchants, nearby houses, and even from government armouries in Hull. Michael S. Cross, "Stony Monday, 1849: The Rebellion Losses
Riots in Bytown," *Ontario History* 63 (1971): 186–9.

67 Letters from G.S. Jarvis, Esquire, and four other Justices of the Peace, 25

November 1844, *Journals of the Legislative Assembly of the Province of Canada, 1844–1845*, Appendix Y.

68 Petition of the Justices of the Peace and other Inhabitants of the County of Dundas, in the vicinity of the Public Works now in progress, 2 November 1844, *Journals of the Legislative Assembly of the Province of Canada, 1844–1845*, Appendix Y.

69 The *Quebec Mercury* took solace in its belief that the arms were of a "very inferior description, and may not be of much service if an attempt is made to use them." *Quebec Mercury*, 8 February 1845, 2.

70 H. Clare Pentland, *Labour and Capital in Canada, 1650–1860* (Toronto: James Lorimer, 1981), 191–3; Pentland, "Lachine Strike of 1843," 264; Ruth Bleasdale, "Class Conflict on the Canals of Upper Canada in the 1840s," *Labour / Le Travailleur* 7 (1981): 33.

71 Provincial Secretary to C. Wetherall, 15 November 1844; C. Wetherall to Provincial Secretary, 20 November 1844; L.G. Brown to Captain Wetherall, 21 November 1844, L.G. Brown to Provincial Secretary, 21 November 1844, *Journals of the Legislative Assembly of the Province of Canada, 1844–1845*, Appendix Y.

72 C. Wetherall to the Provincial Secretary, 21 January 1845, *Journals of the Legislative Assembly of the Province of Canada, 1844–1845*, Appendix Y.

73 Gibbs, *Debates*, vol. 6, pt 2, 1442–3.

74 Ibid., vol. 6, pt 2, 1448, 1513; Louis-Philippe Audet, "Edward Hale," *DCB* online.

75 *An Act for the better preservation of the Peace ...*, S.C. 1845, c.6; *Quebec Mercury*, 8 February 1845, 1; *An Act to continue ... several Acts*, S.C. 1859, c.28.

76 Gibbs, *Debates*, vol. 6, pt 2, 1445, 1446, 1450, 1455, 1477, 1505, 1506, 1511, 1517; Andrée Désilets, "Joseph-Édouard Cauchon," *DCB* online; Michael S. Cross and Robert Lochiel Fraser, "Robert Baldwin," *DCB* online; *Quebec Mercury*, 22 February 1845, 1.

77 "Riots and Assassination in Montreal," *Globe*, 10 December 1844, 2.

78 Quoted in Lois G. Schwoerer, "To Hold and Bear Arms: The English Perspective," in *The Second Amendment in Law and History: Historians and Constitutional Scholars on the Right to Bear Arms*, ed. Carl T. Bogus (New York: New Press, 2000), 215.

79 William Blackstone, as quoted in Schwoerer, "To Hold and Bear Arms," 224.

80 Joyce Lee Malcolm, *To Keep and Bear Arms: The Origins of an Anglo-American Right* (Cambridge, MA: Harvard University Press, 1994); Malcolm, *Guns and Violence*, 58–61.

81 Schwoerer, "To Hold and Bear Arms," 216.
82 Greg Marquis, "In Defence of Liberty: 17th-Century England and 19th-Century Maritime Political Culture," *University of New Brunswick Law Journal* 42 (1993): 69–94; G. Blaine Baker, "Legal Education in Upper Canada, 1785–1889: The Law Society as Educator," in *Essays in the History of Canadian Law*, ed. David H. Flaherty (Toronto: Osgoode Society, 1983), 2:94; Ian McKay, "Canada as a Long Liberal Revolution: On Writing the History of Actually Existing Canadian Liberalisms," in *Liberalism and Hegemony: Debating the Canadian Liberal Revolution*, ed. Jean-François Constant and Michel Ducharme, 347–452 (Toronto: University of Toronto Press, 2009); Ian McKay, "The Liberal Order Framework: A Prospectus for a Reconnaissance of Canadian History," *Canadian Historical Review* 81 (2000): 616–45. Philip Girard suggests that Blackstone had a smaller role in legal education in British North America than in the United States, but still notes that he was usually recommended reading. Philip Girard, *Lawyers and Legal Culture in British North America: Beamish Murdoch of Halifax* (Toronto: University of Toronto Press and the Osgoode Society, 2011), 39–41.
83 Gibbs, *Debates*, vol. 6, pt 2, 1453, 1517. And see Gibbs, *Debates*, vol. 6, pt 2, 1459.
84 In 1837, William Lyon Mackenzie prepared a draft constitution that could be debated by a provisional government in Upper Canada. Among its provisions was a right to bear arms: "The people have a right to bear arms for the defence of themselves and the State." Charles Lindsey, *The Life and Times of Wm. Lyon Mackenzie* (Toronto: P.R. Randall, 1862), 2:347. It is unclear whether Mackenzie simply paraphrased the American Second Amendment or was aware of the older British right in framing his proposal.
85 *An Act to consolidate and amend the several Acts of Assembly relating to the Criminal Law* …, S.N.B. 1849, c.29 (c.5, article 9); R.S.N.B. 1854, c.147, s.10; Scott See, *Riots in New Brunswick: Orange Nativism and Social Violence in the 1840s* (Toronto: University of Toronto Press, 1993), 117–18, 135–7, 145–6, 152–5, 164–8, 194–5.
86 *Of Offences against the Public Peace*, R.S.N.S. 1851, c.160, s.8.
87 *An Act to prevent the carrying of Deadly Weapons about the person*, S.N.B. 1861, c.10, preamble, s.1.
88 "The Legislature," *Morning Freeman* (Saint John), 28 February 1861.
89 *An Act to prevent the carrying of Bowie-knives, Daggers, and other deadly weapons about the person*, S.C. 1859, c.26, s.1; Donald Fyson, "The Trials and Tribulations of Riot Prosecutions: Collective Violence, State Authority,

and Criminal Justice in Quebec, 1841–92," in *Canadian State Trials*, vol. 3, *Political Trials and Security Measures, 1840–1914*, ed. Barry Wright and Susan Binnie (Toronto: University of Toronto Press and the Osgoode Society, 2009), 188.

90 *Journals of the Legislative Council of the Province of Canada*, 1859, 184–5; "Provincial Parliament," *Globe*, 1 April 1859.

91 Morton, *Military History of Canada*, 80–4; Robin W. Winks, *The Civil War Years: Canada and the United States* (Lanham, MD: University Press of America, 1988); Carl L. Davis, *Arming the Union: Small Arms in the Civil War* (Port Washington, NY: Kennikat, 1973), 106; Ross Thomson, "The Continuity of Innovation: The Civil War Experience," *Enterprise & Society* 11, no. 1 (2010): 133–44.

92 J. Brent Wilson, "'That Vast Experiment': The New Brunswick Militia's 1865 Camp of Instruction," *Canadian Military History* 6, no. 2 (1997): 39–53; Facey-Crowther, *New Brunswick Militia*, 100–1; *An Act in reference to the Militia*, S.N.S. 1862, c.9; Sarty, *Guardian of the Gulf*, 31–2, 87; Granatstein, *Canada's Army*, 19–20; *An Act for the regulation of the Militia and Volunteer Forces*, S.P.E.I. 1866, c.2; Morton, *Military History of Canada*, 87.

93 Greg Marquis, *In Armageddon's Shadow: The Civil War and Canada's Maritime Provinces* (Montreal and Kingston: McGill-Queen's University Press, 1998), 20–3; "Notice," *British Colonist* (Halifax), 13 December 1859, 3; Webber, *Thousand Young Men*, 94; Facey-Crowther, *New Brunswick Militia*, 90, 115; Sarty, *Guardian of the Gulf*, 69, 86–7, 93.

94 Granatstein, *Canada's Army*, 18; "A Volunteer Rifle Company," *British Columbian*, 7 November 1863; Peter N. Moogk, assisted by R.V. Stevenson, *Vancouver Defended: A History of the Men and Guns of the Lower Mainland Defences, 1859–1949* (Surrey, BC: Antonson, 1978), 13; *An Act to amend the Laws relative to the Militia*, S.N.S. 1859, c.43; Ian Radforth, *Royal Spectacle: The 1860 Visit of the Prince of Wales to Canada and the United States* (Toronto: University of Toronto Press, 2004), 140–8; Facey-Crowther, *New Brunswick Militia*, 90.

95 "A Volunteer Rifle Company," *British Columbian*, 7 November 1863.

96 Marquis, *In Armageddon's Shadow*, 20; Facey-Crowther, *New Brunswick Militia*, 90, 94, 104, 106; Carman Miller, "The Montreal Militia as a Social Institution before World War I," *Urban History Review* 19 (1990): 57–64; Morton, *Military History of Canada*, 86–7.

97 "Scottish Volunteers," *Halifax Citizen*, 10 December 1863.

98 "Volunteer Rifle Company Meeting," *British Columbian*, 14 November 1863. And see Miller, "The Montreal Militia as a Social Institution before World War I," 60.

99 David A. Hounshell, *From the American System to Mass Production, 1800–1932: The Development of Manufacturing Technology in the United States* (Baltimore, MD: Johns Hopkins University Press, 1984), 46–50; Felicia Johnson Deyrup, *Arms Makers of the Connecticut Valley: A Regional Study of the Economic Development of the Small Arms Industry, 1798–1870* (Northampton, MA: Smith College Studies in History, 1948); Kennett and Anderson, *Gun in America*, 83–93.

100 Boot, *War Made New*, 127; Daniel R. Headrick, *The Tools of Empire: Technology and European Imperialism in the Nineteenth Century* (New York: Oxford University Press, 1981), 88–9; Kennett and Anderson, *Gun in America*, 38–9. Some American revolutionaries also used the "Kentucky rifle" to harass British forces at long range.

101 Boot, *War Made New*, 128–9, 149; Headrick, *Tools of Empire*, 96–104; Carman, *History of Firearms*, 105–12.

102 Carman, *History of Firearms*, 157–65.

103 Boot, *War Made New*, 149–50; Headrick, *Tools of Empire*, 98–9; David J. Naumec, "From Muskets to M4's: Connecticut's Gunmaking Tradition, 1637–2010," *Connecticut History* 49, no. 2 (2010): 192–3; Harold F. Williamson, *Winchester: The Gun That Won the West* (Washington: Combat Forces, 1952).

104 David Miller, *The History of Browning Firearms* (Guilford, CT: Lyons, 2006), 15–17, 96–112.

105 *Globe*, 19 April 1866, 2. A British Columbia merchant advertised a six-chamber repeating rifle in 1862. *British Colonist*, 28 March 1862, 2.

106 "Lessons of the War," *Globe*, 20 July 1866, 2. Also see "The Prussian Breech-Loader," *Grand River Sachem*, 12 September 1866, 1.

107 "Enfield Rifles! Enfield Rifles!," *Globe*, 5 April 1866, 3.

108 Peter Vronsky, *Rigeway: The American Fenian Invasion and the 1866 Battle That Made Canada* (Toronto: Allen Lane, 2011), 66, 109–10; "Arms & Ammunition of War," *Globe*, 30 March 1866; "Spencer Repeating Rifles," *Globe*, 5 April 1866, 3; "Henry Short," *British Colonist*, 4 April 1872, 2.

109 "Rifle Match," *Globe*, 17 February 1862, 2; "Canadian Rifle Association," *Globe*, 19 April 1862, 3; "Upper Canadian Rifle Association," *Globe*, 23 May 1862, 2; "Upper Canadian Rifle Association," *Globe*, 4 June 1862, 2; "The Rifle Matches at Montreal," *Globe*, 6 August 1870, 4; *An Act in relation to a shooting range at St John's*, S.N. 1933, c.12; Prince Edward Island Archives, Acc 4875, Prince Edward Island Provincial Rifle Association fonds, file: Minutes 1875–May 1910; Webber, *Thousand Young Men*, 88; Facey-Crowther, *New Brunswick Militia*, 91; "Rifle Competition," *Halifax Citizen*, 11 October 1864, 2; "The Prize Firing at Truro," *Halifax Citizen*,

15 October 1864, 2; *Journal and Proceedings of the House of Assembly of the Province of Nova Scotia, Session 1865* (Halifax: Compton, 1865), Appendix 5; "Pictou County Rifle Association," *Halifax Citizen*, 22 June 1867, 3; "Provincial News," *Halifax Citizen*, 13 July 1867, 1; "Halifax County Rifle Association," *Halifax Citizen*, 17 August 1867, 3; Susie Cornfield, *The Queen's Prize: The Story of the National Rifle Association* (London: Pelham, 1987), 13–25; Malcolm, *Guns and Violence*, 154.

110 "Grand Rifle Match at Hamilton," *Globe*, 7 September 1864, 2.

111 K.B. Wamsley, "Cultural Signification and National Ideologies: Rifle-Shooting in Late Nineteenth-Century Canada," *Social History* 20, no. 1 (1995): 66; "Upper Canada Rifle Association," *Globe*, 23 May 1862, 2; "Upper Canada Rifle Association," *Globe*, 24 May 1862; "Upper Canadian Rifle Association," *Globe*, 4 June 1862, 2; "Upper Canada Rifle Association," *Globe*, 6 June 1862, 2; "Montreal Rifle Tournament," *Globe*, 24 September 1863, 2; "Grand Rifle Match," *Montreal Herald*, 29 August 1863, 3; "The Great Rifle Match in Montreal," *Globe*, 25 September 1863, 2; "The Rifle Tournament," *Kingston Daily News*, 25 September 1863, 2; "The Rifle Movement," *Kingston Daily News*, 26 October 1863, 2; "The Great Rifle Match at Hamilton," *Hamilton Evening Times*, 7 September 1864, 2; "Rifle Competition," *Halifax Citizen*, 11 October 1864, 2; "The Prize Firing at Truro," *Halifax Citizen*, 15 October 1864, 2; "Provincial Rifle Contest," *Halifax Citizen*, 5 September 1865, 2.

112 "The Great Rifle Match in Montreal," *Globe*, 25 September 1863, 2. Also see "The National Rifle Association," *Globe*, 23 July 1860, 2; "Rifle Matches," *Globe*, 11 July 1863, 3; "The Rifle Movement," *Globe*, 23 October 1863, 2.

113 "Breech-Loading Rifles," *Grand River Sachem*, 25 July 1866, 2. Also see "New Arms for the Volunteer Force," *Hamilton Evening Times*, 23 November 1866, 2.

114 "The National Rifle Association," *Globe*, 23 July 1860, 2. Also see "The Great Rifle Match in Montreal," *Globe*, 25 September 1863, 2; "The Rifle Movement," *Globe*, 23 October 1863, 2; "The Rifle Movement," *Kingston Daily News*, 26 October 1863, 2; "Rifle Shooting," *Kingston Daily News*, 15 August 1864, 1.

115 The *Perth Courier* advocated the creation of a local rifle association in 1861, since doing so would mean that "when the invader does come, if he ever should, every man will be ready to handle his rifle, and will know how to use it." "Canadian Rifle Association," *Perth Courier*, 31 May 1861, 2. Also see "Great Britain," *Globe*, 15 August 1860, 3; "Canadian Rifle Association," *Perth Courier*, 16 August 1861, 2; "Tenth Military District,"

Globe, 11 February 1864, 2. In 1866, the Nova Scotia government reported that the provincial rifle association's work had resulted in "progressive improvement in marksmanship." *Journal and Proceedings of the House of Assembly of the Province of Nova Scotia, 1866* (Halifax: Compton, 1866), Appendix 11.

116 Wamsley, "Cultural Signification and National Ideologies," 67.

117 "The Rifle Movement," *Globe*, 23 October 1863, 2. Also see "The Rifle Match," *Globe*, 14 October, 1861, 2; "The Great Rifle Match in Montreal," *Globe*, 25 September 1863, 2; *Nation*, 8 September 1876, 1.

118 *An Act for the prevention and repression of outrages in violation of the Peace on the frontier ...*, S.C. 1865, c.1.

119 *An Act to prevent the unlawful training of persons to the use of arms ...*, S.C. 1866, c.5, s.3; *An Act to provide for the seizure of Arms and Munitions of War*, S.N.S. 1866, c.37; *An Act to prevent the concealment of Arms or munitions of war ...*, S.P.E.I. 1866, c.3; *An Act to prevent the clandestine training of persons to the use of Arms ...*, S.P.E.I. 1866, c.8. On the raids, see Hereward Senior, *The Last Invasion of Canada: The Fenian Raids, 1866–1870* (Toronto: Dundurn, 1991).

2: Controlling Firearms

1 *An Act respecting the Militia and Defence of the Dominion of Canada*, S.C. 1868, c.40; Desmond Morton, *A Military History of Canada*, 5th ed. (Toronto: McClelland & Stewart, 2007), 90, 95–6; J.L. Granatstein, *Canada's Army: Waging War and Keeping the Peace* (Toronto: University of Toronto Press, 2002), 24.

2 "Latest from Ottawa," *Hamilton Evening Times*, 2 April 1868, 2; "Latest from Ottawa," *Globe*, 2 April 1868, 2; *Globe*, 3 April 1868, 2; "Ontario Rifle Association," *Globe*, 31 August 1876, 4; "Canada's Wimbledon," *Globe*, 3 September 1881, 13; K.B. Wamsley, "Cultural Signification and National Ideologies: Rifle-Shooting in Late Nineteenth-Century Canada," *Social History* 20, no. 1 (1995): 63, 67–8.

3 "Dominion Rifle Association," *Globe*, 25 August 1868, 1; "Canada's Wimbledon," *Globe*, 3 September 1881, 13; Wamsley, "Cultural Signification and National Ideologies," 68. Also see Gerald Redmond, "Imperial Viceregal Patronage: The Governors-General of Canada and Sport in the Dominion, 1867–1909," *International Journal of the History of Sport* 6, no. 2 (1989): 193–217. The list of notables who attended a lunch at the annual meeting of the Ontario Rifle Association in 1873 also evidenced the elite support for rifle shooting. Attendees included prominent figures such as

Casmir Stanislaus Gzowski, Chief Justice William Draper, Senator David Lewis Macpherson, Liberal Ontario Attorney General Oliver Mowat, and well-known Conservative lawyer and politician Robert Harrison. "Ontario Rifle Association," *Globe*, 3 September 1873, 4.

4 Writer and journalist Goldwin Smith told the Ontario Rifle Association in 1875, for instance, that rifle associations "kept up the martial spirit of the nation, which was a part of its manhood." "Ontario Rifle Association," *Globe*, 1 September 1875, 4.

5 *Canadian Military Gazette*, 29 July 1886, quoted in Wamsley, "Cultural Signification and National Ideologies," 68.

6 Wamsley, "Cultural Signification and National Ideologies," 69–70; Susie Cornfield, *The Queen's Prize: The Story of the National Rifle Association* (London: Pelham, 1987), 27, 58; "Wimbledon," *Globe*, 25 July 1873, 2; "Wimbledon," *Globe*, 26 July 1875, 2; "Wimbledon," *Globe*, 3 August 1875, 3; "A Canadian Trophy for Wimbledon," *Globe*, 29 July 1876, 4; "The Wimbledon Shooting," *Globe*, 4 August 1876, 3; "The Wimbledon Meeting," *Globe*, 30 July 1877, 4.

7 "Rifle Practice," *New York Times*, 7 April 1872.

8 *Forest and Stream* 1, no. 4 (4 September 1873): 60. Also see "Rifle Shooting in Canada," *Forest and Stream* 1, no. 11 (23 October 1873): 168.

9 "The Canadian Rifle Team," *Forest and Stream* 5, no. 8 (30 September 1875): 120. Also see "Dominion Rifle Association," *Forest and Stream* 4, no. 6 (18 March 1875): 90. After a Canadian won three of nine competitions at the first annual National Rifle Association shooting competition in 1873, *Forest and Stream* expressed its hope that Canadians' success would "cause a proper amount of emulation, and incite our own men to practice." "Creedmore Prize Contest," *Forest and Stream* 1, no. 10 (16 October 1873): 147. On the success of Canadians at this competition, also see "The Winners at Creedmore," *New York Times*, 13 October 1873, 4.

10 See, for example, *Forest and Stream* 2, no. 26 (6 August 1874): 412; "The Canadian Rifle Matches," *New York Times*, 19 August 1874, 2; "Rifle Matches in Canada," *New York Times*, 24 June 1876, 5.

11 "The Canadian Rifle Team," *Forest and Stream* 5, no. 8 (30 September 1875): 120. On the establishment of the NRA, see Russell Stanley Gilmore, "Crack Shots and Patriots: The National Rifle Association and America's Sporting Tradition, 1871–1929" (PhD diss., University of Wisconsin, 1974), 55; Osha Gray Davidson, *Under Fire: The NRA and the Battle for Gun Control* (New York: Henry Holt, 1993), 20–6.

12 "The Canadian Rifle Team," *Forest and Stream* 5, no. 8 (30 September 1875): 120.

13 *Forest and Stream* 2, no. 20 (25 June 1874): 313; "The Canadian Rifle Team,"
    Globe, 2 October 1875, 7; "The Rifle," *Forest and Stream* 5, no. 8 (30 Septem-
    ber 1875): 121; "Rifle Shooting in Canada," *New York Times*, 10 August
    1877, 3; "The American-Canadian Match: America Victorious," *Forest and
    Stream* 9, no. 5 (6 September 1877): 93; "A Canadian Long-Range Chal-
    lenge," *Forest and Stream* 12, no. 1 (6 February 1879): 13; "The Rifle," *Globe*,
    17 July 1879, 4; "The Gun," *Globe*, 21 January 1888, 14.
14 *Report on the State of the Militia of the Dominion of Canada for the Year 1868*
    (Ottawa: Queen's Printer, 1869), 19; *New Westminster Mainland Guardian*,
    8 April 1882, 2; "Manitoba Rifle Association," *Winnipeg Times*, 7 November
    1883; *Department of Militia and Defence of the Dominion of Canada Annual Re-
    port, 1887* (Ottawa: Maclean, Rogers, 1888), 62; *Report of the Commissioner of
    the North-West Mounted Police Force, 1888* (Ottawa: Queen's Printer, 1889),
    33.
15 *Debates, House of Commons* (27 March 1884), 1159.
16 "The Volunteers," *Winnipeg Times*, 30 April 1884.
17 *Department of Militia and Defence of the Dominion of Canada Annual Report,
    1885* (Ottawa: Maclean, Rogers, 1886), xxiv. Also see *Debates, House of Com-
    mons* (26 April 1883), 857; *Department of Militia Annual Report, 1887*, 8; *De-
    partment of Militia and Defence of the Dominion of Canada Annual Report, 1888*
    (Ottawa: Queen's Printer, 1889), 48.
18 "A Boy's Death Wound," *Globe*, 25 July 1887, 8; David Roberts, "John Kay
    Macdonald," *DCB* online; "The Fatal Rifle Butts," *Globe*, 27 July 1887, 2;
    "A Public Inquiry Demanded," *Globe*, 28 July 1887, 4; "Those Rifle Butts,"
    Globe, 29 July 1887, 8; "The Rifle Butts," *Globe*, 10 August 1887, 4; "'Beware
    of Bullets,'" *Globe*, 19 August 1887, 8; "The Rifle Ranges," *Globe*, 2 March
    1888, 8; "Rifle Practice on King Street," *Globe*, 21 June 1888, 4; "Sport That
    Kills," *Globe*, 10 June 1890, 4; "The Rifle Range Question," *Globe*, 14 Decem-
    ber 1891, 8; *Globe*, 26 April 1892, 4; "Ordered off the Common," *Globe*, 12
    July 1892, 5; "Rifle Association Notes," *Globe*, 18 August 1893, 8; "Ontario's
    Riflemen," *Globe*, 22 August 1893, 3. Safety concerns also led the English
    National Rifle Association to move its range. "The Wimbledon Meet-
    ing," *Globe*, 10 March 1887, 6. The Department of Militia and Defence also
    started reporting on the safety of rifle ranges in its annual report. See, for
    example, *Department of Militia and Defence of the Dominion of Canada Annual
    Report, 1892* (Ottawa: Queen's Printer, 1893), 62–9.
19 Quoted in *Globe*, 21 August 1890, 6.
20 *Debates, House of Commons* (12 April 1892), 1363.
21 Lee Kennett and James LaVerne Anderson, *The Gun in America: The Origins
    of a National Dilemma* (Westport, CT: Greenwood, 1975), 93–5; Harold F.

Williamson, *Winchester: The Gun That Won the West* (Washington: Combat Forces, 1952), 73–4, 114; *Winnipeg Daily Sun*, 16 April 1883, 6.

22 "Firearms," *Globe*, 4 April 1882, 5. Also see *Globe*, 11 April 1882, 5; *Globe*, 7 June 1882, 5.

23 *Debates, House of Commons* (18 December 1867), 309; *An Act to prevent the unlawful training of persons to the use of arms* ..., S.C. 1867, c.15. Also see *An Act respecting Riots, unlawful Assemblies and Breaches of the Peace*, R.S.C. 1886, c.147; *An Act respecting the seizure of Arms kept for dangerous purposes*, R.S.C. 1886, c.149.

24 *An Act imposing Duties of Customs* ..., S.C. 1867, c.7, s.8; *The Customs Act*, R.S.C. 1886, c.32, s.171; R.C. Macleod, *The NWMP and Law Enforcement, 1873–1905* (Toronto: University of Toronto Press, 1976), 3–20.

25 Joseph G. Rosa, *Gunfighter: Man or Myth?* (Norman: University of Oklahoma Press, 1969), vii.

26 Greg Marquis, "Policing Two Imperial Frontiers: The Royal Irish Constabulary and the North-West Mounted Police," in *Laws and Societies in the Canadian Prairie West, 1670–1940*, ed. Louis A. Knafla and Jonathan Swainger (Vancouver: UBC Press, 2005), 198; S.W. Horrall, *The Pictorial History of the Royal Canadian Mounted Police* (Toronto: McGraw-Hill Ryerson, 1973), 60–3; *An Act respecting the Administration of Justice, and for the establishment of a Police Force in the North West Territories*, S.C. 1873, c.35; *Report of the Commissioner of the North-West Mounted Police Force, 1882* (Ottawa, 1883), 21; *Report of the Commissioner of the North-West Mounted Police Force, 1886* (Ottawa: Maclean, Roger, 1887), 10.

27 "Firearms," *Globe*, 4 April 1882, 5. Also see *Manitoba and Northwest Herald*, 1 June 1872, 3; *Manitoba and Northwest Herald*, 8 June 1872, 3; "Manitoba Lands," *Globe*, 16 February 1882, 8; *Globe*, 11 April 1882, 5; *Globe*, 7 June 1882, 5; "Ross Bros." *Edmonton Bulletin*, 13 September 1901; S. James Gooding, *The Canadian Gunsmiths, 1608–1900* (West Hill, ON: Museum Restoration Service, 1962), 11.

28 *Report of the Commissioner of the North-West Mounted Police Force, 1887* (Ottawa: Maclean, Roger, 1888), 12.

29 Tina Loo, *Making Law, Order and Authority in British Columbia, 1821–1871* (Toronto: University of Toronto Press, 1994), 23; Tina Loo, "The Road from Bute Inlet: Crime and Colonial Identity in British Columbia," in *Essays in the History of Canadian Law*, vol. 5, *Crime and Criminal Justice*, ed. Jim Phillips, Tina Loo, and Susan Lewthwaite (Toronto: University of Toronto Press and the Osgoode Society, 1994), 112–42.

30 *Debates, Senate* (4 April 1889), 428.

31 *Debates, House of Commons* (19 May 1892), 2827.

32 Gerald Friesen, *The Canadian Prairies: A History* (Toronto: University of Toronto Press, 1984), 36–8; *Copy of Treaty and Supplementary Treaty No. 7 ...,* CIHM 43117; "Reconnaissance of the North West Provinces ...," in *Report on the State of the Militia of the Dominion of Canada, 1872,* in Canada, *Sessional Papers, 1873,* 5:cxvi–cxvii; Library and Archives Canada (LAC), RCMP fonds, R196-26-3-E, file 69-76, extract of telegram, 19 October 1875. In 1878, David Mills, the minister of the interior and superintendent general of Indian affairs, noted that the government had presented forty-six modern Winchester rifles to chiefs in the North-West. *Debates, House of Commons* (10 April 1878), 1845.

33 *Debates, House of Commons* (17 March 1879), 489.

34 Kennett and Anderson, *Gun in America,* 117; *Report of the Commissioner of the North-West Mounted Police Force, 1876* (Ottawa, 1877), 20, 27, 29, 33, 34–5.

35 Desmond Morton, *The Last War Drum: The North West Campaign of 1885* (Toronto: Hakkert, 1972), 24.

36 *Report of the Commissioner of the North-West Mounted Police Force, 1882* (Ottawa, 1883), 21; *Winnipeg Daily Sun,* 26 February 1884, 1.

37 Concerns that the rebels all possessed modern arms proved overstated. The Metis and Native peoples carried a variety of arms, and some carried no arms. *Debates, House of Commons* (30 March 1885), 813–14; "Military Rifles," *Globe,* 1 May 1885, 4; Friesen, *Canadian Prairies,* 230; Granatstein, *Canada's Army,* 30; Robert H. Caldwell, "'We're Making History, Eh?': An Inquiry into the Events That Occurred near Cut Knife Hill, North West Territories 1–2 May 1885," in *More Fighting for Canada: Five Battles, 1760–1944,* ed. Donald E. Graves (Toronto: Robin Brass Studio, 2004), 107, 111, 121.

38 *Toronto World,* 1 May 1885, 2.

39 "The Queen's in Calgary," *Calgary Weekly Herald,* 28 May 1885, 1.

40 "The Indian Problem," *McLeod Gazette,* 25 April 1885. On the efforts to discourage hunting by Aboriginal Peoples, see Sarah Carter, *Lost Harvests: Prairie Indian Reserve Farmers and Government Policy* (Montreal and Kingston: McGill-Queen's University Press, 1990), 16–22.

41 E. Brian Titley, "Edgar Dewdney," *DCB* online.

42 *An Act respecting the administration of justice, and other matters, in the North-West Territories,* S.C. 1885, c.51, s.14. Also see *An Act respecting the North-West Territories,* R.S.C. 1886, c.50, s.101.

43 *Debates, House of Commons* (1 July 1885), 2966.

44 *Debates, House of Commons* (2 July 1885), 3001.

45 *Debates, House of Commons* (1 July 1885), 2967. Also see *Debates, House of Commons* (2 July 1885), 3002.

46 For a recent discussion of the changing conceptions of liberty in the nine-
    teenth century, see Michel Ducharme, *Le concept de liberté au Canada à*
    l'époque des Révolutions atlantiques (1776–1838) (Montreal and Kingston:
    McGill-Queen's University Press, 2009).
47 *Debates, House of Commons* (2 July 1885), 3001. For other suggestions that
    Canadians had a right to possess arms during the debate over the legisla-
    tion, see *Debates, House of Commons* (16 July 1885), 3428, 3430, 3432. On
    Blake, see R.C.B. Risk, "Blake and Liberty," in *Canadian Constitutionalism,*
    1791–1991, ed. Janet Ajzenstat, 195–211 (Ottawa: Canadian Study of Parlia-
    ment Group, 1992); Ben Forster and Jonathan Swainger, "Edward Blake,"
    DCB online.
48 *Debates, House of Commons* (2 July 1885), 3000.
49 E.A. Heaman, "Rights Talk and the Liberal Order Framework," in *Lib-*
    eralism and Hegemony: Debating the Canadian Liberal Revolution, ed. Jean-
    François Constant and Michel Ducharme (Toronto: University of Toronto
    Press, 2009), 159.
50 *Debates, House of Commons* (2 July 1885), 3000.
51 For examples of this kind of argument, see *Debates, House of Commons* (2
    July 1885), 3002; (16 July 1885), 3428. For studies of the nineteenth-century
    state, see Bruce Curtis, *The Politics of Population: State Formation, Statistics,*
    and the Census of Canada, 1840–1875 (Toronto: University of Toronto Press,
    2001); Bruce Curtis, *True Government by Choice Men? Inspection, Education,*
    and State Formation in Canada West (Toronto: University of Toronto Press,
    1992); Allan Greer and Ian Radforth, eds., *Colonial Leviathan: State Forma-*
    tion in Mid-Nineteenth-Century Canada (Toronto: University of Toronto
    Press, 1992); J.I. Little, *State and Society in Transition: The Politics of Institu-*
    tional Reform in the Eastern Townships, 1838–1852 (Montreal and Kingston:
    McGill-Queen's University Press, 1997).
52 *Debates, House of Commons* (16 July 1885), 3429.
53 "Disarming the Indians," *Calgary Weekly Herald*, 15 July 1885, 2; *Globe*, 2
    September 1885, 4; "Indian Rising Feared," *Globe*, 29 December 1885, 1;
    Debates, House of Commons (28 April 1890), 4054. In fact, the importation
    of guns into the Canadian west boomed in the second half of the 1890s.
    Canada, *Sessional Papers*, 1898, vol. 5, no. 6, 139; 1899, vol. 5, no. 6, 282–3;
    1900, vol. 5, no. 6, 284–5.
54 Order in Council, *Canada Gazette* 19, no. 9 (19 August 1885): 327. The 1884
    act also included the infamous ban on the potlatch. *An Act further to amend*
    "The Indian Act, 1880," S.C. 1884, c.27, s.2; *The Indian Act*, R.S.C. 1886, c.43,
    s.113.
55 Edgar Dewdney to John A. Macdonald, 4 May 1886, LAC MG26A, vol.

213, 90710–1; Edgar Dewdney to John A. Macdonald, 11 May 1886, 90727–8.

56 *Report of the Commissioner of the North-West Mounted Police Force, 1887,* 9.

57 An incident in 1846 in Richmond Hill, Upper Canada, illustrated this weakness. An attempted suicide with a pistol was botched because the bullets meant to pierce the shooter's brain slipped out of the gun. "Attempted Suicide at Richmond Hill," *Globe,* 26 December 1846, 3.

58 W.Y. Carman, *A History of Firearms from the Earliest Times to 1914* (London: Routledge & Kegan Paul, 1955), 131–43; Kenneth Chase, *Firearms: A Global History to 1700* (Cambridge: Cambridge University Press, 2003), 23–6.

59 David A. Hounshell, *From the American System to Mass Production, 1800–1932: The Development of Manufacturing Technology in the United States* (Baltimore, MD: Johns Hopkins University Press, 1984), 46–50; R.L. Wilson, *Colt, An American Legend: The Official History of Colt Firearms from 1836 to the Present* (New York: Abbeville, 1985); Ellsworth S. Grant, *The Colt Legacy: The Colt Armory in Hartford, 1855–1980* (Providence, RI: Mowbray, 1982).

60 Carman, *History of Firearms,* 145–6.

61 For examples, see "Armes a feu Volcaniques," *Le Courrier du Canada,* 18 April 1857, 4; "J. Grainger, Gun and Pistol Maker," *Globe,* 5 November 1857, 3; "Revolvers," *Halifax British Colonist,* 16 October 1858.

62 *Globe,* 31 January 1859, 4; "To Sportsmen," *Quebec Mercury,* 10 June 1863, 1; *Ottawa Times,* 4 August 1866, 3. In 1855, participants in a Hamilton Post Office robbery bought three pistols for the substantial sums of nine dollars, ten dollars, and thirty-five dollars. "Police Intelligence," *Globe,* 27 January 1855, 3. Leading Upper Canada lawyer Robert Harrison purchased a revolver for ten dollars in 1866 in Toronto. Peter Oliver, *The Conventional Man: The Diaries of Ontario Chief Justice Robert A. Harrison, 1856–1878* (Toronto: University of Toronto Press and the Osgoode Society, 2003), 275.

63 Kennett and Anderson, *Gun in America,* 156.

64 *Globe,* 26 August 1882, 5; *Winnipeg Daily Sun,* 16 April 1883, 6; Patrick Brode, *Death in the Queen City: Clara Ford on Trial, 1895* (Toronto: Natural Heritage Books, 2005), 113. Also see "Stark's Guns," *Globe,* 27 October 1894, 18; "McCready's Clearing Out Sale," *Globe,* 18 June 1896, 10. Reports of the low price of revolvers also appeared in murder trial reports. For instance, see "Shelburne Murder," *Globe,* 25 January 1882, 3.

65 "E. Remington & Sons," *Grand River Sachem,* 15 August 1866, 3.

66 *Globe,* 4 November 1895, 6.

67 Gooding, *Canadian Gunsmiths,* 154.

68 *Debates, Senate* (1 March 1877), 120.

69 "Tables of the Trade and Navigation of the Dominion of Canada," *Sessional Papers*, 1870–83. Dominion statistics only once provided an estimate of the number of guns imported. In 1877, Ottawa reported that Canada imported 11,897 firearms valued at $79,827.

70 Susan Binnie, "The Blake Act of 1878: A Legislative Solution to Urban Violence in Post-Confederation Canada," in *Law, Society, and the State: Essays in Modern Legal History*, ed. Louis A. Knafla and Susan Binnie (Toronto: University of Toronto Press, 1995), 233. Also see Susan Binnie, "Maintaining Order on the Pacific Railway: The Peace Preservation Act, 1869–85," in *Canadian State Trials*, vol. 3, *Political Trials and Security Measures, 1840–1914*, ed. Barry Wright and Susan Binnie, 204–56 (Toronto: University of Toronto Press and the Osgoode Society, 2009).

71 "Reckless Use of Firearms," *Globe*, 28 August 1888, 8.

72 "A Fatal Shot," *Globe*, 20 January 1882, 3.

73 "Shot through the Heart," *Globe*, 8 April 1881, 6.

74 "The Dominion," *Globe*, 8 February 1887, 6.

75 "The Gun Was Loaded," *Globe*, 16 July 1891, 10.

76 *Globe*, 5 April 1879, 8.

77 "Accidentally Shot," *Globe*, 2 April, 1887, 16.

78 For examples, see "Fatal Firearms Accident," *Globe*, 30 April 1877, 4; *Globe*, 5 April 1879, 8; "A Revolver Accident," *Globe*, 22 April 1885, 6; "Accidentally Shot," *Globe*, 2 April, 1887, 16; "Shot by a Boy," *Manitoba Daily Free Press*, 30 November 1892, 1; "Fatal Firearms Accident," *Globe*, 30 April 1877, 4; "Notes from the Capital," *Globe*, 8 July 1879, 1; "The Fatal Revolver," *Globe*, 3 August 1888, 1.

79 *Debates, Senate* (1 March 1877), 117. For this practice in the United States, see Kennett and Anderson, *Gun in America*, 156–7. The various ways in which revolvers were concealed was discussed in "The Pistol Pocket," *Woodstock Sentinel-Review*, 18 July 1889, 3. On the appeal of revolvers for murderers, see Randolph Roth, *American Homicide* (Cambridge, MA: Belknap, 2009), 285.

80 "Seduction and Murder," *Globe*, 25 July 1868, 1. Also see *Globe*, 8 October 1875, 2; "A Family Slaughtered," *Globe*, 18 November 1886, 1.

81 *Senate, Debates* (2 April 1889), 377.

82 *Manitoba Daily Free Press*, 16 July 1879, 1; "State of the Streets," *Globe*, 3 November 1885, 2; "Very Nearly a Murder," *Globe*, 2 November 1886, 8; "A Plucky Fight with Burglars," *Globe*, 6 May 1887, 1; "Two Shots Fired," *Globe*, 1 December 1887, 8; *Globe*, "Douglas Also Confesses," *Globe*, 1 January 1892, 1–2; "Brandon Burglary," *Manitoba Morning Free Press*, 18 September 1894, 1.

83 For examples, see "From Pictou," *Halifax Citizen*, 1 February 1870, 2; "Melancholy Suicide," *Halifax Citizen*, 8 August 1870, 3; "Determined Suicide," *Globe*, 10 January 1882, 8; "Canada," *Globe*, 17 June 1882, 3; "Belleville," *Globe*, 17 April 1883, 2; "Manitoba," *Globe*, 30 August 1882, 3; "Suicide at Golden," *Manitoba Daily Free Press*, 11 July 1887, 4; "Attempted Suicide," *Globe*, 31 January 1888, 1; *Globe*, 20 January 1888, 1; "A Deliberate Suicide," *Globe*, 25 February 1888, 16; "Tired of Life," *Globe*, 12 May 1888, 16; "Suicide," *Globe*, 11 August 1888, 1; "Suicide at Fort Saskatchewan," *Calgary Weekly Herald*, 10 July 1890, 4; "The Suicide of Harris," *Manitoba Daily Free Press*, 7 November 1891, 1; "The Suicide of Harris," *Brandon Mail*, 12 November 1891, 6; "A High Park Horror," *Globe*, 25 January 1892, 8; "Shooting Fatality," *Globe*, 4 January 1893, 4; "Another Strange Suicide," *Victoria Daily Colonist*, 3 June 1893, 8. Risa Barkin and Ian Gentles suggest a perhaps not coincidental rise in suicides in Toronto after 1868. Risa Barkin and Ian Gentles, "Death in Victorian Toronto, 1850–1899," *Urban History Review* 19, no. 1 (1990): 15–16.

84 For examples of early incidents of criminals using revolvers, see "Burglar Caught," *Globe*, 3 October 1857, 2; *Globe*, 13 October 1857, 2; "Toronto Spring Assizes," *Globe*, 17 April 1858, 3.

85 "Terrible Results of Carelessness with Firearms," *Globe*, 7 August 1882, 3.

86 *Debates, Senate* (1 March 1877), 120, 121.

87 *Winnipeg Daily Free Press*, 18 April 1876, 3. Also see "City Police Court," *Daily Free Press* (Winnipeg), 21 July 1874, 2.

88 *Report of the Commissioner of the North-West Mounted Police Force, 1885* (Ottawa: Maclean, Roger, 1886), 119; *Report of the Commissioner of the North-West Mounted Police Force, 1886* (Ottawa: Maclean, Roger, 1887), 130; "A Future Metropolis," *Globe*, 16 June 1888, 6.

89 Kennett and Anderson, *Gun in America*, 120. And see Wilbur R. Miller, *Cops and Bobbies: Police Authority in New York and London, 1830–1870* (Chicago: University of Chicago Press, 1977), 115.

90 *Globe*, 25 March 1885, 3.

91 "The Criminal Law," *Manitoba Daily Free Press*, 17 May 1877, 2. A writer in the *Canadian Independent* also railed against young men's proclivity to carry revolvers, suggesting that doing so made them cowards: "There is no surer indication of cowardice than when a man deliberately proposes to protect himself against the ordinary dangers of civilized society, by carrying a revolver." "Revolvers and Pistols," *Canadian Independent* n.s., 30, no. 17 (3 November 1881): 4.

92 "The Knife and the Pistol," *Globe*, 26 September 1881, 4.

93 "A Bit Drunk," *McLeod Gazette*, 16 February 1886. For other examples of incidents involving guns and alcohol, see "Disturbance at Waverley," *Halifax*

Citizen, 25 October 1864; "Latest from Halifax," *Globe*, 27 December 1871, 1; *Manitoba Daily Free Press*, 27 September 1880, 1; *Globe*, 29 September 1881, 2; "Killed in His Tracks," *Manitoba Daily Free Press*, 26 October 1882, 8; "Revolvers and Whisky," *Toronto World*, 20 February 1883, 1; "The York-Street Murder," *Globe*, 9 August 1883, 4; "Penalty for Carrying Firearms," *Globe*, 24 February 1883, 14; "Murder at Brampton," *Globe*, 23 April 1892, 13; "No Mitigating Circumstances," *Calgary Weekly Herald*, 30 July 1890, 6; "A Sensation in London," *Globe*, 14 October 1892, 1.

94 Craig Heron, *Booze: A Distilled History* (Toronto: Between the Lines, 2003), 60.

95 "A Belligerent People," *Halifax Citizen*, 4 August 1866, 1.

96 For examples, see "A Utah Horror," *Daily Free Press* (Winnipeg), 21 April 1875, 2; *Daily Free Press* (Winnipeg), 26 November 1875, 2; "A Deadly Point of Pronunciation," *Manitoba Daily Free Press*, 2 May 1879, 2; "Laying Down Their Arms," *Manitoba Free Press*, 16 August 1879, 3.

97 *Debates, Senate* (1 March 1877), 120. Also see "Notes and Comments," *Globe*, 19 August 1878, 2.

98 *By-Laws of the City of Toronto ...* (Toronto: Henry Rowsell, 1870), 46; *Laws and Ordinances Related to the City of Halifax* (Halifax: James Bowes & Sons, 1876), 36; *The Consolidated By-Laws of the City of Kingston ...* (Kingston: Daily News Office, 1883), 43–4; *Revised By-Laws of the City of Ottawa ...* (Ottawa: J.D. Taylor, 1890), 71; *By-Laws of the City of Winnipeg ...* (Winnipeg: Stovel, 1900), 30.

99 *An Act for the better preservation of the Peace in the vicinity of Public Works*, S.C. 1869, c.24; *An Act to amend an Act for the better preservation of the peace ...*, S.C. 1870, c.28; Binnie, "Maintaining Order on the Pacific Railway," 209.

100 *An Act respecting Offences against the Person*, S.C. 1869, c.20, s.72.

101 Bottomley wrongly suggests that "other offensive weapons" might have included pistols. Samuel A. Bottomley, "Parliament, Politics and Policy: Gun Control in Canada, 1867–2003" (PhD diss., Carleton University, 2004), 94. A similar law against concealed weapons passed in New York in 1866 also omitted pistols. Kennett and Anderson, *Gun in America*, 169.

102 *Debates, House of Commons* (27 April 1869), 91; (4 May 1869), 171.

103 "Canada," *Globe*, 25 July 1871, 4.

104 "East Gwillimbury Murder," *Globe*, 12 January 1872, 4. And see *Globe*, 3 January 1877, 4; Oliver, *Conventional Man*, 275.

105 "York Winter Assizes," *Globe*, 20 January 1876, 3; *Debates, House of Commons* (22 April 1872), 99.

106 *Debates, House of Commons* (5 June 1872), 997.

107 Desmond Morton, "Taking on the Grand Trunk: The Locomotive Engi-

neers Strike of 1876–7," *Labour / Le Travailleur* 2 (1977): 5–34; Susan W.S. Binnie, "Explorations in the Use of Criminal Law in Canada, 1867–1892" (PhD diss., Carleton University, 1992), 184–7; *R. v. Chasson*, 16 (1876) N.B.R. 546; G.F.G. Stanley, "The Caraquet Riots of 1875," *Acadiensis* 2, no. 1 (1972–3): 21–38; Martin A. Galvin, "The Jubilee Riots in Toronto, 1875," *Canadian Catholic Historical Association Annual Report* 26 (1959): 93–107; *R. v. Corcoran*, 26 (1876) U.C.C.P. 134; Binnie, "Blake Act of 1878," 221–2; Desmond Morton, "Aid to the Civil Power: The Canadian Militia in Support of Social Order, 1867–1914," *Canadian Historical Review* 51 (1970): 407–25; *History of the Guibord Case: Ultramontanism Versus Law and Human Rights* (Montreal: Witness Printing House, 1875), 119, 126.

108 *Debates, Senate* (1 March 1877), 117.

109 Ontario responded to the resistance of workers with its own new version of the expired 1845 Province of Canada law that allowed for the prohibition of weapons on public works. *An Act respecting Riots near Public Works*, R.S.O. 1877, c.31.

110 *Debates, House of Commons* (20 March 1877), 850, 851.

111 *An Act to make provision against the improper use of Firearms*, S.C. 1877, c.30.

112 Canada, Criminal Statistics, 1881–1992, in *Sessional Papers*, 1883–93.

113 Donald Fyson notes a substantial use of the 1877 law in Montreal and Quebec City. Donald Fyson, "The Trials and Tribulations of Riot Prosecutions: Collective Violence, State Authority, and Criminal Justice in Quebec, 1841–92," in *Canadian State Trials*, vol. 3, *Political Trials and Security Measures, 1840–1914*, ed. Barry Wright and Susan Binnie (Toronto: University of Toronto Press and the Osgoode Society, 2009), 188.

114 "Twelfth of July Riot," *Montreal Gazette*, 13 July 1877; "The Montreal Troubles," *Globe*, 19 July 1877, 4; "The Hackett Investigation," *Globe*, 3 August 1877, 4; Binnie, "Blake Act of 1878," 224–6.

115 "The Montreal Troubles," *Globe*, 19 July 1877, 4; "Latest from Montreal," *Globe*, 21 July 1877, 8; "The Hackett Investigation," *Globe*, 3 August 1877, 4; "The Elliott Shooting Case," *Globe*, 29 September 1877, 8.

116 *Daily Witness*, 10 July 1877, as quoted in Binnie, "Blake Act of 1878," 228.

117 "The Riot of Monday Night," *Montreal Gazette*, 1 May 1878; Binnie, "Blake Act of 1878," 241.

118 *Montreal Gazette*, 1 May 1878.

119 "The Peace of Our City," *Montreal Gazette*, 4 May 1878.

120 *Debates, House of Commons* (1 May 1878), 2336, 2338, 2339; (4 May 1878), 2411. Quebec MP and lawyer Hector-Louis Langevin, like Blake, said that the act, when proclaimed, would "interfere with our rights and privileges." *Debates, House of Commons* (4 May 1878), 2408. The *Montreal Gazette*

agreed that the act infringed on rights through its search provisions and the limitations the act placed on carrying weapons, though it hoped for an even stronger measure. "The Firearms Bill," *Montreal Gazette*, 7 May 1878.

121 *Debates, House of Commons* (1 May 1878), 2341.

122 *Debates, House of Commons* (4 May 1878), 2409.

123 Binnie, "Blake Act of 1878," 216, 228–9; *The Better Prevention of Crime Act, 1878*, S.C. 1878, c.17; "Mr Blake's Bill," *Montreal Gazette*, 3 May 1878; *An Act to continue in force for a limited time "The better Prevention of Crime Act, 1878,"* S.C. 1879, c.41; *An Act further to continue in force for a limited time "The better Prevention of Crime Act, 1878,"* S.C. 1880, c.5; *An Act further to continue in force for a limited time "The better Prevention of Crime Act, 1878,"* S.C. 1881, c.29; *An Act further to continue in force for a limited time "The better Prevention of Crime Act, 1878,"* S.C. 1882, c.38; *An Act to continue for a limited time the Acts therein mentioned*, S.C. 1883, c.33; "Suppression of Crime," *Manitoba Daily Free Press*, 12 June 1882, 2.

124 "Court of Queen's Bench," *Manitoba Free Press*, 24 October 1878, 1.

125 "Revolvers and Whisky," *Toronto World*, 20 February 1883, 1.

126 LAC, R188-39-8-E, vol. 55, file no. 1882–1829.

127 "Carrying Deadly Weapons," *Globe*, 27 May 1880, 4. Also see "Carrying Arms," *McLeod Gazette*, 18 July 1888; *Canada Presbyterian*, 26 October 1892, 680. Not all commentators agreed there was a problem with revolvers. The *Woodstock Sentinel-Review*, for example, suggested that it had "always been cause for congratulation that Canadians are not given to the vicious habit of carrying revolvers." *Woodstock Sentinel-Review*, 8 November 1887, 2.

128 J.M.S. Careless, "George Brown," *DCB* online; "The Late Mr Brown," *Globe*, 23 June 1880, 4. In 1883, Kingston, Ontario, passed a by-law largely banning the discharge of firearms because the "practice of firing off pistols, revolvers and other firearms" had become "too prevalent for the safety of the inhabitants." *The Consolidated By-Laws of the City of Kingston*, 43.

129 *Debates, Senate* (2 April 1889), 376. Several other senators also argued for the necessity of new legislation. *Debates, Senate* (2 April 1889), 377; (4 April 1889), 427.

130 Desmond H. Brown, ed., *The Birth of a Criminal Code: The Evolution of Canada's Justice System* (Toronto: University of Toronto Press, 1995), 71.

131 His government, however, would pass a new measure that allowed for the punishment of two or more people who together openly carried dangerous or unusual weapons in any public place in such a manner as to create terror. *An Act respecting the improper use of fire-arms and other*

weapons, R.S.C. 1886, c.148, s.8. This measure copied similar provisions found in the law of pre-Confederation Nova Scotia and New Brunswick. R.S.N.S. (3rd ser.), c.162, s.8; and 1 R.S.N.B., c.147, s.10.

132 *Debates, House of Commons* (19 May 1892), 2828.

133 *The Criminal Code*, S.C. 1892, c.29, ss.102, 110.

134 *The Criminal Code*, S.C. 1892, c.29, ss.105, 106.

135 Colin Greenwood, *Firearms Control: A Study of Armed Crime and Firearms Control in England and Wales* (London: Routledge & Kegan Paul, 1972), 17–18, 26–9; Joyce Lee Malcolm, *Guns and Violence: The English Experience* (Cambridge, MA: Harvard University Press, 2002), 117.

3: Arming Britons and Disarming Immigrants

1 John M. MacKenzie, "Hunting and the Natural World in Juvenile Literature," in *Imperialism and Juvenile Literature*, ed. Jeffrey Richards (Manchester, UK: Manchester University Press, 1989), 170. And see Greg Gillespie, "The Empire's Eden: British Hunters, Travel Writing, and Imperialism in Nineteenth-Century Canada," in *The Culture of Hunting in Canada*, ed. Jean L. Manore and Dale G. Miner, 42–55 (Vancouver: UBC Press, 2007); George Colpitts, *Game in the Garden: A Human History of Wildlife in Western Canada to 1940* (Vancouver: UBC Press, 2002), 63–102; John M. MacKenzie, *The Empire of Nature: Hunting, Conservation and British Imperialism* (Manchester, UK: Manchester University Press, 1988).

2 R.G. Moyles and Doug Owram, *Imperial Dreams and Colonial Realities: British Views of Canada, 1880–1914* (Toronto: University of Toronto Press, 1988), 62.

3 John M. MacKenzie, "The Imperial Pioneer and Hunter and the British Masculine Stereotype in Late Victorian and Edwardian Times," in *Manliness and Morality: Middle-Class Masculinity in Britain and America, 1800–1940*, ed. J.A. Mangan and James Walvin (Manchester, UK: Manchester University Press, 1987), 188.

4 British Columbia, *Tenth Report of the Provincial Game Warden, 1914* (Victoria: Government Printer, 1915), J5.

5 Cynthia Comacchio, "Lost in Modernity: 'Maladjustment' and the 'Modern Youth Problem,' English Canada, 1920–50," in *Lost Kids: Vulnerable Children and Youth in Twentieth-Century Canada and the United States*, ed. Mona Gleason, Tamara Myers, Leslie Paris, and Veronica Strong-Boag, 53–71 (Vancouver: UBC Press, 2010); Sharon Wall, *The Nurture of Nature: Childhood, Antimodernism, and Ontario Summer Camps, 1920–55* (Vancouver: UBC Press, 2009).

6　Tina Loo, "Of Moose and Men: Hunting for Masculinities in British Columbia, 1880–1939," *Western Historical Quarterly* 32, no. 3 (2001): 296, 298.

7　"Guns and Gunning," *Globe*, 14 February 1903, 15. Also see Greg Gillespie and Kevin Wamsley, "Clandestine Means: The Aristocratic Hunting Code and Early Game Legislation in Nineteenth-Century Canada," *Sporting Traditions* 22, no. 1 (2005): 99–119.

8　George W. Colpitts, "Fish and Game Associations in Southern Alberta, 1907–1928," *Alberta History* 42, no. 4 (1994): 16–26; Darcy Ingram, "Nature's Improvement: Wildlife, Conservation, and Conflict in Quebec, 1850–1914" (PhD diss., McGill University, 2007); "The Trigger," *Globe*, 12 March 1895, 6; "The Trigger," *Globe*, 11 February 1897, 10; "The Trigger," *Globe*, 14 August 1901, 8; "Crack of Guns at the Woodbine," *Toronto Star*, 12 August 1903, 9.

9　Keith Walden, *Becoming Modern in Toronto: The Industrial Exhibition and the Shaping of a Late Victorian Culture* (Toronto: University of Toronto Press, 1997), 125.

10　David Monod, *Store Wars: Shopkeepers and the Culture of Mass Marketing, 1890–1939* (Toronto: University of Toronto Press, 1996), 16.

11　Loo, "Of Moose and Men," 296–319; Greg Gillespie, *Hunting for Empire: Narratives of Sport in Rupert's Land, 1840–70* (Vancouver: UBC Press, 2007), 38; Greg Gillespie, "'I Was Well Pleased with Our Sport among the Buffalo': Big-Game Hunters, Travel Writing, and Cultural Imperialism in the British North American West, 1847–72," *Canadian Historical Review* 83, no. 4 (2002): 555–84; "Sportsmen's Headquarters," *Manitoba Free Press*, 16 July 1881, 3; *Twillingate Sun*, 9 January 1892, 3; "Greener Guns …," *Globe*, 25 October 1894, 8; *Globe*, 28 August 1903, 6.

12　*Globe*, 23 September 1893, 18; "Sportsmen's Sundries," *Globe*, 31 October 1894, 6. The Timothy Eaton Company also offered a wide variety of goods to hunters. *Globe*, 28 August 1903, 6; *Toronto Star*, 23 September 1904, 12; *Globe*, 15 September 1911, 11.

13　Jean L. Manore, "Contested Terrains of Space and Place: Hunting and the Landscape Known as Algonquin Park, 1890–1950," in Manore and Miner, *Culture of Hunting in Canada*, 140–1; Colpitts, *Game in the Garden*, 71; Bill Parenteau and Richard W. Judd, "More Buck for the Bang: Sporting and the Ideology of Fish and Game Management in Northern New England and the Maritime Provinces, 1870–1900," in *New England and Maritime Provinces: Connections and Comparisons*, ed. Stephen J. Hornsby and John G. Reid (Montreal and Kingston: McGill-Queen's University Press, 2005), 239–44.

14 David Calverley, "'When the Need for It No Longer Existed': Declining Wildlife and Native Hunting Rights in Ontario, 1791–1898," in Manore and Miner, *Culture of Hunting in Canada*, 106. Also see John Sandlos, *Hunters at the Margin: Native People and Wildlife Conservation in the Northwest Territories* (Vancouver: UBC Press, 2007), 236; Loo, "Of Moose and Men," 309.

15 *Debates, Senate* (26 April 1894), 287. Also see *Debates, Senate* (9 May 1894), 339.

16 Parenteau and Judd, "More Buck for the Bang," 247. Also see Darcy Ingram, "'Au temps et dans les quantités qui lui plaisent': Poachers, Outlaws, and Rural Banditry in Quebec," *Histoire Sociale / Social History* 42, no. 83 (2009): 1–34.

17 Tina Loo, *States of Nature: Conserving Canada's Wildlife in the Twentieth Century* (Vancouver: UBC Press, 2006), 23; *The Unorganized Territories' Game Preservation Act, 1894*, S.C. 1894, c.31; Gillespie and Wamsley, "Clandestine Means," 99–120; Kevin Wamsley, "Good Clean Sport and a Deer Apiece: Game Legislation and State Formation in 19th Century Canada," *Canadian Journal of History of Sport* 25, no. 2 (1994): 1–20; Calverley, "When the Need for It No Longer Existed," 112–13; Manore, "Contested Terrains of Space and Place," 132–3. For examples of game legislation permitting the seizure of firearms, see *Game Law*, S.Q. 1887, c.16, s.8; *An Act to amend "The Game Protection Act*," S.M. 1906, c.30; *The Game Act*, S.A. 1907, c.14, s.15; *The Game Act*, S.N.S 1908, c.17, s.30(3); *An Act for the Protection of Game*, S.S. 1909, c.128, s.9; "$10,000 in Licenses," *Perth Courier*, 4 December 1896, 7.

18 See *An Act for the protection of certain Birds and Animals*, S.N.B. 1878, c.45, s.17; *Agriculture, Statistic, and Health Act, 1883*, S.M. 1883, c.19, s.61; *Game Protection Act, 1895*, S.B.C. 1895, c.23, s.23; *The Game Act, 1906*, S.P.E.I. 1906, c.26, s.15; *Ontario Game and Fisheries Act*, S.O. 1907, c.49, s.15; *The Game Act*, S.N.S. 1908, c.17, s.24; *The Game Act*, S.S. 1909, c.128, s.9.

19 See *Game Protection Act, 1898*, S.B.C. 1898, c.20, s.14; *An Act to amend "The Game Protection Act*," S.M. 1904, c.18; *Ontario Game and Fisheries Act*, S.O. 1907, c.49, s.21; *The Game Act*, S.A. 1907, c.14, s.9; *The Game Act*, S.S. 1909, c.128, s.9; *The Game Act, 1909*, S.N.B. 1909, c.46, s.10; *An Act to amend the Game Act, 1906 ...*, S.P.E.I. 1911, c.10, s.1.

20 *Toronto Star*, 28 October 1911, 21.

21 *Toronto Star*, 16 September 1913, 8. Firearms are frequently designated by the diameter of the bullet they fire. A .401 calibre thus fires a bullet that is .401 inches in diameter.

22 "The Gun Accident Season," *Globe*, 30 September 1903, 6. Also see "Deer-Hunting with Long-Range Rifles," *Toronto Star*, 20 November 1901, 6; "The Hunting Rifle," *Toronto Star*, 25 November 1901, 6; "What the Makers of

High-Power Rifles Say," *Toronto Star*, 12 December 1901, 6; "A Needless Danger," *Globe*, 13 May 1904, 6; "Gun-Accident Season," *Globe*, 8 October 1912, 6.

23 "Hints on Handling Guns," *Twillingate Sun*, 20 August 1892, 1. For other examples of such basic advice, see "Sensible Advice," *Weekly Sentinel Review*, 31 October 1884, 7.

24 *Globe*, 27 September 1894, 4. Also see *Globe*, 25 September 1893, 4; "Didn't Know It Was Loaded," *Globe*, 26 September 1896, 22; *Toronto Star*, 11 January 1898, 1; "Guns and the Code of Caution," *Rod and Gun in Canada* 6, no. 1 (November 1899): 117; "Small Bore Rifles," *Toronto Star*, 5 December 1901, 6; "Firearm Foolishness," *Globe*, 28 November 1902, 4; "Criminal Carelessness," *Globe*, 20 February 1903, 6; "The Gun Accident Season," *Globe*, 30 September 1903, 6; *Globe*, 11 September 1905, 6; "Care with Firearms," *Globe*, 27 October 1909, 6.

25 *Globe*, 15 November 1884, 4.

26 "Firearms," *Globe*, 4 February, 1882, 7.

27 "Speaking about Insurance," *Globe*, 14 September 1891, 5.

28 *Toronto Star*, 25 April 1898, 2.

29 *Debates, House of Commons* (6 February 1908), 2590–1; (9 December 1910), 987; *An Act to Amend Chapter 128 of The Revised Statutes of Saskatchewan 1909 ...*, S.S. 1912–1913, c.40, s.13(8); *The Game Act*, S.S. 1916, c.30, s.38.

30 "Dominion Riflemen," *Globe*, 15 April 1897, 5.

31 "Sensible Militia Reform," *Globe*, 30 April 1903, 6. Also see "Canadian Militarism," *Globe*, 25 March 1903, 6.

32 Desmond Morton, *A Military History of Canada*, 5th ed. (Toronto: McClelland & Stewart, 2007), 116–17.

33 "The Rifle," *Edmonton Bulletin*, 1 January 1900.

34 "Learn to Shoot," *Rod and Gun in Canada* 1, no. 10 (March 1900): 194. Also see "Sharpshooters," *Toronto Star*, 2 April 1900, 4; *Rod and Gun in Canada* 2, no. 1 (June 1901); *Debates, House of Commons* (11 March 1901), 1283–4. For discussions of the role of the Anglo-Boer War in stirring and shaping Canadian militarism, see James Wood, *Militia Myths: Ideas of the Canadian Citizen Soldier, 1896–1921* (Vancouver: UBC Press, 2010); Carman Miller, *A Knight in Politics: A Biography of Sir Frederick Borden* (Montreal and Kingston: McGill-Queen's University Press, 2010), 186–7; Morton, *Military History of Canada*, 116–17; Bernd Horn, "'Lost Opportunity': The Boer War Experience and Its Influence on British and Canadian Military Thought," in *Forging a Nation: Perspectives on the Canadian Military Experience*, ed. Bernd Horn, 81–106 (St Catharines, ON: Vanwell, 2002); Mike O'Brien, "Manhood and the Militia Myth: Masculinity, Class and Militarism in

Ontario, 1902–1914," *Labour / Le Travail* 42 (1998): 115–41; Carman Miller, *Painting the Map Red: Canada and the South African War, 1899–1902* (Montreal and Kingston: McGill-Queen's University Press, 1993).

35 Brian A. Reid, "'A Most Daring Advance': Paardeberg," in *More Fighting for Canada: Five Battles, 1760–1944*, ed. Donald E. Graves (Toronto: Robin Brass Studio, 2004), 162; J.L. Granatstein, *Canada's Army: Waging War and Keeping the Peace* (Toronto: University of Toronto Press, 2002), 3–23; Wood, *Militia Myths*, 87–9, 101–2. A similar myth also emerged in French Canada celebrating the role of Canadian militia in fending off British attacks in the eighteenth century. Jay Cassel, "The Militia Legend: Canadians at War, 1665–1760," in *Canadian Military History since the 17th Century*, ed. Yves Tremblay (Ottawa: Department of National Defence, 2001), 59.

36 "Rifle Shooting in Canada," *Rod and Gun in Canada* 3, no. 4 (September 1901): 6.

37 Ronald G. Haycock, *Sam Hughes: The Public Career of a Controversial Canadian, 1885–1916* (Waterloo, ON: Wilfrid Laurier University Press, 1986), 144; *Globe*, 12 June 1900, 6; *Rod and Gun in Canada* 2, no. 3 (August 1900); "Long-Bow and Rifle," *Globe*, 15 January 1901, 6; "Encourage Rifle Practice," *Globe*, 26 August 1904, 6; "Swiss Rifle Clubs," *Temiskaming Speaker*, 19 June 1908, 3; "Encouragement for Rifle Shots," *Globe*, 2 August 1909, 1.

38 *Debates, House of Commons* (29 May 1903), 3772; "Learn Use of Rifle," *Globe*, 29 March 1906, 9; "Shield for the Young Riflemen," *Toronto Star*, 27 February 1907, 13; Morton, *Military History of Canada*, 112; Miller, *Knight in Politics*, 200–1; Haycock, *Sam Hughes*, 13, 110.

39 "Rifle Clubs for Canada," *Globe*, 28 February 1901, 7.

40 *An Act to incorporate the Dominion of Canada Rifle Association*, S.C. 1900, c.99; *The Militia Act*, S.C. 1904, c.23, s.64; Miller, *Knight in Politics*, 188; Morton, *Military History of Canada*, 116–27; "The School of Musketry," *Toronto Star*, 27 February 1901, 1; "New School of Musketry," *Globe*, 31 May 1901, 7; "The School of Musketry," *Globe*, 16 November 1901, 2; *Debates, House of Commons* (11 June 1900), 7135–6.

41 Tables of the Trade and Navigation of the Dominion of Canada, in Canada, *Sessional Papers*, 1892–1914; Wood, *Militia Myths*, 279; "Ontario Rifle Association," *Globe*, 25 August 1896, 10; "With the Rifle," *Globe*, 1 September 1896, 9; "Ontario Rifle Association," *Globe*, 27 February 1897, 28; "At the New Ranges," *Globe*, 18 August 1902, 10; "Thousands Learn to Shoot," *Toronto Star*, 12 April 1904, 9; "Dominion Rifle Meet," *Globe*, 29 August 1904, 2; "Close of the D.R.A. Meeting," *Globe*, 5 September 1904, 11; "Canadians Can Shoot," *Globe*, 24 August 1912, 6; "Last Rifle Meet on Rockliffe Range," *Globe*, 25 August 1913, 2.

42 Prince Edward Island Archives, Acc 3466, HF 79.114.514.5a, Ladies Rifle Association of Charlottetown, Minute Book, 1905–1907; "Ladies' Day at Gun Club," *Globe*, 25 July 1905, 3; Catharine Merritt, "Toronto Ladies Going to Shoot with Rifles," *Toronto Star*, 26 July 1909, 7; "Ladies Shooting in the Armories," *Toronto Star*, 23 September 1909, 11; "Boom in Rifle Shooting," *Montreal Gazette*, 12 January 1909, 1; "Quebec Ladies' Rifle Club," *Globe*, 18 March 1913, 10.
43 *Globe*, 2 October 1913, 6.
44 "Ladies' Rifle Association," *Globe*, 29 June 1909, 8; Catharine Merritt, "Toronto Ladies Going to Shoot with Rifles," *Toronto Star*, 26 July 1909, 7; "Ladies' Rifle Association," *Montreal Gazette*, 29 July 1909, 7; "Ladies' Rifle Club," *Globe*, 25 April 1913, 5; "Women Shoot Accurately at Armories Range," *Toronto World*, 19 September 1914, 5.
45 "Wild West Show Full of Dare-Devil Feats," *Toronto World*, 3 July 1911, 14; "Wild West Show Monday," *Montreal Gazette*, 12 July 1911, 3.
46 Laura Browder, *Her Best Shot: Women and Guns in America* (Chapel Hill: University of North Carolina Press, 2006), 86.
47 "Shooting," *Globe*, 2 August 1902, 13.
48 Catharine Merritt, "Toronto Ladies Going to Shoot with Rifles," *Toronto Star*, 26 July 1909, 7.
49 Prince Edward Island Archives, Acc 3466, HF 79.114.514.5a, Ladies Rifle Association of Charlottetown, Minute Book, 1905–1907; *Toronto Star*, 28 October 1895, 4; "Women's Revolver Club Is Flourishing," *Toronto Star*, 11 January 1915, 8; *Globe*, 18 January 1915, 4; "Why Not a Shooting Gallery," *Temiskaming Speaker*, 12 November 1915, 1.
50 *Rod and Gun in Canada* 5, no. 6 (November 1903). Also see *Rod and Gun in Canada* 5, no. 12 (May 1904). A few of these women may also have practised with rifles because of the militarist rhetoric of the day. In 1909, twenty-three women of the Ladies' Rifle Association of Canada took the oath of allegiance and signed the service roll. The outbreak of war in 1914 further encouraged the participation of women in rifle shooting. A Montreal Ladies' Rifle Association formed in 1915 and had ninety-nine members after just three weeks. The Ladies' Rifle Club of Toronto turned out forty members for rifle practice in October 1914 and reported a large waiting list of potential members. The club, however, suffered from a lack of ammunition during the Great War – a problem that bedevilled all rifle associations. "Lady Rifle Shots Sworn In; Liable for Military Service," *Toronto Star*, 14 October 1909, 1; "Ladies Drill Tonight," *Montreal Gazette*, 19 July 1915, 2; "Women Are Crack Shots," *Globe*, 10 October 1914, 9; "Girls Would Shoot," *Toronto Star*, 5 November 1914, 10.

51 *Globe*, 17 July 1914, 8.

52 *Rod and Guns in Canada* 6, no. 2 (July 1904). On American gun-makers' attempts to entice women to shoot, see Browder, *Her Best Shot*, 3–7.

53 K.B. Wamsley, "Cultural Signification and National Ideologies: Rifle-Shooting in Late Nineteenth-Century Canada," *Social History* 20, no. 1 (1995): 63–72; Mark Moss, *Manliness and Militarism: Educating Young Boys in Ontario for War* (Don Mills, ON: Oxford University Press, 2001), 112; Lynne Marks, *Revivals and Roller Rinks: Religion, Leisure, and Identity in Late-Nineteenth-Century Small-Town Ontario* (Toronto: University of Toronto Press, 1996), 81–6; Steven Maynard, "'Horrible Temptations': Sex, Men, and Working-Class Male Youth in Urban Ontario, 1890–1935," *Canadian Historical Review* 78, no. 2 (1997): 191–235; Susan E. Houston, "Victorian Origins of Juvenile Delinquency," in *Education and Social Change: Themes from Ontario's Past*, ed. Michael B. Katz and Paul H. Mattingly, 83–109 (New York: New York University Press, 1975); Susan E. Houston, "The 'Waifs and Strays' of a Late Victorian City: Juvenile Delinquents in Toronto," in *Childhood and Family in Canadian History*, ed. Joy Parr, 129–42 (Toronto: McClelland & Stewart, 1982).

54 Garry J. Burke, "Good for the Boy and the Nation: Military Drill and the Cadet Movement in Ontario Public Schools, 1865–1911" (PhD diss., University of Toronto, 1996), 122–34; Desmond Morton, "The Cadet Movement in the Moment of Canadian Militarism," *Journal of Canadian Studies* 13, no. 2 (1978): 59; R.S.S. Baden-Powell, "The Boy Scout Movement," *Empire Club Speeches*, vol. 8 (1910–11), http://speeches.empireclub.org/62214/data?n=1; Patricia Dirks, "Canada's Boys: An Imperial or National Asset? Responses to Baden-Powell's Boy Scout Movement in Pre-War Canada," in *Canada and the British World: Culture, Migration, and Identity*, ed. Phillip Buckner and R. Douglas Francis (Vancouver: UBC Press, 2006), 121. On the role of scouting in inculcating cultural values, see Jeffrey P. Hantover, "The Boy Scouts and the Validation of Masculinity," *Journal of Social Issues* 34, no. 1 (1978): 184–95; J.O. Springhall, "The Boy Scouts, Class and Militarism in Relation to British Youth Movements, 1908–1930," *International Review of Social History* 16 (1971): 135–6; Allen Warren, "Popular Manliness: Baden-Powell, Scouting, and the Development of Manly Character," in Mangan and Walvin, *Manliness and Morality*, 199–216.

55 Quoted in Moss, *Manliness and Militarism*, 118.

56 Minutes of Executive Committee Meeting of Dominion Council, Canadian Boy Scouts (16 May 1914); Canadian General Council of the Boy Scouts Association, *Report of the Third Annual Meeting Held in Ottawa, April 21, 1917;*

Annual Report of the Canadian General Council of The Boys Scouts Association, March, 1919 (Ottawa: n.p. 1919), 8, LAC, MG28-173.

57 *The Militia Act*, S.C. 1904, c.23, s.67; Wood, *Militia Myths*, 150–61, 279; Morton, "Cadet Movement," 56–68; Haycock, *Sam Hughes*, 140–1.

58 "Toys for the Million," *Halifax Citizen*, 2 November 1869, 3.

59 "Celebrate!," *Commercial* 18, no. 36 (12 May 1900): 1128; "Fire Works and Flags," *Commercial* 19, no. 36 (11 May 1901): 864; *Simpson's Christmas Catalogue*, 1906, 92, LAC, http://www.collectionscanada.gc.ca/mailorder/index-e.html. Also see "Spencer's Arcade," *Victoria Daily Colonist*, 10 December 1897, 4.

60 "Air Guns," *Globe*, 22 September 1896, 8. On the sale of air guns as parlour games in the United State, see Gary Cross, *Kids' Stuff: Toys and the Changing World of American Childhood* (Cambridge, MA: Harvard University Press, 1997), 24, 66. On Daisy, see Michael Landry, "It's a Daisy!," *Michigan History* 90, no. 1 (2006): 28–38.

61 *Saint John Daily Sun*, 20 May 1896, 7; *Edmonton Capital*, 5 September 1913, 9. For other examples of inexpensive air guns, see *Cycling* 1, no. 14 (10 June 1891), 155; *Toronto Star*, 17 December 1901, 8; *Red Deer News*, 16 December 1914, 4.

62 *T. Eaton Co. Spring and Summer 1899 Catalogue*, Archives of Ontario (AO), F229-1-0-17. Also see *Morning Telegram* (Winnipeg), 26 July 1900, 2; *T. Eaton Co. Fall and Winter 1913–1914 Catalogue*, AO, F229-1-0-47; *Red Deer News*, 21 August 1912, 9; *Red Deer News*, 20 August 1913, 7.

63 *Simpson's Christmas Catalogue*, 1906, 93, LAC, http://www.collectionscanada.gc.ca/mailorder/index-e.html. A Red Deer, AB, retailer in 1914 advertised an air rifle as a "good toy for boys 7 to 15 years old." *Red Deer News*, 16 December 1914, 4. Also see *Red Deer News*, 9 December 1908, 1; *Edmonton Capital*, 12 September 1913, 9; "Business Locals," *Red Deer News*, 10 December 1913, 8.

64 *T. Eaton Co. Spring/Summer 1910 Catalogue*, AO, F229-1-0-40; "Spencer's Arcade," *Victoria Daily Colonist*, 10 December 1897, 4; *T. Eaton Co. Fall/Winter 1892–93 Catalogue*, AO, F229-1-0-6; *T. Eaton Co. Fall/Winter 1902–03 Catalogue*, AO, F229-1-0-24.

65 Cross, *Kids' Stuff*, 50–1.

66 *Calgary Weekly Herald*, 22 March 1900, 7; *Calgary Weekly Herald*, 11 May 1900, 8; *Globe*, 21 April 1900, 3; *Globe*, 23 March 1901, 4; *Toronto Star*, 22 February 1902, 3; *Globe*, 1 November 1902, 4; "Free Rifle," *Globe*, 31 January 1903, 4; *Globe*, 24 February 1905, 11; *Twillingate Sun*, 30 October 1909, 3; *St John's Evening Telegram*, 19 November 1909, 3; *Twillingate Sun*, 27 November 1909, 3; *Waterford Star*, 9 December 1909, 6; *Toronto Star*, 22 January

1910, 7; "Free to Boys," *Wetaskiwin Times*, 28 March 1912, 3; *Rod and Gun in Canada* 16, no. 9 (February 1914): 1001.

67   T. Eaton Co. *Spring/Summer 1911 Catalogue*, AO, F229-1-0-42.

68   *Rod and Gun in Canada* 3, no. 12 (May 1902). Also see *Rod and Gun in Canada* 4, no. 11 (April 1904).

69   *Globe*, 17 October 1914, 16. Also see "The Ross Rifle," *Rod and Gun in Canada* 18, no. 1 (June 1916): 69; Roger Phillips, *The Ross Rifle Story* (Sydney, NS: J.A. Chadwick, 1984), 47.

70   *Saint John Daily Sun*, 23 May 1896, 7.

71   *Grain Growers' Guide*, 15 June 1910, 2.

72   *Toronto Star*, 17 December 1904, 9.

73   *Grain Growers' Guide*, 23 November 1910, 15.

74   *Rod and Gun in Canada* 5, no. 7 (December 1903). For other examples of retailers advertising guns as Christmas gifts, see "Xmas," *Globe*, 21 December 1896, 10; *Red Deer News*, 9 December 1908, 1; *Victoria Daily Colonist*, 20 December 1908, 9; *Edmonton Capital*, 14 December 1911, 11; "Xmas Gifts," *Red Deer News*, 16 December 1914, 5; "Christmas Suggestions," *Globe*, 2 December 1916, 8; *Bassano Mail*, 18 December 1919, 10.

75   *Rod and Gun in Canada* 5, no. 7 (December 1903).

76   Cross, *Kids' Stuff*, 111–12; Steven Mintz, *Huck's Raft: A History of American Childhood* (Cambridge, MA: Belknap, 2004), 217. On liberalism and the connection between liberalism and consumption, see Donica Belisle, "Toward a Canadian Consumer History," *Labour / Le Travail* 52 (2003): 191–4; Ian McKay, "The Liberal Order Framework: A Prospectus for a Reconnaissance of Canadian History," *Canadian Historical Review* 81, no. 4 (2000): 616-78.

77   "Thomas Ryan Was Careless," *Toronto Star*, 28 May 1901, 3.

78   "Sixteen-Cent Pistols," *Chicago Daily Tribune*, 4 July 1880, 7.

79   "The Deadly Toy Pistol," *Chicago Daily Tribune*, 29 July 1880, 3; "The Deadly Toy Pistol," *New York Times*, 16 July 1881, 4; "The Deadly Work of the National Toy Pistol," *Chicago Daily Tribune*, 12 July 1882, 2; "The Toy Pistol Pursuing Its Deadly Course," *Chicago Daily Tribune*, 13 July 1882, 7; "Twenty-Eight Toy Pistol Deaths," *New York Times*, 21 July 1882, 2; "General Notes," *New York Times*, 26 July 1882, 4; "The Toy Pistol Prohibited," *New York Times*, 7 July 1883, 1; "Chicago Bars Toy Pistol," *New York Times*, 11 November 1903, 1; "A Safe July 4," *Toronto Star*, 29 June 1912, 11; "Toy-Pistol Tetanus," *Quarterly Epitome of American Practical Medicine and Surgery*, March 1882 (New York: W.A. Townsend, 1882), 512–13; "The Toy Pistol Again," *Medical Standard* 24, no. 7 (July 1901): 347–8; C.H. Claudy and Clarence Maris, "The Deadly Toy Pistol," *Technical World Magazine* 11, no. 1 (1909): 476–82.

80 See "Latest from London," *Globe*, 28 July 1877, 8; "American Mail," *Victoria Daily Colonist*, 8 August 1880, 3; "American Mail," *Victoria Daily Colonist*, 26 July 1881, 3; *Canada Presbyterian* 10, no. 30 (26 July 1882): 475; "The Toy Pistol," *Globe*, 24 March 1884, 6; "The 'Toy Pistol' Again," *Globe*, 22 October 1887, 1; "Local Briefs," *Globe*, 30 July 1892, 12; "Dangerous Toy Pistols," *Wetaskiwin Times*, 23 August 1901, 2; "Lad Shot with Toy Gun," *Toronto Star*, 2 September 1902, 7; "What It Costs to Celebrate Independence Day," *Advertiser and Central Alberta News*, 9 July 1908, 4; "Uncle Sam's Fourth," *Claresholm Review*, 10 July 1908, 1; "What It Costs to Celebrate Independence Day," *Wetaskiwin Times*, 16 July 1908, 6; *Victoria Daily Colonist*, 6 July 1909, 13; *Maritime Medical News* 21, no. 8 (August 1909): 316.

81 "Municipal Police Court," *Victoria Daily Colonist*, 12 October 1880, 3.

82 "Toy Cigars," *Pleasant Hours* 4, no. 4 (23 February 1884): 30. Also see "Notes and Comments," *Globe*, 31 July 1882, 4; *Globe*, 6 July 1883, 4; "Warning to Little Boys," *Victoria Daily Colonist*, 24 February 1888, 4; "Men and Things," *Victoria Daily Colonist*, 23 July 1903, 4; "In Woman's Realm," *Victoria Daily Colonist*, 19 March 1908, 8.

83 *Debates, Senate* (4 April 1889), 429; (25 February 1890), 140.

84 "Played Wild West," *Globe*, 26 October 1907, 1. For a sample of other accidents involving air rifles, see "Police Court," *Saint John Daily Sun*, 14 June 1906, 2; "Boy Shot in the Eye," *Montreal Gazette*, 20 January 1910, 6.

85 "The Law on Air Guns," *Manitoba Morning Free Press*, 12 November 1898, 12.

86 "City and District," *Montreal Gazette*, 12 May 1913. For a sample of other incidents, see "Shot in the Eye," *Globe*, 5 November 1895, 10; "Shooting Accident at London," *Globe*, 14 April 1900, 20; "Another Shooting Accident," *Globe*, 30 May 1901, 12; "Hamilton Boy Killed," *Globe*, 7 September 1903, 1; "Boy Sportsman Killed," *Globe*, 20 July 1904, 9; "Hamilton Boy Shot," *Globe*, 20 March 1905, 1; "Shot through the Brain," *Globe*, 11 July 1905, 1; "Another Gun Victim," *Montreal Gazette*, 17 December 1908, 11; "Youth with Rifle Kills Companion," *Globe*, 27 October 1913, 8.

87 *Cayley Hustler*, 20 September 1911, 5. Also see "Accidentally Shot," *Victoria Daily Colonist*, 23 September 1896, 5; "Shot through the Head," *Victoria Daily Colonist*, 29 October 1897, 2; "Gun License," *Victoria Daily Colonist*, 11 January 1901, 7.

88 *Globe*, 23 May 1885, 9.

89 "The Mirror," *Saturday News*, 13 January 1906, 4. Also see "Bad Boys at the Bijou," *Manitoba Morning Free Press*, 24 March 1896, 6; *Globe*, 6 August 1887, 4; "Influence the Imagination," *Educational Journal* 5, no. 16 (1 January 1892): 604.

90 "Boys Handling Fire Arms," *Temiskaming Speaker*, 29 October 1909, 1. Also
see "The Boy and the Gun," *Temiskaming Speaker*, 8 November 1912, 1.

91 "Engaged in a Noble Work," *Victoria Daily Colonist*, 4 November 1903, 6.

92 "Small Boys with Rifles a Menace in the Country," *Toronto Star*, 26 October
1911, 17. Also see "The Killing of Birds," *Toronto Star*, 7 May 1904, 6; "The
Boy and the Gun," *Toronto Star*, 6 November 1911, 6; "Firearms in Suburbs," *Toronto Star*, 24 October 1913, 1; British Columbia, *Eighth Report of
the Provincial Game Warden and Forest Warden, 1912* (Victoria: Government
Printer, 1913), O6–O7.

93 Cynthia Comacchio, *The Dominion of Youth: Adolescence and the Making
of Modern Canada, 1920–1950* (Waterloo, ON: Wilfrid Laurier University
Press, 2006), 28.

94 Ibid., 29; Tamara Myers, "Nocturnal Disorder and the Curfew Solution:
A History of Juvenile Sundown Regulations in Canada," in Gleason et al.,
Lost Kids, 95–113; Tamara Myers, *Caught: Montreal's Modern Girls and the
Law, 1869–1945* (Toronto: University of Toronto Press, 2006); Dorothy E.
Chunn, "Boys Will Be Men, Girls Will Be Mothers: The Legal Regulation
of Childhood in Toronto and Vancouver," in *Histories of Canadian Children
and Youth*, ed. Nancy Janovicek and Joy Parr, 188–206 (Don Mills, ON: Ox-
ford University Press, 2003).

95 *An Act to make provision against the improper use of Firearms*, S.C. 1877, c.30.

96 *Debates, Senate* (4 April 1889), 427–9; (9 April 1889), 449–50; *The Criminal
Code*, S.C. 1892, c.29, s.106(1); Chunn, "Boys Will Be Men, Girls Will Be
Mothers," 194. In 1890, British Columbia banned most boys under fourteen
from carrying a gun without the accompaniment of a father or guardian.
An Act to prevent Minors from carrying Fire-arms, S.B.C. 1890, c.18. This was
increased to those under sixteen in 1913. *Firearms Act Amendment Act, 1913*,
S.B.C. 1913, c.23. There were, however, complaints that this legislation was
not enforced. "Gun License," *Victoria Daily Colonist*, 11 January 1901, 7.

97 *The Criminal Code*, S.C. 1892, c.29, s.106(1).

98 "The Law on Air Guns," *Manitoba Morning Free Press*, 12 November 1898,
12; *Toronto Star*, 27 September 1898, 3. Accidents with air guns led the Toronto Board of Police Commissioners to make renewed efforts to enforce
the law forbidding boys under sixteen from acquiring air guns. "The Boy
and the Gun," *Toronto Star*, 17 April 1901, 7.

99 "The Deadly Flobert," *Globe*, 25 November 1913, 6. Also see "Children and
Firearms," *Toronto Star*, 29 April 1896, 2. Concern with safety led Eaton's to
note that Stevens .22 calibre "Little Scout" rifle was "Not a toy," but was a
"safe dependable gun." *T. Eaton Co. Spring / Summer 1913 Catalogue* (Winnipeg ed.), AO, F229-2-0-17.

100 *Debates, House of Commons* (29 May 1903), 3777; (10 July 1905), 9120. Also
     see "The Mail Bag," *Grain Growers' Guide*, 27 May 1914, 23.
101 "Feminine Fancies and the Home Circle Chat," *Victoria Daily Colonist*,
     8 March 1908, 22. Also see "Let the Boys Shoot," *Victoria Daily Colonist*,
     26 May 1890, 3; "Young Sportsmen," *Strathmore Standard*, 6 May 1914, 3;
     "Young Sportsmen," *Gleichen Call*, 14 May 1914, 7.
102 "Police Court," *Saint John Daily Sun*, 14 June 1906, 2; "Had Received No
     Authority," *Globe*, 17 September 1887, 20; "Lad Had Air Gun, Mother
     Censured," *Toronto Star*, 24 March 1906, 7; "Youth with Rifle Kills Com-
     panion," *Globe*, 27 October 1913, 8.
103 *Fowell v. Grafton* (1910), 22 O.L.R. 550, upholding *Fowell v. Grafton*, 20
     (1910) O.L.R. 639; "Responsible for Gift," *Edmonton Capital*, 12 April 1910,
     8.
104 *Moran v. Burroughs*, 10 (1912) D.L.R. 181.
105 *The Offensive Weapons Act*, S.O. 1911, c.66; *The Offensive Weapons Act*, S.M.
     1912, c.57; *The Offensive Weapons Act*, S.S 1912, c.24; *Offensive Weapons Act*,
     S.B.C. 1913, c.83.
106 "Permit Is Now Necessary for Keeping an Air Rifle," *Toronto Star*, 21
     April 1911, 1.
107 *The Criminal Code Amendment Act*, 1913, S.C. 1913, c.13, s.5.
108 *An Act to amend ... An Act imposing duties of Customs*, S.C. 1868, c.44; *An
     Act to amend the Act respecting the Duties of Customs*, S.C. 1887, c.39. In
     1878, the commander of the militia lamented that cartridges had to be
     "imported from England, as I regret to say we have no manufactories in
     this country to produce them." *Report on the State of the Militia of the Do-
     minion of Canada for the Year 1878* (Ottawa: Maclean Rogers, 1879), xli.
109 Harold F. Williamson, *Winchester: The Gun That Won the West* (Washing-
     ton: Combat Forces , 1952), 63; Kennett and Anderson, *Gun in America*, 95;
     Debates, House of Commons (13 April 1882), 855; *An Act further to amend ...
     duties of Customs*, S.C. 1881, c.10; *An Act to amend the Acts respecting the Du-
     ties of Customs*, S.C. 1890, c.20.
110 S. James Gooding, *Trade Guns of the Hudson's Bay Company, 1670–1970*
     (Bloomfield, ON: Museum Restoration Service, 2003), 123; Miller, *Knight
     in Politics*, 216; "Canada," *Globe*, 3 January 1883, 2; *Debates, House of Com-
     mons* (14 May 1886), 898, 1302; (29 May 1903), 3771; "The Dominion
     Riflemen," *Globe*, 31 August 1887, 1; "Dominion Riflemen," *Globe*, 15
     March 1888, 2; "Good Scoring," *Globe*, 23 August 1894, 5; *Department of
     Militia and Defence of the Dominion of Canada Annual Report, 1889* (Ottawa:
     Queen's Printer, 1890), xii; Kennett and Anderson, *Gun in America*, 98;
     Williamson, *Winchester*, 122–4.

111 "Big Game," *Globe*, 6 December 1907, 9. Also see *Rod and Gun in Canada* 5, no. 6 (November 1903); *Rod and Gun in Canada* 4, no. 10 (March 1904); *Rod and Gun in Canada* 6, no. 1 (June 1904); *Globe*, 25 October 1913, 23.

112 S. James Gooding, *The Canadian Gunsmiths, 1608–1900* (West Hill, ON: Museum Restoration Service, 1962), 12; Tim Cook, *The Madman and the Butcher: The Sensational Wars of Sam Hughes and General Arthur Currie* (Toronto: Allen Lane, 2010), 41–2; Phillips, *Ross Rifle Story*, 28.

113 Morton, *Military History of Canada*, 118.

114 *The Customs Tariff, 1897*, S.C. 1897, c.16; Phillips, *Ross Rifle Story*, 43–50; "'Champion of the Year,'" *Globe*, 1 May 1909, 20; "Ross Rifle Barrels," *Globe*, 11 September 1909, 20; "The Ross Sporting Rifle," *Globe*, 9 October 1909, 19.

115 "The Ross Rifle Factory," *Globe*, 24 October 1903, 6. Also see "Ross Rifle Company," *Globe*, 2 July 1904, 1.

116 Phillips, *Ross Rifle Story*, 58–61; Miller, *Knight in Politics*, 223.

117 *Debates, House of Commons* (23 November 1909), 339. Also see "Success of Ross Rifle," *Perth Courier*, 6 August 1909, 2.

118 "A Feather in Canada's Cap," *Calgary Daily Herald*, 9 August 1913, 16.

119 *Globe*, 23 May 1910, 10; "With a Ross Rifle," *Globe*, 26 July 1911, 12. Also see Phillips, *Ross Rifle Story*, 5; "'Champion of the Year,'" *Globe*, 1 May 1909, 20; "Experience Overcomes Prejudice," *Globe*, 8 May 1909, 16; "Long-Range Champion," *Globe*, 12 June 1909, 16; "Good for the Ross Rifle," *Globe*, 17 July 1909, 1; "At Bisley," *Globe*, 11 April 1910, 10; "The Ross Rifle," *Toronto Star*, 2 September 1911, 9.

120 "Mounted Police Discard Ross Rifles," *Red Deer News*, 6 November 1906, 4; "Mounted Police Reject Ross Rifle?," *Toronto Star*, 30 October 1906, 1; "Ross Rifle Is Again under Fire," *Toronto Star*, 20 January 1908, 7; S.W. Horrall, *The Pictorial History of the Royal Canadian Mounted Police* (Toronto: McGraw-Hill Ryerson, 1973), 61; Tim Cook, *At the Sharp End*, vol. 1, *Canadians Fighting the Great War, 1914–1916* (Toronto: Viking, 2007), 312–14; Bill Rawling, *Surviving Trench Warfare: Technology and the Canadian Corps 1914–1918* (Toronto: University of Toronto Press, 1992), 63–6; Phillips, *Ross Rifle Story*, 5–6.

121 "'Possibles' at the O.R.A.," *Globe*, 8 August 1935, 4. For discussions of how the machine gun revolutionized the battlefield in the Great War, see C.J. Chivers, *The Gun* (New York: Simon & Schuster, 2010), 118–40; John Ellis, *The Social History of the Machine Gun* (NY: Pantheon Books, 1975), 111–47.

122 "What Ails Rifle Shooting?," *Globe*, 5 July 1930, 1, 10. Also see "Shooting as a Sport," *Globe*, 8 July 1930, 4.

123 *Debates, House of Commons* (13 May 1938), 2886.

124 *The Criminal Code*, S.C. 1892, c.29, ss.105, 106.

125 W.Y. Carman, *A History of Firearms from the Earliest Times to 1914* (London: Routledge & Kegan Paul, 1955), 148; "Colt Automatic Pistol," *Rod and Gun in Canada* 1, no. 12 (May 1900): 236; "A Unique Pistol," *Victoria Daily Colonist*, 30 December 1903, 6; *Manitoba Morning Free Press*, 16 March 1906, 6.

126 *T. Eaton Co. Fall/Winter 1910–11 Catalogue* (Winnipeg ed.), AO, F229-2-0-11.

127 *Chief Constables' Association of Canada, Eighth Annual Convention, 1912*, (n.p.: n.d.), 6.

128 *T. Eaton Co. Spring and Summer 1899 Catalogue*, 231 AO, F299-1-0-17. For other examples of inexpensive handguns, see *Morning Telegram* (Winnipeg), 26 July 1900, 2; *Toronto Star*, 21 November 1902, 8; *Toronto Star*, 27 October 1905, 6; *Manitoba Morning Free Press*, 16 March 1906, 6; *Toronto Star*, 7 September 1906, 8; *Toronto Star*, 16 October 1906, 12; *Toronto Star*, 6 September 1907, 12.

129 G.H. Robinson to Wilfrid Laurier, 17 March 1909, LAC, MG26G, vol. 566, 153648; "A Tragedy at Kingston," *Globe*, 29 April 1902, 1; *Globe*, 30 April 1902, 14; "Killed the Girl Who Teased Him," *Toronto Star*, 29 April 1902, 7. Also see "Second-Hand Dealers," *Globe*, 15 June 1904, 11.

130 "The Murder Gun," *Toronto Star*, 31 March 1909, 6. Also see "Banish the Revolver," *Globe*, 18 September 1901, 9; "Crimes of Violence," *Globe*, 4 December 1903, 6; *Globe*, 28 May 1912.

131 "Judge Scores the Sale of Revolvers," *Manitoba Morning Free Press*, 17 October 1912, 16.

132 *Globe*, 28 May 1901, 6.

133 On social and moral reform in the period, see Carolyn Strange and Tina Loo, *Making Good: Law and Moral Regulation in Canada, 1867–1939* (Toronto: University of Toronto Press, 1997); Craig Heron, *Booze: A Distilled History* (Toronto: Between the Lines, 2003); Mariana Valverde, *The Age of Light, Soap, and Water: Moral Reform in English Canada, 1885–1925* (Toronto: McClelland & Stewart, 1991).

134 John Herd Thompson, *Ethnic Minorities during Two World Wars* (Ottawa: Canadian Historical Association, 1991), 3; Valerie Knowles, *Strangers at Our Gates: Canadian Immigration and Immigration Policy, 1540–1990* (Toronto: Dundurn, 1992), 58–92; Ninette Kelley and Michael Trebilcock, *The Making of the Mosaic: A History of Canadian Immigration Policy* (Toronto: University of Toronto Press, 1998), 111–63.

135 For examples of such incidents, see "Miners Assaulted by a Masked

Mob," *Manitoba Morning Free Press*, 23 March 1903, 9; "Striking Italians Stab Policemen," *Winnipeg Morning Free Press*, 29 June 1906, 1.

136 *Toronto Star*, 9 May 1906, 6. On the connection between immigration and gun control before the Great War see Pelletier, "Le Code criminel canadien," 57–60.

137 Kelley and Trebilcock, *Making of the Mosaic*, 139–40; Bruno Ramirez, *The Italians in Canada* (Ottawa: Canadian Historical Association, 1989), 5–12; Roberto Perin and Franc Sturino, eds., *"Arrangiarsi": The Italian Immigration Experience in Canada* (Montreal: Guernica, 1989); Karen Dubinsky and Franca Iacovetta, "Murder, Womanly Virtue and Motherhood: The Case of Angelina Napolitano, 1911–1922," *Canadian Historical Review* 72, no. 4 (1991): 505–31.

138 *Montreal Gazette*, 23 January 1911, 10. For other examples, see "Striking Italians Stab Policemen," *Winnipeg Morning Free Press*, 29 June 1906, 1; "Charged with Wounding," *Globe*, 7 July 1906, 11; "Italian Used Pistol," *Globe*, 24 May 1909, 2; "A Ward Shooting Affray," *Globe*, 23 June 1909, 14; "Shot through Ear in Italian Row," *Montreal Gazette*, 10 August 1912, 3; "Murder Trial Opens at Hamilton Assizes," *Globe*, 22 January 1915, 6; "Italian Lies Dead: Indian Is Arrested," *Globe*, 26 March 1915, 2.

139 "Italians and Their Weapons," *Globe*, 4 December 1905, 3.

140 "Montreal Second-Hand Stores Arsenals Which Issue Hundreds of Guns Daily," *Montreal Herald*, 22 January 1911, 21. On the criticism of Italians, also see "Still Another Italian Shooting Reflects on Free Sale of Arms," *Montreal Herald*, 24 January 1911, 1.

141 *Montreal Herald*, 23 June 1911, 1.

142 *Montreal Herald*, 24 January 1911, 1.

143 Michael Barnholden, *Reading the Riot Act: A Brief History of Riots in Vancouver* (Vancouver: Anvil, 2005), 35, 38; W. Peter Ward, *White Canada Forever: Popular Attitudes and Public Policy toward Orientals in British Columbia*, 3rd ed. (Montreal and Kingston: McGill-Queen's University Press, 2002); Kelley and Trebilcock, *Making of the Mosaic*, 143–7; Knowles, *Strangers at Our Gates*, 86–7; "Very Bad News from Vancouver," *Globe*, 10 September 1907, 1; Ken Adachi, *The Enemy That Never Was: A History of the Japanese Canadians* (Toronto: McClelland & Stewart, 1991), 75–6.

144 Bryan Williams to W.J. Bowser, British Columbia Archives, GR 446, box 32, file 8. Williams repeated many of the same concerns in his 1912 and 1913 annual reports. British Columbia, *Eighth Report of the Provincial Game Warden and Forest Warden, 1912* (Victoria: Government Printer, 1913) O6–O7; British Columbia, *Ninth Report of the Provincial Game Warden and Forest Warden, 1913* (Victoria: Government Printer, 1914), N5.

145 *Game Protection Act Amendment Act, 1913*, S.B.C. 1913, c.27; *Game Act*, S.B.C. 1914, c.33.

146 *Criminal Statistics*, in Canada, *Sessional Papers* 1893–1914.

147 "Against Carrying Fire-Arms," *Globe*, 14 August 1909, 6.

148 "Grand Jury against Weapon Carrying," *Manitoba Morning Free Press*, 8 July 1911, 17.

149 "Will Round Up Armed Italians," *Montreal Gazette*, 24 March 1911, 14; "Crimes of Violence Are on the Increase," *Manitoba Morning Free Press*, 24 January 1914, 22.

150 Kennett and Anderson, *Gun in America*, 167–82; Colin Greenwood, *Firearms Control: A Study of Armed Crime and Firearms Control in England and Wales* (London: Routledge & Kegan Paul, 1972), 27–9; Joyce Lee Malcolm, *Guns and Violence: The English Experience* (Cambridge, MA: Harvard University Press, 2002), 136–8.

151 *Ontario Game and Fisheries Act*, S.O. 1907, c.49, s.22. For an example of this legislation being used, see "Fire Arms Seized," *Temiskaming Speaker*, 20 January 1921, 1.

152 "Foreigners, Firearms, and Liquor," *Globe*, 26 January 1910, 6. Also see "The Concealed-Weapon Problem," *Globe*, 11 December 1907, 6. For descriptions of the incident, see "Shot His Foreman Dead: Brutal Crime at Grafton," *Globe*, 26 January 1910, 1; "Drink the Cause of Grafton Crime," *Globe*, 27 January 1910, 1.

153 *Debates, House of Commons* (15 January 1908), 1285. Also see *Debates, House of Commons* (22 January 1908), 1669; (1 March 1909), 1716. MP Thomas Joseph Stewart of West Hamilton introduced another bill to curtail the use of guns by foreigners. *Debates, House of Commons* (9 March 1909), 2217–18.

154 "Parliament and the Pistol: Restrict Sale of Weapons," *Toronto Star*, 26 March 1909, 11; "Dealers Protest," *Ottawa Citizen*, 29 March 1909, 4; *An Act to amend the Criminal Code*, S.C. 1909, c.9, s.2.

155 *Debates, House of Commons* (13 January 1911), 1642, 1643.

156 *The Offensive Weapons Act*, S.O. 1911, c.66, s.5. The Ontario law received mixed reviews. "Permit Is Now Necessary for Keeping an Air Rifle," *Toronto Star*, 21 April 1911, 1; "Decided Drop in Sale of Revolvers under the New Law," *Toronto Star*, 10 May 1912, 10; "The Revolver Habit," *Globe*, 20 May 1912, 6; "Far Too Many Revolvers Sold," *Toronto World*, 14 May 1913, 7.

157 *The Offensive Weapons Act*, S.M. 1912, c.57; *An Act respecting Offensive Weapons*, S.S. 1912, c.24; *Offensive Weapons Act*, S.B.C. 1913, c.83.

158 *Chief Constables' Association of Canada, Eighth Annual Convention, 1912* (n.p.: n.d.), 5–6; "Term in Prison Penalty for Carrying Dangerous Weapons," *Toronto World*, 22 February 1913, 1.

159 "Revolvers," *Canada Law Journal*, n.s., 49 (1913): 135.

160 *Debates, House of Commons* (16 May 1913), 10071.

161 *The Criminal Code Amendment Act, 1913*, S.C. 1913, c.13. Eaton's requested and got permission for its employees to carry revolvers when they took money to banks. OA, F229-35, Eaton's Legal Section general files, Revolver Permits (1913–1915). There were complaints in Montreal that authorities failed to enforce the law. "Revolver Law Clear as Day; Not Enforced," *Montreal Daily Mail*, 15 November 1913, 4; "Police to Enforce Law re Sale of Weapons," *Montreal Daily Mail*, 18 November 1913, 4.

162 *Debates*, House of Commons (5 February 1914), 468.

163 "Object to Firearms," *Globe*, 21 September 1907, 5; "Indiscriminate Use of Firearms Aimed At," *Globe*, 6 February 1914, 14.

4: Suppressing Gun Ownership

1 Bohdan S. Kordan, *Enemy Aliens, Prisoners of War: Internment in Canada during the Great War* (Montreal and Kingston: McGill-Queen's University Press, 2002); John Herd Thompson, *Ethnic Minorities during Two World Wars* (Ottawa: Canadian Historical Association, 1991), 4, 7, 79; John Herd Thompson, *The Harvests of War: The Prairie West, 1914–1918* (Toronto: McClelland and Stewart, 1978), 79; Donald Avery, *"Dangerous Foreigners": European Immigrant Workers and Labour Radicalism in Canada, 1896–1932* (Toronto: McClelland and Stewart, 1979), 65-6.

2 Order in Council, PC 2283 (3 September 1914), *Canada Gazette* 48, no. 10 (5 September 1914): 768–9.

3 LAC, RCMP fonds, R196-48-2-E, vol. 1784, file 619; vol. 1786, file 689; vol. 1787, file 715; vol. 1793, file 935.

4 LAC, RCMP fonds, R196-48-2-E, vol. 1789, file 783.

5 LAC, RCMP fonds, R196-48-2-E, vol. 1778, file 385. Also see LAC, RCMP fonds, R196-152-8-E, vol. 2174, file: Stuhr and Garbet.

6 LAC, RCMP fonds, R196-48-2-E, vol. 1778, file 383; vol. 1780, file 460; R196-152-8-E, vol. 2174, file: Frank Mino; vol. 2174, file: August Miller; vol. 2174, file: Joseph Schmirler. For other instances of enemy aliens claiming to have been unaware of the law, see LAC, RCMP fonds, R196-48-2-E, vol. 1783, file 601; vol. 2174, file: Steve Strady; R196-152-8-E, vol. 2174, file: Artland.

7 LAC, RCMP fonds, R196-152-8-E, vol. 2174, file: Stuhr and Garbet.

8 LAC, RCMP fonds, R196-48-2-E, vol. 1783, file 601.

9 LAC, RCMP fonds, R196-48-2-E, vol. 1789, file 784. Also see LAC, RCMP fonds, R196-152-8-E, vol. 2174, file: Julius Ritter.

10 See LAC, RCMP fonds, R196-48-2-E, vol. 1793, file 936.

11 Larry Hannant, *The Infernal Machine: Investigating the Loyalty of Canada's Citizens* (Toronto: University of Toronto Press, 1995), 7. On the Canadian left in this period, see Ian McKay, *Reasoning Otherwise: Leftists and the People's Enlightenment in Canada 1890–1920* (Toronto: Between the Lines, 2008).

12 "Demands of Veterans on Government and the City," *Toronto Star*, 7 August 1918, 13. Also see Desmond Morton and Glenn Wright, *Winning the Second Battle: Canadian Veterans and the Return to Civilian Life, 1915–1930* (Toronto: University of Toronto Press, 1987), 120–1.

13 D.C. Masters, *The Winnipeg General Strike* (Toronto: University of Toronto Press, 1950), 85–7; Kenneth McNaught and David J. Bercuson, *The Winnipeg General Strike: 1919* (Don Mills, ON: Longmans, 1974), 91; David Jay Bercuson, *Confrontation at Winnipeg: Labour, Industrial Relations, and the General Strike* (Montreal and Kingston: McGill-Queen's University Press, 1974), 173; *Debates, House of Commons* (1 July 1919), 4357; (7 October 1919), 876; "The Sort of 'Equipment' Found on Many Aliens," *Globe*, 14 June 1919, 13; "Bouquet to Winnipeg from Montreal Press," *Manitoba Morning Free Press*, 21 November 1919, 1; *Chief Constables' Association of Canada, Fifteenth Annual Convention, 1919* (n.p.: n.d.), 58–60; Gérald Pelletier, "Le Code criminel canadien, 1892–1939: Le contrôle des armes à feu," *Crime, Histoire & Sociétés* 6, no. 2 (2002): 57–67.

14 *Debates, House of Commons* (1 July 1919), 4357, 4358.

15 *Debates, House of Commons* (1 July 1919), 4357, 4358, 4361. Also see *Debates, House of Commons* (7 October 1919), 878

16 *Debates, House of Commons* (1 July 1919), 4358.

17 *An Act to amend the Criminal Code*, S.C. 1919, c.46, s.2. In late 1919, the government clarified that it targeted the possession of all weapons, not just concealable weapons. *An Act to amend the Criminal Code*, S.C. 1919, c.12; *Debates, House of Commons* (6 October 1919), 841; (7 October 1919), 871–84.

18 *An Act to amend the Criminal Code*, S.C. 1920, c.43; "All Suspects Are to Be Searched," *Toronto World*, 10 December 1920, 14; "Permits Necessary for Having Weapons," *Globe*, 15 January 1921, 1. Britain passed similar gun control measures in 1920. The British act introduced several new restrictions on gun ownership and use. First, the act required firearm certificates for anyone who wanted to purchase a weapon, possess a firearm, use a weapon, or carry a gun or ammunition. The act gave local police chiefs responsibility for determining who should get a certificate and on what ground such certificates should be granted or refused. Applicants needed a "good reason" for a certificate, which expired every three years. Joyce Lee Malcolm, *Guns and Violence: The English Experience* (Cambridge, MA: Harvard University Press, 2002), 148–9.

19 *Debates, House of Commons* (10 June 1920), 3410; *Debates, Senate* (23 June 1920), 694.

20 *Debates, House of Commons* (29 March 1933), 3519.

21 *Debates, Senate* (23 June 1920), 696.

22 Ibid., 695.

23 *Debates, House of Commons* (10 June 1920), 3412.

24 "Law against Firearms," *Toronto Star*, 19 February 1921, 14.

25 "The Law against Firearms," *Toronto Star*, 22 February 1921, 4. Also see "Burglar's Point of View," *Toronto Star*, 17 February 1921, 13; "The Arms Act," *Manitoba Free Press*, 12 March 1921, 13.

26 "Firearm Restrictions," *Manitoba Morning Free Press*, 4 January 1921, 3.

27 "The Carrying of Weapons," *Toronto Star*, 10 February 1921, 6. Also see "The Settler and His Gun," *Toronto Star*, 14 April 1921, 6; "The Law on Firearms," *Temiskaming Speaker*, 14 April 1921, 11. There were also worries about possible fees. "Fire Arms Seized," *Temiskaming Speaker*, 20 January 1921, 1; "'Fire-Arms,' Again," *Temiskaming Speaker*, 31 March 1921, 1.

28 *Debates, House of Commons* (6 May 1921), 191. Also see *Debates, House of Commons* (26 May 1921), 3906–7.

29 *An Act to amend the Criminal Code*, S.C. 1921, c.25, s.2.

30 *Debates, Senate* (23 June 1920), 695.

31 *Debates, House of Commons* (13 March 1930), 550.

32 "Use of Revolvers," *Montreal Gazette*, 12 October 1920, 6; "Sale of Revolvers," *Vancouver Sun*, 15 November 1921, 4; "The Useless Revolver," *Toronto Star*, 18 July 1924, 6; "Ban the Revolver," *Globe*, 18 July 1924, 4; "Too Many Pistols," *Globe*, 26 August 1924, 4; "The Overpowering Gun," *Globe*, 15 November 1927, 4; "Eliminate Firearms," *Globe*, 21 March 1928, 4; *Globe*, 12 April 1928, 5; "Revolvers Are Too Easy to Get," *Calgary Daily Herald*, 16 November 1928, 16; "Confiscate Weapons," *Toronto Star*, 27 December 1930, 7; *Chief Constables' Association of Canada, Sixteenth Annual Convention, 1920* (n.p.: n.d.), 51–3; *Chief Constables' Association of Canada, Twentieth Annual Convention, 1924* (n.p.: n.d.), 65–6; *Chief Constables' Association of Canada, Twenty-First Annual Convention, 1925* (n.p.: n.d.), 42–9.

33 *Rex v. Smart*, 49 (1927) C.C.C. 75 at 77. Also see "Judge Is Alarmed at Number of Guns," *Globe*, 23 October 1924, 10; *Debates, House of Commons* (13 March 1930), 550. A belief that aliens tended to use handguns persisted. See "Lethal Tools Are Collected in Police Raids," *Globe*, 17 January 1921, 6; "Woman Is Arrested; Revolver and Knife Used on Her Husband," *Globe*, 13 June 1921, 7; "Revolver Play after Slashing," *Globe*, 19 September 1921, 9; "Italian Is Arrested Following Gunplay on Walton Street," *Globe*, 4 March 1929, 13; John C. Weaver, *Crimes, Constables, and Courts: Order*

and Transgression in a Canadian City, 1816–1970 (Montreal and Kingston: McGill-Queen's University Press, 1995), 221.

34 F.H. Leacy, ed., *Historical Statistics of Canada*, 2nd ed. (Ottawa: Statistics Canada, 1983), Z21. Population figures are drawn from Statistics Canada, "Estimated Population of Canada, 1605 to Present," http://www.statcan .gc.ca/pub/98-187-x/4151287-eng.htm.

35 However, in 1925 Newfoundland dictated that no person could purchase or possess a pistol unless he or she held a firearm certificate. The inspector general of the Newfoundland Constabulary issued such certificates in St John's, while stipendiary magistrates could issue certificates outside of St John's. The issuer had to be satisfied that the applicant had a good reason for requiring a certificate, and that the potential owner of the firearm was not a public danger. Reasons for refusing a permit included intemperance or an unsound mind. A person who carried a pistol without a certificate faced a fine of up to two hundred dollars and/or imprisonment for up to three months. *An Act relating to Firearms and other Weapons*, S.N. 1925, c.18.

36 *Debates, Senate* (22 June 1920), 675; *Debates, House of Commons* (21 June 1926), 4812–14; (23 April 1929), 1857–9; N.A. Belcourt to William Lyon Mackenzie King, 30 June 1926, LAC MG26 J1, vol. 128, 108613.

37 *Debates, Senate* (29 May 1930), 383.

38 "Goose Missteps," *Toronto Star*, 24 August 1928, 6.

39 "The Armed Policeman," *Toronto Star*, 21 February 1902, 6; *The King v. Smith* (1907), 13 C.C.C. 326; "Better without Revolvers," *Toronto Star*, 17 February 1910, 8.

40 "Armed or Unarmed?," *Montreal Gazette*, 10 January 1911, 8.

41 "Revolvers," *Canada Law Journal*, n.s., 49 (1913): 134.

42 Wilbur R. Miller, *Cops and Bobbies: Police Authority in New York and London, 1830–1870* (Chicago: University of Chicago Press, 1977), 48–52; Stanley H. Palmer, "Cops and Guns: Arming the American Police," *History Today* 28, no. 6 (1978): 382–9. Also see Dennis C. Rousey, "Cops and Guns: Police Use of Deadly Force in Nineteenth-Century New Orleans," *American Journal of Legal History* 28, no. 1 (1984): 41–66.

43 Weaver, *Crimes, Constables, and Courts*, 122–3.

44 "The Police Force," *Globe*, 13 October 1886, 9; "Winnipeg Police Will Carry Arms," *Manitoba Morning Free Press*, 26 August 1911, 28; "Police Revolvers Thirty Years Old," *Toronto World*, 12 November 1919, 13; "Police Instructed to Return Fire," *Toronto World*, 13 November 1919, 8; "Will Take Charge of Police at Fair," *Toronto World*, 24 August 1920, 16; "New Arms for Toronto Police," *Montreal Gazette*, 9 July 1921, 1; Greg Marquis, "Henry James Grasett," *DCB* online; Michael Boudreau, *City of Order: Crime and Society in*

Halifax, 1918–1935 (Vancouver: UBC Press, 2012), 242; Kelly Toughill, "Police Force Bites the Bullet," *Toronto Star*, 24 May 1998, 1.

45 LAC, R188-39-8-E, vol. 20, file 1868-507.

46 S.W. Horrall, *The Pictorial History of the Royal Canadian Mounted Police* (Toronto: McGraw-Hill Ryerson, 1973), 60–2; Zhiqiu Lin, *Policing the Wild North-West: A Sociological Study of the Provincial Police in Alberta and Saskatchewan, 1905–32* (Calgary: University of Calgary Press, 2007), 52.

47 *Criminal Code*, S.C. 1892, c.29, s.33.

48 "Guns and the Police," *Toronto Star*, 22 August 1928, 6.

49 "The Use of Firearms," *Globe*, 6 November 1928, 4. Also see "Shooting by the Police," *Globe*, 5 September 1928, 4; "Would Prosecute Person Ordering Use of Firearms," *Toronto Star*, 9 October 1928, 3; "Would Disarm All Policemen, Declares Ont. Chief Justice," *Calgary Daily Herald*, 6 November 1928, 8.

50 Greg Marquis, *Policing Canada's Century: A History of the Canadian Association of Chiefs of Police* (Toronto: University of Toronto Press, 1993), 177; "Law Giving Police Power to Shoot Called Barbarous," *Montreal Gazette*, 3 May 1929, 10; "Contends Police Must Only Shoot in Self-Defence," *Toronto Star*, 3 May 1929, 21; "Would Limit Use Pistols by Police," *Edmonton Journal*, 21 May 1931, 18. On the Samson case, see "Crown to Claim Shooting by Police Unjustifiable," *Toronto Star*, 23 October 1928, 1–2; "Constable Dinnen Acquitted by Jury," *Montreal Gazette*, 25 October 1928, 15; "Dinnen Reinstated as Police Constable," *Toronto Star*, 25 October 1928, 29. For other examples, see *Rex v. Smith* (1907), 17 M.R. 282; "Will Lay Charges of Manslaughter," *Globe*, 30 October 1923, 13; *Rex v. Purvis*, [1929] 51 C.C.C. 273; "Shooting to Kill," *Globe*, 19 February 1929, 4; "Arrest of Constables Is Sequel to Inquest into Brennan's Death," *Globe*, 22 February 1929, 1–2; "Not Guilty, But—," *Toronto Star*, 9 November 1933, 6.

51 "Officer Must Decide When Use of Firearms in Public Interest," *Toronto Star*, 22 August 1928, 1–2. Also see "Police Need to Be Armed Says Inspector Guthrie," *Toronto Star*, 4 May 1929, 17; *Chief Constables' Association of Canada, Twenty-Fifth Annual Convention, 1929* (Winnipeg: n.d.), 141–3; *Chief Constables' Association of Canada, Twenty-Seventh Annual Convention, 1931* (Winnipeg: n.d.), 65–6; "Police Commission Supports Officers Lately Acquitted," *Globe*, 8 December 1933, 11–12; Marquis, *Policing Canada's Century*, 177.

52 "Many Young Canucks Win Marksman Medals," *Globe*, 8 November 1923, 3; "'Scouts and Firearms' Is a Book Every Lad Should Possess and Peruse," *Calgary Daily Herald*, 16 May 1924, 36; "Cadet Training," *Toronto Star*, 11 April 1931, 6; "Editorial," *Rod and Gun in Canada and Canadian Silver Fox*

News 36, no. 7 (December 1934): 5; Cynthia R. Comacchio, *The Dominion of Youth: Adolescence and the Making of a Modern Canada, 1920–1950* (Waterloo, ON: Wilfrid Laurier University Press, 2006), 113–14.

53 *Cardston News*, 6 December 1934; *Eaton's Fall 1934 / Winter 1935 Catalogue*, LAC, http://www.collectionscanada.gc.ca/mailorder/index-e.html; *Nerlich & Co. General Catalogue, Season 1938–1939*, LAC, http://www.collectionscanada.gc.ca/mailorder/index-e.html; Gary Cross, *Kids' Stuff: Toys and the Changing World of American Childhood* (Cambridge, MA: Harvard University Press, 1997), 114–15.

54 "Death Was Accidental Blame Make of Rifle," *Toronto Star*, 15 October 1924, 16; "Boys and Firearms," *Temiskaming Speaker*, 30 April 1925, 4; "Children Should Be Warned of All Accident Dangers," *Calgary Daily Herald*, 2 May 1925, 24; "Would Check Fire-Arms Kept in Private Homes," *Toronto Star*, 8 December 1930, 1; "Curb Urged by Jury on Ammunition Sale," *Globe*, 20 March 1930, 11; "Child Is Fatally Wounded by Sister," *Winnipeg Free Press*, 27 October 1930, 1; "Children and Firearms," *Globe*, 23 December 1931, 4; "Ten-Year-Old Boy Allegedly Shot by His Playmate," *Globe*, 4 August 1932, 3; "Danger in Air Guns," *Vancouver Sun*, 21 January 1936, 8; "Boys with Guns Prove Dangerous," *Calgary Daily Herald*, 24 June 1936, 12. Courts found in favour of plaintiffs injured by young people in this period. For example, in Saskatchewan in 1922, eleven-year-old George Hunter accidentally shot the six-year-old son of his father's housekeeper. The trial court found in favour of the plaintiff, and the Saskatchewan Court of Appeal upheld the decision, declaring doubt "whether under any circumstances, it is not negligent to allow a boy of 11 years of age to use a gun, or to leave a gun and shells in a place where they are so easily accessible to children of that age." *Black v. Hunter et al.*, [1925] 4 D.L.R. 285 at para 11. Similarly, in 1939 an eleven-year-old shot a twenty-year-old housekeeper in the eye with a gun taken from an unlocked cupboard. The British Columbia Court of Appeal refused to overturn a trial decision to award the young woman damages. *Edwards v. Smith*, [1941] 1 D.L.R. 736. Also see *Kennedy et al. v. Hanes et al.*, [1940] O.R. 461; *Hanes v. Kennedy*, [1941] S.C.R. 384.

55 Canada, *Vital Statistics*, 1921–1939; "Prohibit Firearms among Young Boys," *Toronto Star*, 28 October 1924, 2; "'Rabbit Hunters' on Pheasant Land to Be Prosecuted," *Calgary Daily Herald*, 29 September 1928, 28; "Boys with Rifles Warned of Danger near City Homes," *Calgary Daily Herald*, 5 April 1932, 3; "Asks Fish and Game Association to Help in Saving Pheasants," *Calgary Daily Herald*, 9 April 1932, 22; "Steps to Stop Shooting near Red Deer Urged," *Calgary Daily Herald*, 22 April 1933, 26; "To Restrict

Firearms," *Waterford Star*, 15 June 1933, 2; "The Boy and the Gun," *Globe*, 17 April 1933, 4; "Rifles in Hands of Young," *Calgary Daily Herald*, 29 May 1936, 4; "Handling of Guns," *Toronto Star*, 19 February 1937, 4; "Editorialets," *Cardston News*, 27 April 1937, 4; "Local Curb on Firearms Denied," *Globe and Mail*, 5 April 1938, 17; "Parents to Pay for Damage Done by Young Gun Toters, Says Children's Aid Head," *Calgary Daily Herald*, 8 July 1938, 9; "Notice re Shooting," *Cardston News*, 19 March 1940. The town of Cardston subsequently offered a five-dollar reward for information leading to the conviction of persons committing such damage. "Warning to Boys Using 22 Rifles," *Cardston News*, 4 May 1937; "Reward," *Cardston News*, 8 June 1937, 2.

56 *Chief Constables' Association of Canada, Twenty-Sixth Annual Convention, 1930* (Winnipeg: n.p., n.d.), 27. Also see *Chief Constables' Association of Canada, Thirty-Seventh Annual Convention, 1942* (Montreal: n.p., n.d.), 110–11. For other criticisms of parents who provided arms to children, see "Menace of the Boy with a Gun," *Globe*, 2 March 1936, 4.

57 Joan Sangster, "Creating Social and Moral Citizens: Defining and Treating Delinquent Boys and Girls in English Canada, 1920–65," in *Contesting Canadian Citizenship: Historical Readings*, ed. Robert Adamoski, Dorothy E. Chunn and Robert Menzies, 337–58 (Toronto: Broadview, 2002). Also see Comacchio, *Dominion of Youth*, 17–43.

58 "Dime Novels Lead Youth Astray," *Globe*, 1 March 1919, 16.

59 Quoted in "Should Forbid Movie Gun," *Edmonton Journal*, 9 August 1930, 4. Also see "More about Children and the Movies," *Globe*, 14 August 1917, 8; "Boy Fatally Shot by His Playmate," *Globe*, 16 April 1923, 1; "Wants Gun-Play Cut in Children's Films," *Toronto Star*, 29 March 1928, 4; *Debates, House of Commons* (29 March 1933), 3522; "Ban on Air Rifles Urged as Boy Nearly Loses Eye," *Toronto Star*, 13 December 1938, 21. On the appeal of gangster films in the 1930s, see Jack Shadoian, *Dreams & Dead Ends: The American Gangster Film* (New York: Oxford University Press, 2003), 29–61. For criticisms of toy guns, see "Carrying Weapons," *Globe*, 28 April 1928, 4; "A Peril to Children," *Globe*, 28 November 1931, 4; "Cause and Effect," *Globe*, 28 November 1931, 4; "The Child and the Gun," *Globe*, 8 December 1931, 4; "Guns and the Child," *Globe*, 11 March 1936, 4. The *Globe* also published a series of articles by American syndicated columnist Angelo Patri, who argued strongly against giving small rifles, air guns, and toy guns to boys. See, for example, "Holds Shooting No Pastime for Small Boy," *Globe and Mail*, 10 June 1939, 28.

60 *Chief Constables' Association of Canada, Twenty-Ninth Annual Convention, 1934* (Toronto: n.p., n.d.), 43.

61 D. Peter Morris, *Embattled Shadows: A History of Canadian Cinema, 1895–1939* (Montreal and Kingston: McGill-Queen's University Press, 1992), 55; David C. Jones, "The Reflective Value of Movies and Censorship on Interwar Prairie Society," *Prairie Forum* 10, no. 2 (1985): 388; Mary Vipond, *The Mass Media in Canada*, 3rd ed. (Toronto: James Lorimer, 2000), 33–4; "Exchanges Dislike 'No Revolver' Order," *Toronto Star*, 14 March 1921, 3; "Ban Poster Revolvers," *Toronto Star*, 14 March 1921, 3.

62 *Debates, House of Commons* (28 June 1938), 4321–2.

63 *Debates, House of Commons* (5 November 1945), 1807–8.

64 Speakman also declared that he was "quite certain that the majority of boys in my county between the ages of twelve and sixteen own and carry .22 rifles and shoot small game, gophers, rabbits and so on. The law is completely ignored at present." *Debates, House of Commons* (29 March 1933), 3529.

65 *An Act to amend the Criminal Code (Offensive Weapons)*, S.C. 1933, c.25; *An Act to amend the Criminal Code*, S.C. 1938, c.44, s.9; *Debates, House of Commons* (29 March 1933), 3526–31; "Danger in Air Guns," *Vancouver Sun*, 21 January 1936, 8; "Danger in Toys," *Globe*, 28 May 1936, 4. Also see "Trustees Urge Ban upon Air Rifle Sale," *Toronto Star*, 27 May 1937, 17; "Ask Control of Air Guns," *Globe and Mail*, 8 June 1937, 4; "Students Warned of Air-Gun Danger," *Toronto Star*, 19 November 1937, 8; "Ban on Air Rifles Urged as Boy Nearly Loses Eye," *Toronto Star*, 13 December 1938, 21.

66 Leacy, *Historical Statistics of Canada*, Z66–78. Population figures are drawn from Statistics Canada, "Estimated Population of Canada, 1605 to Present," http://www.statcan.gc.ca/pub/98-187-x/4151287-eng.htm.

67 *Debates, Senate* (6 April 1933), 398.

68 "Stricter Control over Firearms," *Calgary Daily Herald*, 13 July 1933, 4.

69 *Debates, House of Commons* (29 March 1933), 3517.

70 "Copp Dies and City Launches Hunt for Slayer," *Globe*, 4 December 1933, 1–2; "Citizens Join Intensive Search for Copp Slayer," *Globe*, 6 December 1933, 9; "Draper Asks All to Co-operate in Trapping Killer," *Globe*, 7 December 1933, 11.

71 C.T. Currelly to R.B. Bennett, 18 December 1933, LAC, MG26K, vol. 407, 259326.

72 "Disarm the Thugs!," *Globe*, 5 December 1933, 4; "The Weapon of Murder," *Toronto Star*, 28 December 1933, 6.

73 *Debates, House of Commons* (29 March 1933), 3512; "Revolvers Should Be Banned," *Calgary Daily Herald*, 22 December 1931, 4; "The Carrying of Weapons," *Globe*, 31 March 1933, 4; "Revolver Menace Emphasized," *Calgary Daily Herald*, 5 November 1934, 4; C.V. Heward to R.B. Bennett, 16

February 1931, LAC, MG26K, vol. 433, 274692–5; J.R.L. Starr to R.B. Bennett, 16 December 1933, LAC, MG26K, vol. 407, 259324; C.V. Heward to R.B. Bennett, 18 February 1931, LAC, MG26K, vol. 433, 274697–8; C.T. Currelly to R.B. Bennett, 18 December 1933, LAC MG26K, vol. 407, 259326–7; C.T. Currelly to R.B. Bennett, 9 January 1933, LAC MG26K, vol. 407, 259335–6.

74 "Mrs Macnaughton Made Life Member by Women Liberals," *Globe*, 23 January 1931, 16.

75 LAC, MG 26K, vol. 798, 493456; *Chief Constables' Association of Canada, Twenty-Ninth Annual Convention, 1934* (Toronto: n.p., n.d.), 26; Marquis, *Policing Canada's Century*, 176–7. Also see "Police Here Laud Move to Add Teeth to Law on Arms," *Winnipeg Free Press*, 23 June 1934, 24; "Police Favor Registration of Revolvers," *Calgary Daily Herald*, 5 September 1934, 12; "Registration of Revolvers to Be Started Today," *Winnipeg Free Press*, 7 September 1934, 7; "Would Ban Revolvers," *Montreal Gazette*, 17 July 1937, 4; "Ban on Firearms Proposed at Police Meeting," *Globe and Mail*, 17 July 1937, 13; LAC, R188-39-8-E, vol. 2205, file no. 1930-712.

76 *Debates, House of Commons* (21 June 1926), 4815; (29 March 1933), 3520, 3522.

77 Gregg Lee Carter, *Guns in American Society: An Encyclopedia of History, Politics, Culture and the Law* (Santa Barbara, CA: ABC-CLIO, 2002), 2:427; Kennett and Anderson, *Gun in America*, 187–215; Malcolm, *Guns and Violence*, 152–4.

78 *An Act to amend the Customs Act*, S.C. 1920, c.10, s.1; *Customs Act*, R.S.C. 1927, c.42, s.122; *Debates, House of Commons* (17 March 1933), 3147.

79 William Price to R.B. Bennett, 2 January 1934, LAC, MG26K, vol. 407, 259330.

80 R.B. Bennett to J.R.L. Starr, 18 December 1933, LAC, MG26K, vol. 407, 259325.

81 *An Act to amend the Criminal Code (Offensive Weapons)*, S.C. 1933, c.25.

82 "Drastic Changes in Firearms Law Effective July 15," *Winnipeg Free Press*, 5 July 1933, 16.

83 *An Act to Amend the Criminal Code*, S.C. 1934, c.47; "More Teeth Put in Law against Owning Firearms," *Winnipeg Free Press*, 22 June 1934, 3; "Jail or Fine for All Unregistered Revolver Owners," *Winnipeg Free Press*, 24 December 1934, 2.

84 "Guns Far Exceed Register Forms," *Globe*, 2 January 1935, 5; "Total of 6,000 Guns Registered by Owners with Police to Date," *Winnipeg Free Press*, 22 September 1934, 29; "Armed Citizens Have Taken 7,000 Guns to Police Headquarters," *Winnipeg Free Press*, 25 September 1934, 4; "Time for

Registration of Firearms Is Extended," *Winnipeg Free Press*, 5 January 1935, 27.

85 *Report of the Royal Canadian Mounted Police for the Year ended March 31, 1936* (Ottawa: King's Printer, 1936), 15.

86 *Report of the Royal Canadian Mounted Police for the Year ended March 31, 1937* (Ottawa: King's Printer, 1937), 14. Some law enforcement officials suggested a low rate of compliance with the act. Toronto Chief Constable D.C. Draper reported in 1937 that Toronto citizens had registered 17,105, but he guessed that this represented only half the small arms requiring registration. "Many Citizens Glad to Yield Firearms," *Toronto Star*, 9 January 1937, 9; "No Gun-Toting in England," *Globe and Mail*, 19 January 1937, 6.

87 "Ownership of Firearms," *Winnipeg Free Press*, 4 October 1934, 15; "Permits for Small Arms," special issue, *Canadian Marksman* 6 (January 1935): 13.

88 *Report of the Royal Canadian Mounted Police for the Year ended March 31, 1938* (Ottawa: King's Printer, 1938), 18. Also see *Chief Constables' Association of Canada, Thirty-Fourth Annual Convention, 1939* (Montreal: n.p., n.d.), 120–1; "Pistol Registration Great Aid to Police," *Calgary Daily Herald*, 16 January 1939, 3.

89 *Report of the Royal Canadian Mounted Police for the Year ended March 31, 1941* (Ottawa: King's Printer, 1941), 58–9; *Report of the Royal Canadian Mounted Police for the Year ended March 31, 1949* (Ottawa: King's Printer, 1949), 45; *Report of the Royal Canadian Mounted Police for the Year ended March 31, 1950* (Ottawa: King's Printer, 1950), 48; "Enough Pistols in City for Every Tenth Man, Police Record Shows," *Globe and Mail*, 22 March 1938, 19; "Hold Crime Reduced by Gun Registration," *Toronto Star*, 23 March 1938, 7.

90 *An Act to amend the Criminal Code*, S.C. 1936, c.29, s.2; *An Act to amend the Criminal Code*, S.C. 1938, c.44; "Criminal Code Bill Passes," *Winnipeg Free Press*, 29 June 1938, 3; "Curbing the Guns," *Winnipeg Free Press*, 21 July 1938, 11. The 1944 re-registration was postponed for one year. *An Act to amend the Criminal Code*, S.C. 1943–44, c.23, s.4; *Debates, Senate* (21 July 1943), 348; "Firearms Registration," *Winnipeg Free Press*, 3 March 1944, 8. Ottawa abolished the re-registration process in 1950. Each of the handgun registration processes (in 1934, 1939, and 1945) had been somewhat incomplete, with the result that the RCMP had three collections of records to consult, rather than just one. *Chief Constables' Association of Canada, Forty-Fourth Annual Conference, 1949* (n.p., n.d.), 11–12. The RCMP instead felt it could adequately track such arms through the requirement that a permit be attained to acquire a registered weapon. *Debates, House of Commons* (29 May 1950), 2968; Marquis, *Policing Canada's Century*, 220.

91 J. de N. Kennedy, *History of the Department of Munitions and Supply: Canada*

in the Second World War, vol. 1, *Production Branches and Crown Companies* (Ottawa: King's Printer, 1950), 76, 186, 197–202; Wartime Prices and Trade Board, Order No. 501, in Canada, Wartime Prices and Trade Board, *Canadian War Orders and Regulations, 1942: Office Consolidation* (Ottawa: King's Printer, 1943), 599–600; Wartime Prices and Trade Board, Order No. 251, in Canada, Wartime Prices and Trade Board, *Canadian War Orders and Regulations, 1943: Office Consolidation*, vol. 2 (Ottawa: King's Printer 1943); Wartime Prices and Trade Board, Order No. 350, in Canada, Wartime Prices and Trade Board, *Canadian War Orders and Regulations, 1943: Office Consolidation* (Ottawa: King's Printer 1944), 3:170–4; LAC, R112-67-1-E, file No. 1/ Pistols Sig /1; LAC, R112-552-8-E, file no. 8997-1-1; "Army Voices Appeal to Revolver Owners," *Winnipeg Free Press*, 23 April 1943, 2.

92 Canada, Criminal Statistics, 1935, 1940, in *Sessional Papers*; Order in Council, PC 3042 (11 October 1939), in *Proclamations and Orders in Council Passed under the Authority of The War Measures Act* (Ottawa: King's Printer, 1940), 1:123–4; *Debates, House of Commons* (23 May 1940), 145; Order in Council, PC 2505 (15 June 1940), in *Proclamations and Orders in Council Passed under the Authority of The War Measures Act* (Ottawa: King's Printer 1940), 2:111–12. There had been several calls for the government to disarm naturalized citizens. See "Canadian Corps Asks Government to Disarm Aliens," *Saskatoon Star-Phoenix*, 20 May 1940, 3; "Ask Action on 'Fifth Column,'" *Leader Post*, 27 May 1940, 5; Ken Adachi, *The Enemy That Never Was: A History of the Japanese Canadians* (Toronto: McClelland & Stewart, 1991), 193–4. Newfoundland issued regulations empowering the government to require residents to report gun ownership, and permitting the requisitioning of these guns. *Regulations Made under Defence Act, 1939 and Emergency Powers (Defence) Act, 1940, Sept. 1st, 1939, to Dec. 31st, 1941* (St John's: King's Printer, 1942), 60–4, 71–3, 87–9.

93 *Report of the Royal Canadian Mounted Police for the Year ended March 31, 1941* (Ottawa: King's Printer, 1941), 10, 61. The RCMP later reported that it held fourteen thousand weapons. *Report of the Royal Canadian Mounted Police for the Year ended March 31, 1950* (Ottawa: King's Printer, 1950), 29.

94 Order in Council, PC 253 (22 January 1940), in *Proclamations and Orders in Council Passed under the Authority of The War Measures Act* (Ottawa: King's Printer, 1940), 2:17; *Report of the Royal Canadian Mounted Police ... 1941*, 60; *Report of the Royal Canadian Mounted Police for the Year ended March 31, 1943* (Ottawa: King's Printer, 1943), 44; *Report of the Royal Canadian Mounted Police for the Year ended March 31, 1945* (Ottawa: King's Printer, 1945), 34.

95 Order in Council, PC 3506 (29 July 1940), *Canada Gazette* 74, no. 5 (3 August 1940): 353–4. Also see *Defence of Canada Regulations (consolidated)* (Ottawa:

King's Printer, 1940), 41–3; "Ottawa Moving to Register Rifles and Shot-guns in Canada," *Winnipeg Free Press*, 26 July 1940, 1. Pressure came from British Columbia for this action because of concerns with fifth column activity. *Debates, House of Commons* (11 June 1940), 677; "B.C. Plans Roundup of Every Gun," *Vancouver Sun*, 25 July 1940, 1.

96 Order in Council, PC 4086 (21 August 1940), *Canada Gazette* 74, no. 8 (21 August 1940), 664. "Boost Penalty," *Windsor Daily Star*, 26 August 1940, 19; "Penalties Up," *Windsor Daily Star*, 28 August 1940, 23.

97 *Report of the Royal Canadian Mounted Police ... 1941*, 11. Also see *Report of the Royal Canadian Mounted Police ... 1943*, 44; *Report of the Royal Canadian Mounted Police ... 1944*, 38.

98 *Report of the Royal Canadian Mounted Police ... 1941*, 59; *Report of the Royal Canadian Mounted Police ... 1943*, 44; *Report of the Royal Canadian Mounted Police ... 1945*, 40; *Chief Constables' Association of Canada, Journal of Proceedings of the Thirty-Ninth Annual Conference, 1944* (Montreal: n.p., n.d.), 18–22, 124.

99 Hannant, *Infernal Machine*, 180.

100 Canada, *Report of the Royal Canadian Mounted Police for the Year ended March 31, 1942* (Ottawa: King's Printer, 1942), 10, 32; Hannant, *Infernal Machine*, 171, 179–80, 250.

101 *Debates, House of Commons* (22 October 1945), 1351; (25 October 1945), 1518; *An Act to amend the Criminal Code*, S.C. 1950, c.11, s.2; *Report of the Royal Canadian Mounted Police for the Year ended March 31, 1947* (Ottawa: King's Printer, 1947), 29–30; *Report of the Royal Canadian Mounted Police for the Year ended March 31, 1949* (Ottawa: King's Printer, 1949), 27; Marquis, *Policing Canada's Century*, 220–1; "Price of 'Hot' Guns in Toronto is $20: Illegal Sales Boom," *Globe and Mail*, 5 September 1945, 4; "Firearm Menace," *Globe and Mail*, 26 October 1945, 15. For concerns with pistol souvenirs, see "A Useful Regulation," *Globe and Mail*, 29 October 1945, 6; "Considers Law on Concealable Guns," *Winnipeg Free Press*, 3 November 1945, 6; Warren Baldwin, "Ottawa Abandons Plan to Seize Most Guns," *Globe and Mail*, 10 December 1945, 3; H.R. Armstrong, "Plan Law Change Covering Guns from War Zone," *Toronto Star*, 10 December 1945, 1; D'arcy O'Donnell, "Unregistered Small Arms Criminal Code Offense," *Saskatoon Star Phoenix*, 15 January 1946, 1; "Unregistered Weapons," *Winnipeg Free Press*, 19 February 1946, 11; "Police Chief Warns Gun-Owners," *Winnipeg Free Press*, 23 September 1946, 1; LAC, RG2, Privy Council Office, series A-5-a, vol. 2637 (31 October 1945), 1–2; (14 November 1945), 3.

102 *Debates, House of Commons* (22 October 1945), 1351.

103 Canada, Criminal Statistics, 1943, 1946, 1952 in *Sessional Papers*; *Report of the Royal Canadian Mounted Police …1945*, 40; *Report of the Royal Canadian Mounted Police for the Year ended March 31, 1946* (Ottawa: King's Printer, 1946), 39–40; Canada, *Report of the Royal Canadian Mounted Police for the Year ended March 31, 1948* (Ottawa: King's Printer, 1948), 29; "Attention!," *Winnipeg Free Press*, 7 June 1945, 2; "Firearm Registration before July 1st Is Urged," *Winnipeg Free Press*, 27 June 1945, 11; "Government Rule Bans Firearms as War Trophies," *Globe and Mail*, 27 July 1945, 13; "Move to Control 'Souvenir' Arms," *Globe and Mail*, 27 October 1945, 2; "The Firearm Menace," *Canadian Police Bulletin* (December 1945); *Chief Constables' Association of Canada, Fortieth Annual Conference, 1945* (n.p., n.d.), 63; *Debates, House of Commons* (25 October 1945), 1518. In addition, the government used a wartime Order in Council to require the registration of automatic weapons. Ottawa banned the possession of automatic guns except by designated government officials or people who had acquired a permit issued by a provincial attorney general or the RCMP commissioner. The commissioner of the RCMP ordered that such permits should be kept to a minimum and should be granted only when the firearm had been rendered useless for firing. As a result, authorities granted few such permits, and by March 1946, the RCMP reported the seizure of 270 submachine guns. *Debates, House of Commons* (25 October 1945), 1518; "Government Rule Bans Firearms as War Trophies," *Globe and Mail*, 27 July 1945, 13; Order in Council PC 1055 (20 February 1945), in *Canada Gazette* 74, no. 16 (21 April 1945): 1694; *Statutory Orders and Regulations, Consolidation 1949*, vol. 1, *A to D* (Ottawa: King's Printer, 1949), 447–9.

5: Resistance to Gun Control in Canada

1 Stephen Clarkson, *The Big Red Machine: How the Liberal Party Dominates Canadian Politics* (Vancouver: UBC Press, 2005), 209.
2 *Report of the Royal Canadian Mounted Police for the Year ended March 31, 1945* (Ottawa: King's Printer, 1945), 45; *Report of the Royal Canadian Mounted Police for the Year ended March 31, 1955* (Ottawa: Queen's Printer, 1955), 27; *Report of the Royal Canadian Mounted Police for the Year ended March 31, 1968* (Ottawa: Queen's Printer, 1968), 29.
3 *Debates, House of Commons* (29 May 1950), 2969. The *Canadian Police Bulletin* expressed concern with the large number of unregistered handguns in circulation. "That Firearms Problem," *Canadian Police Bulletin* (November 1949), 12–13. MP Thomas Langton Church pressed for new measures in the late 1940s. *Debates, House of Commons* (27 September 1949), 293. For

other expressions of concern with firearms in the 1950s and early 1960s, see "Urge Ban on Guns," *Canadian Police Chief* (June 1957): 17; *Debates, House of Commons* (30 June 1959), 5298; (30 June 1960), 5615–16, 5619; (25 May 1961), 5349–50.

4 *R. v. Quon*, [1947] O.R. 856; "Plugging the Loopholes," *Globe and Mail*, 2 July 1947, 6; *Debates, Senate* (8 July 1947), 552. For examples of crimes committed with toy guns, see "Brothers with Toy Gun Kidnap and Compel Lad to Marry Their Sister," *Toronto Star*, 21 May 1924, 1; "Charge Boy with Toy Robbed London Fireman," *Globe*, 29 August 1933, 3; "The Robber's Toy Gun," *Globe*, 22 April 1935, 4; "'Toy Gun' Pair Sent to Prison," *Globe and Mail*, 5 February 1943, 4.

5 *An Act to amend the Criminal Code*, S.C. 1947, c.55, s.15.

6 *Chief Constables' Association of Canada, Forty-Third Annual Conference, 1948* (n.p., n.d.), 167–8. Also see "Police Chief Wants Some Toy Pistols Classed 'Offensive,'" *Winnipeg Free Press*, 18 September 1954, 1. For examples of such incidents in British Columbia in the 1950s, see "Toy Pistol Bandits Get Break from Magistrate," *Vancouver Sun*, 15 December 1950, 21; "Police Seize Mask, Pistol," *Vancouver Sun*, 5 January 1953, 8; "Boys Blamed for Weekend Crime," *Vancouver Sun*, 12 December 1955, 25; "Whiskey-Bottle Bandit Admits 7 Armed Hold Ups," *Vancouver Sun*, 16 November 1957, 9; "Thug Uses Toy Pistol," *Vancouver Sun*, 5 January 1959, 8.

7 *An Act to amend the Criminal Code*, S.C. 1951, c.47, s.1(4).

8 *An Act to amend the Criminal Code*, S.C. 1959, c.41, s.5.

9 *An Act to amend the Criminal Code*, S.C. 1951, c.47, s.7.

10 *Debates, House of Commons* (25 June 1951), 4657.

11 *An Act to amend the Criminal Code*, S.C. 1960, c.37, s.1; *Debates, House of Commons* (12 July 1960), 6120–2; LAC, RG2, Privy Council Office, series A-5-a, vol. 2745 (24 November 1959), 3; (26 November 1959), 5; "Ottawa Cancels Sale of Surplus .22 Rifles," *Globe and Mail*, 18 November 1959, 11; M.L. Friedland, "Gun Control: The Options," *Criminal Law Quarterly* 18 (1975–6): 45; *Chief Constables' Association of Canada, Forty-Fourth Annual Conference, 1949* (n.p., n.d.), 12–16.

12 Newfoundland, *Annual Report of the Department of Mines and Resources for the year ended 31st March, 1957*, 100; Newfoundland, *Annual Report of the Department of Mines, Agriculture and Resources for the year ended 31st March 1961*, 58; British Columbia, *Department of Recreation and Conservation, Annual Report, 1969*, 16; British Columbia, *Department of Recreation and Conservation, Annual Report, 1971*, 38; Ontario, Department of Lands and Forests, *A Statistical Reference of Lands and Forests Administration, 1968*, 27; Lee Kennett and James LaVerne Anderson, *The Gun in America: The Origins of a National*

Dilemma (Westport, CT: Greenwood, 1975), 217–18. For examples of the sale of cheap war surplus rifles, see *Globe and Mail*, 3 September 1959, 23; *Toronto Star*, 15 October 1959, 82; *Toronto Star*, 22 October 1959, 71.

13 "Don't Do This with Guns, Reckless Hunters Warned," *Globe and Mail*, 18 October 1947, 15; "How Many Dead Hunters?," *Globe and Mail*, 24 September 1955, 6; Bruce West, "Be Careful While Hunting," *Globe and Mail*, 31 October 1960, 21; Michael Bolton, "Hunters Go Forth – but 20 Aren't Coming Back," *Toronto Star*, 29 September 1962, 8; "Firearm Warning," *Winnipeg Free Press*, 18 October 1969, 3; Canada, *Vital Statistics*, 1944–60 (Ottawa: Dominion Bureau of Statistics).

14 Christopher Dummitt, "A Crash Course in Manhood: Men, Cars, and Risk in Postwar Vancouver," in *The Sixties: Passion, Politics, and Style*, ed. Dimitry Anastakis (Montreal and Kingston: McGill-Queen's University Press, 2008), 76.

15 Nova Scotia, *Report of the Department of Lands and Forests, 1959* (Halifax: Queen's Printer, 1959), 27; Nova Scotia, *Report of the Department of Lands and Forests, 1960* (Halifax: Queen's Printer, 1960), 30.

16 *An Act to amend The Game and Fisheries Act*, S.O. 1958, c.31, s.12; "Hunter Safety Training," *Canadian Police Bulletin* (March 1960): 58; Michael Bolton, "New Ontario Gun-Training Course May Save Lives," *Toronto Star*, 30 October 1957, 36; "New Hunters Will Get Test on Gun Handling," *Globe and Mail*, 8 October 1958, 4; "Need Experience Now to get Gun License," *Globe and Mail*, 22 August 1959, 26; Alan Dawson, "Getting First License May Take Full Month," *Globe and Mail*, 5 September 1959, 27; "Teen-Agers Learn Gun Safety," *Globe and Mail*, 24 October 1959, 24; Alan Dawson, "Hunter Safety Course Fascinating," *Globe and Mail*, 18 December 1965, 28; Alan Dawson, "Instructors Needed Even More under New Hunting Regulations," *Globe and Mail*, 1 April 1967, 33; Manitoba Reg. 103/69; B.C. Reg. 131/72; Memorandum on Provincial Hunting Laws, LAC, MG31, E54, vol. 8, file 14.

17 "New Hunters Will Get Test on Gun Handling," *Globe and Mail*, 8 October 1958, 5; "Plan Safety Tests for Ontario Hunters," *Globe and Mail*, 24 January 1959, 26; Elisabeth Scarff, *Evaluation of the Canadian Gun Control Legislation: Final Report* (Ottawa: Minister of Supply and Services, 1983), 27–9; "Hunting Safer Than Ever," *Toronto Star*, 31 December 1964, 10; Ontario, Department of Lands and Forests, *A Statistical Reference of Lands and Forests Administration, 1968*, 109; Ontario, Department of Lands and Forests, *Statistics, 1971*, 113; Canada, *Vital Statistics*, 1960–4 (Ottawa: Dominion Bureau of Statistics); Canada, *Causes of Death*, 1965–82 (Ottawa: Dominion Bureau of Statistics / Statistics Canada).

18 *Debates, House of Commons* (12 December 1945), 3350; LAC, RG2, Privy
Council Office, series A-5-a, vol. 6192 (15 January 1962), 5.

19 Kennett and Anderson, *Gun in America*, 242–5; Joyce Lee Malcolm, *Guns
and Violence: The English Experience* (Cambridge, MA: Harvard University
Press, 2002), 197–200; Colin Greenwood, *Firearms Control: A Study of Armed
Crime and Firearms Control in England and Wales* (London: Routledge and
Kegan Paul, 1972), 81–90.

20 *Debates, House of Commons* (23 January 1969), 4721.

21 Gordon Pape, "Turner Ignores Lobbyist Pressure and Pushes a Revised
Omnibus Bill," *Montreal Gazette*, 21 November 1968, 9; letter re: Joint Brief
on Section 6 of Bill C-195, 9 August 1968; Office of the Minister of Justice,
news release, 15 March 1968; R.C. Passmore to John Turner, 8 October
1968, LAC, MG31, E54, vol. 9, file 1; "Bill C-151 Discussed with Justice
Minister Turner," *Canadian Handgun* (November–December 1968): 1; *Debates, House of Commons* (23 January 1969), 4860.

22 R.C. Passmore to John Turner, 8 October 1968, LAC, MG31, E54, vol. 9, file
1. Also see R.C. Passmore to Commons Committee on Justice and Legal
Affairs, 5 March 1969, LAC, MG31, E54, vol. 9, file 1.

23 *Criminal Law Amendment Act, 1968–69*, S.C. 1968–69, c.38, s.6. The Canadian Wildlife Federation had proposed such a division between prohibited,
restricted, and sporting firearms in 1967. This suggested the important role
gun groups played in shaping the 1969 legislation. "Advocates Strict Firearm Legislation," *Winnipeg Free Press*, 13 January 1967, 28.

24 Restricted Weapons Order, P.C. 1974-2186 (1 October 1974), LAC, MG31,
E54, vol. 8, file 10; Friedland, "Gun Control," 37–8.

25 John Saywell, "Parliament and Politics," in *Canadian Annual Review for
1964*, ed. John Saywell (Toronto: University of Toronto Press, 1965), 45;
Louis Fournier, *F.L.Q.: The Anatomy of an Underground Movement* (Toronto:
NC, 1984), 53–4, 97, 120; James Stewart, *Seven Years of Terrorism: The FLQ*
(Richmond Hill, ON: *Montreal Star* and Simon & Schuster, 1970), 22–3;
Debates, House of Commons (23 November 1970), 1361; (25 February 1971),
3733; Peter Whitehouse, "Guns Are for Experts Only," *Winnipeg Free Press*,
14 August 1971, 101.

26 "Not a Gun Review, Action," *Globe and Mail*, 20 November 1970, 6.

27 F.H. Leacy, ed., *Historical Statistics of Canada*, 2nd ed. (Ottawa: Statistics
Canada 1983), Z1–Z14, Z21; Martin L. Friedland, *My Life in Crime and
Other Academic Adventures* (Toronto: University of Toronto Press and the
Osgoode Society, 2007), 219; Cheryl Marie Webster and Anthony N. Doob,
"Punitive Trends and Stable Imprisonment Rates in Canada," in *Crime
and Justice: A Review of Research*, vol. 36, *Crime, Punishment, and Politics in*

Comparative Perspective, ed. Michael Tonry (Chicago: University of Chicago Press, 2007), 302–3; John Hagan, "Comparing Crime and Criminalization in Canada and the U.S.A.," *Canadian Journal of Sociology* 14, no. 3 (1989): 361–71; Canada, *Causes of Death*, 1966–74 (Ottawa: Dominion Bureau of Statistics / Statistics Canada); Solicitor General of Canada and Minister of Justice, "Questions and Answers on Firearms Control," LAC, MG31, E54, vol. 8, file 13; "Murders in Canada Increase 14% to Record 545," *Globe and Mail*, 21 August 1975, 39. Population figures are drawn from Statistics Canada, "Estimated Population of Canada, 1605 to Present," http://www .statcan.gc.ca/pub/98-187-x/4151287-eng.htm. The suicide statistics include suicides involving firearms and explosives.

28 *Debates, House of Commons* (28 April 1972), 1725. Also see *Debates, Senate* (20 March 1973), 360.

29 For examples, see "Slow Draw," *Globe and Mail*, 20 January 1971, 6; "Stiffer Gun Control," *Montreal Gazette*, 28 October 1974, 8; "Gun Lobby Is off Target," *Ottawa Citizen*, 16 September 1976.

30 Grand Jury Report, 15 March 1974, LAC, MG31, E54, vol. 10. Also see "Gun Control: The Grand Jury Reports," *Canadian Forum* 54, no. 5 (May–June 1974): 5, 66; *Debates, Senate* (20 March 1973), 360.

31 Leacy, *Historical Statistics of Canada*, Z167; Doug Owram, *Born at the Right Time: A History of the Baby-Boom Generation* (Toronto: University of Toronto Press, 1996), 202–3; Marcel Martel, "'They Smell Bad, Have Diseases and Are Lazy': RCMP Officers' Reporting on Hippies in the Late Sixties," in *The Sixties in Canada: A Turbulent and Creative Decade*, ed. M. Athena Palaeologu, 165–92 (Montreal: Black Rose Books, 2009); Bryan D. Palmer, *Canada's 1960s: The Ironies of Identity in a Rebellious Era* (Toronto: University of Toronto Press, 2009), 181–209.

32 Doris Hopper, "The Gun: 'Its Purpose Is to Kill,'" *Winnipeg Free Press*, 14 July 1973, 78; Friedland, "Gun Control," 30; Donald Grant, "100 Students and Three Teachers Held by Boy, 13, Carrying Rifle," *Globe and Mail*, 3 May 1975, 2; Geoffrey Stevens, "The Need for Gun Controls," *Globe and Mail*, 30 May 1975, 6; "Brampton Slayings Trigger Gun Control," *Winnipeg Free Press*, 4 June 1975, 24; "Slobodian Jury Recommends Gun Controls," *Ottawa Journal*, 26 June 1975, 8; William Hanley, "Gun Control Urged," *Winnipeg Free Press*, 26 June 1975, 1; Rudy Platiel, "Inquest Jury Seeks Stiffer Gun Control after School Deaths," *Globe and Mail*, 26 June 1975, 1–2; "Parents of Slain Youth Confident Gov't Serious," *Ottawa Journal*, 22 July 1975, 12; "Ottawa Serious on Gun Controls, Slinger Says," *Globe and Mail*, 22 July 1975, 8; "Controlling People Instead of Guns Wins Support in B.C.," *Globe and Mail*, 6 October 1975, 8; "Tighter Gun Laws Sought,"

Winnipeg Free Press, 6 October 1975, 6; Robin Barstow, "Gun Control: How Much Longer?," *Ottawa Citizen*, 29 October 1975, 6; Geoffrey Stevens, "Youth and Gun Control," *Globe and Mail*, 12 November 1975, 6; "Poulin Inquest Jury Supports Police Investigation of High School Deaths," *Winnipeg Free Press*, 5 December 1975, 10; *Debates, House of Commons* (28 October 1975), 8604; (20 November 1975), 9276–7; (26 January 1976), 10271; (30 March 1976), 12283, 12298; Central Students Council of the Ottawa Board of Eductaion, news release, 26 January 1976, LAC, MG31, E54, vol. 8, file 4.

33   *Debates, House of Commons* (26 January 1973), 699.

34   Grand Jury Report, 15 March 1974, LAC, MG31, E54, vol. 10; Robert Sherrill, *The Saturday Night Special* (New York: Charterhouse, 1973); *Debates, Senate* (15 March 1973), 353.

35   Osha Gray Davidson, *Under Fire: The NRA and the Battle for Gun Control* (New York: Henry Holt, 1993), 28.

36   Research Branch, Library of Parliament, "The Gun Control Controversy: The Situation in Canada, the United States and Selected Other Countries," 12–13, LAC, MG32, C55, vol. 6, file 9; Scott Melzer, *Gun Crusaders: The NRA's Culture War* (New York: NYU Press, 2009), 35–42.

37   *Debates, Senate* (15 March 1973), 354; "Canadians Should Oppose Gun Propaganda, Davey Says," *Globe and Mail*, 16 March 1973, 8; Jonathan Manthorpe, "Compulsory Registration of All Guns May Be Feature of Allmand's Control Laws," *Globe and Mail*, 7 July 1975, 9.

38   *Debates, Senate* (4 April 1974), 238. Also see *Debates, Senate* (14 February 1973), 241; "Gun Control," *Montreal Gazette*, 14 August 1972, 6.

39   *Debates, House of Commons* (20 December 1971), 10612–13; (28 January 1975), 2666; (30 May 1975), 6277; *Debates, Senate* (14 February 1973), 240; (26 March 1974), 164; "Allmand to Fight Crime," *Winnipeg Free Press*, 28 November 1972, 5; "MP's Bill Urges All Firearms Be Restricted," *Globe and Mail*, 7 February 1973, 9; "Gun Controls Pushed," *Winnipeg Free Press*, 15 February 1973, 1; "Senator's Bill on Gun Restrictions Goes to Legal Affairs Committee," *Globe and Mail*, 22 March 1973, 8; "Up on the Hill," *Canadian Police Chief* 62, no. 2 (April 1973): 13–14, 20; "Up on the Hill …," *Canadian Police Chief* 63, no. 3 (July 1974): 21.

40   *Criminal Law Amendment Act, 1972*, S.C. 1972, c.13, s.76.3; *Debates, House of Commons* (27 April 1972), 1699.

41   *Debates, House of Commons* (5 February 1973), 949. Also see *Debates, House of Commons* (13 March 1973), 2197–8; Ian Hunter, "Gun Limits Out," *Winnipeg Free Press*, 6 February 1973, 1; "Still Careless with Guns," *Globe and Mail*, 14 July 1973, 6; Geoffrey Stevens, "The Need for Gun Controls," *Globe and Mail*, 30 May 1975, 6; "Lang Won't Alter Gun Control Law,"

Winnipeg Free Press, 31 May 1975, 12; Jonathan Manthorpe, "Gun Control Laws Acceptable to Both Sides Likely," *Globe and Mail*, 2 July 1975, 8.

42 George A. Kerr to W.H. Bush, 8 July 1974, LAC, MG31, E54, vol. 9, file 1; Robert Williamson, "Tory Backbenchers Press for Tight Gun Control in Ontario," *Globe and Mail*, 17 April 1974, 31; "Clement Says Control of Sales Would Add to Weapon Problem," *Globe and Mail*, 7 June 1975, 14; Robert Williamson, "Kerr Wants Ontario Licencing System to Control Sale of Guns, Ammunition," *Globe and Mail*, 10 July 1975, 1; "Stiffer Gun Laws Planned," *Winnipeg Free Press*, 16 August 1975, 1; Peter Mosher, "Ontario to Require Licence to Buy Gun Unless Ottawa Acts," *Globe and Mail*, 16 August 1975, 1; *FARO Bulletin*, September 1975, LAC, MG31, E54, vol. 8, file 11; *Ottawa Citizen*, 16 September 1975, 31; *Debates, House of Commons* (16 October 1975), 8257; Friedland, "Gun Control," 31–2; "Ontario Solicitor General Outlines Government Policy," *Canadian Handgun* 4 (1975); Ontario Arms Collectors Association, Memorandum to Members, n.d., LAC, MG31, E54, vol. 8, file 12.

43 Friedland, "Gun Control," 59–60; Friedland, *My Life in Crime and Other Academic Adventures*, 216–22; Jonathan Manthorpe, "Canada Already Has Enough Gun Controls, Government Research Document Concludes," *Globe and Mail*, 16 September 1976, 47; *Canadian Handgun* 2 (1 October 1976): S3. For Du Perron's thoughts on gun control, see "Issues on Gun Control," *Canadian Police Chief* 64, no. 3 (July 1975): 17–20, 37–8.

44 Research Branch, Library of Parliament, "The Gun Control Controversy," 7, LAC, MG32, C55, vol. 6, file 9; *Debates, House of Commons* (28 October 1975), 8602–3; "Gov't Starts 'Crash Study' of Gun Laws," *Ottawa Journal*, 7 June 1975; Roy Romanow to Ron Basford, 17 February 1976, LAC, MG31, E54, vol. 8, file 12.

45 Memorandum from NCO I/C Firearms Registration Section, 18 April 1975, LAC, MG31, E54, vol. 9, file 2.

46 Statistics Canada, Justice Statistics Division, "Special Bulletin: Statistics of Estimated Gun Ownership and Use in Canada," May 1977, LAC, MG31, E54, vol. 8, file 13; Don Seller, "Complexities of Gun Control Weaken Government's Stand," *Montreal Gazette*, 22 May 1976, 10. The federal government decided to err on the high side in some of its official publications. For example, in a flyer meant to explain new gun control measures in 1977, the government estimated that Canadians possessed about 10.2 million firearms. Solicitor General of Canada and Minister of Justice, "Questions and Answers on Firearms Control," LAC, MG31, E54, vol. 8, file 13.

47 Friedland, *My Life in Crime and Other Academic Adventures*, 223; LAC, RG2, Privy Council Office, series A-5-a, vol. 6457 (18 December 1975), 12, 25.

48 *Debates, House of Commons* (8 March 1976), 11579.

49 "Control Favored," *Winnipeg Free Press*, 11 August 1975, 19; Friedland, "Gun Control," 32; *Canadian Police Chief* 65, no. 2 (April 1976): 19; "Up on the Hill ...," *Canadian Police Chief* 65, no. 3 (July 1976): 23; Solicitor General of Canada, *National Attitudes towards Crime and Gun Control* (1977), 17–18; John Saywell, "Parliament and Politics," in *Canadian Annual Review of Politics and Political Affairs, 1976*, ed. John Saywell (Toronto: University of Toronto Press, 1977), 7.

50 *Debates, House of Commons* (12 April 1976), 12721.

51 See Christopher MacLennan, *Towards the Charter: Canadians and the Demand for a National Bill of Rights, 1929–1960* (Montreal and Kingston: McGill-Queen's University Press, 2003); Dominique Clément, *Canada's Rights Revolution: Social Movements and Social Change, 1937–82* (Vancouver: UBC Press, 2008).

52 "Native Group Seeking Exclusion from Curbs," *Globe and Mail*, 23 April 1976, 2; Nora T. Corley, "The Yukon and Northwest Territories," in Saywell, *Canadian Annual Review of Politics and Political Affairs, 1976*, 296; Council for Yukon Indians Position: Views and Recommendations on Bill C-83, 14 July 1976, LAC, MG32, C55, vol. 6, file 10.

53 National Indian Brotherhood Presentation on Proposed Gun Control Legislation ..., 29 June 1977, LAC, MG31, E54, vol. 8, file 13.

54 Statistics Canada, Justice Statistics Division, "Special Bulletin: Statistics of Estimated Gun Ownership and Use in Canada," May 1977, LAC, MG31, E54, vol. 8, file 13.

55 Bob Scammell to K.A. Brynaert, 12 March 1975, LAC, MG31, E54, vol. 9, file 2. Also see Ted Tillack, "Against Gun Control," *Winnipeg Free Press*, 22 February 1975, 12.

56 Lyle Whealy to H. Carl Goldenberg, 14 June 1973, LAC, MG32, C55, vol. 6, file 8; Susan Goldenberg, "Gun Makers Link Arms to Fight Controls," *Financial Post* (11 August 1973); Submission of the Canadian Sporting Arms and Ammunition Association to the Senate Committee on Legal and Constitutional Affairs, 4 February 1975, LAC, MG32, C55, vol. 6, file 9; Gary Jones to L.H. Nicholson, 27 May 1976, LAC, MG31, E54, vol. 9, file 3; "C-83 vs You," *Canada GunSport* 1, no. 7 (July 1976): 1; M.L. Friedland, "Pressure Groups and the Development of the Criminal Law," in P.R. Glazebrook, ed., *Reshaping the Criminal Law: Essays in Honour of Glanville Williams* (London: Stevens & Son, 1978), 210.

57 Robert Lewis, "The Hidden Persuaders," *Maclean's* (13 June 1977), 40b.

58 Lorne White, "'Let George Do It' Could Cost You Your Sport," *Ottawa Journal*, 7 December 1972; *Debates, Senate* (14 February 1973), 241.

59 "'Virtually Impossible' to Register Sub-machine Gun, Lobbyist Says," *Globe and Mail*, 29 July 1975, 3.

60 *RAGO Bulletin*, no. 6, February 1977, LAC, MG31, E54, vol. 8, file 13. Another Alberta group was the Calgary-based Firearms Legislation Action Committee (FLAC). "Government Plans Another Assault on Gun-Owners ...," *Canada GunSport* 1, no. 10 (December 1976): 3; Dave Tomlinson, Bill Jones, and Ray Laycock, "The Beginning of Sound Firearms Legislation," *Canada GunSport* 1, no. 11 (February 1977): 22–3, 30.

61 "Gun Control Faces Heavy Artillery," *Globe and Mail*, 22 September 1976, 6; "Gun Lobby Is off Target," *Ottawa Citizen*, 16 September 1976, 9.

62 Memorandum from L.H. Nicholson, 10 August 1976; Minutes of the Canadian Association for Sensible Arms Legislation, 11–12 September 1976; news release, CASAL, 13 September 1976, LAC, MG31, E54, vol. 8, file 1; "New Group Loaded for Bear on Gun Controls," *Winnipeg Free Press*, 14 September 1976, 23; "The CASAL Story," *Canadian Handgun* 2 (July 1977): 5.

63 *Canadian Handgun* 2 (1 October 1976): S2.

64 Tom Sarsfield, "Gun Control Legislation Threat to Sportsmen," *Ottawa Citizen*, 4 March 1976, 23.

65 Tom Sarsfield, "Federation Policy Makes Sense," *Ottawa Citizen*, 27 February 1975, 28; Tom Sarsfield, "Gun Controls Not the Solution," *Ottawa Citizen*, 30 October 1975, 31; Friedland, "Pressure Groups and the Development of the Criminal Law," 212.

66 Memorandum to CWF Directors and Provincial Affiliates from L.H. Nicholson, 29 October 1976; Submission by the Canadian Association for Sensible Arms Legislation to the Government of Canada, November 1976; Canadian Association for Sensible Arms Legislation, news release, 13 December 1976, LAC, MG31, E54, vol. 8, file 1.

67 British Columbia Federation of Shooting Sports, newsletter 5, 15 January 1975, LAC, MG31, E54, vol. 9, file 2; Ontario Arms Collectors' Association, Memorandum to Members, n.d., LAC, MG31, E54, vol. 8, file 12; Friedland, "Pressure Groups and the Development of the Criminal Law," 213.

68 Jonathan Manthorpe, "Gun Controls a Hotter Issue Than Hanging," *Globe and Mail*, 25 March 1976, 3. Also see Geoffrey Stevens, "Gun Controls," *Globe and Mail*, 25 February 1975, 6; *Debates, House of Commons* (7 April 1976), 12593; Report on the Review of Bill C-83 by the Standing Committee on Justice and Legal Affairs, LAC, MG32, C-55, vol. 6, file 10.

69 "Government Crime-Bill Case Called Contradictory," *Globe and Mail*, 8 April 1976, 63.

70 Dominion of Canada Rifle Association to members, 28 September 1976,

LAC, MG31, E54, vol. 8, file 8. Also see "Political Lesson for the Month," *Canadian Handgun* 5 (20 December 1976).

71 *FARO Bulletin*, December 1976, LAC, MG31, E54, vol. 8, file 12. Also see Canadian Wildlife Federation, Survey of Positions Taken by Members of Parliament on the Firearms Provisions in Bill C-83 (Second Reading), August 1976, LAC MG31, E54, vol. 8, file 1; D.D. Macdonald, President, Quebec Rifle Association to Ron Basford, 3 September 1976, LAC, MG31, E54, vol. 8, file 12.

72 "Former RCMP Commissioner against Firearms Restriction," *Prince Albert Daily Herald*, 13 February 1975, 3; "RCMP Head against Gun-Control Proposal," *Ottawa Citizen*, 24 February 1975, 18; "Former Mountie Chief Hits Firearm Bill," *Vancouver Province*, 3 May 1975; "He'd Put Gun Control in Provinces' Hands," *Telegraph Journal*, 29 March 1976; "Ex-RCMP Chief Riddles Proposed Gun Legislation," *Ottawa Citizen*, 1 March 1976, 12. Opponents of gun control frequently complained that the media undermined their cause, and instead amplified public concerns with firearms. See, for example, L.H. Nicholson to *Ottawa Journal*, 20 December 1976, LAC, MG 31, E54, vol. 8, file 1. The voice of the Ontario Handgun Association, *Canadian Handgun*, complained consistently about media reports. "It's Time to Speak Out," *Canadian Handgun* 4 (1972): 1; "Read These Talking Points," *Canadian Handgun* 1 (1973). The CBC came under particular criticism. The Ontario Arms Collectors' Association complained of "a C.B.C. inspired mass hysteria concerning guns." Ontario Arms Collectors' Association, news release, n.d., LAC, MG31, E54, vol. 8, file 12. Also see *FARO Bulletin*, May 1977, LAC, MG31, E54, vol. 8, file 13. *Out of Doors* magazine collected donations for a "Proud to Be a Hunter" fund to contest critical statements made about hunters and guns. *Out of Doors* (May 1976): 7; "Brampton's CHIC Radio Insults Hunters: Proud Hunter Association Demands Apology," *Out of Doors* (October 1976): 8; Daniel J. Thomey, "Proud Hunter Association Demands Apology from Television Programme," *Out of Doors* (October 1977): 6–7.

73 "Allmand Booed on Gun Legislation Views, but He Shoots Back at Scarborough Crowd," *Globe and Mail*, 13 April 1976, 5. For other examples, see Max Heath, "Peace and Security Bill Continues to Draw Flak," *Wallaceburg News*, 28 April 1976, 1; "Control Foes Loudest Voice in Gun Debate," *Globe and Mail*, 3 June 1976, 8; Susan A. Brown, "Gun Control Opponents Debate with Milne," *Orangeville Citizen*, 9 June 1976, 1.

74 "The National Firearms Safety Association," *Globe and Mail*, 9 August 1975, 36; Lowell Green, "Safety in Their Sights," *Winnipeg Free Press*, 14 October 1975, 29; Friedland, "Pressure Groups and the Development of the Criminal Law," 210.

75 British Columbia Federation of Wildlife, "Bill C-83: What It Means to You as a Hunter and as a Legitimate Firearms Owner," LAC, MG31, E54, vol. 8, file 12. Also see Sarsfield, "Gun Controls Not the Solution."

76 D.D. Macdonald, President, Quebec Rifle Association to Ron Basford, 3 September 1976, LAC, MG31, E54, vol. 8, file 12.

77 F. Paul Fromm, "Canada Faces Gun Confiscation," *Review of the News* (22 January 1975), 8; D.D. Macdonald, President, Quebec Rifle Association to Ron Basford, 3 September 1976, LAC, MG31, E54, vol. 8, file 12.

78 R.T. Runciman to David Lewis, 20 February 1973, LAC, MG32, C-55, vol. 6, file 8; D.L. Aiton, "… The Myth of Gun Registration," *B.C. Outdoors* (August 1975): 47; D.A. Tomlinson, "Shooting Politics," *Canada GunSport* 1, no. 11 (February 1977): 8–9, 13; *Debates, House of Commons* (29 March 1976), 12258; (30 March 1976), 12285, 12287, 12296–7; (31 March 1976), 12328, 12338–9; (7 April 1976), 12601.

79 Shooting Federation of Canada, Brief to the Committee on Legal and Constitutional Affairs, Senate of Canada, n.d., Leonard Nicholson fonds, LAC, MG 31, E54, vol. 8, file 9.

80 "Editorial," *Canadian Handgun* (March 1968): 2.

81 White, "'Let George Do It'"; Robert Campbell, "Gun Control: More of a Problem Than a Solution," *Ottawa Citizen*, 17 February 1975, 6; Glen MacKenzie, "Gun Owners Fire Volley," *Winnipeg Free Press*, 11 March 1976, 1.

82 Responsible Alberta Gun Owners (R.A.G.O.), 16 September 1976, LAC, MG31, E54, vol. 8, file 1. Also see H.R. Jonah to Senate Legal Affairs Committee, 26 March 1973, LAC, MG32, C55, vol. 6, file 8; Bob Scammell, "Herald Outdoors," *Calgary Herald*, 19 December 1974, 14; Bob Scammell to K.A. Brynaert, 12 March 1975, LAC, MG31, E54, vol. 9, file 2; Dominion of Canada Rifle Association to members, 28 September 1976, LAC, MG31, E54, vol. 8, file 8; Doreen McClocklin, "Confiscation of Guns Next," *Winnipeg Free Press*, 25 March 1976, 38; Burton J. Myers, "Editorial," *Out of Doors* (November 1976): 4; *Minutes of Proceedings and Evidence of the Standing Committee on Justice and Legal Affairs*, issue 18 (2 June 1977), 34; Ontario Arms Collectors' Association, Memorandum to Members, LAC, MG31, E54, vol. 8, file 12; Fromm, "Canada Faces Gun Confiscation," 1.

83 Brief by the Shooting Federation of Canada to the Committee in Legal and Constitutional Affairs, Senate of Canada, n.d., LAC, MG31, E54, vol. 8, file 9. Also see *FARO Bulletin*, 1 April 1975, LAC, MG31, E54, vol. 8, file 11; *FARO Bulletin*, December 1976, LAC, MG31, E54, vol. 8, file 12; C.P. Barager, "Sportsmen," *Winnipeg Free Press*, 28 February 1976, 157.

84 "New Gun Legislation," *Out of Doors* (May 1976): 15; Ontario Arms Collectors' Association, Memorandum to Members, LAC, MG31, E54, vol. 8, file 12.

85 Brown, "Gun Control Opponents Debate with Milne."
86 British Columbia Federation of Wildlife, "Bill C-83: What It Means to You as a Hunter and Legitimate Firearms Owner," LAC, MG31, E54, vol. 8, file 12.
87 FARO Brief, October 1975, LAC, MG31, E54, vol. 8, file 11.
88 Statistics Canada, Justice Statistics Division, "Special Bulletin: Statistics of Estimated Gun Ownership and Use in Canada" (May 1977), LAC, MG31, E54, vol. 8, file 13.
89 D.J. Thomey, "Minister Says We Misunderstand Bill C-83," *Out of Doors* (September 1976): 13.
90 *Out of Doors* (May 1976): 7.
91 Cleve Kidd to Warren Allmand, Otto Lang, and Donald Cameron, 19 September 1975, LAC, MG31, E54, vol. 8, file 11.
92 Daniel J. Thomey, "Second-Class Citizen Status," *Out of Doors* (June 1976): 8. Also see "New Gun Legislation," *Out of Doors* (May 1976): 7.
93 *Out of Doors* magazine warned that firearm licences might require applicants to provide "mug shots" and fingerprints. *Out of Doors* (June 1976): 13; Daniel J. Thomey, "New Firearm License Could Require Mug Shot," *Out of Doors* (October 1976): 8.
94 Brown, "Gun Control Opponents Debate with Milne."
95 *FARO Bulletin*, September 1975, LAC, MG 31, E54, vol. 8, file 11. This fear was not entirely unwarranted. See Steve Friedman, "'Sport' of Hunting Must End," *Winnipeg Free Press*, 20 October 1976, 50.
96 Manitoba Association of Gun Owners' Parameters for a Firearms Control Act, 14 December 1976, LAC, MG 31, E54, vol. 8, file 2. Other gun-control opponents made similar appeals for an amendment to the Canadian Bill of Rights. See *Winnipeg Free Press*, 8 February 1962, 12; D.A. Tomlinson, "The Absolute Rights of the Individual," *Canada GunSport* 1, no. 11 (February 1977): 6, 18.
97 British Columbia Federation of Shooting Sports, A Brief on Bill C-83 …, May 1976, LAC, MG32, C55, vol. 6, file 10 (emphasis in original). Also see Burton J. Myers, "Editorial," *Out of Doors* (August 1976): 4. Also see Ontario Arms Collectors' Association, Memorandum to Members, LAC, MG31, E54, vol. 8, file 12; Gord McIntyre, "Firearms Ownership: A Right or a Privilege," *Out of Doors* (June 1976): 10–11, 34–5; Tomlinson, "The Absolute Rights of an Individual," 6, 18.
98 Responsible Alberta Gun Owners (RAGO), 16 September 1976, LAC, MG31, E54, vol. 8, file 1.
99 Brief prepared by the Ontario Federation of Anglers and Hunters, Inc., concerning Firearms Legislation …, n.d., LAC, MG31, E54, vol. 8, file 9.

100 L.H. Nicholson to S.R. Basford, 11 August 1976, LAC, MG31, E54, vol. 9, file 3. Also see "Senator Cameron Introduces Anti-Firearm Bill for Third Time," *Canadian Handgun* 1 (1975): 1; "A Good Gun Law?," *Canadian Handgun* 1 (March 1977): 8; W.A. Milroy to S.R. Basford, 1 June 1977, LAC, MG31, E54, vol. 8, file 8.

101 Aiton, "… The Myth of Gun Registration," 48.

102 Ibid., 49.

103 Thompson's Sporting Goods flyer, LAC, MG31, E54, vol. 9, file 3. Also see Reginald Richardson to Stuart Leggatt, 20 February 1973, LAC, MG32, C55, vol. 6, File 8; F. Paul Fromm, "Canada Faces Gun Confiscation," *The Review of the News* (22 January 1975): 6; W. John Farquharson, "The Anti-Gun Bandwagon," *Winnipeg Free Press*, 6 December 1975, 36; L. Martynec, "Gun Control Is Just the Start," *Winnipeg Free Press*, 13 March 1976, 37; *Canada GunSport* 1, no. 6 (May 1976): 1; D. Storozuk, "Gun Control," *Winnipeg Free Press*, 20 May 1977, 22.

104 "Alberta Socreds See Socialism in Gun Control," *Globe and Mail*, 15 November 1976, 9.

105 *Debates, House of Commons* (29 March 1976), 12258.

106 A. Paul Pross, *Group Politics and Public Policy*, 2nd ed. (Toronto: Oxford University Press, 1992), 66.

107 *Debates, House of Commons* (9 March 1976), 11644.

108 *Debates, House of Commons* (31 March 1976), 12339.

109 British Columbia Federation of Shooting Sports, A Brief on Bill C-83, May 1976, LAC, MG32, C55, vol. 6, file 10. Also see *FARO Bulletin*, September 1975, LAC, MG31, E54, vol. 8, file 11; T.P. Edwards, "The True North: No Longer Strong and Free," *Canadian GunSport* 1, no. 6 (May 1976): 3; Ontario Arms Collectors Association, news release, n.d., LAC, MG31, E54, vol. 8, file 13.

110 British Columbia Federation of Shooting Sports, A Brief on Bill C-83 …, May 1976, LAC, MG32, C55, vol. 6, file 10. Also see Burton J. Myers, "Editorial," *Out of Doors* (April 1976): 4; "Dangerous Bureaucratic Red Tape," *Canada GunSport* 2, no. 6 (February 1978): 4.

111 British Columbia Wildlife Federation, Submission to Commons Standing Committee on Justice and Legal Affairs, May 1976, LAC, MG31, E54, vol. 8, file 12. Also see Saskatchewan Wildlife Federation, *Bulletin*, 23 September 1976, MG31, E54, vol. 9, file 3.

112 Saywell, "Parliament and Politics," 7–8; Ken Pole, "Gov't Limits Gun Bill Debate," *Ottawa Journal*, 1 April 1976, 4; Ontario Arms Collectors Association, *Bulletin*, n.d., LAC, MG31, E54, vol. 8, file 12; "Peace-and-Security Bill No Longer a House Priority," *Globe and Mail*, 2 June 1976, 8; Iain Hunter, "PCs Want Simpler Firearm Restriction," *Winnipeg Free Press*, 5

October 1976, 4; "Gun Control Back to Square One in Commons," *Winnipeg Free Press*, 21 January 1977, 17; John English, *Just Watch Me: The Life of Pierre Elliott Trudeau, 1968–2000* (Toronto: Alfred A. Knopf, 2009), 342.

113 "Gun Control: How Much Longer?," *Globe and Mail*, 8 September 1976, 6. On the incident, see Friedland, *My Life in Crime and Other Academic Adventures*, 224; "Sniper Incident Raises Gun Rules," *Winnipeg Free Press*, 9 September 1976, 8.

114 LAC, RG2, Privy Council Office, Series A-5-a, vol. 6496 (23 December 1976), 15–16; news release of Ralph Goodale, 12 May 1977, LAC, MG31, E54, vol. 9, file 3; Otto Lang to Tom Motta, 18 November 1976, LAC, MG31, E54, vol. 8, file 8.

115 Tom Traves and John Saywell, "Parliament and Politics," in *Canadian Annual Review of Politics and Political Affairs, 1977*, ed. John Saywell (Toronto: University of Toronto Press, 1979), 17. Similarly, *Maclean's* concluded that the proposed legislation met "virtually every objection raised by the gun associations." Robert Lewis, "The Hidden Persuaders," *Maclean's*, 13 June 1977, 40. Also see "Watered-Down Version of Gun Control Presented," *Calgary Herald*, 21 April 1977.

116 *Debates, House of Commons* (11 May 1977), 5525.

117 The legislation did not require existing owners of automatic weapons to give up their guns. Rather, existing owners could retain automatic weapons through a grandfather clause in the legislation.

118 News release, CASAL, 3 December 1976, LAC, MG31, E54, vol. 8, file 1; Friedland, "Pressure Groups and the Development of the Criminal Law," 219; "The CASAL Story," LAC, MG31, E54, vol. 8, file 2; Shooting Federation of Canada, An Analysis of Bill C-51, n.d., LAC, MG31, E54, vol. 8, file 13; "A Letter to Basford," *Out of Doors* (January 1977): 7, 51; Notes for a speech by the Hon. Ron Basford ... to the Ontario Federation of Anglers and Hunters, 18 February 1977, LAC, MG31, E54, vol. 9, file 5; "No Guarantors to Be Required for Gun Licence," *Globe and Mail*, 19 February 1977, 5; Mary Trueman, "Softer Gun-Control Bill Not Likely to Get Rough Treatment," *Globe and Mail*, 9 May 1977, 11; "No Guarantors to Be Required for Gun Licence," *Globe and Mail*, 19 February 1977, 5; Responsible Alberta Gun Owners, *Bulletin* no. 7, (May 1977) 27, LAC, MG31, E54, vol. 8, file 8; Canadian Wildlife Federation, Report of the Firearms Legislation Committee, 27 May 1977, LAC, MG 31, E54, vol. 9, file 4; G.N. [Ted] Dentay, "A Conversation with Justice Minister Basford," *Canada GunSport* 2, no. 1 (June 1977): 42–4, 49.

119 "The CASAL Story," LAC, MG 31, E54, vol. 8, file 2; P.C. 1977-186 (17

March 1977), LAC, MG31, E54, vol. 8, file 10; Daniel J. Thomey, "Warning: Unreasonable Gun Control Bill about to Be Made Law," *Out of Doors* (August 1977): 8; John R. Youmans and others to Carl Goldenberg, 8 September 1977, LAC, MG32, C55, vol. 6, file 11; "Dangerous Bureaucratic Red Tape," *Canada GunSport* 2, no. 6 (February 1978): 4; Harry Jennings, "Gun Laws: Where to from Here?," *Ottawa Citizen*, 11 September 1980, 32. Ottawa restricted a handful of other semi-automatic weapons, including the Thompson Model 27 A-1, a semi-automatic version of the infamous "Tommy gun."

120 L.H. Nicholson to all directors and provincial affiliates of CWF, 15 June 1977, LAC, MG31, E54, vol. 8, file 2. Also see Friedland, *My Life in Crime and Other Academic Adventures*, 226.

121 *Minutes of Proceedings and Evidence of the Standing Committee on Justice and Legal Affairs*, issue no. 19 (7 June 1977), 51.

122 Ibid., 57–8.

123 Memorandum by R.H. Campbell, 16 June 1977, LAC, MG31, E54, vol. 8, file 2.

124 Friedland, "Pressure Groups and the Development of the Criminal Law," 212–3; L.H. Nicholson to all directors and provincial affiliates of the Canadian Wildlife Federation, 15 June 1977, LAC, MG31, E54, vol. 8, file 2; L.H. Nicholson to Rick Morgan, 12 November 1977, LAC, MG31, E54, vol. 9, file 5; L.H. Nicholson to CWF Government Relations Committee, 6 September 1977, LAC, MG31, E54, vol. 9, file 4.

125 Friedland, *My Life in Crime and Other Academic Adventures*, 226.

126 Ron Basford to L.H. Nicholson, 19 August 1977, LAC, MG31, E54, vol. 9, file 4.

127 *Criminal Law Amendment Act, 1977*, S.C. 1977, c.53; "Gun Control: Working Together to Save Lives," *Winnipeg Free Press*, 17 January 1978, 86; "Gun Control: Working Together to Save Lives," *Globe and Mail*, 18 January 1978, 4; "Gun Control: Working Together to Save Lives," *Calgary Herald*, 18 January 1978, 19; "Notes from Address by James Hayes ...," *Canadian Police Chief* 67, no. 4 (October 1978): 54.

128 Ted Gorsline, "Owners Slow to Register Restricted Weapons," *Globe and Mail*, 22 March 1978, 47; "Ottawa Grants Month-Long Amnesty on Illegal Firearms," *Globe and Mail*, 27 October 1978, 10; Andy Blicq, "No Rush to Return Fire-Arms," *Winnipeg Free Press*, 3 November 1978, 4; "Few Calgarians Take Advantage of Gun Amnesty," *Calgary Herald*, 8 November 1978, B1; "5,346 Firearms Turned In during Amnesty," *Globe and Mail*, 16 November 1978, 60; Donald Grant, "700 Gun Owners in Metro Respond to Amnesty," *Globe and Mail*, 21 November 1978, 1, 5; "Ottawa Extends

Period for Firearm Registration," *Calgary Herald*, 2 December 1978, C4;
"The Growing Threat of Civilian Firepower," *Globe and Mail*, 26 June
1990, A16; "Minister Announces National Firearms Amnesty," *Canadian
Police Chief Newsletter* 11, no. 2 (Summer 1992): 12.

129 "National Advisory Council on Firearms Created," *Canadian Police Chief*
68, no. 2 (April 1979): 33; John L. Evans, "A Research Strategy for the
Evaluation of Canada's Gun Control Legislation," *Canadian Police Chief*
68, no. 3 (July 1979): 22–4; Scarff, *Evaluation of the Canadian Gun Control
Legislation*, xviii–xix.

130 FARO *Bulletin*, January 1978, LAC, MG31, E54, vol. 9, file 6; "National
Firearms Association," *Canada GunSport* 2, no. 6 (February 1978): 9; Mel
Dagg, "Outdoors," *Winnipeg Free Press*, 30 March 1978, 76; *Winnipeg Free
Press*, 15 September 1978, 76; Harry Jennings, "Gun Laws: Where To
from Here?," *Ottawa Citizen*, 11 September 1980. In September 1978, the
National Firearms Association had 3500 members. "Firearms Group to
Take Battle to the Hustings," *Winnipeg Free Press*, 7 September 1978; "Gun
Enthusiasts Suggest Repeal of Lawmakers," *Ottawa Citizen*, 9 September
1978. It claimed thirty thousand members by March 1979 (but it is unclear
how many were individual members). Mary Trueman, "Special Issues
Pushed," *Globe and Mail*, 31 March 1979, 11.

   Representatives of mainstream organizations discouraged their members from joining the NFA, which some deemed FARO with a new name.
Groups that laboured to make the federal legislation palatable and to preserve their respectability worried that the NFA made outrageous claims
to drum up support. *Canada GunSport* 2, no. 6 (February 1978): 9–11;
"Sinister Repercussions from C-51," *Canada GunSport* 2, no. 7 (June 1978):
8–10; L.H. Nicholson to CWF Government Relations Committee, 31 January 1978; Jack O'Dette to L.H. Nicholson, 12 February 1978, Jack O'Dette
to L.H. Nicholson, 29 April 1978, Jack O'Dette to L.H. Nicholson, 17 June
1978, LAC, MG31, E54, vol. 9, file 6; Memorandum from D.A. Stewart to
CWF committee, 13 February 1979, LAC, MG31, E54, vol. 9, file 7. Mainstream organizations, for example, criticized the NFA when the association publicized a fraudulent document indicating that Ottawa secretly
intended to disarm the Canadian public. National Firearms Association
letter and document, n.d., LAC, MG31, E54, vol. 9, file 6; "Group Calls
Gun Control Govt. Plot, but Offers No Proof," *Winnipeg Free Press*, 28
November 1978, 2; Jean-Jacques Blais to H. Goldsmith, 17 January 1979;
Jean-Jacque Blais to all Members of Parliament, 23 February 1979; K.A.
Brynaert to CWF Board of Directors and Provincial Affiliates, 18 May
1979, LAC, MG31, E54, vol. 9, file 7; "Gun Clubs Get Fake Memo," *Globe*

and Mail, 18 May 1979, 11; "Memo on Disarming a Fake," *Winnipeg Free Press*, 18 May 1979, 6.

131 "Justice Minister Ron Basford to Quit Politics," *Canadian Handgun* 1 (May 1978): 8. Basford, however, said he left politics to spend more time with his children. "Basford Tells Why Kids Come before Career," *Montreal Gazette*, 17 January 1978, 6; "Family Reason for Basford's Exit," *Calgary Herald*, 18 January 1978, A5.

132 "Tories in Their Debt, Gun Owners Say," *Globe and Mail*, 26 June 1979, 8. Also see "Gun Lobby Demands 'Repayment,'" *Calgary Herald*, 26 June 1979; "Gun Lobby to Call in Election Debt," *Winnipeg Free Press*, 26 June 1979, 38; "Gun Lobby Claims Credit for Tory Win," *Ottawa Citizen*, 26 June 1979; "The NFA's Mythical Bag," *Globe and Mail*, 2 July 1979.

133 "Clark Proposes Quick Redraft of Gun Controls," *Edmonton Journal*, 12 April 1979; "Tories Undertake to Correct 'Flaws' in Gun Control Laws," *Vancouver Sun*, 17 November 1979; W.H. Bush, "Colt AR-15 Sporter Removed from List of Restricted Weapons," *Canadian Handgun* 1 (April 1980): 8.

6: Flexing the Liberal State's Muscles

1 Elisabeth Scarff, Ted Saharchuk, Terrence Jacques, and Michael McAuley, *Evaluation of the Canadian Gun Control Legislation: First Progress Report* (Ottawa: Supply and Social Services, 1981); Elisabeth Scarff, *Evaluation of the Canadian Gun Control Legislation: Final Report* (Ottawa: Minister of Supply and Services, 1983); "Canadians Aren't Gunning Each Other Down as Much," *Winnipeg Free Press*, 21 May 1981, 25; Diane Ellson, "Courts Not Using Gun Bill, Study Says," *Globe and Mail*, 27 May 1981, 1–2; "Gun Safety Plan Aimed at Children," *Globe and Mail*, 8 November 1982, 15; "New Firearms Program Aims to Cut Accidents," *Winnipeg Free Press*, 10 November 1982, 23; "Gun Use in Crimes down since 1979 Control Law," *Globe and Mail*, 20 August 1983, 11; "Report Cites Gun Law in Firearm Crime Drop," *Winnipeg Free Press*, 20 August 1983, 9.

2 See "Lennon Shooting Brings New Outcry over Gun Control," *Globe and Mail*, 10 December 1980, 4; "Security Is Just a 'Tiny Little Gun,'" *Globe and Mail*, 12 December 1980, 1; Joe Hall, "Anti-Gun Outcry in U.S. a Wasted Effort," *Toronto Star*, 26 December 1980, A10; "Firearms Take Bloody Toll," *Globe and Mail*, 31 March 1981, 11; Val Sears, "Frontier Land Where Guns Spit Solutions," *Toronto Star*, 31 March 1981, A12; "'Guns Don't Kill People' Slogan Comes Back to Haunt President," *Toronto Star*, 31 March 1981, A18; Christie Blatchford, "Americans Won't Give Up Guns Despite

Outcry over Shooting," *Toronto Star*, 1 April 1981, A24; John Honderich, "Reagan Sticks to His Guns," *Toronto Star*, 14 August 1981, B12; Lawrence Martin, "Money, Emotion Kill Gun-Control Bid," *Globe and Mail*, 5 November 1982, 12; "Firearm Control 'Die Cast' in Vote," *Winnipeg Free Press*, 10 April 1986, 29; "Gun Controls under Fire," *Globe and Mail*, 20 July 1985, 9; "A Mad American Way," *Globe and Mail*, 1 May 1987, A6; "Gun Laws Trigger Shootout Fears," *Winnipeg Free Press*, 28 September 1987, 28; "Arms and Mania," *Globe and Mail*, 2 November 1987, A6; Stephen Brunt, "Sticking to Their Guns," *Globe and Mail*, 14 November 1987, D1, D5; Colin MacKenzie, "Land of the Gun," *Globe and Mail*, 8 October 1988, A8.

3 Val Werier, "Canada's Gun Controls Have Serious Flaws," *Winnipeg Free Press*, 24 April 1980, 132; *Globe and Mail*, 10 December 1986, A6; Commissioner of the RCMP, *Annual Firearms Report to the Solicitor General of Canada* (1980–90); Resolution of the Canadian Association of Chiefs of Police re: Firearms (1986), on file at Canadian Association of Chiefs of Police head office, Ottawa.

4 *Debates, House of Commons* (4 May 1983), 25140–1; (5 March 1986), 11210; (7 October 1986), 129; (8 October 1986), 197; (12 March 1986), 11463; (5 June 1987), 6806–8; (15 September 1987), 8971–3.

5 *Debates, House of Commons* (24 February 1986), 10909.

6 *Debates, House of Commons* (3 December 1982), 21278; (4 November 1985), 8334–7; (14 November 1985), 220. Federal Justice Minister John Crosbie reported in 1986 that his department was studying ways to strengthen the nation's firearm laws, but no legislation was immediately forthcoming. "Firearms on Agenda," *Winnipeg Free Press*, 11 February 1986, 15; "Tougher Gun Control on Crosbie's Agenda," *Globe and Mail*, 11 February 1986, A4.

7 C.P. Barager, "Gun Owners Left in Dark," *Winnipeg Free Press*, 10 October 1980, 51; Don Hinchley, "FN-FAL Rifle Placed on Restricted Weapons List," *Canadian Handgun* (Spring 1983); Don Hinchley, "FN/FAL Update," *Canadian Handgun* (Summer 1983). Allmand's 1982 private member's bill generated a number of petitions. For a sample, see *Debates, House of Commons* (20 April 1982), 16402; (21 April 1982), 16462–3; (13 May 1982), 17379; (18 May 1982), 17536; (21 May 1982), 17685; (26 May 1982), 17788; (1 June 1982), 17968; (10 June 1982), 18316; (22 June 1982), 18726.

8 *Debates, House of Commons* (3 December 1982), 21281.

9 Samuel A. Bottomley, "Locked and Loaded: Gun Control Policy in Canada," in *The Real World of Canadian Politics: Cases in Process and Policy*, ed. Robert M. Campbell, Leslie A. Pal, and Michael Howlett, 4th ed. (Toronto: Broadview, 2004), 32–3; Zuhair Kashmeri, "Mac-10's Potential Worries

Police Forces," *Globe and Mail*, 24 June 1985, M3; Timothy Appleby, "Guns Banned in U.S. on Sale in Canada," *Globe and Mail*, 4 March 1989, A13; Terry Weber, "Gun Buffs Take Aim at Proposals," *Winnipeg Free Press*, 27 August 1989, 2; *Debates, House of Commons* (27 October 1989), 5228; "Ottawa to Ban Imports of Modified Assault Weapons," *Globe and Mail*, 28 October 1989, A9; Resolution of the Canadian Association of Chiefs of Police re Ban the Importation of Military Weapons of War (1988), on file at Canadian Association of Chiefs of Police head office, Ottawa.

10 Teresa K. Sourour, *Report of Coroner's Investigation* (1991), http://www.diarmani.com/Montreal_Coroners_Report.pdf; "Paul Wiecek, "Mini-14 Rifle Easy to Purchase," *Winnipeg Free Press*, 8 December 1989, 3.

11 Heidi Rathjen and Charles Montpetit, *December 6: From the Montreal Massacre to Gun Control, The Inside Story* (Toronto: McClelland & Stewart, 1999), 3; Samuel A. Bottomley, "Parliament, Politics and Policy: Gun Control in Canada, 1867–2003" (PhD diss., Carleton University, 2004), 149–50.

12 *Debates, House of Commons* (8 December 1989), 6663, 6666; (27 September 1990), 13538; "Gun-Control Reform Renewed as MPs Refuse to Call for Ban," *Winnipeg Free Press*, 8 December 1989, 19; Richard Cleroux and Craig McInnes, "Opposition MPs Demand Long-Promised Gun Control Amendments," *Globe and Mail*, 8 December 1989, A13; Graham Fraser, "Lewis Willing to 'Look at' Need for Safety Course in Gun Law Amendments," *Globe and Mail*, 9 December 1989, A6.

13 "The Semi-Automatic Response," *Globe and Mail*, 9 December 1989, D6; "Angus Reid Poll," *Toronto Star*, 29 December 1989, A4; "After the Montreal Massacre (2)," *Globe and Mail*, 7 December 1990, A16; "Public Favors Tougher Gun Control Law," *Toronto Star*, 15 April 1991, A15.

14 W.A. Wilson, "Taking a Look at Gun Control," *Winnipeg Free Press*, 14 December 1989, 6. Also see Val Werier, "Firearm Screening Inadequate," *Winnipeg Free Press*, 7 February 1990, 6.

15 "Canadian Gun Control under Fire for Cursory Screening of Licencees," *Globe and Mail*, 26 December 1989, A17.

16 "Stricter Gun Laws Sought," *Winnipeg Free Press*, 15 December 1989, 18; *Debates, House of Commons* (12 March 1990), 9089; (25 April 1990), 10651–2; (2 May 1990), 10913; (1 October 1990), 13628; Geoffrey York, "Ottawa to Change Gun-Control Bill," *Globe and Mail*, 27 March 1991, A5.

17 For examples, see Heidi Rathjen, "'Their Sole Function Is to Kill People,'" *Globe and Mail*, 4 June 1993, A31; Wendy Cukier, "Tragedy Was Catalyst for Change," *Winnipeg Free Press*, 7 December 1993, A7; Wendy Cukier, "The Guns of Canada: Several Million and Counting," *Globe and Mail*, 15 April 1994, A25; Wendy Cukier, "A Gun to Parliament's Head," *Toronto*

Star, 15 April 1994, A27; Wendy Cukier, "Gun Control," *Globe and Mail*, 30 June 1994, A26; Rathjen and Montpetit, *December 6*; Wendy Cukier, "Changing Public Policy on Firearms: Success Stories from Around the World," *Journal of Public Health Policy* 26, no. 2 (2005): 227–30; Wendy Cukier and Victor W. Sidel, *The Global Gun Epidemic: From Saturday Night Specials to AK-47s* (Westport, CT: Praeger Security International, 2006); Philip J. Cook, Wendy Cukier, and Keith Krause, "The Illicit Firearms Trade in North America," *Criminology and Criminal Justice* 9, no. 3 (2009): 265–86.

18 Wendy Cukier, "Gun Control," *Globe and Mail*, 30 June 1994, A26; Virginia Galt, "Oshawa Shooting Sparks Controversy over Gun Control," *Globe and Mail*, 16 September 1994, A6; Kirk Makin, "A Gun Lobby with No Bang," *Globe and Mail*, 26 November 1994, A1, A6; "Justice Minister Sticks to His Guns on Registration," *Globe and Mail*, 15 February 1995, A1, A4.

19 "Tighten Gun Laws, Slain Student's Mother Says," *Globe and Mail*, 17 January 1991, A6; Graham Fraser, "Gun Bill 'Uniquely Canadian,'" *Globe and Mail*, 7 November 1991, A8; *Debates, House of Commons* (11 December 1989), 6744; (23 November 1990), 15670–1; (26 March 1991), 19014; (30 September 1991), 2876; (6 November 1991), 4691–2; (23 September 1994), 6081; (4 November 1994), 7682; (6 December 1994), 8660–1, 8685; (13 March 1995), 10400–1; (27 March 1995), 11092–3; Canada, *Causes of Death*, 1980–93 (Ottawa: Statistics Canada).

20 Geoffrey York, "Ottawa to Change Gun-Control Bill," *Globe and Mail*, 27 March 1991, A5.

21 Canadian Advisory Council on the Status of Women, *Cease-Fire: A Brief to the Legislative Committee Studying Bill C-17 on Gun Control* (Ottawa: Canadian Advisory Council on the Status of Women, 1991), 8.

22 Angus Reid estimated 86 per cent of Canadian gun owners were men. Murray Campbell, "Gun Debate to Heat Up as Rock Tables Bill," *Globe and Mail*, 14 February 1995, A3.

23 Makin, "Gun Lobby with No Bang."

24 Larry Whitmore, "As I See It," *Canadian Handgun* (January 1992): 2. A columnist in the *Winnipeg Free Press* alleged that feminists employed the Montreal Massacre to pursue a broader anti-male agenda. The murders in Montreal "sent the anti-gun lobby into full frenzy, not to mention the anti-male lobby among the more extreme elements of the feminist movement." Tom Oleson, "The Magnificent Folly of Gun Control," *Winnipeg Free Press*, 2 December 1994, A6.

25 *Debates, House of Commons* (1 November 1990), 15023; Donn Downey, "Tighter Gun Controls on Way, Lewis Says," *Globe and Mail*, 9 January 1990, A13; "Private Member's Bill," *Canadian Handgun* (Winter 1990): 11.

26 *Debates, House of Commons* (22 November 1990), 15576–8; Timothy Apple-by, "One Certificate Gets Endless Guns," *Globe and Mail*, 27 June 1990, A8; "Automatic Guns Face Ban," *Globe and Mail*, 27 June 1990, A8; "Firearms and the Committee," *Globe and Mail*, 21 January 1991, A14.

27 "Legislative Update – Bill C-80," *Canadian Handgun* (April 1991): 10. Also see Kevin Rollason, "Critics Say Law Off-Target," *Winnipeg Free Press*, 27 June 1990, 1; Hugh Winsor, "Gun Control Critics Fire Salvos at Bill," *Globe and Mail*, 14 December 1990, A4; "The O.H.A. and Bill C-80," *Canadian Handgun* (April 1991): 8.

28 "Group Opposes Gun Limits," *Toronto Star*, 18 December 1989, A18; André Picard, "Victims' Families Express Anger over Non-Voice," *Globe and Mail*, 12 January 1991, A5; *Globe and Mail*, 16 October 1991, A12; Larry Whitmore, "As I See It," *Canadian Handgun* (February 1993): 2.

29 *Debates, House of Commons* (22 November 1990), 15574, 15615.

30 Graham Fraser, "Gun Control Legislation Stuck in Committee," *Globe and Mail*, 7 December 1990, A6; *Report of the Special Committee on the Subject-Matter of Bill C-80 (Firearms)* (February 1991); Susan Delacourt, "Gun Control Divides Tory Women," *Globe and Mail*, 8 February 1991, A4; David Vienneau, "Gun Bill Puts Tories on the Firing Line," *Toronto Star*, 15 February 1991, A23; "Better Gun-Control Law Promised Despite Divisive Report," *Globe and Mail*, 16 February 1991, A5; Geoffrey York, "Ottawa to Change Gun-Control Bill," *Globe and Mail*, 27 March 1991, A5; David Vienneau, "Outspoken Tory MP Fights Caucus Sexism," *Toronto Star*, 14 October 1991, A1; *Debates, House of Commons* (2 October 1991), 3133; (6 November 1991), 4691.

31 *Debates, House of Commons* (6 June 1991), 1257.

32 Geoffrey York, "Tories Battle over Gun-Control Bill," *Globe and Mail*, 2 October 1991, A6; David Vienneau, "Mulroney Spikes Bid by Tory MPs to Weaken Proposed New Gun Law," *Toronto Star*, 3 October 1991, A3; "Mulroney Intervenes in Tory Fight on Gun Control," *Globe and Mail*, 3 October 1991, A5; Bob Cox, "House Passes Gun Bill, but Neither Side Happy," *Winnipeg Free Press*, 8 November 1991, C34; Ross Howard, "MPs Vote to Tighten Gun Control Regulations," *Globe and Mail*, 8 November 1991, A1–A2; Paul Wiecek, "Gun Law Misses Mark," *Winnipeg Free Press*, 10 November 1991, B13.

33 *An Act to amend the Criminal Code and the Customs Tariff in consequence thereof*, S.C. 1991, c.40; "Summary of Major Points in Bill C-17…," *Canadian Police Chief Newsletter* 10, no. 4 (1991): 12–13; Timothy Appleby, "Police Officials Welcome Gun Amnesty Plan," *Globe and Mail*, 10 April 1992, A8; "Canadian Firearms Safety Program to Come into Effect January 1, 1994,"

Canadian Police Chief Newsletter 12, no. 4 (Winter 1993): 16. For lists of restricted and prohibited arms, see *Prohibited Weapons Order, No. 11*, Order in Council 1992-1668 (16 July 1992), and *Restricted Weapons Order*, Order in Council, PC 1992-1670 (16 July 1992).

34 "Bill C-17 Gun Control," *Canadian Police Chief Newsletter* 10, no. 4 (Winter 1991): 1.

35 Presentation on Behalf of the Canadian Association of Chiefs of Police to the Special Parliamentary Committee on Bill C-80, 19 December 1990; Resolution of the Canadian Association of Chiefs of Police re: "Grandfather" Clause – Bill C-80, 1990; Presentation on Behalf of the Canadian Association of Chiefs of Police to Legislative Committee H – Bill C-17 (Gun Control), 1 October 1991, on file at Canadian Association of Chiefs of Police head office, Ottawa; *Canadian Police Chief Newsletter* 9, no. 8 (October 1990): 10–11; "Bill C-17 Gun Control," *Canadian Police Chief Newsletter* 10, no. 2 (Summer 1991): 2; Geoffrey York, "2 Sides Prepare for Intense Fight over Gun Bill," *Globe and Mail*, 1 June 1991, A10; *Canadian Handgun* (June 1991): 7; Robert Matas, "Gun Regulations Greeted with Mixed Reviews," *Globe and Mail*, 28 July 1992, A3; "The Marc Lepine Law," *Globe and Mail*, 29 July 1992, A12; "Parry Sound–Muskoka Riding Association Victory: Score One for the Good Guys," *Canadian Handgun* (August 1992): 5.

36 Stephen Clarkson, *The Big Red Machine: How the Liberal Party Dominates Canadian Politics* (Vancouver: UBC Press, 2005), 209.

37 Alvin Finkel, *Social Policy and Practice in Canada: A History* (Waterloo, ON: Wilfrid Laurier University Press, 2006), 281, 283–91; Brooke Jeffrey, *Hard Right Turn: The New Face of Neo-Conservatism in Canada* (Toronto: HarperCollins, 1999), 48; Neil Nevitt et al., "The Populist Right in Canada: The Rise of the Reform Party of Canada," in *The New Politics of the Right: Neo-Populist Parties and Movements in Established Democracies*, ed. Hans-Georg Betz and Stefan Immerfall (New York: St Martin's, 1998), 187–8; *Canadian Handgun* (June 1991): 9.

38 *Debates, House of Commons* (6 November 1991), 4684.

39 "Reform Party Platform," *Canadian Handgun* (February 1993): 7; "Who Will You Vote For?," *Canadian Handgun* (May 1997): 2.

40 Brooke Jeffrey, *Divided Loyalties: The Liberal Party of Canada, 1984–2008* (Toronto: University of Toronto Press, 2010), 299–300; Bottomley, "Locked and Loaded," 37.

41 Jean Chrétien, *My Years as Prime Minister* (Toronto: Vintage Canada, 2008), 209.

42 *Debates, House of Commons* (25 February 1994), 1859; (24 March 1994),

2706–7; (2 June 1994), 4774; (3 June 1994), 4823; (15 June 1994), 5344;
(4 November 1994), 7689–90; Timothy F. Hartnagel, "Gun Control in
Alberta: Explaining Public Attitudes concerning Legislative Change,"
Canadian Journal of Criminology 44, no. 4 (2002): 404–5; Auditor General
of Canada, *Report of the Auditor General of Canada, 1993* (Ottawa: Auditor General of Canada), chap. 27; Eric Siblin, "Third Prof Dies after Col-
league Faces Charges," *Winnipeg Free Press*, 26 August 1992, A3; "How He
Got His Gun," *Globe and Mail*, 27 August 1992, A14; Barry Came, "Death
in a Classroom," *Maclean's* 105, no. 36 (7 September 1992): 44; Timothy
Appleby, "Firearms Trigger Homicide Increase," *Globe and Mail*, 7 October
1992, A1, A9; "Gun Control Wake Up," *Globe and Mail*, 16 November 1993,
A26; "Guns and Crime," *Globe and Mail*, 19 April 1994, A22; "Taking Aim
on Guns: A Rash of Brutal Murders Sparks Calls for More Controls on
Firearms," *Maclean's* 107, no. 17 (25 April 1994): 10; James Rusk, "Ontario
Moves to Fight Illegal Guns," *Globe and Mail*, 21 May 1994, A6; Brian Berg-
man, "Conflict at Concordia," *Maclean's* 107, no. 24 (13 June 1994): 12; Bob
Brent and Leslie Papp, "Rae Urges Ban on Handguns," *Toronto Star*, 18
June 1994, A8; "Majority Supports Registry of Guns," *Winnipeg Free Press*,
1 December 1994, B3; Jeffrey Simpson, "The Only Real Debates Are Found
within the Caucus of the Liberal Party," *Globe and Mail*, 16 February 1995,
A22; Henry Hess, "U.S. Is Source of Rising Flood of Illegal Guns," *Globe
and Mail*, 13 May 1995, A1, A6.

43 Bottomley, "Locked and Loaded," 38; Ross Howard, "Chrétien Promises
Tougher Gun Law," *Globe and Mail*, 16 May 1994, A1, A2.

44 Susan Delacourt, "Ottawa Ponders Gun Ban in Cities," *Globe and Mail*, 12
April 1994, A1, A2. Also see Portia Priegert, "Liberals Consider Ban on
Pistols to Cut Crime," *Winnipeg Free Press*, 12 April 1994, A3; "Legislative/
Court Update," *Canadian Handgun* (April 1994): 26.

45 *Debates, House of Commons* (22 September 1994), 6031. Also see Fred Cleverley, "More Gun Control Won't Help," *Winnipeg Free Press*, 4 July 1994,
A6; Tom Oleson, "'Gun Nuts' Were Right, after All," *Winnipeg Free Press*,
1 August 1996, A10.

46 "Firearms Control Program Announced," *Canadian Police Chief Newsletter*
13, no. 4 (Winter 1994), 7–8.

47 *Debates, House of Commons* (9 December 1994), 8884; (16 February 1995),
9706–11; Luke Fisher, "In the Crossfire," *Maclean's* 107, no. 40 (3 October
1994): 14; Tu Thanh Ha, "Rock Readies New Gun Laws," *Globe and Mail*, 28
November 1994, A1, A4; "Irresistible Force Meets Immovable Object: Rock
Comes to Alberta to Sell Gun Owners on More Controls, and Fails," *Western Report* 9, no. 52 (23 January 1995): 26.

48 Canadian Advisory Council on the Status of Women, 18–19; Presentation on Behalf of the Canadian Association of Chiefs of Police to Legislative Committee H – Bill C-17 (Gun Control), 1 October 1991; Resolution of the Canadian Association of Chiefs of Police re: Registration of All Firearms, 1994; Presentation by the Canadian Association of Chiefs of Police (CACP) to the Standing Senate Committee on Legal and Constitutional Affairs, 29 June 1995, on file at Canadian Association of Chiefs of Police head office, Ottawa; *Canadian Police Chief Newsletter* 13, no. 3 (Fall 1994): 12; "Why Canada's Police Chiefs Favour Gun Registration," *Globe and Mail*, 13 March 1995, A11; "Canada's Top Police Bullish on Bill C-68," *Winnipeg Free Press*, 24 September 1995, B4; "President's Report (Chief Vince MacDonald)," *Canadian Police Chief Newsletter* 14, no. 3 (Fall 1995): 4–5.

49 Auditor General of Canada, *Report of the Auditor General of Canada, 1993* (Ottawa: Auditor General of Canada), chap. 27.2; *Debates, House of Commons* (15 April 1994), 3104; (22 September 1994), 6037.

50 Ross Howard, "Up in Arms at Ban Talk, Gun Owners Coalesce," *Globe and Mail*, 13 June 1994, A1, A4; Tu Thanh Ha, "Gun Bill Triggers Strong Emotions," *Globe and Mail*, 23 September 1994, A1, A8; Tony Davis, "Gun Lovers Take Aim at Feds," *Winnipeg Free Press*, 9 October 1994, A1; Fred Cleverley, "Gun Controls Going Too Far," *Winnipeg Free Press*, 24 October 1994, A6; "Massive Pro Gun Rally," *Canadian Handgun* (May 1995); Larry Whitmore, "From the Office," *Canadian Handgun* (May 1995): 2; Mary Nemeth, "Fighting Back," *Maclean's* 108, no. 23 (5 June 1995): 14; "Petition," *Canadian Handgun* (July 1995); "Hamilton Pro-Gun Rally: Where Was Everyone?," *Canadian Handgun* (July 1995): 12.

51 John Barber, "Now Gun Lobbyists Can Take Aim at Toronto," *Globe and Mail*, 3 May 1995, A2. Also see "Gunowners Are Fed Up: Over 2,500 at Wainwright Warn Ottawa to Stop Blaming Them for Rising Crime," *Western Report* 9, no. 20 (13 June 1994): 22; Dalton Camp, "Gun Owners See Controls as Just Another Eastern Plot," *Toronto Star*, 11 January 1995, A19; Scott Feschuk, "Rock Gets a Blast from Gun Lovers," *Globe and Mail*, 11 January 1995, A1, A7; Tom Oleson, "Putting the Blame on Guns," *Winnipeg Free Press*, 21 April 1995, A6; Peter C. Newman, "Gun Control: The CF-18 of the 1990s?," *Maclean's* 108, no. 22 (29 May 1995): 51; Alanna Mitchell, "Gun Ownership in Alberta Approaches U.S. levels," *Globe and Mail*, 30 April 1999, A1, A2.

52 Feschuk, "Rock Gets a Blast from Gun Lovers"; Larry Whitmore, "As I See It," *Canadian Handgun* (May 1993): 2; "Registration Will Mean Confiscation: Don't Believe Otherwise," *Canadian Handgun* (May 1995): 8–9. The

fear of confiscation remained a concern after the passage of the *Firearms Act*. See Fred Cleverley, "Wait for It: Anne Will Get Your Guns," *Winnipeg Free Press*, 2 October 2000, A10.

53 *Debates, House of Commons* (17 November 1994), 7924.

54 *Debates, House of Commons* (6 February 1995), 9191.

55 Scott Feschuk, "Albertans Might Defy Gun Law, Minister Says," *Globe and Mail*, 10 January 1995, A4.

56 Larry Whitmore, "As I See It," *Canadian Handgun* (May 1995): 6–7; Tu Thanh Ha, "Rock Hints at Yielding More Ground on Guns," *Globe and Mail*, 16 May 1995, A4; Tu Thanh Ha, "Gun Penalties Could Violate Charter, Legal Groups Say," *Globe and Mail*, 18 May 1995, A4; "Questions about Gun Control," *Globe and Mail*, 25 May 1995, A20.

57 *Debates, House of Commons* (15 November 1994), 7811; Gary A. Mauser, "Gun Control Is Not Crime Control," *Fraser Forum*, supplement (March 1995): S28; "Revisiting Gun Registration," *Globe and Mail*, 7 July 1995, A12; "Politics," *Globe and Mail*, 7 February 1995, D1; Bottomley, "Parliament, Politics and Policy," 223–4.

58 *Debates, House of Commons* (5 December 1994), 8645; (16 February 1995), 9711–14; (5 April 1995), 11556–7; Tu Thanh Ha, "Foes of New Gun Bill Muster Forces," *Globe and Mail*, 22 September 1994, A1, A11. On third reading, however, Harper voted against the bill because a subsequent poll indicated his constituents were opposed. *Debates, House of Commons* (12 June 1995), 13631–2; Tu Thanh Ha, "Reform MPs Split over Gun Reform," *Globe and Mail*, 13 June 1995, A3.

59 *Debates, House of Commons* (13 June 1995), 13685–6, 13758–60; Susan Delacourt, "MPs' Ouster Raises Question of Tolerance," *Globe and Mail*, 7 April 1995, A4; "Bending on Gun Control," *Maclean's* 108, no. 22 (29 May 1995): 37; Tu Thanh Ha, "Rock Suggests Ways to Soften Gun Legislation," *Globe and Mail*, 20 May 1995, A4; Robert Lewis, "Taking Dead Aim," *Maclean's* 108, no. 23 (5 June 1995): 2; "Gun Bill Sees Few Changes in Committee," *Globe and Mail*, 7 June 1995, A7; Tu Thanh Ha, "Firearms Registry Ottawa's Next Project," *Globe and Mail*, 14 June 1995, A1, A7; Dan Lett, "MPs Brave Wrath in Vote on Gun Bill," *Winnipeg Free Press*, 14 June 1995, A9; "Senate Stalls Gun Bill," *Globe and Mail*, 21 June 1995, A2; Scott Feschuk, "Gun Law Faces Fight in Senate," *Globe and Mail*, 28 July 1995, A2; Tu Thanh Ha, "PC Senators Play Gun-Bill Roulette," *Globe and Mail*, 17 November 1995, A1, A9; To Thanh Ha, "Bitter Gun Debate Silenced as Senate Passes Bill," *Globe and Mail*, 23 November 1995, A4; "Gun-Control Law Takes Effect," *Globe and Mail*, 6 December 1995, A4.

60 *Firearms Act*, S.C. 1995, c.39; Department of Justice, *Firearms Act Regulations*

(March 1998); Registrar, Canadian Firearms Registry, *Report on the Admin-istration of the Firearms Act to the Solicitor General* (1999), 6.

61 *Report on the Administration of the Firearms Act to the Solicitor General* (1999), 6; Registrar, Canadian Firearms Registry, *Report on the Administration of the Firearms Act to the Solicitor General* (2000), 4.

62 Peter Moon, "Gun Laws Wide of Mark in Native Communities," *Globe and Mail*, 1 May 1995, A1, A4; *Debates, House of Commons* (19 May 1995), 12844; "The Natives Are Getting Restless," *Western Report* 10, no. 18 (29 May 1995): 7; "Mercredi Denounces Gun Law," *Globe and Mail*, 4 February 1997, A4; Brian Laghi, "Easier Native Hunting Rules Proposed," *Globe and Mail*, 11 September 1997, A4; *Aboriginal Peoples of Canada Adaptations Regulations (Firearms)*, in Department of Justice, *Firearms Act Regulations* (March 1998), 61–7.

63 Bottomley, "Parliament, Politics and Policy," 264–5; "NRA Involved in Gun Registry Debate," *CBC News* (website), 4 September 2010; Makin, "Gun Lobby with No Bang."

64 Ross Howard, "Canada's Gun Problem Hard to Take Aim At," *Globe and Mail*, 23 May 1994, A6.

65 David Vienneau, "Gun Lovers Set Sights on the Liberals," *Toronto Star*, 3 May 1997, E4; Bottomley, "Parliament, Politics and Policy," 262–3; Jeffrey, *Hard Right Turn*, 373, 393, 432–4.

66 CORFOS included a number of organizations, although these organiza-tions included fewer hunting groups and more gun owners' associations. CORFOS included the Responsible Firearm Owners of Alberta, Respon-sible Firearm Owners of Ontario, Sporting Clubs of Niagara, the Alberta Arms and Cartridge Collectors Association, National Firearms Associa-tion, Alberta Civil Society Association, the Alberta Fish and Game Associ-ation, and Responsible Firearms Coalition of British Columbia. Bottomley, "Parliament, Politics and Policy," 266.

67 Erin Anderssen, "Gun Owners Rally against Registry," *Globe and Mail*, 23 September 1998, A3; Erin Anderssen, "The Good, the Bad, and the Angry," *Globe and Mail*, 26 September 1998, 1, D2.

68 *Debates, House of Commons* (15 November 1994): 7811; "Support for Reg-istration is a Mile Wide but Only an Inch Deep," *Canadian Handgun* (May 1995): 12; "What Has the OHA Done for You Lately?," *Canadian Handgun* (April 1997): 8. For examples of Mauser's writing, see Gary A. Mauser, "A Comparison of Canadian and American Attitudes towards Firearms," *Canadian Journal of Criminology* 32, no. 4 (1990): 573–89; Gary A. Mauser and Richard Holmes, "An Evaluation of the 1977 Canadian Firearms Leg-islation," *Evaluation Review* 16, no. 6 (1992): 603–17; Gary A. Mauser and

Michael Margolis, "The Politics of Gun Control: Comparing Canadian and American Patterns," *Government and Policy* 10 (1992): 189–209; Gary A. Mauser, *Misfire: Firearm Registration in Canada* (Vancouver: Fraser Institute, 2001); Gary Mauser, "One Thing's for Sure, Crime Causes Gun Laws," *Globe and Mail*, 18 September 2006, A17; Gary Mauser, "Firearm Bans Haven't Worked," *Toronto Star*, 4 June 2007, A7.

69 Gary Mauser, "Do Canadians Use Firearms in Self-Protection," *Canadian Journal of Criminology* 37 (1995): 556–62; Gary Mauser, "Canadians Do Use Firearms for Self-Protection," *Canadian Journal of Criminology* 38, no. 4 (1996): 485–8; Ross Howard, "Canadians Use Firearms for Self-Defence, Gun-Registration Critic Says," *Globe and Mail*, 17 March 1995, A9.

70 Michael Valpy, "The U.S. Cavalry Is Called In on Gun Control," *Globe and Mail*, 7 April 1995, A2. Allan Rock also felt it necessary to write to the *Globe and Mail* to undermine Mauser's credibility on the gun control issue. "The Efficacy of Gun Registration," *Globe and Mail*, 14 June 1995, A15.

71 For references to Mauser, see Diane Francis, "A Case against Rock's Gun Controls," *Maclean's* 108, no. 23 (5 June 1995): 13; Henry Hess, "Rock Ignoring Figures on Gun Control, Critics Say," *Globe and Mail*, 8 June 1995, A9; Dawn Walton, "Right-Wing Think Tank Takes Aim at Gun Law," *Globe and Mail*, 19 March 2001, A3; Ingrid Peritz, "Accused Man Had Two Illegal Rifles, Police Say," *Globe and Mail*, 17 December 2005, A22. The Conservative government of Prime Minister Stephen Harper eventually appointed Mauser to an advisory panel on gun laws. Susan Delacourt, "Panel Loaded with Gun Buffs," *Toronto Star*, 28 May 2007, A21; Susan Delacourt, "Day Tries to Dampen Storm over Gun Panel," *Toronto Star*, 29 May 2007, A14.

For examples of other academic critiques of the *Firearms Act*, see David Bercuson and Barry Cooper, "Provinces Target Gun Bill in Court," *Globe and Mail*, 23 August 1997, D2; Philip C. Stenning, "Gun Control: A Critique of Current Policy," *Policy Options* 15 (1994): 13–17; Philip C. Stenning, "Solutions in Search of Problems: A Critique of the Federal Government's Gun Control Proposals," *Canadian Journal of Criminology* 37 (1995): 184–94; Philip C. Stenning, "Long Gun Registration: A Poorly Aimed Longshot," *Canadian Journal of Criminology and Criminal Justice* 45, no. 4 (2003): 480–8.

72 Liberal Party of Canada, *Securing Our Future Together: The Liberal Plan – 1997* (Ottawa: Liberal Party of Canada, 1997), 89.

73 Bottomley, "Parliament, Politics and Policy," 237–8; Brian Bergman, "'We Are Left Numb,'" *Maclean's* 118, no. 12 (21 March 2005): 22–5; Ross Howard, "Slayings Reveal Limitations in Gun Control," *Globe and Mail*, 10 April 1996, A4; "Mark Got His Gun," *Globe and Mail*, 12 April 1996, A18.

74 Donald McKenzie, "Killer Not Banned from Owning Guns," *Winnipeg Free Press*, 10 April 1996, A10.

75 William Neville, "It Wasn't about Arms and Dope," *Winnipeg Free Press*, 11 March 2005, A13.

76 Davis Sheremata, "Free People Don't Register," *Alberta Report* 26, no. 7 (1999): 24; Bill Whatcott, "A Significant Blaze," *Report / Newsmagazine* (Alberta ed.) 28, no. 21 (2001): 6; Patrick Brethour, "Gun-Registry Foes Lack Defendant for Court Battle," *Globe and Mail*, 6 January 2003, A4; "First Gun-Registry Charge to Be Laid Today?," *Winnipeg Free Press*, 13 January 2003, A7; Daniel Leblanc, "1.6 Million Guns Elude Registry," *Globe and Mail*, 1 July 2003, A1, A2; Allister Muir, "Taking Aim at Injustice," *Globe and Mail*, 26 August 2003, A19.

77 *Report on the Administration of the Firearms Act to Solicitor General by the Registrar* (2000), 14; Jill Mahoney, "Half of Guns Unregistered as Deadline Approaches," *Globe and Mail*, 12 December 2000, A1, A9; Brian Laghi and Jill Mahoney, "New Gun Law Won't Work, Ottawa Warned," *Globe and Mail*, 13 December 2000, A7; Lily Nguyen and Caroline Alphonso, "Gun Owners Hit Crunch at Licensing Deadline," *Globe and Mail*, 2 January 2001, A2; John Ward, "Procrastinators Clog Gun Registry," *Winnipeg Free Press*, 3 January 2001, B2; Ken MacQueen, "Armed, Angry and Defiant," *Maclean's* 114, no. 8 (19 February 2001): 26; Leblanc, "1.6 Million Guns Elude Registry."

78 Ontario, Ministry of Natural Resources, *Statistics, 1986*, 37; Ontario, Ministry of Natural Resources, *Statistics, 1988–1989*, 30; New Brunswick, Department of Natural Resources and Energy, *Annual Report, 1986–1987*; New Brunswick, Department of Natural Resources and Energy, *Annual Report, 1997–1998*, 23; Manitoba, *State of the Environment Report for Manitoba, 1993*, 69; GPC Research, *Fall 2001 Estimate of Firearms in Canada* (Ottawa: GPC Research, 2001), 18, 21.

79 *R. v. Northcott* (1980), 5 W.W.R. 38. Also see *Canada (Attorney General) v. Pattison* (1981), 123 D.L.R. (3d) 111.

80 *R. v. Krug*, [1985] 2 S.C.R. 255; "Law on Gun Control Is Upheld by Court," *Globe and Mail*, 11 October 1985, A8; *R. v. Kelly (Ont. C.A.)* (1990), 59 C.C.C. (3d) 497; Thomas Claridge, "Ontario's Firearm Provision Upheld," *Globe and Mail*, 10 September 1990, A8.

81 *Martinoff v. Canada (Royal Canadian Mounted Police)* (1990), 57 C.C.C. (3d) 482. For earlier legal disputes involving Martinoff, see "Collector Can Keep Machine Guns," *Calgary Herald*, 6 October 1977, 17; "Machinegun Martinoff Wins One Round," *Leader-Post*, 16 December 1977, 22.

82 *R. v. Martinoff*, [1990] B.C.J. 2337; *R. v. Martinoff*, [1991] 2 B.C.A.C. 227.

83 *R. v. Hasselwander*, [1993] 2 S.C.R. 398; *Ontario Handgun Assn. v. Ontario (Solicitor General)*, [1993] O.J. No. 2336; *Ontario Handgun Assn. v. Ontario (Solicitor General)*, [1993] O.J. 4614. Business interests, represented by the Canadian Sporting Arms & Ammunition Association, helped pay for the Ontario Handgun Association's legal challenge. "Legislative/Court Update," *Canadian Handgun* (April 1994): 26.

84 Dale Gibson, "The Firearms Reference in the Alberta Court of Appeal," *Alberta Law Review* 37 (1999): 1071–93; Allan C. Hutchinson and David Schneiderman, "Smoking Guns: The Federal Government Confronts the Tobacco and Gun Lobbies," *Constitutional Forum* 7, no. 1 (1995): 16–22; David M. Beatty, "Gun Control and Judicial Anarchy," *Constitutional Forum* 10, no. 2 (1999): 45–9.

85 *Reference re Firearms Act (Can.)* (1998), 65 Alta. L.R. (3d) 1; Gibson, "The Firearms Reference in the Alberta Court of Appeal," 1071–93.

86 *Reference re Firearms Act*, [2000] 1 S.C.R. 783; John T. Saywell, *The Lawmakers: Judicial Power and the Shaping of Canadian Federalism* (Toronto: University of Toronto Press and the Osgoode Society, 2002), 287–8.

87 Nahlah Ayed, "Firearms Laws: An Emotional Issue for Both Sides," *Western Star* (Corner Brook), 16 February 2000, 19; F.L. (Ted) Morton, "How the Firearms Act (Bill C-68) Violates the Charter of Rights and Freedoms," unpublished paper; Richard Foot, "Gun Lobby Planning Charter Challenge," *National Post*, 7 February 2000, A1.

88 *R. v. Wiles*, [2005] 3 S.C.R. 895 at para 9.

89 Canadian Association of Chiefs of Police, *Position Paper on Gun Control Laws* (1973), 1, 5, on file at Canadian Association of Chiefs of Police head office, Ottawa.

90 Tu Thanh Ha, "Gun Plan 'Final,' Rock Declares," *Globe and Mail*, 1 December 1994, A1, A11; *Debates, House of Commons* (16 February 1995), 9709.

91 Auditor General of Canada, *2002 December Report of the Auditor General of Canada to the House of Commons*, chap. 10 (Ottawa: Office of the Auditor General, 2002); Jonathon Gatehouse, "Bureaucracy Multiples at Gun Registry," *National Post*, 20 May 1999, A7. Also see Scott Feschuk, "Price Tag of Registry for Guns May Rise," *Globe and Mail*, 28 November 1996, A3; Rod Edwards, "New Ads Add to Ballooning Cost of Gun Registry," *Medicine Hat News*, 14 September 2000, A4; Brian Bergman, "Handing Out Heavy Ammo," *Maclean's* 115, no. 50 (16 December 2002): 30; Kim Lunman, "Gun Owners Get $6-million in Fee Rebates," *Globe and Mail*, 1 January 2003, A4; Neil Boyd, "Gun Control: Placing Costs in Context," *Canadian Journal of Criminology and Criminal Justice* 45, no. 4 (2003): 473–8.

92 Bottomley, "Parliament, Politics and Policy," 285; "The Right to Bear

Arms: U.S. and Canada," Gallup, 10 December 2002, http://www.gallup
.com/poll/7381/right-bear-arms-us-canada.aspx.

93 Kim Lunman, "Liberals Want $172-Million for Firearms Program," *Globe
and Mail*, 27 February 2003, A10. Also see Lloyd Axworthy, "Guns 'N Registries: Right-Wing Rage Must Not Prevail," *Winnipeg Free Press*,
19 December 2002, A13.

94 Kim Lunman, "Martin Health Plan Gets 48% Support," *Globe and Mail*,
2 February 2004, A4.

Conclusion

1 "Another Gun Law," *Winnipeg Free Press*, 9 December 2005, A14. Also see
Jane Taber, "Liberals Plan New Gun Rules," *Globe and Mail*, 8 December
2005, A1; "Rural, Urban Ridings Take Aim at Proposed Handgun Ban,"
Globe and Mail, 15 December 2005, A7.

2 Canada, *Causes of Death*, 1974–2010 (Ottawa: Statistics Canada); Tina
Hotton Mahony, *Homicide in Canada, 2010, Juristat*, cat. no. 85-002-X (Ot-
tawa: Statistics Canada, 2011), 1; Mia Dauvergne and Leonardo De Socio,
"Firearms and Violent Crime, 2006," *Juristat* 28, no. 2 (cat. no. 85-002-XIE)
(Ottawa: Statistics Canada), 11; Robert D. Sopuck, "Long-Gun Registry
Opponents Are In for the Long Haul," *Winnipeg Free Press*, 30 May 2009,
D4; Mia Rabson, "Bill to Kill Long Gun Registry RCMP Released Data
to Polling Agency," *Winnipeg Free Press*, 26 September 2009, A8; Stephen
Thorne, "Police vs Police," *St John's Telegram*, 7 May 2010, A9; Chris Mor-
ris, "Gun Debate Fires Up," *Telegraph-Journal*, 5 April 2011, A1.

3 RCMP, "Firearms: Canada / United States Comparison," June 1998,
http://www.rcmp-grc.gc.ca/cfp-pcaf/res-rec/comp-eng.htm.

Index

Earl Grey (Governor General), 92
Eaton's, 83, 85, 103, 104, 119, 120,
   144, 289n161
École Polytechnique (Montreal), 12,
   199, 203, 204
Edmonton, 103, 109, 146, 168
Edmonton Bulletin, 91
Elbow River Rifle Club, 48
election violence, 25
England. *See* Britain
environment/environmentalism/en-
   vironmentalist, 6, 86, 107, 163, 185
Europe, 119, 121, 133, 138, 141

Fabrikant, Valery, 214
Fairbank, John, 58
Fanning, Edmund, 22
Federation of Canadian Municipalities, 205
Federation of Saskatchewan Indian
   Nations, 228–9
Feminism / feminist movement, 203,
   320n24
Fenians, 10, 41, 43–4, 52, 53, 70, 141
Ferguson, J.S., 155
"fifth column," 132, 135, 156, 300n95
Firearm Legislation Action Committee (FLAC), 309n60
firearm permits and licences, 11, 19,
   28, 44, 75, 76, 78, 113, 123–4, 125,
   127, 129–30, 133, 136, 137, 138, 139,
   147, 150–1, 153–5, 166, 173–4, 178,
   182, 184, 188, 190, 211, 220–1, 225,
   230, 238, 290n18, 292n35, 298n90,
   301n103; amnesty, 195–6, 211, 235;
   Canadian Safety Firearms Test,
   221; "certificate of exemption," 78,
   119, 127, 129, 153, 237; Firearms
   Acquisition Certificate (FAC), 190,
   194, 195, 202, 208, 211, 226; Firearm

Possession Certificate, 216; Form
   76 permit, 129–30, 137, 151
firearms: ammunition, 22, 38–9, 47,
   52, 58, 60, 81, 114–16, 119, 130,
   133, 153, 169, 177, 213, 214, 238,
   275n21, 284n108, 290n18; and
   Christmas 103–6; antique/vintage,
   176, 178, 219; AR-15 rifle, 190, 192;
   "arquebus," 14, 15; automatic/
   semi-automatic weapon, 7, 87,
   119, 122, 125, 150, 156, 161, 167,
   168, 172, 178, 190, 192, 195, 203,
   204, 207, 209, 211, 227, 301n103,
   314n117, 315n119; breech-loading
   rifle, 9, 37, 39, 40, 41, 42, 44, 52, 53,
   55, 88, 237; Bren gun, 153; "British
   bull-dog" revolver, 63; Bullard
   Repeating Rifle, 88; cap gun, 102;
   carbine, 22; costs, 52–4, 62–3, 103,
   119–20, 267n62; Colt revolver, 61,
   142; Daisy air rifle, 103–4, 111;
   "double-action" revolver, 62;
   Dreyse rifle, 38; flintlock musket,
   15, 55, 64; Henry repeating rifle,
   39; Hornet rifle, 161; hunting rifle,
   8, 11, 88, 116, 140, 158, 159, 160,
   162, 166, 169, 176–7, 228, 251n35;
   imitation gun, 150, 160–1; Lee-
   Enfield rifle, 116, 153; long gun,
   9, 39, 40, 46, 61, 119, 138, 139, 159,
   173, 176; "long tom" (sealing gun),
   248n14; machine guns, 117–18, 144;
   magazines, 39, 209, 211, 227, 237;
   Marlin Repeating Rifle, 88; matchlock mechanism, 14–15; Mauser
   rifle, 91, 134; musket, 15, 16, 17, 22,
   23, 37–8, 236, 237; muzzle-loading
   rifle, 37, 236, 245n13; "needle gun,"
   38, 39; Peacemaker revolver, 62;
   "pepperbox" pistol, 61; percussion

2012   R. Blake Brown, *Arming and Disarming: A History of Gun Control in Canada*
       Eric Tucker, James Muir, and Bruce Ziff, eds., *Property on Trial: Canadian Cases in Context*
       Shelley Gavigan, *Hunger, Horses, and Government Men: Criminal Law on the Aboriginal Plains, 1870–1905*
       Barrington Walker, ed., *The African Canadian Legal Odyssey: Historical Essays*
2011   Robert J. Sharpe, *The Lazier Murder: Prince Edward County, 1884*
       Philip Girard, *Lawyers and Legal Culture in British North America: Beamish Murdoch of Halifax*
       John McLaren, *Dewigged, Bothered, and Bewildered: British Colonial Judges on Trial, 1800–1900*
       Lesley Erickson, *Westward Bound: Sex, Violence, the Law, and the Making of a Settler Society*
2010   Judy Fudge and Eric Tucker, eds., *Work on Trial: Canadian Labour Law Struggles*
       Christopher Moore, *The British Columbia Court of Appeal: The First Hundred Years*
       Frederick Vaughan, *Viscount Haldane: 'The Wicked Step-father of the Canadian Constitution'*
       Barrington Walker, *Race on Trial: Black Defendants in Ontario's Criminal Courts, 1858–1958*
2009   William Kaplan, *Canadian Maverick: The Life and Times of Ivan C. Rand*
       R. Blake Brown, *A Trying Question: The Jury in Nineteenth-Century Canada*
       Barry Wright and Susan Binnie, eds., *Canadian State Trials, Volume III: Political Trials and Security Measures, 1840–1914*
       Robert J. Sharpe, *The Last Day, the Last Hour: The Currie Libel Trial* (paperback edition with a new preface)
2008   Constance Backhouse, *Carnal Crimes: Sexual Assault Law in Canada, 1900–1975*
       Jim Phillips, R. Roy McMurtry, and John T. Saywell, eds., *Essays in the History of Canadian Law, Volume X: A Tribute to Peter N. Oliver*
       Greg Taylor, *The Law of the Land: The Advent of the Torrens System in Canada*
       Hamar Foster, Benjamin Berger, and A.R. Buck, eds., *The Grand Experiment: Law and Legal Culture in British Settler Societies*

2007   Robert Sharpe and Patricia McMahon, *The Persons Case: The Origins and Legacy of the Fight for Legal Personhood*

Lori Chambers, *Misconceptions: Unmarried Motherhood and the Ontario Children of Unmarried Parents Act, 1921–1969*

Jonathan Swainger, ed., *A History of the Supreme Court of Alberta*

Martin Friedland, *My Life in Crime and Other Academic Adventures*

2006   Donald Fyson, *Magistrates, Police, and People: Everyday Criminal Justice in Quebec and Lower Canada, 1764–1837*

Dale Brawn, *The Court of Queen's Bench of Manitoba, 1870–1950: A Biographical History*

R.C.B. Risk, *A History of Canadian Legal Thought: Collected Essays*, edited and introduced by G. Blaine Baker and Jim Phillips

2005   Philip Girard, *Bora Laskin: Bringing Law to Life*

Christopher English, ed., *Essays in the History of Canadian Law: Volume IX – Two Islands: Newfoundland and Prince Edward Island*

Fred Kaufman, *Searching for Justice: An Autobiography*

2004   Philip Girard, Jim Phillips, and Barry Cahill, eds., *The Supreme Court of Nova Scotia, 1754–2004: From Imperial Bastion to Provincial Oracle*

Frederick Vaughan, *Aggressive in Pursuit: The Life of Justice Emmett Hall*

John D. Honsberger, *Osgoode Hall: An Illustrated History*

Constance Backhouse and Nancy Backhouse, *The Heiress versus the Establishment: Mrs Campbell's Campaign for Legal Justice*

2003   Robert Sharpe and Kent Roach, *Brian Dickson: A Judge's Journey*

Jerry Bannister, *The Rule of the Admirals: Law, Custom, and Naval Government in Newfoundland, 1699–1832*

George Finlayson, *John J. Robinette, Peerless Mentor: An Appreciation*

Peter Oliver, *The Conventional Man: The Diaries of Ontario Chief Justice Robert A. Harrison, 1856–1878*

2002   John T. Saywell, *The Lawmakers: Judicial Power and the Shaping of Canadian Federalism*

Patrick Brode, *Courted and Abandoned: Seduction in Canadian Law*

David Murray, *Colonial Justice: Justice, Morality, and Crime in the Niagara District, 1791–1849*

F. Murray Greenwood and Barry Wright, eds., *Canadian State Trials, Volume II: Rebellion and Invasion in the Canadas, 1837–1839*

2001   Ellen Anderson, *Judging Bertha Wilson: Law as Large as Life*

Judy Fudge and Eric Tucker, *Labour before the Law: The Regulation of Workers' Collective Action in Canada, 1900–1948*

Laurel Sefton MacDowell, *Renegade Lawyer: The Life of J.L. Cohen*

Jim Phillips, Tina Loo, and Susan Lewthwaite, eds., *Essays in the History of Canadian Law: Volume V – Crime and Criminal Justice*

Brian Young, *The Politics of Codification: The Lower Canadian Civil Code of 1866*

1993 Greg Marquis, *Policing Canada's Century: A History of the Canadian Association of Chiefs of Police*

Murray Greenwood, *Legacies of Fear: Law and Politics in Quebec in the Era of the French Revolution*

1992 Brendan O'Brien, *Speedy Justice: The Tragic Last Voyage of His Majesty's Vessel Speedy*

Robert Fraser, ed., *Provincial Justice: Upper Canadian Legal Portraits from the Dictionary of Canadian Biography*

1991 Constance Backhouse, *Petticoats and Prejudice: Women and Law in Nineteenth-Century Canada*

1990 Philip Girard and Jim Phillips, eds., *Essays in the History of Canadian Law: Volume III – Nova Scotia*

Carol Wilton, ed., *Essays in the History of Canadian Law: Volume IV – Beyond the Law: Lawyers and Business in Canada, 1830–1930*

1989 Desmond Brown, *The Genesis of the Canadian Criminal Code of 1892*

Patrick Brode, *The Odyssey of John Anderson*

1988 Robert Sharpe, *The Last Day, the Last Hour: The Currie Libel Trial*

John D. Arnup, *Middleton: The Beloved Judge*

1987 C. Ian Kyer and Jerome Bickenbach, *The Fiercest Debate: Cecil A. Wright, the Benchers, and Legal Education in Ontario, 1923–1957*

1986 Paul Romney, *Mr Attorney: The Attorney General for Ontario in Court, Cabinet, and Legislature, 1791–1899*

Martin Friedland, *The Case of Valentine Shortis: A True Story of Crime and Politics in Canada*

1985 James Snell and Frederick Vaughan, *The Supreme Court of Canada: History of the Institution*

1984 Patrick Brode, *Sir John Beverley Robinson: Bone and Sinew of the Compact*

David Williams, *Duff: A Life in the Law*

1983 David H. Flaherty, ed., *Essays in the History of Canadian Law: Volume II*

1982 Marion MacRae and Anthony Adamson, *Cornerstones of Order: Courthouses and Town Halls of Ontario, 1784–1914*

1981 David H. Flaherty, ed., *Essays in the History of Canadian Law: Volume I*